FANNY BURNEY AND THE BURNEYS

ADDITIONS TO MADAME D'ARBLAY'S DIARY ᴥ
LETTERS BY SUSAN BURNEY ᴥ A JOURNAL OF
THE WORCESTER BURNEYS ᴥ SELECTIONS FROM
THE WORKS OF DR. BURNEY, HIS CHILDREN,
AND GRANDCHILDREN

NEW PORTRAITS OF THE FAMILY AND
DRAWINGS BY EDWARD F. BURNEY

Allegorical Sketch by Edward Burney.

from the original.

FANNY BURNEY AND THE BURNEYS

EDITED, WITH INTRODUCTION, BY

R. BRIMLEY JOHNSON

*" I love all of that breed whom I can be said to know,
and one or two I hardly know, I love on credit."*

Dr. Johnson

FULLY ILLUSTRATED

☙

LONDON
STANLEY PAUL & CO. LTD.

First published 1926

*Made and Printed in Great Britain
by Hazell, Watson & Viney Ld.
London and
Aylesbury*

PREFACE

For the new material in this volume I am indebted to the generous courtesy of Mr. Leverton Harris, who has given me full access to, and permission to print from, his unrivalled collection of Burneyiana, as a second time brought together by him after the disastrous fire at Camilla Lacey.

The additions to Madame D'Arblay's *Diary and Letters* were, fortunately, copied before the fire, and consist of passages from her journals in France which were omitted—by her or her editor—from the published volumes.

The summary of, and selections from, the *Journal of the Worcester Burneys*, in the possession of Mr. Harris, are here printed by the kind permission of Miss G. H. Burney, of Woburn Sands. The selection from unpublished Letters of Susan Burney has been kindly permitted by the Right Hon. the Earl of Ferrers and Mr. Harry A. Johnston, representing the family of Molesworth Phillips. The manuscript was recently presented to the Public Library at Armagh, and has been kindly lent to me by the Librarian, the Dean of Armagh.

Both the Journal and Susan's Letters contain many genealogical trees and biographical notes, which have enabled me to add dates and other items of information to the family biographies.

The illustrations are nearly all reproduced from photographs given to me, or taken for me, by Mr. Harris: the miniature of Fanny Burney being reproduced by permission of the Lord Aldenham; the portraits of Norbury Phillips and General D'Arblay by per-

5

mission of Miss Wauchope; those of James Burney, and Norbury Phillips by Edward Burney, and of Charlotte Barrett, by permission of Mr. Cecil H. R. Hensley. The allegorical painting by Edward Burney (frontispiece) was drawn for a scrap-book belonging to a grand-daughter of the "classic" Dr. Burney, now in the possession of his great grand-daughter Lady Douglas Powell, by whose permission it is reproduced.

The oil portrait of Sarah Harriet Burney, incorrectly supposed to be Fanny Burney, belongs to Mr. G. Buxton Browne, M.D., and is reproduced by his permission.

The sketch of Mrs. Locke belongs to Mrs. Atherton Cumming, grand-daughter of Archdeacon Burney, and is reproduced by her permission.

The extracts I have taken from published books by Dr. Burney and other members of the family are arranged to illustrate the phenomenal activity and varied output of the whole clan: many of the illustrations showing the artistic gifts of Edward Burney.

R. B. J.

CONTENTS

CHAPTER   PAGE

INTRODUCTION 13

I. MADAME D'ARBLAY IN FRANCE . . 18
ADDITIONS TO THE DIARY . . . 19

II. FRANCES BURNEY 108
"APOLOGY" FOR *Emigrant French Clergy* 108
A FAMILY SCENE: *Camilla* . . 110
A CHARACTER: *Camilla* . . . 114
THE HEROINE: *Camilla* . . . 114
THE HERO: *Camilla* 114
IMPRUDENCE AND SUSPICION: *Camilla* . 115
"DEDICATION" TO *The Wanderer* . 115

III. SUSAN BURNEY 118
UNPUBLISHED LETTERS 125

IV. DR. BURNEY 306
ADVERTISEMENT: *Essay on Comets* . . 308
DEDICATION: *Essay on Comets* . . 308
SUPERSTITION: *Essay on Comets* . . 309
INTRODUCTION: *State of Music in France and Italy* 310
TAKING THE VEIL: *State of Music in France and Italy* . . . 311
DEDICATION: *History of Music* . . 314
FROM THE PREFACE: *History of Music* . 315
"THE BEGGAR'S OPERA" AND NOTE: *History of Music* 316

7

CHAPTER   PAGE

A FRAGMENT OF AUTOBIOGRAPHY: *Memoirs* 317

FURIOUS INDUSTRY: *Memoirs* . . 320

LETTER TO HIS WIFE: *Memoirs* . . 321

LETTER TO FANNY: *Memoirs* . . 322

ON DEATH OF HIS (SECOND) WIFE: *Memoirs* 323

OF OLD AGE: *Memoirs* . . . 324

TO MISS BIDDY BELLAIR (VERSE): *Memoirs* 325

IN MEMORY OF SUSAN (VERSE): *Memoirs* 326

AS THE YEARS PASS (VERSES): *Memoirs* 326

V. JAMES BURNEY 328

"ADVERTISEMENT": *Discoveries in the South Seas* 331

ETHICS OF BUCCANEERING: *Discoveries in the South Seas* . . . 333

BRIEF INSTRUCTIONS: *Essay on Whist* . 338

GENERAL MAXIMS: *Essay on Whist* . 340

OF IMPROPRIETIES: *Essay on Whist* . 343

VI. CHARLES BURNEY, D.D. 344

INTRODUCTORY: *Milton's Greek Verses* . 345

PREFACE: *Exposition of the Creed* . . 346

VII. SARAH HARRIET BURNEY—AND RICHARD THOMAS BURNEY 351

OF HEROES AND HEROINES: *Geraldine Fauconberg* 354

JEALOUSY: *Country Neighbours* . . 355

THE PERFECT BRIDE: *Country Neighbours* 356

CONTENTS

CHAPTER   PAGE

VIII. CHARLOTTE ANN BURNEY, HER CHILDREN
       AND GRAND-CHILDREN   .   .   . 357
       PREFACE: *Charades by a Cantab*. .
        [CHARLOTTE BARRETT]   .   .   . 358
       A NATIVE FEAST: *Letters from Madras*
        [JULIA CHARLOTTE MAITLAND] .   . 361

IX. FRANCES BURNEY (DAUGHTER OF ESTHER) 366
       PREFACE: *Tragic Dramas*   .   .   . 367

X. THE WORCESTER JOURNAL   .   .   . 372
       THE MACBURNEYS, RICHARD OF WORCES-
       TER AND DR. CHARLES   .   .   . 374
       RICHARD'S CHILDREN 381
       THE THIRD GENERATION .   .   . 386

INDEX 401

LIST OF ILLUSTRATIONS

ALLEGORICAL SKETCH, by Edward Burney   *Frontispiece*

FACING PAGE

FANNY BURNEY, MINIATURE, by S. Shelley .   .⎫

DESK GIVEN TO FANNY BY THE QUEEN, in the pos-⎬ 32
    session of Mr. Leverton Harris   .   .   .⎭

GENERAL D'ARBLAY, by Vernet.   .   .   .   48

TWO BREVETS OF GENERAL D'ARBLAY   .   64 and 80

PROOF-SHEETS OF CAMILLA   .   .   .   112, 113

SUSAN BURNEY, by Edward Burney   .   .   .   128

MRS. LOCKE   144

MOLESWORTH PHILLIPS, by A. Geddes   .   .   160

BABY NORBURY, by Edward Burney .   .   .   176

DRAWINGS FOR ILLUSTRATION, by Edward Burney   192

FANNY PHILLIPS, by Edward Burney   .   .⎫
                                     ⎬ 208
NORBURY PHILLIPS, by Edward Burney   .⎭

DR. BURNEY (probably by Miss Reynolds) .   .   320

JAMES BURNEY (SILHOUETTE)   336

CHARLES BURNEY, D.D., from a bust by Nollekens   352

SARAH HARRIET BURNEY   368

CHARLOTTE BARRETT, by Edward Burney   .   .   384

SOPHY, CHARLES, AND FRANCES BURNEY (CHILDREN
    OF ESTHER), by Edward Burney   .   .   .   400

FANNY BURNEY AND THE BURNEYS

INTRODUCTION

" Next to the balloon," wrote Mrs. Barbauld, " Miss Burney is the object of public curiosity " ; and her words precisely represent the attitude of those days towards a " professional."

I have always felt that Fanny's pioneer work in fiction and her remarkable advance towards modernity from Richardson and Fielding have been curiously little appreciated ; but there are two other unique features of her novels which have been scarcely even observed : the social inheritance which inspired them, and the personality behind their emotional good taste.

Many Burneys wrote copiously, with some measure of distinction and abnormal industry ; but they were not properly men of letters. As musicians, more or less amateur artists, above all, dancing masters, they belonged rather to what is still called " the profession " ; that is a class, of old frankly associated with " rogues and vagabonds," who played a part to amuse the plebs, patronised by the Peers.

Dr. Johnson, indeed, had only just extorted some kind of respect from Society, which was still denied Garrick ; Mrs. Thrale and the " learned ladies " held their own in an emerging middle-class that was largely independent of aristocrats ; the culture of Mrs. Delany and her friends was never allowed to interfere with their social prestige.

These classes mingled, with intimacy and friendship indeed, but not fundamentally on equal terms. Dr. Burney was a very prince among entertainers ; but the great folk crowded to him as a popular " diversion," whose charm and power to collect " stars " had made him the fashion. As one of the girls herself gaily hit off an evening at the house in St. Martin's Street : " We had a very *singular* party : Italians, French, Irish, English, Jews, Protestants, Catholics, Deists, and what not ! "

In the fuller records of the Burney forbears, collateral relations, and descendants of the " Worcester " journal and other vignette biographies of this volume, we see how persistently the whole clan had, for generations, adventured without the pale, and yet commanded attention from more correct persons by their energy and artistic gifts. Nearly all did *something*, scarcely one quite conformed to the social rule, or applied himself to the regular business of life. Three, of later generations, appear as " characters " in the *Essays of Elia*. A genuine Bohemianism pervades the breed.

II

I do not suggest that Fanny was accurately conscious of the family position, or that she arranged her fictions as a star turn for " the show." But the daring social confusions of her *dramatis personæ*, the " character " parts on which her humour so much depends, the vivacity of her dialogue, her " heroics," and the melodrama of her passion-scenes, were obviously theatrical— gay reflections of life as she knew it among her family and friends.

Evelina, no doubt, was a spontaneous expression of genius, that will out ; invented because she loved the children of her gay and busy imagination. *Cecilia*, I think, was no less personally inspired, though constructed with more self-conscious art—to keep up the reputation that had so completely taken her by surprise, to please Daddy Crisp and Dr. Johnson.

But in form both novels are written for the stage or

the concert platform ; and, for this reason, stand almost outside regular literature, of which she knew neither the vision nor the rules. All the Burneys were given to self-expression—jesters, minstrels, and chroniclers to the nobility and at court. She was following the family way : only destined among them for pre-eminence, because in her alone dwelt the immortal fire of Art.

It is misleading to picture her as a neglected child, uneducated, and more or less gutter-bred. The home atmosphere, of course, was not scholarly or academic, certainly not cultured or high-brow. They had almost no instinct for written style. But it supplied the best of all education : a knowledge of men indifferent to the conventions, in mental " undress " revealing their true selves, enjoying life, and eager about the realities of heart and mind. Such were Dr. Burney's chosen friends, always at their best in his company ; such—in varying degrees—were all the Burneys ; and one can almost say that the whole family had their part in her achievement and her success.

III

The second personal characteristic of her work is almost more completely exemplified in Susan than in Fanny herself, as it is perhaps more fully or emphatically expressed in *Camilla* than in the well-known novels. This is a combination of eager and strong family affection—itself most remarkably universal among so large a connection nearly all of pronounced individuality, with a subtle refinement of moral and emotional taste. In many ways they were indifferent to, or unaware of, good form ; their taste in humour, while not actually coarse, was scarcely at all in advance of their age ; their easy cosmopolitanism did not save them from cheap jokes on foreigners ; but there was a strain of fundamental fastidiousness at least among the " inner " family circle, pre-eminent in Fanny and Susan, which is clearly reflected as the ruling characteristic of all her heroines.

It was known as " Sensibility "—that is, refinement

of mind and heart ; a grace which lent itself to the wildest extravagances of passion-storms, fainting-fits, morbid romance, and super-sentimentality ; but which, in a genuine and really superior nature, meant that they were ladies in the best sense of the word ; or, if you will, true women—with a higher private standard than most of their sex and than any but very exceptional men.

Because the Burneys were not quite well-bred, this quality sometimes found expression in what we can only call the language of a snob ; because they had no sense of style, and lacked emotional balance, it was also sometimes expressed,—fictionally in burlesque emotion, privately in over-sweet words of love.

But the essential fineness of which only a few women have ever known the secret is no less absolute in Evelina, Cecilia, and Camilla than in the sisters themselves. There exists, moreover, a masculine variant (false in Sterne and *The Man of Feeling*, but real and charming in Lord Orville, real and perverse in Delville and Edgar Mandelbert), which occasionally, I think, peeped out in Dr. Burney, was very striking in cousin Edward, both enhancing and weakening the personal charm of their dear friend, the younger William Locke.

Her somewhat stiffly phrased estimate of the gentle D'Arblay further reveals the need she felt for something rare and fundamentally refined in anyone she could call a friend, or be content to live with in any intimate relation : " A person *most peculiarly to my taste*, and whom I think most peculiarly formed for my happiness of any mortal I ever knew in my life."

It is here, in the very subtle and altogether charming " partiality " of Evelina and the gentlemanly perfection of Orville, that Fanny Burney shows such a striking advance upon the conventional psychology of Richardson or even Fielding, and strikes the first clear note of all that women were destined to do for fiction towards cleanliness, sincerity, truth to life, and feminine perception.

As she once remarked : " For my part, I wish the

story to be natural, tho' the sentiments are refined, and
the characters to be probable, thô their behaviour is
excelling."

Her objection, referred to in Susan's " Letters,"
against calling *Camilla* a " novel," reveals a criticism
(expressly stated by Fielding and Richardson) of the
" tendencies " in so-called romance ; and Susan's answer
defines what Fanny had done for the novel : " *Evelina*
and *Cecilia* alone would ennoble the word in my mind ;
even had there never existed a Richardson, or a Cervantes, or a Le Sage."

As I have endeavoured to prove elsewhere,[1] the actual
eighteenth-century ways and manners of Sensibility are
most literally pictured in *Camilla*, with all the enthusiasm
of extreme youth, as they were burlesqued in *Northanger
Abbey* and tenderly reincarnated in Marianne Dashwood ;
but it remains the most distinguishing charm and virtue
of the Burney sisters, which kept them a little apart
among the cruder spirits of professional Bohemia.

IV

The story of Fanny Burney's " Life " has been told
many times, with loyal care and critical understanding ;
her incomparable pictures of men and manners in the
eighteenth century are familiar to all who care for the
past.

Susan's " Letters " and the " Worcester " journal, I
think, materially assist us to understand the innermost
feelings of one of the shrewdest observers of human
nature who ever created fictions in the likeness of man,
and to appreciate the gallant industry, public spirit,
and loving-kindness of the race from which she sprang.

R. Brimley Johnson.

[1] *The Women Novelists* (Collins, 1918 and 1922).

I

MADAME D'ARBLAY IN FRANCE.

THE habit of copying, revising, and suppressing was so common among all the Burneys,—Madame D'Arblay, in particular, destroyed or erased for publication so much written by Fanny Burney and her respected father; her editors, again, exercised their own judgment in preparing the Diaries and Letters,—that we need not seriously concern ourselves to conjecture the precise reasons that have hitherto detained the following passages from print.

The relations between France and England at the time obviously account for copies being carefully preserved, when the originals, if sent away at the time, were of necessity despatched by private channels, and *possibly* never reached their destination. Similar precautions, also, suggested the elaborate " table of flowers " used for different members of the Royal Family—already, however, adopted in the Letters between Susan at Mickleham and Fanny at " the Queen's House."

Windsor would naturally be interested in every detail about their high-born neighbours at this particular time, and these narratives to Miss Planta—for Royalty—are scarcely less characteristic and illuminating for us than the " Journal " intimacies and private letters which Fanny herself chose to omit.

Although, strictly speaking, many of the paragraphs belong to and link parts of the published narrative, they can be read and enjoyed without reference to the book; but, to ensure a clear understanding of every extract, I have indicated its subject and supplied names for pronouns, in addition to stating precisely where each should have been inserted, by references to Mr. Austin Dobson's standard edition of 1905. I have retained her irregular spelling, etc., but corrected a few copyist slips.

The bulk of this new material, however, is itself consecutive, relating scenes, describing persons, and expressing opinions altogether omitted from the Diaries. It reveals much of her personal attitude on foreign politics, naturally coloured by earlier intimacies with distinguished *émigrés* and by her marriage, to some extent curiously limited, again, by the moral fastidiousness with which Dr. Burney had forbidden her certain friendships, and she had obeyed !

We know too little, indeed, of these last days, when the authoress of *Evelina* once more became, above all, a loving and loyal daughter, with the added domesticity of a mother and wife—too little of D'Arblay and the young Alex. While, in another view, the full and complete statement of her unjust judgment on Mrs. Thrale's second marriage further explains a foolish and unfortunate break in her literary social experience, as the boy's charming letter to one of the Lockes recalls the " best friend " chosen to replace Mrs. Piozzi.

Finally, I think, we can see here that the exasperating Johnsonese of her later books was in part put on for stage effect. These journals and letters are not, certainly, written in pure English ; but they *are* less tortured than the vexatious *Memoirs of Dr. Burney* or than *The Wanderer*. They are very nearly Fanny herself.

ADDITIONS TO MADAME D'ARBLAY'S DIARY AND LETTERS

Diary (addressed to Dr. Burney)

[Following the words " seeing his loved hand with some return."—V, p. 493.]

Thursday, April 15, 1802.—Good little faithful Molly, and Beckey, will let you know they[1] sat up till 4 o'clock in the morning to help, as well as see me off ; I could not

---
[1] The Lockes.

endure to wake my dear Fanny Phillips, though I had made, for the purpose of persuading her to go to rest, a sort of tacit agreement to embrace her again before my departure. She is one amongst those I very anxiously leave, and with all my true willingness to follow my Mate, my Heart was full, and heavy, and my spirits only supported by excess of business, which allowed no time for rumination.

[Replacing the " dots " . . . .—V, p. 494.]

My companions, or rather fellow travellers—for that Englishism of reserve for which I am so noted even in the circles in which I am known, was not very likely to be metamorphosed into companionabilityness in a diligence with these whose names were as unknown to me as their faces. As I stayed to converse with my dear Mrs. Lock, to the last moment, my friend the Book-keeper, etc. . . .

[Further details of Madame Raymond, following words " whether she might rest there or not."—V, p. 495.]

She [Madame Raymond] had a femme de chambre who travelled in the basket, and who waited upon her very assiduously, whenever we stopt for refreshments, or changing Horses. She refused, the whole way to Dover, to quit the carriage, having a little basket of provisions, of which she partook with her maid when the rest alighted at the Inns. I thought this an excess of penury to avoid the eating Bills, and longed to have made her partake of our fare without that draw-back; but though I tried various means of bringing this about, I could never succeed; she was polite but firm in all her refusals : and had only one defect to prevent etc. etc.

[Following words " as if she had been attired in a hoop for Courtt."—VI, p. 495.]

This strict formality put apart, she [Madame Ray-

mond] was far the first person of the set ; her language,
manners, and deportment, all announcing her superiority to the rest.

["A fellow-traveller" not described in printed Diary,
following the words "last ten eventful years"—V, p.
496.]

The 4th and last I have to name is a young Irishman,
immensely tall, very awkward, and excessively bashful ;
with eyes that dared look at nobody, yet leered at everybody ; manners utterly unformed, a face marking eager
curiosity, and a figure the most gawky. He was going
to France to study the language, and I presume, the
graces ; for he could not have more work for the one
than for the other ; but he was civil, good natured,
inoffensive, and I believe pretty well informed. In a
few months, he will perhaps be quite new modelled, for
he is still at that pliant age when accident, new scenes,
or new connexions may change or new mould the whole
character. My two little ones, and myself slept the
first two hours. Alex, delighted with the novelty of all
he saw then lost every sleepy sensation. I, though tired
with a whole night's watching, had Adrienne in my
arms, and no power to repose.

PARIS, *April* [18].

MY DEAREST FATHER,

When I began my journal, I meant to give you
immediately the full detail of my journey ; but the [un]-
speakable hurries and fatigue which prevented my writing
the first week, and the illness of my poor Boy, which has
wholly occupied me the second, make it impossible for
me now to go back with the alacrity which would accord
with my opening, and my intentions : I will devote
however every moment I can spare to that part of my
adventures, and then usher you with me into this great
Capital of the Great Nation ! *To the* 15*th April* once
more. We breakfasted at *Rochester,* almost famished,

but had not a moment for seeing the City, except as we passed through it, that and Brompton and Chatham, all appearing as one Town. The Country was always beautiful, and the children were always gay and happy.

[Between the second and third paragraphs.—V, p. 496.]

The road thence [from Canterbury] to Dover is so extremely pleasant, that it kept my fatigue in such good order, as to make it set sleep at defiance. Nor could Alex once close his eyes, though Adrienne took several short naps, which extremely refreshed her.

[Manuscript note in General D'Arblay's handwriting to the words "the examination was so slight."—V, p. 496, l. 24.]

As soon as the *red trunk* of poor Adrienne [1] was taken and the examiner unlocked it, the poor little thing burst into a flood of tears and threw herself upon me quite in despair. I instantly explained to the old gentleman, who was opening it, that it contained all the child's gifts; and her fright lest they should be seized; upon which, with a good humour I wish you could have seen, he exclaimed: "O poor little dear! Pray comfort her! I will touch nothing that can make her uneasy!" and he immediately locked the little trunk, without having put a finger within it; and gave the key into her own hand. I wish, too, you could have seen how her face brightened, and the conscious smile which exulted in her little triumph. Indeed she was the best little Traveller imaginable; never ill, never sick, and sleeping when tired without difficulty. But with a comical incipient coquetry, always preferring the official services of the *Gentlemen*, to that of we poor fair sex, whenever any choice was in her power! She will be a true little french demoiselle, for all Norbury, and for all *La Bonne*: a spirit of coquetry is in her nature, and her arch-smile

---

[1] Daughter of Madame de Chavagnac, who had been in the care of Mrs. Locke, and was now being taken back to France by the D'Arblays.

and meaning eyes will not repress the adoration for which she will have, I fear, but too much taste.

[Last moments at sea. Preceding the final paragraph —last two lines.—V, p. 496.]

The rain had now ceased, and my purpose was to remain on deck during the whole passage, as by that means, I escaped sickness, when I went in the commissioners' yacht to the Isle of White with Mr. and Mrs. Thrale (though in the 2nd passage which was in the cabin, I suffered severely as did Miss Thrale now Lady Keith). We had seats brought us and I placed my children before me. Alex was delighted with the grandeur and manliness of the idea of being at sea, and astonished to find it a matter of so little apparent danger or toil : Adrienne was playful and happy, and the first quarter of an hour, during which we were steering from the Port, all was pleasant and agreeable the whole party remaining on deck and expecting to arrive to a 3 o'clock dinner at Calais. We were joined by some other parties, from the Inn : one, consisting of a Lady and her daughter ; another of a dutchman and his English wife ; and a third of 3 young Bucks, who were crossing the sea for a frolic, wholly undetermined whether to go only to Calais, or to Dunkerk, or to *Bologn*, or to Paris, or to return sharp in the vessel, which was to be again at Dover as quickly as possible. Scarcely however were we out of the harbour, when my poor Alex was taken sick ; the steward of the vessel carried him down to the cabin, while I rose to accompany him ; but before I could move a step the contagion of his example so suddenly prevailed, that I was compelled to take a side view of the vessel, not to shock all the party by a front view of my poor self. Here I was stopt and re-stopt, in spite of every effort to follow my poor boy, a considerable time ; and at last was compelled to commit myself in silence to the guidance of the same steward, hopeless of reaching him by any more active means ; and only by signs able to summon Adrienne to be of our party : but the little girl still perfectly well, was so much amused, and so much courted by all, that my signal was not obeyed, and I was forced to be drawn on alone. I threw myself on the first bed, and can with difficulty pronounce whether I suffered most in body or in mind ; for I was unable to utter a single word, from a sickness without a moment's interruption, that tore me to pieces ; while I was wretched to join my poor boy, who was unfortunately on a bed in the next cabin ; and I was still more miserable for Adrienne, lest any accident should befal her while with only strangers on the deck. I really think I was two hours in this terrible situation, before I could utter a phrase of sufficient length to pray the steward to bring me the two children. My poor Alex was then placed on the other end of my Hammock and as much relieved as myself by the approximation, though neither of us were above a few minutes at a time allowed any respite ! but Adrienne, still well, positively refused to leave the deck, where she sat and sung and chatted with all around : and my helplessness to obtain her, caused me an incessant inquietude. Unused to consider me as a person who had any authority over her, and delighted to find herself the plaything of the party, she was too young to have any compunction for my uneasiness ; and, as I never could pronounce more than three words without a stoppage to my eloquence as little inviting to the beholder, as to the speaker, I could never frame a message of sufficient energy to counterbalance the little gypsey's delight in her amusement and her liberty. When at length, I heard some one say it was three o'clock, I was endued with sudden power to exclaim : " I hope, then, we are in sight of Calais ? " but what was my check, when I was answered " Of Calais ? You are hardly out of the Port of Dover," and I was then told a dead calm had completely stopt our course. In this suffering state Alex and I passed the day ; Adrienne was tempted to come down to us at about 5 o'clock, and when once I could speak to her, I found voice and breath to assure her she would be drowned, inevitably, if she left us any more : and her innocent credulity then detained her ; this relieved me from nearly the most painful solicitude I ever experienced. The daughter of the lady I have mentioned came down also, and as both were quite well, they danced and sung together, clambered up and down the beds, and told each other little stories. Adrienne, young as she is, became the confident of the other, though ten years old ; and heard from her " that she was carried over to her papa, who was in France, by her Mama, who was very unkind to her ; and meant to leave her ; because her papa hated her Mama, and they could not live together. She regretted nothing but school, where she had friends, and where alone she was happy ! " Poor little Girl !—At night, the calm continuing, no further attempt was made at sailing, and the whole party came down to the cabins. When the beds were filled, the *overplus* laid on the floor, getting what they could reach for mattrasses and pillows : and now it was that our three Town Bucks became diverting, for they ranted out such unmeaning rattle of their unmeaning excursion, that it was just bad enough to be good enough for laughable folly. Anything ridiculous in a higher style would have failed, if requiring attention or combination to give it effect. Adrienne now submitted to lie down in the same bed with her new friend, and fell fast asleep, and enjoyed the most perfect repose all night. Alex and myself had no such rest ; a few intervals from suffering were all we could obtain, and those of that unquiet sort that demanded the most perfect stillness, and were instantly broken by the smallest motion or even speech. Towards morning, however, the poor little Boy grew better, and from about 6 o'clock he had no further return of sickness. At 9, my own sufferings abated ; and as I heard we were at length in sight of Calais, I ventured to rise and crawl, with my children, to the deck : and as there was now sufficient air for the vessel to get on, I presently in some measure recovered ; and, though never quite easy, found myself able to keep above, and saw my Alex entirely revive, though still as pale as death from so wretched a day and night. A dutch vessel made up to us, with offers to tow us to shore ; but we all refused, except our Bucks, who were enchanted at a sort of new enterprise, and skipt on board with the smart vulgar agility of city apprentices skipping on a Form to look around them, at Sadler's Wells, or Vauxhall.

[Further examination of passports. Between second and third paragraphs.—V, p. 498.]

My gentle carrier [1] gave up his charge without resistance, however, and I parted from it no more. It was still very formidable to me to mount a sort of Tower, where were seated two civil officers, who examined our passports. They wrote in them. I never examined what, and I was desired to go into a round closet on one side the room. I took my two children, for my protectors, and a formal, but civil old gentleman, asked me if I brought anything that was contrary to the laws of the Republic ? Another added this was the room where an oath was to be taken to that effect. I did not chuse to give a very categorical answer to this demand, all my new mock peticoats jumping in the mouth of my conscience, which answered inwardly, it would rather I should lose them all than give a plump negative. I merely therefore replied, that I brought nothing for sale. This, to my equal surprise and pleasure, satisfied them ; they took hold of my écritoire ; I assured them it only contained letters ; and they returned it unexamined. I told them the simple truth in both my answers ; but was much gratified by their so readily believing it. They bowed, and we returned to the other passengers, and were conducted by the same commissary, and all our first companions of the shore, to some other municipal association, as I suppose ; for I understood nothing that passed, through the tremor I experienced from all these ceremonies ; and my many previous fears, joined

[1] Porter carrying her *écritoire*, in which was her passport.

to total ignorance of travelling, and constant solicitude
about the children through the impossibility of always
having a hand for each.   All this kept me in a state of
apprehension not very favourable to observation at the
time, nor to memory afterwards.   Nevertheless, through
all these impediments, the novelty of the scene and of
the persons surrounding me, afforded me, in the intervals
of my cowardice, much entertainment.

[Following the words : " We set off for Paris " (from
Calais), at 5 o'clock in the morning."—V, p. 502.]

I had just time to get my children ready, but had not
dared risk undressing myself.   You may believe, therefore, I was not much refreshed, and the poor things
were unwilling enough to rise ; but Alex, once awaked,
could sleep no more, and Adrienne, more happy as a
traveller, reposed upon my lap till she had finished her
night's requisite rest.   There was not, indeed, much
lost by those who spared their eyes in this part of the
journey !

[Between first and second paragraphs.—V, p. 502.]

At Boulogne we dined, and here, most unexpectedly,
we were joined at Table by a tall well made young
woman, not handsome, but of a rather striking countenance, and singularly ceremonious in reverences and
gestures, and sententious and self-complacent in discourse, as well as fashionable, though not indecent, in
attire : and she travelled in the Basket ! though she
begged leave to join the inside company at Table.
There was something so civil in her manners, it was impossible not to be civil in return ; yet so little *as usual*,
it was equally impossible not to draw back from any
acquaintance.

[After first meeting Madame Raymond.   Following
first paragraph.—V, p. 503.]

When we began our journey, Madame Raymond informed us that she had learnt from her femme de chambre, that the lady who now joined us at meals, was an actress. This was not surprising to me, from her appearance, though I felt a little awkward in her junction, without knowing something of her character. However, it was amongst the chances I was forced to run. But our merry hearted Gouvernante now conceived a plan, to make this dame undertake to form, and to teach french, to the young Irishman ; who declared, half frightened, half amused, that he had rather put himself under the protection of Madame Raymond : but the highland chief entered into the project, and from this time, when-ever the coach stopt, whether for our refreshments, or simply for that of our Horses, the Gentleman and lady were brought to a conference by the lively gouvernante, encouraged by the highlander, and listened to with some, though more dignified amusement by Madame Raymond, who seeing my shyness of this Farce, whis-pered me that, in France, actresses, when they had talents, were always received if they behaved with pro-priety. I told her I was amongst the last not to do them justice ; and where they had character as well as talents, I should be the first to do them honour : this might be the case here, but I always prefer *holding* back to *drawing* back, and therefore I was constantly silent and absorbed by the children. The approbation of the High-lander so stimulated the Gouvernante, that her spirits now were above her discretion, and she knew no bounds to her laughing scheme ; which I soon saw brought the Actress rather more into the front ground than shewed her to advantage. Madame Raymond luckily perceived it too, and by a grave though mild interference, checked the progress of the essay ; as much, I really believe, to the relief of the poor young Irishman, as to mine. The High-lander, who would have kept up the sport, and the Gouvernante were now such friends, that they sung, chatted, told stories and were alive to each other's pleasantries with mutual joy in lightening the tediousness of the night journey ; the

highlander glad to be diverted out of his haughty sulki-
ness, and the gouvernante delighted with all and every
opportunity of making mirth. This lasted till, tired all
around, one by one, the whole party dropt asleep, except
myself and my two charges, who were too miserably
accomodated themselves, both leaning entirely upon me,
to obtain any repose. An hour or two passed now in
darkness and in silence ; my sole amusement arose from
the poor Irishman's head, which dropt down on Madame
Raymond's shoulder, from its tall and thin height above
it, twenty times in a quarter of an hour ; and which she
repulsed, with a dignity that would have been anger,
had not her own sleepiness been so potent that she could
only awake for the single instant requisite to push the
unfortunate pate away from her : but about 4 o'clock
in the morning, the highland chief suddenly awaking,
let down the window : the Gouvernante, who was fast
asleep, awoke by a sharp blast of air, suddenly lost her
good humour by the cold, and pulled it up. The high-
lander, motioning her to be quiet, resumed his first
sullen pride, and again let it down : " What for you do
that," cried she, " I won't suffer no such thing to get
my nose full of cold at such time of night." He, however, roughly insisted ; and the gouvernante, not chusing
to submit, exclaimed, " What for you think only of
yourself ? Nobody will let no gentleman do such
thing ! " and she held the glass up with both her hands.
The highlander seemed indignant beyond words, and
looked as if he could have felt no small solace to his
wounded pride, had it been convenient to have taken
such a measure, by some manual exertions with his
broad hand upon her broad plump cheeks. He forbore
however ; but spoke to her no more ; and though, when
she had taken another nap and awoke to the sun beams
which succeeded to the nightly blast, she was as gay and
chatty as before, and told her stories, and sung her
songs, all were cast away ; the highlander neither heard
nor saw her. He spoke only with the young Irishman,
whom he had not before heeded ; and shewed every

mark of respect he could devise to Madame Raymond,
by way of manifesting her superiority to the poor gouvernante, who was by no means unmoved by the change,
and so angry that she could only look at him with disgust.   Two spirits of such fiery materials, both offended,
were not likely to remain long without striking against
each other ; and, in a few hours, upon some new change
from hot to cold, the highlander put down the glass,
et the gouvernante pulled it up.   This was repeated
with the pristine vivacity of the original struggle, till
the gouvernante, natural as well as violent, called out
" What for you think conquer a lady ? you rude man ? "
" A lady ? " repeated he, " what do you mean by a
lady ? you are a mere poor low-bred woman ; and never
till now sat at the same table with such a man as me ! "
" Did not I ? who told you so, Mr. ? you are nothing
but for a Brute to talk so ! I have been at the same
table with you many times enough ! "   " Yes," cried
he, " to stand behind the chair, when I have been
seated upon it ! "   " How dare you say such thing ? "
cried she ; " I will shew you what a lady I am the next
town I come to ! you may speak so to your English, if
they will let you, English as you are, for a Brute, to
speak so to me ! I will have you to the municipality ! "
He had just got his head out, to call to the conductor,
when this word *Municipality*, checked and alarmed him :
he drew back, and applied to Madame Raymond ; who
gravely told him he was in the wrong, but consented to
let him change place with her, to be on the side where
the glass was down by general consent.   He accepted
the offer, making her many compliments upon her being
a gentlewoman, and protesting he would no longer sit
opposite to so low a creature.   The Gouvernante again
declared she would take him to the municipality at
Amiens ; and from that time nobody spoke till we
arrived there, except the dear children.
Arrived at Amiens, where we were to dine, Madame
Raymond, after a private conference with our enraged
but really good hearted Gouvernante called me to assist

at the discussion ; I would fain have retreated for every possible reason ; but could not get excused : what however was my surprise, when she told me that she must send for the conductor, and make him come before us, while in a body, we declared the offence offered to Madame Blaizeau ; that justice must be done and that we must all join to vindicate her right to have one glass up, while the other was down as well as to let the mistaken gentleman know that, in public machines, the majority always prevailed ; and therefore, since by our joint opinions, he had offended a lady, we must desire, in a body, that the conductor would insist upon his relinquishing his place, and proceeding in some other conveyance.

I can hardly tell you my consternation at this proposal. To make my entrance into France run the risk of being announced by a dispute so likely to end by our all being called before the Municipality of Amiens, and thence, perhaps, sent with some guard to Paris ! English, too, myself, to appear against a member of our own United Kingdom !—but my fright luckily made me eloquent enough to save me from this exposition. I represented so urgently my hopes that the culprit was already alarmed, which indeed, in defiance of his rage, I had observed to be the case ; and that the victory was sufficient, if he were forced to offend no more, that the good humoured gouvernante gave way, and it was agreed we should let him have one more trial before we proceeded to extremities.

This foolish affair swallowed up all the time in which I might have strolled a little about the Town of Amiens. When we returned to the carriage, the High-lander, getting in first, and sitting forward, said to Madame de Raymond who followed him, " Mettez vous la Madame " pointing to the seat opposite him. " Pardonnez moi, Monsieur," answered she and composedly added, that she begged him to alight a moment and speak with the conductor who had been prepared to give him a little counsel. This effectually quieted him ; and he left the

Glass to the discretion of his triumphant vis-à-vis, but the painful care with which they each determined never to look at the other, was ridiculous to behold, though it must have been very difficult to sustain. At Chantilly, however, at about 5 o'clock in the following morning, this Highland Chief descended to make some enquiries concerning that famous place, and then sending for his baggage into the Inn, appeared no more : how deeply regretted, by our Gouvernante, I leave you, dearest Sir, to imagine.

[On the road to Paris : between third and fourth paragraphs.—V, p. 503.]

Where ever the coach stopt to change, or only feed the horses, my children and I alighted, and walked on, to stretch our limbs ; or else entered some cottage, or some shop, for some refreshment ; without which management, I know not how the poor little souls could have endured continual confinement for 2 days and 2 nights, after so fatiguing a passage. Indeed the change of posture was equally necessary to myself ; perhaps more, for so crampt I sometimes felt myself that I could hardly descend from the coach.

[Manuscript continuation (in General D'Arblay's handwriting) of the letter to Dr. Burney, describing journey to Paris, which ends V, p. 504.]

PARIS, 1, 1802.

I go on with the day of our arrival (April 20) from its peculiar interest to my dearest Padre. We entered Paris with perfect quietness, and found it as quiet as ourselves. The carriages, indeed, from some peculiarity in their construction, make triple the noise of those in London,—a noise so stunning as to nearly deafen me ; but the people move so gently, make way for one another so civilly, and look so peaceably, that in streets without carriages, you may walk through crowds of men and women as tranquilly and unmolested as through so many

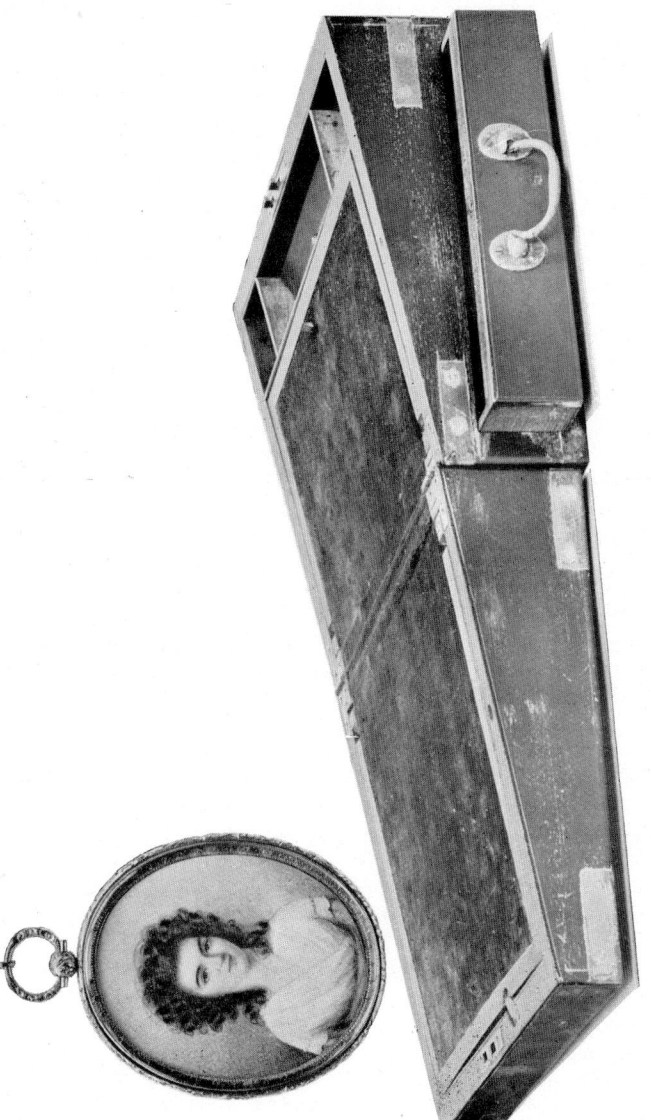

FANNY BURNEY.
By S. Shelley.

DESK GIVEN TO FANNY BY THE QUEEN.
From the original, now in the possession of Mr. Leverton Harris.

32]

flocks of sheep. I was forcibly, however, struck with
the immense superiority of London in the appearance
of the streets. Their narrowness here, and the surprising
height of the houses, gives them the air of what in
England, we should merely denominate *lanes* ; while the
breadth of ours, and our noble foot pavement, give a
facility of intercourse to the passengers, and a healthy
and pleasant airyness to the inhabitants, as much more
agreeable as I should suppose it to be more salubrious.
Against this, however, for constant residence, our coal-
fires and smoke must be balanced :—and then, perhaps,
with respect both to health and pleasure, the scales may
become even.

When we drove to the Hotel where we were to alight,
Rue Notre Dame des Victoires, the first object I saw
was M. D'arblay awaiting us : it was between 10 and
11 o'clock, and there he had stationed himself from 7 !
It was not what I wished, so publickly to meet him,
after so painful and eventful an absence ; yet it might
not have been, perhaps, what I should have expected,
had he stayed quietly at home till we could have joined
him there. To the kind heart of my dearest Father,
which but too feelingly knows the perfection of conjugal
partnership, I need not enter upon the solace of this
moment to all its preceding conflicts. Even my little
Alex, seized, with speechless fondness, to his Father's
breast, felt his loquacious and ardent spirit softened by
joy into silent tenderness. I took a brief leave of my
fellow travellers, who by their congratulations, showed
they discovered by my looks the happiness which not a
word, I am sure, betrayed, and M. D'a. ordered a fiacre
which conveyed us to Rue de Miromenil, where, in the
Hotel Marengo, he had prepared for our reception. We
have a very pretty apartment, consisting of a salloon,
a salle-à-manger, notre chambre, a dressing room within
it, which we make Alex's Bed-room, a little dark closet
for a fille de chambre, and an anti-room, which separates
all this from our little kitchen ; and the whole has been
papered, with new linen, beds, and much new furniture,

3

put up entirely to prevail with M. D'ar. to fix his little
Family for the present, where he had all the winter, in
a single room, fixed himself. We are up 3 pairs of stairs,
to be sure—but *The nearer the Gods*, you know! and
we see the Gardens of the ci-devant Hotel de Beauvau
from our windows and we have the fields open to us at
one end of the street, and we are close to the Champs
Elysees from the other. The situation is all that I can
wish; entirely out of the violent bustle and close air
of Paris. M. D'Arblay had been most kindly assisted
in preparing for me by Made. la cy-devant P'cesse
d'Henin d'Alsace, whom I had known particularly in
England and who has a claim to my respect and affection
from having inspired both in one whose feeling and
judgment in the characters she appreciated was *nearly*
unerring! Scarcely had we looked around us, when this
truly amiable Lady, whose apartments are nearly opposite, arrived to welcome me to Paris. M. de Narbonne
came also; he lives also immediately vis-a-vis to us,
and, as far as I can gather, in the most retired private
life. I was much affected by many recollections at his
sight; and so he seemed himself. He was extremely
pleased with his little God-son cordially embracing and
blessing him.

Made. d'Henin had already prepared me Tea, sugar,
an urn, a Tea-pot, &c. *a l'anglaise*; and three pots of
groseille, for little Alex, with small articles [in]numerable
of immediate use and comfort. She received me with
the extremist kindness, was charmed to see Adrienne so
much improved, and talked of my dearest friend, Mrs.
L., and all her's, with a warmth of regard and respect
and affection very delightful to my ears and my heart,
but alas! with what a pang, a sadness did I see her!
We had not met since my ever and for ever irremediable
loss[1]; and the knowledge she had of it, and the value
that angel set upon her, and her friendship—all rushed
upon my mind, and I was so much overpowered as I
fear to distress her. But this place, my dearest padre,

[1] The death of Susan.

this scene,—this country,—this society,—all which she
naturally loved, and all which she would so have delighted
to have joined, whether personally or by accounts—o
my beloved padre! what a constant,—a gnawing—an
endless drawback to all perfect enjoyment is that fatal
separation! Feelingly, and prudently, she hastened
away, advising me to take some rest. But she had only
descended the stairs, when Augustin mounted them to
bring me the compliments of Mlle. de L. who desired
to know how I did after my journey. I sent my thanks
and that I was tolerably well, but meant to take a week's
rest before I should feel recovered. My dear padre
will not think this quite so elegant as it was sincere:
but here comes another alas! Certain reports against
this lady, with respect to her amitie for an old and admired friend of ours, had made me anxious to defer the
acquaintance, till I could know better with what degree
of intimacy, or coldness, to begin it. I soon found,
however, my precaution rather too late ; she had already
formed the project of a free connexion, had sent, also
des confitures for Alex ; and persuaded M. D'Ar. to let
her chuse me a cap and a hat from her own Milliner.
This was embarrassing ; especially as I had no time to
speak upon the subject before there came another message, that she would enquire herself how I did, if it
would not be indiscreet. M. D'A . . . said it would be
impossible to refuse : and upstairs she took the trouble
to mount. She is still even *pretty*, nay almost *more*,
almost beautiful, except for very bad teeth ; her complexion is fair and smooth, her eyes very fine, and all
her features good ; her dress was a very elegant *des-
habillé*, though not in first repair, and she has a look
that, had I not been prejudiced against her, would have
struck me as mingling benevolence of character with
spirit of disposition. But I held back, involuntarily,
from thinking the best, lest I should again have to crush,
as with Mde. de Staël, an intimacy too hastily, and
unhappily formed. Her civilities were unspeakable ; her
offers of service had the solicitude of begging them ; and

her whole mind seemed at work to oblige, and to engage me. She would not, however, she said, so soon have forced her way, but that, understanding how much I was fatigued, she concluded I should be invisible for some days, and she could not command her forbearance so long a time. She seemed, indeed, so ardent and so kind that I was truly disturbed by my incertitude what to think of her ; which, joined to my entire disuse to speaking french, made the visit extremely, *to be sincere*, oppressive to me. I made, however, no engagement, anxious first to discuss the subject with M. D'Arblay ; but not a moment was now to be allowed for it, as I was obliged to seize the instant of her retreat to look for the small packet of dear Adrienne, to prepare her for her friends. I had not, however, taken out the first pin (all sewing being demolished at the custom-house) when Augustin returned, with the compliments of M. de N. and a request to know if I was too tired to receive him before I took my projected long repose. There was again no denying ;—but o what bitter pangs of bitterest recollection, and retrospection, accompanied this interview ! It was long before I could speak to him—even a word ; and he was pale as death, and trembling all the time : and though, in introducing to him his little Godson, I a little recovered, I believe it was nearly an equal relief to us both when Mr. D'a . . . said, I ought now to take a little rest. For rest, how-ever, I had as little time as, at that moment, power ; my poor Adrienne's pacquet was still unpinned, when Made. de Montecler was announced. She was received of course, instantly ; she was accompanied by M. de Chavagnac, M. Louis de C., his little son, and a young lady, who was not named, but who seemed a relation, and appeared to be about 12 years of age. Poor Adrienne now changed colour,—she ran to me, and clung to me, was pale and trembling ; but nevertheless, though this first emotion conquered her, and I saw her ready to burst into tears, and longing to cry *o take me back to my Mama Locke !* she subdued it with a presence of mind, and power over her feelings, that announce uncommon fortitude and sense in so young a creature; for when her Papa opened his arms, and fondly called her, she instantly went to him, and affectionately embraced him. Made. de Montecler called her next; Made. de Montecler bears a character of highest respectability, and I think it very fortunate for the future welfare of Mrs. Lock's dear little protégée that she will be in such worthy hands : but for the present Melle. de M. has an air so naturally austere and cold, though studiously kind to the child, that the contrast from the *other* maman was irresistibly felt, and the poor thing's head droopt and her eyes filled with tears; wisely, however, dispersed, even untouched, as slowly and reluctantly she obeyed the call. The young lady then took her hand, and, courtesying, made her a compliment on her arrival with the ceremony she would have done to a woman of forty. To this Adrienne only hung her head. I never heard who she was, but while I thought, from her youth and stiffness, she had been allowed to come out one day in the year from some strict school discipline, judge my surprise, to find, from Made. de Montecler's ceremonials with her, when they were departing, and from the word *Madame*, that she was already a married woman ! The fourth call for our Adrienne was by no means the most melancholy,—it was from her young Brother, and presently getting into a corner with him, she caressed him very fondly, and they soon chatted, and laughed together as if they had never been parted. What now was her joy, that all her cakes, etc. which Mamma Lock had intended for her journey had been fortunately so packed up, by the conductors, that we could never get at them ! Untouched, she had the pleasure of carrying them all home ; and the thought of making a feast with her Brother soon lightened all her rising sorrows. Everyone was anxious to make her happy, and M. de Chavagnac admired her beauty with the fondest paternal partiality. Poor little Adrienne told me *she would write to Mama Locke every day.*

Mr. Bourdois and Maria came next, looking in high spirits, and very happy. They are in a house as yet all unfinished and unfurnished, but as Time only is wanting not *money*, for its completion, their condition is not very deplorable.

Some other persons called also, and I had a young maiden brought to me who had already been hired for my *femme de chambre*, et *femme de cuisine*, et *Bonne pour Alex* etc. etc. while *la portière* of the House was to undertake all the drudgery. This young maiden, Pauline, is remarkably pretty, and very well made; *douce*, in voice and manner, a good milliner, a tolerable *mantua-maker*, and really fitted to be *really femme de chambre*: but she undertakes the rest, *moyennant* a *generous* salary, which for us is extremely cheap, as her various talents make her constantly useful and comfortable, and she is extremely pleasing.

April 21*st*.—I spent the whole morning in Bed, while at least a score of M. D'Ar. 's friends came to enquire after me. But when Bood and Maria were of the number, I arose; not however, much refreshed, for I had been too much fatigued for sleep. My little Adrienne also came to see me and her good father and Grandmother; and I was struck to observe how serious the poor little girl was grown, not however, from any apprehensions of her future welfare and happiness, for she could have had no heart to be gay at once upon leaving such an adopting Mother as Mrs. Locke, such a house as Norbury Park. Mr. Huber called also; and after the terrific account he had given to Mrs. Huber, communicated no small comfort to me, by saying that, many as were the licentious and profligate here, there was no City in Europe where Foreigners were more completely at liberty to chuse their own society, and their own plans, than the visitors of Paris: and that those who thought they must needs follow the stream, were entirely mistaken. "And, Madam," he added, "however many people and things you may see here to shock you, you will find many persons of real worth, ready to receive you, and to do you every service in their power." He then particularly instanced Made. de Sessa, an old lady, cy-devant first Dame d'honneur to the Queen, poor Marie Antoinette, whose wishes, he said, to know me, were stimulated *en outre* other civil reasons, by her long esteem and personal regard for M. D'ar. Made. de H. he also named as particularly amiable and benevolent ; and he gave me a hint, in very flattering terms, that I required nothing but care to pretty much chuse for myself throughout Paris, my own Society.

We closed this day by a visit in the evening, from M. Bazille Junr. the son of M. D'arblay's so much beloved uncle. He seems a very amiable young man, and is remarquably handsome *for* our Alex has a strong family resemblance to him !—*n'cest ce pas tout dire ?* That excellent uncle has written us the kindest, most cordial invitation to Joigny, where he would have us fix our residence.

[Letter to Miss Planta. Paris, April 27, 1802. Telling again of their journey. Filling the space shown by dots. . . .—VI, p. 2.]

I had heard so much of the plainness and mahogany skins I should view when I had crossed the strait of Dover, that I was amazed at the number of pretty women, and of lovely children I saw in Calais, most of them very fair. Mentioning this circumstance afterwards to an English gentleman, he hastily replied : " Don't you recollect the reason ? Calais was so long in possession of the English, that the Race is not yet extinct." You will acknowledge this was modest, whether true or not. Two days and two nights we then travelled to reach Paris, Adrienne leaning upon my arms and Alex resting against my knees.—Need I enter in further detail to give you a notion of my *fatigue* ? Indeed I am not yet recovered from it, though I will confess to you, I forgot it all for some hours after my arrival, from the reception my exertions met with from the person for whom I made them.

[From the same letter. Filling space shown by dots . . . .—VI, p. 3.]

I must pass by however, all other to speak of one introduction in which I was most peculiarly interested —that to Mademoiselle de Mortemar, whom I have already seen four times, and always with added pleasure : a certain Honeysuckle message with which I was honoured for her, has caused her so much delight, that I believe she can never see me without a pleased sensation from its recollection. I find her lively, agreeable, interesting and intelligent ; and her beautiful sister, Madame de Beauvau, seems a composition of grace and virtue. Their lives, by all I have observed or have gathered, are exemplary for discretion, right conduct, and domestic seclusion. Most fortunately for me, Madame d'Henin d'Alsace, whom I had known in England, and who had assisted M. D'Arblay in all his preparations for making me comfortable upon my arrival, had already settled a meeting for me with these ladies before I came ; and while I was recruiting to enable myself to wait upon them with my letter, and my *Honeyed* message, they were so good as to come to me themselves, arm in arm with M. le P. de Beauvau whom M. D'A. had known intimately when a child, though they have hardly, I believe, met since. I can scarcely tell you with what sensibility and delight the Honeyed-words and the letter of Mrs. Harcourt, were received by Mademoiselle de Mortemart. I was only sorry I had not a similar pleasure to bestow upon her charming sister, whose beauty and whose gentle manners rival each other in attraction. As two ladies who had called upon me were in the room, our conversation upon what I most covetted to talk, the Oak, the Magnolia, and the fair flowers of England was brief though expressive, and heartfelt ; but not so as to Mrs. Harcourt. They both spoke of her with fondest admiration and friendship, and seemed quite solaced to meet with one who had been personally known to her—to the General, to Lord and Lady Harcourt, and could enter upon a subject that enabled them to

give vent to their affection and gratitude for that noble
family in general and Mrs. Harcourt in particular. We
returned their visit as speedily as possible, Madame
d'Henin d'Alsace having the goodness to conduct us. I
have the pleasure to find they live very near us, and that
the walk between our habitations is, at this season, clean
and pleasant. They were so kind as to let me see all
their children, except a little one of eight months old,
who was sleeping. M. de Beauveau fetched us the others
himself, and seems as fond a Parent, and as good a husband as any our own dear Isle, so famed for parental
and conjugal characters, can boast. You will believe,
my dear Miss P. I name him not as *singular* for those
domestic qualities, though born in France! The children are healthy, blooming and well behaved, though
none of them have half the beauty of their mother. I
forgot to mention how much I was charmed and surprised by both sisters, as well as by M. de Beauvau, in
being addressed by them in English. I am still so very,
very little accustomed to speaking French, that the
attempt always embarrasses even my thoughts.

A party was now formed for our all meeting again by
Madame d'Henin who wished to take me to the Italian
opera buffa, and who had the loge, with eight Tickets,
of M. de Choiseul, for a day or two after. There accordingly we all met, the 8 tickets being disposed of by
Madame d'Henin to M. et Mde. de Beauveau, Melle.
de Mortemart, Mr. Charles de Poix, Mr. Malhouet and
ourselves : but Mr. Malhouet failing, M. de Guignes
formerly ambassador in England, took his place. The
Music was by Sarti, and very pretty, but the *altogether*
was so very long, that, little used as I now am to public
places I was so oppressively tired, that being unable to
disguise my weariness, and, in defiance of all my efforts
to be pleased, on the very point of falling asleep, Mde.
D'H. et Mr. D'A. had the charity, at the end of the
second act, to convey me away. I must, however,
observe that I saw, with much satisfaction, a general
decency of *costume* at this Theatre that was wholly

unexpected; neither in *les loges*, nor on the stage, was there anything that could shock the most scrupulous spectator; the exceptions being so few as to be rather objects of mingled pity and curiosity, than of the horrour and disgust with which I was prepared to behold them. Entre nous, nevertheless, it is but right to notice, in this favourable account, that I am horribly near-sighted!

Again I met these two charming sisters at a very select and elegant Assembly and *petit soupé*, chez Mde. D'Henin, consisting of Mr. et Mde. de Tessé, Made. la Psse. de Poix, Mr. Charles de Poix son fils, Mr. de Guignes, Mr. Crillon and his son, who are preparing to visit England; Mr. et Mademoiselle Mounier, Mr. de Noailles, Mr. Adrien de Meun, Mr. de Montagu, Mr. de Damas, Mr. de Beauveau, and a very few others whose names I forget, though the ceremonial of introduction passed with almost all, for it is impossible for me to give any idea of the politeness and kindness that are shown me. I dare not even attempt it.—My own ease and delight, however, was chiefly with the two sisters, and I had now an opportunity to converse at full length with Mademoiselle de Mortemar upon the Trees, plants, and flowers she had seen in England, and which she spoke of with a warm admiration that came close to my heart. We sat together at supper, and talked of nothing else. That exquisite plant, the Magnolia, which she seems to have had good opportunity of seeing, and which, though not a native of our soil, has taken root in its very heart, she agreed with me in thinking it possessed the highest and most elegant perfume possible; she indeed was chiefly listener here, my own opportunities of seeing and studying the virtues and sweetness of that plant having far exceeded hers; and I may say the same, also of our Rose, which has a flavour always so peculiarly delicious to me, that it is difficult for anyone to keep pace with me in its commendation. Our Honeysuckle, however, and our Lily, she disputed with me which should praise most, thinking them the loveliest flowers she had ever smelt. You will easily believe with how much pleasure I joined in her panegyric, but the glowing carnation, and my dear, dear, beautiful violet, she permitted me to describe entirely in my own way, being, compared with myself, almost a stranger to their odour.

Need I tell you how delightful to me was a conversation such as this ? or how animated I became when she talked of our noble Oak, acknowledging no such tree grew in any other Country ! Mademoiselle de Mortemar could discourse upon England as long, and with just or near as much eagerness as myself. She regards it, she says, completely as her native land, having spent in it the last important 10 years of her life, and its customs, manners and inhabitants, were all highly esteemed by her. She never, she said, suffered so much as in quitting it ; especially as the last four days she spent in it were passed in waiting for a passage at Dover ! " to have left " she said, " everything most dear to me, and then to be detained from coming on, in a place where I had no interest, no pleasure ! for, once fixed that I must leave England, my next wish was to arrive in Paris." She and M. d'Ar. then recollected that they had crossed the sea together, though without knowing each other's names : but the burthen of every stanza was Mrs. Harcourt, whom she almost adores. She had just written to that lady by Mr. Jackson.

My letters for Mr. Merry—one of which was from Lord Pelham, M. D'Arblay carried to that Gentleman a few days after my arrival. He was out, but so polite as to call here the next morning. I could not see him, having laid down, in a fit of almost insufferable fatigue, and unluckily he mounted our high stairs in vain : he left tickets for us both, and for me an especial message, with an offer the most obliging of his services, and a desire I would not scruple to employ him, if anything occured in which he could be of use to me. I shall avail myself of his civility by enclosing this to him, and requesting he will forward it with his next despatches. I have been 3 days writing it, by odd minutes, from the illness of my dearest Boy, who has been seized with a fever that has almost terrified us to death,—and forced us to see two physicians, though till now, I have never once had recourse to any since I married. I attribute it to the fatigue of our journey, joined to change of water to wine, diet and hours, and his too violent sensations of joy in seeing his Father, who in return, overpowered by pleasure, took him about, till his eager spirits, and excess of animation, were heated and inflamed into fever. I write still by his bed-side, having positively renounced every sort of engagement till I see him well : but he is so much recovered, that I have every reason to hope his re-establishment will be as rapid as the attack. One of his physicians, M. Bourdois, is an old friend of Mr. D'Ar ; the other Mr. Cöet, was recommended to me by Madame de Beauveau. Both assure me all danger is over ; but are of opinion he has narrowly escaped a putrid disorder ! O my dear Miss P. how thankful am I for such an escape.

Your *favourite* Hero[1] is excessively popular at this moment from three successive grand-events, all occurring within the short time of my arrival—The Ratification of the Treaty of Peace,—The restoration of Sunday and catholic worship,—and the amnisty of the Emigrants. At the Opera Buffa, the loge in which I sat was exactly opposite to that of the First Consul ; but He and his family are all at Lamort-maison.—Malmaison.

Shall I never have done ? Yes, yes—Adieu, my dear Miss P. and believe me ever

Your affecti. friend and servt.

F. D'AR.

M. D'Ar entreats you to accept his best compliments.

RUE MIROMENIL,
    No. 1185,
        PARIS.

[The following passage was written in the form of

---

[1] This was an appellation agreed upon previously for Buonaparte, as a flattering one, and therefore safe one, in case of a letter's seizure or miscarriage.

"Notes or rather margins," which "were copied by my partial Partner, willing to keep my first sentiments of his country and countrymen, from parts of my Letters to my beloved Friend *Frederica Lock*."—Ed.]

M. de Beauvau has a serious count[e]nance, but without much mark, and his dress and air are both very English, and in the Style of an English man of Fashion but not of elegance; his wife, ah my dearest F. . not so his wife.— She too, has an English air—but it is of elegance and not of fashion; t'is a look of sweetness with dignity, not *pretention*, t'is beauty of so chaste a character, as far as features and countenance and complexion can combine to give an idea of mental through bodily perfection, that my imagination flattered itself with seeing something like my own beloved F . . in the early years of her marriage. Do you think then, I did not feel myself drawn, attracted, almost bewitched by her? Mademoiselle de M. has by no means as much beauty, nor as much grace; but she has extremely fine speaking eyes, a look that is highly *spirituelle*, great native gaity and quickness, and feelings as strong, perhaps, or stronger than her sister's; but not so well curbed for herself, nor so soothing for others. Warm, energ[e]tic, enthusiastic, for all she loves, she seems prone to an indifference bordering upon disdain for all else: while Mde. de B. has an air, a voice and a manner of such fascinating sweetness, as to inspire whomever she addresses with an opinion, a hope, at least, of her personal kindness. If their appearance and deportment pleased me, you will easily imagine my added gratification upon their addressing me in my own language. I am so little able to say *what* I mean *as* I mean in French, that I am perpetually entangled in difficulty when I attempt a phrase of more than 5 or 6 words: and the moment any embarassment begins, my very ideas become obscure from the horrible provocation of searching in vain for words that may explain them. Yet everybody assures me *I speak so well*, that I am not without hopes they fill up all the chasms, formed by my ignorance how to fill them up myself, with so high an opinion of my untold meaning, as to make it pass for something excellent—beyond expression !

[Journal again—to Dr. Burney. Between first and second paragraphs.—VI, p. 4.]

M. de Beauveau is extremely tall, rather large, and though not handsome, has a very pleasing smile, when to smile seems good to him, but he seems very reserved, and distant, and rather taciturn. His wife who looks not yet twenty, and is not many years more, though she was married so early as to have a son near 9 years old ! is quite beautiful : fair with a high, yet soft tinted colour, lively blue eyes, an aquiline nose, and a mouth and teeth extremely pretty. She has a look of modesty, goodness and dignity joined to an air, a manner, and a voice of the most interesting softness ; you would be in love with her my dear daddy, immediately. I felt myself quite charmed with her. She has four children, and yet you would think she was but just brought forth from some convent, in which she had received an exemplary education, to be disposed of in marriage. Nevertheless there is not the least look of our *mauvaise honte* ; no embarassing because embarassed timidity ; on the contrary, though everything she said had a tone that shewed the most unaffected diffidence of her own merits, there is an ease as well as grace in her deportment to others, evidently resulting from a consciousness of what is due to her situation in life, which she feels without vanity, and sustains without pride, because the humility of her character saves her from annexing to it any idea of self. In this she reminded me of my lovely Princesses. Indeed she is a sweet creature, and I am the more tempted to admire and to like her, from the novelty to my expectations of beholding in France, so much loveliness of youth and beauty in a faithfully attached wife, and tenderly affectionate mother. At this very moment she nurses herself her youngest child, Gabriella who is about 6 months old. Mademoiselle

de Mortmart, her sister, has more spirit in her countenance, but less beauty. She appears to be lively and
clever, yet full of sensibility. She has spent 10 years in
England, which as she is not yet 25 makes so much the
greatest part of her conscious life, that she always, she
says, thinks it her real country. She has been returned
but two or three months, and came over in the same
packet with Mr. D'Ar. though they then did not know
each other. She loves England with such enthusiasm,
that she talks of it with a rapture that presently fills her
eyes with tears in bitter regret at having left it; and
her heart's first wish, she assured me, was to return
thither as soon as possible. Mrs. Harcourt had been a
mother to her, she told me, and her reception everywhere had been as if born her daughter. She hinted
not that her own birth had yet higher claims as to all
ceremonial of respect; but though her sense and judgment silenced her on this subject, there is something
in her look and manner, that always announce she does
not forget what she was born to think her due. They
are two charming creatures, and if Madame de Beauveau,
from superior beauty, and winning softness of voice and
manner, is more immediately engaging, it is very possible
that Mademoiselle de Mortmart, from the animation
of her character, and the quick feeling displayed in her
very fine eyes, may be equally attractive where she fixes
her own desire to please. They made me a long and
extremely pleasant visit, assuring me that they came the
very moment they heard of my arrival. I have the
more reason to be obliged to them, as I am informed
it is not the custom of the French ladies to visit any
strangers, till they are waited upon first. This however, was not more agreeable to me, than another over-
ture of intercourse which followed was painful and
perplexing. A lady whom M. D'Ar. called upon soon
after, told him she had had a visit from Madame de
Staël, who having heard I was come to Paris, mentioned
her expectation of soon receiving my visit: the lady
—a little in the confidence of our notions upon that

subject, said she doubted my going much abroad, and understood I meant to live in a very retired manner. That was nothing Mme. de St. answered, with regard to her, as she had been so much acquainted with me in England ; the lady again expressed her doubt of my calling myself into notice by any voluntary action. She then said : " Croyex vous qu'elle me recevra avec amitié ? En ce cas j'irais la voir ; qouique ce ne soit point l'usage." A hesitation of our friend to this demand, changed the tone of its condescension into scornful resentment. She added—" Si non—à la bonne heure ! qu'est ce que Madame D'Ar. pour moi ! " Here the matter rested ; and here, though sorry to offend, we yet concluded it best to let her own pique end the difficulty.

Mr. B. junior, son of Mr. D'Ar.['s] beloved uncle was admitted to our little dinner to-day, we have resolved never to attempt giving dinners, from the beginning, lest soon we ourselves should be without them ! excepting only the sons of Mr. Bazille, when in Paris, and M. Lajard who, having partaken of our Hermit fare at West Humble, we judged sufficiently initiated in the secret of bad living to be continued a member of our Table. Young Baz. was going the following day to Joigny, where we are all expected with the kindest impatience ; though Mr. Baz.—l'aine, with the best grace possible, yields to the desire of his nephew to keep me in Paris while the season is yet favourable for my seeing it.

April 22nd.—The good and respectable M. Lajard this morning breakfasted with us. I was rejoiced to see him, and felt myself received by a sincere and worthy friend. Having lost everything during his exile, he has been soliciting ever since his return, for his *retraite* and is living, meanwhile, in the most penurious manner, from delicacy to the friends by whom he is aided, though by them, a mother and two brothers, he is loved with the utmost tenderness. Just as he went, arrived M. Chevallier ;—Do you remember him in England ? He

GENERAL D'ARBLAY.
By Vernet.

enquired after you and after Charles, with warm expressions of gratitude; to you he owed, he said, the kind proposition of translating Baretti's Dialogues for Miss Thrale; and to Charles much kindness and service. You are of his party, I well know, in support of *Troy*, —both of you!—Heavens! undermine the very existence of belief so classic! What is to become of every allusion in every poet? Who is to understand a single simile in an ancient author? T'is almost teaching one to read without an alphabet. His visit was presently succeeded by one from M. de Narbonne—whom I amused—amazed at least, not a little, when in return to innumerable offers of service and kindness, in procuring me Tickets, admissions, or accompanying me to public places, or celebrated people I answered I required nothing at present but repose, for I lived *so much in the world* that I must rest before I could undertake anything new. And this, ridiculous as it sounds to those accustomed to the life of a Capital, is with me, so long a real Hermit for retirement, a simple matter of fact.

After him came our Bood and Maria, with M. Bourdois l'ainé who is a physician of eminence and a perfectly well bred and much admired man. I was very happy to find that Marie likes him extremely, as much of her life will be spent in his society.

Madame d'Henin had made us promise to dine with her, to meet only Mr. Malhouet. She is so friendly and amiable that I am always pleased in her society; and so inexpressibly kind to me, that I apply to her upon every difficulty. She lives nearly opposite us, in apartments which she has made elegant by the fitting up, and which her friends had ornamented by various presents at once useful and decorative, before her return from England. It is up two pairs of stairs! and she resigns herself to it with as much modest cheerfulness of content, as if she had never been Mistress of any more spacious residence: though her former Hotel, which I have been shewn, is superb!

In the evening we were joined by la cy-devant Prin-

4

cesse de Poix, who for 30 years past has been the confidential and intimate friend of Madame d'Henin. You may recollect, my dearest Sir, a letter written by M. le cy-devant Prince de Poix to Mr. D'Arb. upon our marriage. That Gentleman is husband to Madame de Poix, who is of highest estimation in this country alike for her virtues, her wit and her accomplishments. As she is quite, by some accident, lame, and has dreadful health, she was litterally incapable of emigration; but great as were her sufferings and danger in remaining, during the dread reign of Terror, when hardly a relation or a friend survived but by flight, in the result it has left her so much of her own fortune as to enable her to receive her husband, when erazed from the fatal list, to pay his debts, which were enormous, to save him from his creditors, and to live with him in a style the nearest to elegant of any I have yet seen, though far, far removed from what they had been born and bred to before the revolution. Madame de Poix looks near 60 but has still fine bright piercing eyes, and the most pleasing remains of beauty; her manner is vivacious, striking, and highly agreeable; her speech has a rapidity that does not seem the mere effect of female volubility and love of prate, but of quick ideas, which demand immediate vent, because others are crowding upon them, which insist upon making way. Her civility was of the most distinguished and elegant sort, and though, as I could only speak my miserable french, I could not be at my ease with her, I liked her too much to form my usual wish of retreat, She soon glided the discourse into Cecilia; but with an adroitness of turning her eyes every way but towards me, that prevented its being oppressive; I was not, I own, much surprised to find, by what I observed in her, that the character with which she seemed the most deeply impressed was Mrs. Delville. She declared this visit was not to Madame d'Henin, but merely to begin an acquaintance which her lameness alone had prevented her opening by mounting my stair-case at the Hotel Marengo.

HOME LIFE UNDER THE STUARTS

By ELIZABETH GODFREY

Author of "English Children in the Olden Time"

GEORGE VILLIERS AND HIS BROTHER

Fully Illustrated. Cloth Gilt. Demy 8vo. 12s. 6d. net

MISS GODFREY'S charming volume covers the period of forty-five years from the death of Queen Elizabeth to the triumph of Parliament—the reigns of James I and Charles I. It illustrates from contemporary materials, chiefly familiar letters and private diaries and memoirs, the inner life of the home. That it is a book of gossip and personal details of a bygone age is one of the great attractions of the volume.

The author's themes reach from the cradle to the grave ; the baby in the nursery, the boy with his games and lesson-books, the public school, the private tutor, the university : girlhood, marriage, dress, fashion, housekeeping, gardening, and the various domestic crafts. She steps aside from the beaten path to tell the romantic stories of several young ladies who defied the conventions of their time and were so bold as to choose their own husbands, let parents and guardians rage never so furiously. Indeed the most thrilling chapter of the book is that which deals with the love-story of Anne Murray who bestowed her affection successively upon three cavaliers, the last of whom, Sir James Halkett, won her hand into the bargain. Her first lover, M.H., being a " dangerous detrimental," Anne's mother extracted a promise that she would not see him again. This, Anne kept to the letter by blindfolding herself before she received him secretly " in the blanketting house in the garden."

Many curious details may be picked up, as one travels through these pages. There is the mention of a schoolmaster, who " in winter would ordinarily on a cold morning whip his boyes for no other purpose but to heat himself."

There is a pleasing story of a young gentleman who had sought to remedy a defect in nature. Being in company he caught the calf of his leg upon a nail, " whereupon instead of blood—the bran came running out." A young lady of quality, writing to ask her father's consent to a marriage of which he disapproved, urges that if she may not marry the man of her choice, she will be left at five-and-twenty " a forlorn Cat and Flirt, caring for any one with 8,000 pounds."

The author gives a description of the beautiful needlework of the period, with its elaborate stitches and quaint design. Also there is a delightful chapter on gardens, with a description of John Parkinson's fascinating book on the " Terrestrial Paradise." In his list of all " the pleasant flowers which our English ayre will permit to be nours'd up," we are told that " carnations and gilloflowers are the chiefest flowers of account in all our English gardens," and that one variety of " stocke gilloflower " figures as " the melancholicke gentleman." Some quaint old recipes for invalid cooking are included, of which the following for making water-gruel is characteristic :—

> " *Water-gruel ought to be boiled till it rises in great ebullition in great galloping waters, when the upper surface hath no gross visible oatmeal in it, it should be skimmed off, and it will be found much better than the part which remaineth below of the oatmeal. Yet even that will make good water-gruel for the servants* " *!*

Surely this is a volume of which we can say that it is nothing less than delightful and that there is a great deal of pleasant knowledge to be gleaned from its pages.

London : Stanley Paul & Co. Ltd. 8 Endsleigh Gardens

[Journal continued.   Between second and third paragraphs of VI, p. 4.]

The two eldest, [children of Madame de Beauvais] who are boys, and will soon look like the brothers of their beautiful young mother, speak English pretty well ; the third who is a little girl about 5 years old *looks* English only, for she is wholly without that early formed womanhood of which I have heard so much in France. The youngest who is still in arms and nursed by her mother, we did not see.   When I praised the healthy, blooming looks of those who appeared, Mademoiselle de Mortemart said, with a meaning smile, " They were all three born in England, you know ! "   She delights to be taken for English herself, and thinks nothing excellent but what will bear comparison with that country.   I was quite charmed with the domestic *menage* and apparent domestic happiness of this house, and could not refrain, like Mademoiselle de Mortemart, continually exclaiming : " How English is all this ! " for they appear to live a completely happy as well as virtuous family life.

[A visit not mentioned in the published Journal. Between third and fourth paragraphs.—VI, p. 4.]

Madame d'Henin then took us to leave cards at Madame de Tessé's and at Madame de Poix'.   With the last I was most ready to do it, as it became a devoir after the meeting of the preceding evening, and as I was so much pleased with her : but I should have thought it a liberty to begin myself an acquaintance with Madame de Tessé, her age, former rank, high talents, and remaining distinction in all the society she yet associated with, considered ; but that I was assured where French ladies desired to make an acquaintance, it was the settled etiquette for strangers, foreigners, to wait upon them.
They were both out, and to my no small surprise, I found upon my returning home, a card left for me of Madame de Staël-Holstein, Neckar !—This was a re-

newal of a perplexity I had thought ended, and a renewal that caused me a good deal of uneasiness, from the fear that a determination of intercourse was formed, that resolved to resist all offence from manifest coldness. We concluded, however, still to try its chilling influence, and that my card only should be returned ; and that not for 3 days. The courage, however, which this required, was by no means of a pleasant sort ; for as I could declare no reasons, I seemed not only forgetful of the intimacy so unfortunately begun in England, but insulting to the civility so eagerly offered me here. How truly sorry I am to find her now in Paris ! for nothing is so painful as repressing kindness, and nothing seems so odious as returning condescension by contempt.

[After the opera. Between first and second paragraphs.—VI, p. 5.]

In our way home, which was through the Boulevards, we turned into Rue Choiseul, to call on Bood and Maria, but they were preparing for bed, little expecting such dissipation on my part as a visit after the play ! I have heard much of the visit of Mrs. Damer etc.

[First entry for April 25. Between third and fourth paragraphs.—VI, p. 6.]

April 25.—Yesterday M. D'Arblay waited upon M. Merry, with my letters and a note from me, and his own card : and this morning Mr. Merry very politely came to our apartments, taking the trouble to mount our heights : but I was a good deal indisposed, and, to my great mortification, obliged to decline seeing him ; and Mr. D'Arblay was abroad. He left me an extremely obliging message, desiring me at any time to make use of him, if he could be of the least service to me. Had I seen him, I might have turned this extensive but vague compliment into something rather more limited, but more useful, in soliciting his permission to send him a few letters for England.

[At the Opera Buffa. At bottom of VI, p. 6.]

M. Charles de Poix, eldest son of M. de Poix finished
our party. He is lively and intelligent, has been much
in England and speaks our language extremely well.
When I remarked this to him, he answered with great
vivacity, " When there are but two nations in the world,
surely they ought reciprocally to know each other's
language ! " " It is not for us," cried I, " to whom
you allow this participation to dispute the point, but
t'is modest you must confess to set Austrians, Russians,
Prussians, and all the rest of mankind down for nothing ! "

[Personal trouble not mentioned in published Diary.
After the first paragraph.—VI, p. 7.]

The next day, however, *April* 26, my own menaced
illness yielded to a very serious alarm for my Alex, who
had looked pale and unwell ever since our arrival, but
whose spirits had always deceived our expectations for
his health. A fever however now took place of our
hopes, and but for my faith in my experienced success
with James' powders, I should have been terrified
beyond expression. I gave him 3 grains, and the quickness with which the fever subsided was exactly propor-
tioned to the rapidity with which it had broken out.
But though he was so well before the evening that all
rational fear was passed, you will easily believe how little
I felt disposed to quit him : yet I had an appointment
for meeting Madame de Beauveau et Mademoiselle de
Mortemart at Madame d'Henin's which it was difficult
to relinquish, as it had made expressly for me, and on
my arrival. However M. D'Ar. went over to endeavour
to effect what I so much wished. Madame d'Henin
unluckily dined out, and he could not see her, and
soon after, her femme de chambre came to me, and
with an earnestness that amazed me, entreated I would
not disappoint her lady, who was still out, but who, she
knew had appointed Madame de Tessé et Madame de

Poix, as well as the other 2 ladies, purposely to meet me. The affectionate creature so interested herself in her lady's feelings, even upon such a trivial affair, that her eyes were full of tears while she pleaded for them ; and when, upon Mr. D'Arblay's representing I could be called in a moment, should my Alex be again worse, I thought it incumbent upon me to consent to go, the good creature brightened up, and smiled, and courtsied, and thanked me, as warmly and gratefully as if I had presented her with a purse of guineas. How rare is a character of an attachment of this sort, minutely entering into the happiness as well as interest of a Master or Mistress, to be found in our Country ! You, however, my dear Sir, I really believe, possess one in our good little Molly ; and I could name one or two others, but not more : chiefly at Norbury Park and Twickenham Meadows.

[An "Assembly" at Madame d'Henin's, April 26, after the words "a meeting within the number of twenty."—VI. p. 7.]

We went very late, as I could spare but an hour from my little Boy, whom I left in a sweet and refreshing sleep. I was immediately presented to Madame de Tessé, who received me with every display of the most flattering distinction. She seems between 60 and 70, is upright, and of a stiff and formal deportment, her speech is slow and her words are delivered with an air of precision that appears the result of weighing every one she utters, and the whole of her manner is ceremoniously affable and therefore depressingly discouraging. When I have said all this, from the first shock of observation, I must tell you the far more pleasant result of what I have heard than of what I have seen. Mr. D'Ar says she has high principles, elevated sentiments, and talents for conversation, equal though not of a similar nature to those of Madame de Staël. She is sister to the cy devant Duc d'Ayen and was lady of the first rank with the cy devant Court. She had a very large fortune, and appointments of the first dignity and profit joined ; M. de Tessé being Master of the Horse to the Queen. All however, has been lost, in the revolution, except what enables them to live in modest comfort. But neither this account, nor my own remarks, put me much, you will believe, at my ease in this [i]nterview, especially as I saw, on her own part, expectations excited that I was horribly sure to disappoint.

Such being my embarassed and almost frightened situation in this opening intercourse, you will not marvel, my dearest Father, that I was relieved very agreeably by the entrance of the Bauveaus and Mademoiselle de Mortemart, and by being placed between the two charming sisters by Madame d'Henin. The *how d'ye do ?* of Mademoiselle de Mortemart transported me immediately to England, and we began an English chat with mutual eagerness and openness in which Mademoiselle de Mortemart told me, with a very hearty laugh that she had been informed, at the time of my marriage, that Mr. D'Arblay could speak no English and I could speak no French !—a natural enough exageration of our habit of each speaking our own language. M. de Crillon, a gentleman who by continuing here during the variations of the seasons, has retained a considerable portion of his property, and who now, with his son, is proposing to visit England, Ireland, and Scotland, for a summer excursion, came to converse with Mademoiselle de Mortemart upon his route, etc., and she expatiated upon the pleasure she had derived from English society, english custom and english places, people, and things with a joy and delight in the subject truly animating. Madame de Poix after this, invited me to a little conference, forcing me to take a *fauteuil*, while she seated herself on a *chaise-de-paille* close to me ! Yet though this excess of condescension from a person of her rank and peculiar situation confounded me, her manners soon put me at my ease, in some measure ; or rather, though I attained not ease, succeeded

in giving me pleasure ; for her vivacity is of such quick
and ready conception, that her penetrating eyes not
only aid her to express her own meaning, but to seize
that of others, and therefore while the grave, nay respectful attention of Madame de Tessé not to lose a
word I uttered, made me regularly forget any idea I
meant to convey ; the rapidity with which Madame de
Poix conceived every half-pronounced phrase, always
helped me on to something new, by appearing to comprehend, though unsaid, all that should have preceeded.

We were separated by her being summoned to a
Card-table, and I did not love cards the better for
taking her away.

M. Mounier also was there, but some engagement
made him depart as soon as we had been named to each
other. His daughter and a son remained ; of the latter
I say little or nothing ; but Mademoiselle Mounier
fixed herself upon me without mercy, paying me compliments incessant with such full smiles as to fatigue
my poor muscles in keeping up a decent return. The
rest of the names that I heard were M. de Noailles, de
Damas, de Meun, de Guignes. . . .

Madame d'Henin had provided a very elegant little
supper, of cream biscuits, cakes, and various confec-
tionaries, all arranged with Taste and effect, at which
the ladies alone sat down, and the men helped themselves as they could, while waiting upon them. It was
very pleasant, and Madame d'Henin placed me between
herself and Mademoiselle de Mortemart, with whom, as
I speak English, I am always quite at home :

[After the Assembly. At the bottom of VI, p. 7.]

On our return I found my dear little boy still asleep
but very feverish, and so thin and weak, that I grew
much alarmed, and his Father still more, and when we
found in the morning, no amendment, Mr. D'Ar. went
in search of Dr. Bourdois the Physician, and missing
him, brought home le Docteur Coët, a physician who

had been recommended to me by Madame de Beauveau. The operation of James' powders not being yet decidedly over, he wisely forbore giving any new medicine, and only ordered cooling drinks. In the morning he was abundantly better, and M. Bourdois and M. Coët both allowed nothing more was required but care and gentle doses of bark; and both also granted that the timely administration of James' powders had, in all probability saved him a putrid fever!—I omit the journal of this week, which was devoted to my dear boy, only mentioning that Mr. and Madame de Tessé called upon us the next day, and kindly accepted my apologies for the intended diner at their house. Madame de Poix came also, and lame as she is, insisted on mounting our high stairs, and yet was so tenderly considerate to my inquietudes she would not let me be called from my Alex, but stayed and conversed a few minutes with Mr. D'Arblay, in our Saloon, and then quietly descended.

[Between fourth and fifth paragraphs.—VI, p. 9.]

May 3rd.[1]—I pass now to the week following my poor Boy's illness: which we began by carrying him on this May 3rd. to Moussaux in Madame de Poix' carriage, which Madame d'Henin borrowed. The morning was delightful, and the little excursion did infinite good to the poor Alex.

[Filling the space shown by dots . . . .—VI, p. 10.]

May 4th. was therefore, a very full day indeed, and began deliciously: for we first went to Maria, and there, as soon as I had embraced the dear girl, cordially, and not without wet eyes congratulating her upon her happy and almost superb establishment, in la Rue de Choiseul, she told me she had just received letters from her dear

[1] This date and the next show that, in preparing her Journal for print the dates of each entry were not accurately preserved. In the published Diary the whole passage from p. 7 to p. 13 appears continuously under April 26.

Parents informing her of the legacy of good Mrs. Bateman to little Amelia. I have seldom heard more delightful intelligence. I felt all the joy of her fond Father and mother, and the mental relief to so great a portion of their cares. How kindly has prosperity of late, shone upon them through the same medium that caused their solicitudes and difficulties, their children! I wanted Maria to accompany us in our next visit, which was to her brother and sister in law Mr. et Madame Bourdois ; but there was some impediment of pavement that made the street impassable for a carriage and she is not yet strong enough to undertake a long walk. I was glad afterwards she was spared the trouble, as we found no one at home. The fine weather had drawn out also Mesdames de Poix, de Tessé, de Muras, de Luynes et de *Montagu*, which 3 latter I have never seen, and therefore will pass by to mention to my dear Father those of whom I can give some sketch from having obtained admission. And first, we were let in to a cy devant Princesse, Madame de Beaufremont, a lady of the cy devant *Franche Comté* and of the neighbourhood of Joigny, who had been excessively urgent with Mr. D'Arblay for my introduction to her ; but who, I fear, will find her desire subside, now into sickened rather than satisfied curiosity ; for, being a good deal fatigued with so many presentations, and somewhat indisposed, I never felt more forcibly my want of ease in the french language than during this visit—in so much, that I could not twice open my mouth. She has still fine prominent and lustrous eyes, though her person is immense, and her youth is passed : she has a pleasing voice, and high bred manner ; and I wonder now, why I was so *dumbfounded* in her presence ; but I had heard so much of her wish for the acquaintance, that it frightened me. Mr. D'Arblay however made amends for my silence, as he had so much to enquire or communicate, relative to Joigny and its vicinity, that the conversation never flagged, though I only appeared to assist [it] in [the] character of Audience. Her daughter, Madame de

Listenois, a tall thin and elegant young lady, formerly, *dame de Remiremont*, was one of the interlocutors, and seemed lively and sensible ; but an accident happened on my entrance that was truly comic. Madame de Listenois after I had been saluted in the usual way by her mother, approached me with an eagerness that seemed so determined to be affectionate, that judging by her youth and her manner she really meant to embrace me, as soon as she jutted forward, with vivacious smiles and sparkling eyes, her cheek, I met it with my lips, but to my no little surprise, it was withdrawn before they touched it ; yet the other side was presented with a precipitancy of expressive pleasure that again deceived me, and again my lips did their office ; so that twice in the same moment I kissed the air. This served me, however, for a lesson, during the rest of my first visits, against a similar simplicity of credulity in etiquette's tenderness. We next were admitted by Madame de Chastel, wife to the elder brother of M. de Boinville. She is a french american by birth, and fair, fresh, and of elegant but entirely decent appearance. She surprised me a little by apologising for not having come to see me immediately, in saying she should certainly have done it but that she was informed there were *tant de curieuses qui l'avoient fait*, that she would not risk being included in their number !

We then went to see the lady of General d'Hennezel, who is an ancient camarade of Mr. D'Ar. and was an intimate friend of his eldest and favourite brother in their mutual youth. The General was at home with his wife, who appears a perfectly good sort of woman, strongly attached to her husband, whose immensely tall person is striking, and whose attentively polite manners speak the early *cy devant* military education. They had 3 children in the room with them, whom they appear to love with great fondness ; and indeed their whole *menage* seems that of complete domestic comfort, and quite a l'anglaise—as we English have the modesty to say of every thing we much approve amongst Foreigners.

We were received, also, by Mademoiselle La Jacqueminiere, daughter to an old friend and Townsman and
relation of M. D'Arblay and who is a very worthy, upright man, and now of the Tribunat, which if composed
of many such, must be truly respectable : but—well,
Mademoiselle La Jacqueminiere has just the air of a
modest, quiet, silent, shy and dull young English woman.

Last we went to Madame de Monteclerc, to see my
dear Adrienne, as I wished to make that my longest
visit.   Madame de Montecler seeing us from the window
brought down her little Grand-child to the Gate to
receive me : Madame de M. is extremely stiff and
formal, but perfectly good.   I believe her amongst the
cy devants the most to be pitied, because suffering most,
in lost dignity and consequence, from the new order
of things.   Monsieur de Chavagnac, also, is truly sad
and serious, and I should trouble for the happiness of
my poor little Adrienne, but that there is a brother in
law, Mr. Rozely who resides with them, and who is
naturally gay, and very pleasing, and who is fond of the
child, and plays with her, and is almost adored by her
in return, already.   I was sorry not to carry my Alex
there, but he has been too ill for such a course as we
took in the middle of the heats of Paris.   Indeed, . . .

[May 5.—Parade of General Hulin, at the Tuillieries.
Note to words " The Scene now."—VI, p. 16.]

The extraordinary variety and superb shewyness of
the several uniforms far exceeded whatever can be
imagined ; it was a scene of military splendour scarcely
possible to describe.   To see Mr. D'Arblay among them
in his dear old plain West H[u]mble coat, was I own, to
me, not an indifferent spectacle ; and to see his reception from those officers of old date enough to have known
him, was honourable to both parties, and to me, very
touching ; for they seemed so eager to shew the impression his character has left upon their minds, that they

come forward to shake hands with or embrace him, with a warmth, and a respect that gave, in my eyes, as much of grace to their finery as of honour to his want of it.

[After the Review. Conclusion of " Journal account," preceding letter to Mrs. Burney.—VI, 27.]

Arrived at this Terrace,[1] we missed M. de Beauveau who had been unable to keep near us during the Review, or to find us after it. Mr. D'ar. desired us to remain upon the Terrace while he sought him. We had it entirely to ourselves, except for two foreign officers, in gay, but not splendid Regimentals, who offered their services, and Madame d'Henin, extremely fatigued, accepted an arm of one of them, while Madame de Beauveau, tired also, held by another. We had all stood the whole time. Mademoiselle de Mortmart and I walked up and down the Terrace talking over the past scene : but Madame d'Henin seated herself on the steps, and presently the direction of her Eye shewed she was speaking of me, to the officer attending her, who hastily quitting her, and coming up to me, said in English, " I understand, Ma'am you are English ? "

" Yes, Sir," I answered, surprized ; " and I fancy by your accent, you have learnt my language in my own country ? "

" True, Ma'am," replied he, smiling, " I learnt it there—for I was born there ! "

" And you have entered," said Madame de Beau, " into the Austrian service ? "

" No, Ma'am, into the Prussian—I have been engaged in the Prussian service twenty four years." Then turning to me while he looked at Madame de Beauveau, " That Lady," he added, " is English too, I'm sure ! "

" No," I cried, " she is not ! but I know why you think her so ! "

" And why Ma'am," said he, " And why ? " repeated Madame de B. eagerly.

---

[1] Leading to a quiet exit from the palace into the gardens.

" I must not tell *you*," I answered, " but I will tell my countryman."

He leant down his head, very envious, and I added : " Whenever an Englishman sees a female beautiful, fair and modest, he concludes, nay takes it for granted, she must come from his own country ! "

Mr. D'Arblay now joined us, and these Gentlemen, having no pretence for remaining made their bows.

[The position of this extract is conjectural. But as they went with Madame d'Hénin to the Review on May 5, 1802, I believe this is the correct date.]

To Dr. Burney. Account of *Madame de Maisonneuve* and La *Princesse d'Henin*, and her villa in le Bois de Boulogne.

To Dr. Burney

May 6th [1802].

Madame d'Henin having borrowed the carriage of Madame de Poix took us this morning to Passy, a very pretty village about 2 miles from Paris, to pay a visit to Madame de Maisonneuve a great favourite of Mr. D'Arblay and a lady of singular estimation for her private character. She is sister to M. La Tour Maubourg, but young enough, I believe, to be his daughter. She is nearly beautiful, certainly beyond pretty ; particularly in her profile, which is in a very noble style. Dignity and modesty divide the expression of her fine and serious countenance ; the first announcing all that is reported of her unblemished character, the second, seeming to indicate a purity that rendered its preservation *even in France*, perfectly indispensable to her. She devotes her virtuous life to giving the rudiments of education to an only little son, in this retirement, where her brother, and his family, also spend much of their time ; but whence she never departs for any spectacle, of amusement, though so near their first attraction, Paris. Her husband is still, I believe, in emigration. She received us with a gentleness which though nearly timid, was

extremely graceful. M. D'Arblay's admiration of her
is not bestowed on an Ingrate, for she has long been
anxious he should fix himself and his little family at
Passy, and she had been sedulously employed herself in
seeking us an habitation. She had one immediately to
propose, which we all went to examine ; but it smelt of
fresh paint, and would not do. We were led next to an
interesting-melancholy sight, that of a small villa,
belonging, before the revolution, to Madame d'Henin :
a place constructed while here, for elegant retirement
from her more magnificent mansions ; and where she
most loved to receive the favourite Friends of her youth,
Madame de Biron, Madame de Poix, et Madame de
Bouillon ; with whom she had been connected in strictest
friendship above 30 years, the intercourse being formed
while they were all in their teens. The dreadful fate
of the first of these ladies, made the sight of the room,
which in early days Madame d'Henin had appropriated
for her, and fitted up to her taste, saddening indeed !
The second lady still happily lives, and delights all who
know her by worth mingled with talents : the third, after
they had all been separated 9 years, returned from her
exile to meet once more the yet remaining two of the
quartette, Madames de Poix et d'Hénin, and almost
immediately after expired in their arms. My kind
Padre's interest in them will not be diminished by
hearing they had all read Cecilia together I think 3
times, While we were examining outwardly the windows, and listening to some incident of every room,
some people belonging to the house came and offered
poor Madame d'Henin to enter it : but this she hastily
declined feeling unable to bear. She had resolution
enough however, to walk over the grounds, which had
been laid out by her own orders, and are extremely
pretty . . . for France . . . for I must confess I have
seen nothing here, as yet, to bear comparison with what
is really beautiful, in the disposition of grounds in England. The time however, may come, when I travel
further and see more.

After spending with the amiable and deserving Madame de Maisonneuve the whole morning, Madame d'Henin took us back through le Bois de Boulogne, that my Alex, —indulged by all who wish to indulge us, might have the longer airing.   The mischief done in this very pretty Bois during the time of turbulence, in slashing and hacking trees, was such as greatly to shock M. D'Arblay who had not seen it since its almost desolation, and declared I could scarcely form a notion of what it had been.

Letter to Miss Planta

[Preceding letter to Mrs. Burney—VI, p. 27.]

RUE CYSALPINE À MONCEAUX, PARIS,

July 20, 1802.

MY DEAR MISS PLANTA,

I hope my last long letter arrived safely.   I had expected to have had another to have written upon the 14th the only day in which I have been anywhere in public since my boy's third relapse ;   but the Fete, though it excited a curiosity that had been big with conjecture for some months previous to its taking place failed in satisfying it.   Nothing was done in the famous Champ de Mars, where it was expected the *Consulat a vie* would have been declared and proclaimed ;   no spectacles were given to the people and Paris was as tranquil, and business was as placidly pursued, as upon any other day.   The Parade, however, was far more numerous than upon any former occasion, for not only the Court of the Tuileries, but the carrouzel were filled with troops, the preparations for which were nothing less than trifling, since not only all common incumbrances were removed to make place for them, but houses were levelled to the ground, and whole hosts were employed in filling up cellars and hollows, removing rubbish and making an even pavement of the whole space.   The condition in which I saw it, covered with ruins and dirt, but two days before, as we drove through

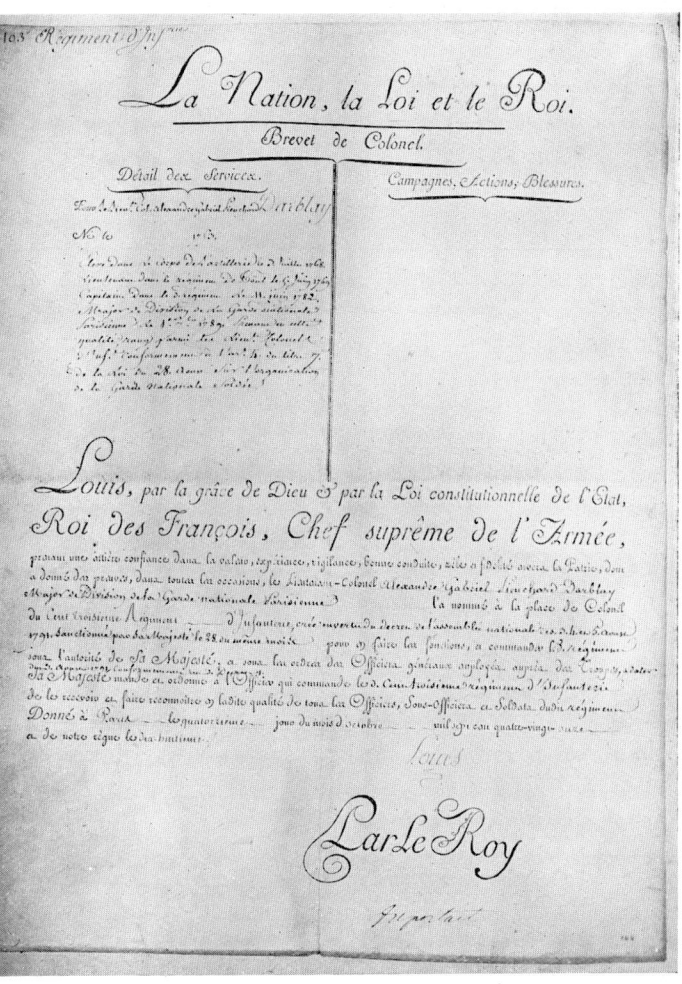

BREVET OF GENERAL D'ARBLAY.
From the original document.

it upon our return from la *Bouigogne*, made me conclude it to be utterly impossible that the parade could extend to that spot ; and indeed, the celerity with which the workmen finished it continues a wonder to me.

Our imaginations not being less awake than our neighbour's upon the approach of this day, we hurried from our visit to Joigny in order to be present at the interesting, or eventful scenes to which all looked forward. Mr. D'Arblay applied for places too late to obtain them anywhere but on a scaffolding in the carrouzel,[1] belonging to a begun house of M. Auguste, formerly orfevre to the Queen of France. The Parade, however, had no difference from that which I saw in May, except in exhibiting double the number of troops and adding the Mamelucks to those of this country. These last, in their gay coloured full drapery, and large Turbans, riding the most beautiful light and spirited arabian horses, gave all that was novel to the sight ; and though we had excellent places for a complete view of the whole, you will not, I believe, wonder that I, who do not, you know, pique myself upon being military, should by no means have been as well entertained as at the Parade of which I have already given you an account ; when, in fact, it was not the Parade, but my situation for seeing various persons and characters and ceremonies, that amused me.

In the evening, we walked, with a large party, in the Thuileries Gardens to see the illuminations, which were very pretty, though for Paris, I am told by the knowing in these things, they were inferior to all rejoicings of that kind hitherto manifested.

N.B.—It seems to me, however, as if every rejoicing commemoration of the various separate epochs of the Revolution were enfeebling at least, if not dying away.

Except upon this 14th I have not been in Paris these two months, and the change of air with liberty of run-

---

[1] Note of M. D'A. : Il eut assurément été impossible de trouver une meilleure place que sur cet echaffaudage ou Mdme. D'Arblay etait en ler. rang avec Mdes. de Timidof, de Salmours. &c. &c. &c.

ning about, succeed completely with my little Boy,
who has had no return of fever since we left the capital.
Monceaux where we now abide in Rue Cisalpine, may
on one side be reached through streets, but on the other,
which alone we frequent, it is divided from the City by
fields, and it has the great inducement of being near a
very charming Garden, open at present to the Public,
abounding in pleasant walks, interspersed with groves,
lawns, seats, shade, flourishing trees, and flowering
shrubs.   It was the *cy devant Folie de Chartres* made by
the late *Duke d'Orleans*, under the direction of an
English gardener, who is now, I am told, forming, or
improving the Gardens of La Mal-maison.   We can go
there at any hour and in any dress, and it is so near our
apartments, that it is little more trouble than to step
into another room.   There are still the remains of
various slight, but very pretty structures, which, *jadis*
ornamented this spot; temples, Bridges, mounts, colon-
ades, Ruins, &c., and mile stones, with directions in
English;   and rooms imitating Bowers;   and walks
imitating cloisters; but the devastation which violence,
not time, has made, I *here* regard without any of those
emotions, of pity, or resentment, with which I view
desolation from similar causes elsewhere; since to the
owner of this Folie de Chartres, so much of the general
destruction may be radically attributed.   I did not
quite so unmoved hear, but yesterday, the lamentation
of Mdme. de Poix upon the degradation of the Hotel de
Beauveau, into an Hotel Carni (the Prince of Wales)—
Hotel du Prince de Galles.   She had spent there, she said,
so much of her youth, so many of her happiest hours!
and, *la Marechale* de Beauvau, her belle mere, still living,
was a person of such eminent worth and virtue, that to
see her driven into small hired apartments, while her
sumptuous mansion was made an Inn, was a circumstance
so poignantly painful, that she had not yet been able to
completely resign herself to its shock.   At the house of
this truly charming lady, Mdme. de Poix, who seems now
to have as many talents and virtues as formerly she had

beauty and attractions, we had the pleasure of meeting
the two fair sisters I have so often mentioned to you, on
the last day that one of them, the young Mdme. de
Beauvau spent in Paris for this season.   She is now,
with her husband, and three youngest children at a
seat still belonging to them near Strasbourg : the eldest
son is left at school at St. Germain en laye, under the
protection of the Marechale de Beauveau, whom Mdme.
de Poix spoke of with such praise and such pity.   We
were engaged to spend a day with that Mar^{ale}. under
the auspices of Mdme. d'Henin, just as my poor Boy
made me a Prisoner to his room.   We are still, however, to
have that honour when Mdme. de Poix has finished [her]
previous summer excursion.   The same sort of captivity
as *garde-malade*, has kept me from again seeing Mdlle.
Mortmart, who, however, has been so kind, before my
journey to Joigny, to send me a noble pacquet of a
month's English news-papers.   How greedily I devoured
them !   It is now 7 weeks ago, and I have not seen one
since.   Mdlle. de Mortemart has great hopes of recovering something of her fortune, which in her situation,
will be of considerable importance to her happiness, and
probably to her establishment.   She is with her *Belle-
mère* cy-devant Duchesse, still I believe in Paris, and as
soon as I am able I shall endeavour to regale myself with
waiting upon her.   I wish I could tell you how Mdme.
de Poix delighted to make me talk to her of our *English
Garden* (a) !—with our noble *Tree* (b) of the Forest which
she speaks, as well as hears of, with rapture.   Indeed I am
frequently astonished—and o how gratified !—by the
manner in which I find that Tree appreciated in this
country, while that graceful, fragrant, fascinating *plant* (c),
which so much to our honour and happiness we have
naturalized and fostered, is a matter of frequent enquiry
and discussion, in a manner, so deeply interesting to my
feelings, that whenever the subject is started, I forget
all my impediments to speaking french, lose my embarassment in my eagerness, and my shame and fears in the
pleasure, the gratitude, and the love of justice which

excite me, and I believe I may faithfully say there is no
occasion upon which I express myself so nearly the same
as in my own language. The favourite Flowers of that
Garden, also, Madame de Poix loves to make me describe
at very full length; the Rose (d); The Lily (e), The
Honeysuckle (f), The Carnation (g), and the Violet (h).

(a) Royal Family of England.
(b) George IIId.
(c) The Queen Charlotte.
(d) Princess Augusta.
(e) Princess Elizabeth.
(f) Princess Mary.
(g) Princess Sophia.
(h) Princess Amelia.

To Miss Cambridge

August 1st, 1802.

.   .   .   .

.   .   .   .   .   .

I must now come to ourselves beginning with the little
boy you and my dear Sally so kindly take to your hearts.
Alas, my dear friends, he is not yet re-established into
anything like permanent health ! he has had another
fever since I wrote last, and though it is now over, for
I could not, and I would not have written while it
existed—it is his 4th attack within 4 months ! and the
little flesh he gains upon every recovery is always
shrunk away upon every relapse. How discouraging,
how distressing this is, I need not say.—I cannot !—Yet
he is so well between every attack, that all around me
think my fears mere maternal exagerations, till a sudden
seizure shews what too—too just reason I have for
apprehension. The dear little soul also has spirits that
deceive all but myself into a belief of his security ; but
I know well they make no part of his health, since neither
sickness, nor fever, nor weakness rob him of them,
except during the time of immediate pain. I am often

told this is a critical year, his eigth,—and that when he
has turned it, his constitution may radically strengthen.
I am sure your kind prayers, and my kind Sally's will
join yours that this may be granted us. Amen! Amen!

I have told you we have been to Joigny, and as I
know the kind interest you will feel upon the subject
of that visit, I shall put aside other more general matters,
to give you some account of it.

The Town, built upon the side of a high hill, or
rather mountain, is full of scrambling, narrow, ill-built,
and worse paved up and down streets.   Here and there,
the prospect[s], especially from the heights of the houses,
are fine in the extreme ; but this is the good fortune
of the favoured very few.   I saw nowhere a view so
beautiful as from the house in which M. D'Arblay was
born.   It is still inhabited by a relation of the family,
a distant cousin, Mdlle. Chollet, an ancient virgin of
the most courteous manners, with which she mixes a
degree of dignity that ensures her receiving as much
good breeding as she bestows.   She perfectly remembers
M. D'Arblay's Father, who has been dead these 40 years,
and she invited me to a meeting of 20 of his cousins,
that I might dine with all that remained of him, in the
very room in which my mate was born.   She gave us a
noble repast, and a dessert fit for an Emperor's Table.
We would have scolded, but she said it was *le diner de
noces*, and promised *to do so no more*. We saw here
many curious family portraits, but all that had had, in
the old style, the family arms painted in the corner, had
that part either cut out, or pasted over! This precaution had been taken in the reign of Rob. to preserve
not merely the pictures but the lives of those who were
so hardy as to possess them !

As Mr. D'Ar. was the only son of an only son, all the
cousins are very distant, though my Alex, upon hearing
this remarked, innocently exclaimed : " Distant ? how
can they be my distant cousins, when they are all so
near me ? " It is singular that amongst the whole
tribe, though there are almost countless children, not

one from the principal stock, bearing the old family real name, Piochard, has a rising male. Our Alex is the last and the only one existing. Perhaps 'tis from instinct he has so prodigious a desire to be Papa to all those hundreds of children he enumerated to you and your Cornelia !

To have done, however, with these *distants* on the male side, let me come to the more interesting near ones on the female. M. Bazille brother to the mother of Mr. D'Ar. answered all my expectations, both in character and kindness, though he disappointed them by his feebleness and infirmities. He is a man of high and honourable sentiments and conduct, strikingly gentlemanlike in his person and his manners, and to a deep and sagacious judgment, joining a dry pleasantry extremely entertaining, which he communicates with a sort of arch gravity, that for a while, makes his listener in doubt whether he is in jest or in earnest. He doats upon his nephew,—not one of his children can be dearer to him, and his kindness to him and to *his* was so great, that he wanted us to settle with him during the whole of our stay in this Country. This, however, was impossible, as Mr. D'Ar. has still a pursuit, urged on by his friends in Paris, which he thinks right to follow up. We shall, return nevertheless to Joigny in about a fortnight to spend there the time of les *vendanges*. Mdme. Bazille, wife of this dear and worthy Gentleman, is one of the most excellent, nay, exemplary characters I have ever met with. Every thought and every hour of her life are devoted to the service of others. To see the use she is of to her husband, whom she quite adores, you would think she had not a moment for anyone else ; yet to see what she does and contrives for each and all her children, would make you conclude, next, that they alone employed her. For her domestics, her house, her guests, you may almost say the same. I can hardly tell you how much I love and admire her ; yet I could never make her believe either ; for amongst her perfections is that of humility, which characterizes to herself

every exertion and every task as a simple duty, culpable
to withhold, but not laudable to fulfil.

I must now say adieu, entreating you to remember
me to all your house, and singularly to our revered Mrs.
Boscawen; and let her know all she has the goodness
to desire hearing of my affairs. My reception in this
country has been the most flattering possible, as far as
I have been able to see of it: and I have kept out of the
way of all those whose civility could only have shocked
or worried me.

For the *Queen Charlotte*, and the *Princesses*, directed
to Miss Planta. Account of the Institution of
Madame Campan at St. Germain en loye. Journey;
Mdme d'Henin; Mdme de Belloy; M. Malhouet;
Mr. Jerningham; Salle Examination of the Pupils;
The Murats; Mdme Le Brun; Mdme. Louis
Bonaparte; Valence; visit to La Marechale de
Beauveau; M. de Lally Tolendal.

(This account was destined for my Royal Mistress Queen
Charlotte and her 5 lovely and loved single daughters; but it was directed to Miss Planta.)

Mrs. C.n's School
Madame Campan.

The Institution of *Madame Campan* is for a limited
and not very small number of young ladies, who under
the superintendence of Mdme. Campan are educated
from childhood to,—I cannot say to maturity,—but to
the age at which they are regarded, in this country, to
be wise enough, experienced enough, and steady enough
to become wives, mistresses of large household establish-
ments, and mothers. You will not wonder they have,
generally, such success in these characters, when I add
that the most common period upon which they commence them, is when they have just reached their fourteenth year! It was here that the youngest sister of

le Premier Consul, Made. Murat, and his daughter, now sister-in-law, Made. Louis Bonaparte, were brought up ; and in consequence, probably of such a patronage the daughters of most of the principal Generals in the army are sent to this seminary.

The occasion of my going to St. Germain en loye to see it, was that I might be present at an examination of the young pupils before two members of the *Institut*, previous to the distribution of the prizes adjudged to those who excelled in writing, Ortography, grammar, Geography, Music, Recitation, history and disposition of temper. Made. Campan wrote to Made. d'Henin inviting her to be at the ceremony, and to use *her influence*, for bringing with her M. Malhouet, and your very humble servant. You may easily imagine my surprise at such a distinction, as well as my readiness to avail myself of the opportunity of viewing such an establishment.

Me. d'Henin borrowed, or hired, a carriage in which she took 6, after making them all *The*, *a l'anglaise*, *in her* modest but very elegant small lodging. Our party consisted of Me. d'Henin, Made. de Belloy (*niece to the archevêque de Paris*), M. Malhoust Mr.—formerly called le Chevalier de Jerningham, Mr. D'Ar. and his mate. We had a very pleasant little journey, by the borders of the Seine, and passed *la malmaison*, which looked very small for your favourite Hero, though the grounds about it are considerable, and it is furnished and still furnishing with plenty of cazernes for troops and stabling for cavalry. It is well *walling* (*Note* the Walls were then only begun) also around. The country and views in its neighbourhood are extremely beautiful. On a summit near one of the boundaries of the Park is an elegant little villa, which has been given to the young *Beauharnais*, son of Madame Bonaparte. And, on another summit, further on, and much higher, is a beautiful Pavillon, built for, and *erst* inhabited by, the wretched and too famous Mdme. Dubarry.

Arrived at St. Germain en laye, we gave in our

Tickets, and entered the Garden, whence we proceeded to the *Salle de Compagnie*. We were so late, owing to some accidents, that the ceremony of examination was begun, and the room was so full that we were all crowded to death, and with difficulty could squeeze ourselves into the worst and most uneasy places imaginable.

The appartment was pretty equally divided between the audience, seated in rows, and the pupils, who were upon a sort of stage, or elevated floor, parted from the rest, not by an orchestra, but by those gentlemen who were appointed as judges of the Prize-claimers. Two of these, placed conspicuously in the middle, and still more conspicuous by dark coats, embroidered richly down the front, and at the pocket-holes, with large green laurel leaves, were the two members of the national Institut, of which the premier Consul is president.

The young ladies were all dressed alike, very simply, and very elegantly in white muslin, with white shoes, coquelicot sashes, and their hair in ringlets without any other sort of ornament, either for their heads or robes : a prohibition very wise to prevent any rivalry in the vanity of finery, so hurtful, I should say to all youth, if I knew not a lovely six-fold [1] exception, which has often made me reflect, how many mental errors and folies, may be spread and prevented, even in the very bosom of danger and temptation, by timely and regular attention to pointing out their evils and futility.

What had preceeded our entrance, I cannot tell ; but the younger pupils had already passed their examination, and were all out of sight. Those who remained were from the ages of 10 to 14. Amongst these, the most juvenile was Mademoiselle de Valence, a daughter of the General, and a grand-daughter of the celebrated Madame de Genlis. They—the pupils—were at this time all seated round a large table. I think there were about twenty. They were all employed in writing, from the dictates of their judges or masters, who pro-

[1] Meaning the six English princesses, i.e. Princess Royal, Augusta, Elizabeth, Mary, Sophia, and Amelia.

nounced a phrase at a time, which they all committed to paper at once, till a very long paragraph was completed by everyone. They then each delivered what they had separately written to one of the judges, who was to pronounce which was the most perfect in orthography, and correctness of accent and punctuation, The honour, however, was to be announced, and the prizes distributed, all together, at the end of the ceremony.

This over, the great table was removed, and the young ladies were seated on chairs, in a semy-circle, so as all to be in sight of the audience, which chiefly consisted of their own relations and friends, or acquaintances. Madame Campan herself sat at the corner of the stage, from which a kind of box was lightly railed off, in expectation of the premier Consul and his family. He has attended two or three times when the young ladies have performed Athaliah or Esther.

Madame d'Henin being now discovered by Madame Campan, she took the opportunity of the interval between the writing and the next exhibition, to descend from the stage to the audience, and express her satisfaction ; but as she spoke rather loud, at least not in a whisper, I had such a dread of being named, and marked, that I entreated Mdm. d'Henin not to mention me ; and she could stay so short a time, and was so much hurried, that she had not a moment for any questions. Mdme. d'H. nevertheless enquired if there was any chance that the first Consul would come ; Mdme. Campan answered that she had prepared him his place, but could not be sure, as he was particularly engaged : for this was just before the declaration of the Consulat à vie.

I was extremely glad I had taken my precaution in time, for soon after she had returned to her seat, some one whispered her the name of Mr. Malouët, and she immediately arose and called to him aloud, to say how she rejoiced in his presence, and begged him to come forward, and take a seat amongst the judges. Mr.

Malouët gently declined the honour, and got to the farthest end of the Salle to avoid its repetition.

Above our heads were two galleries, in which many of the most distinguished persons of the audience were seated. Mdme. d'Henin had desired to have her places below, that she might have a better view, should he come, of the first Consul. In one of these galleries sat Madame *Louis Bonaparte*, late Mademoiselle Beauharnais. She is not at all handsome, but has singularly the look and countenance of a *good* character. She was educated in this seminary and has very lately quitted it, for her marriage. She retains great fondness for Made. Campan, and all her fellow students, and for the place itself, frequently, when at liberty, going thither for two or three days following, and behaving and even dressing as a pensionnaire, and going through, as such, all her former exercises ; a kind of taste and of industry, which reflect upon her much honour. She has done this ever since her marriage ! Next to her was a sister of General Laclerc, now at St. Domingo, and then Made. Lauriston, wife of the friend of M. D'arblay, who brought over the preliminaries of peace to England ; and then a young lady who was waiting for only 3 days to begin her fourteenth year, when she was to be married to M. Duroc, an aide de Camp of the first Consul, and Governor of the Palais of the Thuilleries.

The next trial of skill was in Grammar. A book—I did not hear its title—was given to one of the young ladies, who was desired to read the first paragraph, stopping upon every word to declare its part of speech. When she had done, she sat down, and gave the book to her next neighbour, who in like manner, analysed the following paragraph : and so on, till every one had gone through the same task. This took an immense time, and was not very lively. Mr. Jerningham—who is brother to Sir William, and to the Poet,—behaved very indiscreetly upon the fatigue he felt upon this part of the examination, whispering to me every other minute—" Can you stand this ? "—" A'nt you half

dead ? "—" How would this do in England ? "—and
other such sneers, making the whole time such abominable faces of weariness and contempt, that I was almost
afraid to remain in his company, lest he should give
some offence. Nor did he content himself with what
he risked upon this subject ; for whenever he observed
any lady, amongst the audience, particularly in the
height of the French costume, he turned to me and bid
me look at her, with such grimaces of disgust and abhorrence, that I hardly knew whether to laugh or be frightened. " What say you to that Madame D'Arblay ?—
what say you to that ?—Good God ! what a shocking,
figure !—Did you ever see the like ? ever behold such a
nasty creature ? " Yet no one was *nasty*, I assure you,
though his indignation at the light drapery could find
no softer term. Indeed I saw more of the costume of
les elegantes here than I had yet beheld in France, as
the room was almost filled with the rich and gay who first
set afloat, or first adopt the modes of the day.

After this, followed Geography. The stage was filled
with large sheets of strained paper, framed and hung up,
on which various of the most skilled in this science
sketched maps of every quarter of the Globes, on which
they drew the outlines of the terrestrial Sphere, and
marked the longitude and latitude. While this was
performing, one young lady was selected to come forward, and point upon a Map, ready made, to all the
countries of Europe, naming their relative positions,
and chief cities ; for each of which another called out
its latitude and longitude.

This lasted so long, that Madame d'Henin, tired of
sitting on a form where she had no means of procuring
rest by leaning, insisted upon going for a while into the
air to refresh herself. I was very sorry to remove, as
the whole was curious, however its parts were tedious :
but I could not risk staying without her, and we both
went into the Garden. Here, while we were strolling,
we were accosted by Madame—somebody, whose name
I cannot recollect, but who is first female assistant to

Madame Campan, and who asked if we would not go upstairs to the Gallery.

Madame d'Henin declined this, saying " Madame D'Arblay et moi nous nous promenons pour prendre l'air, et puis nous retournerons à la Salle." Away went Mdme. Somebody,—and in two minutes, out came Mdme. Campan herself, flying up to us, and exclaiming that she had not heard my name till that moment, and knew not I was in her house. Much civility ensued— which I shall spare writing without much fear of reproach ; but she said that as we were so ill placed, we should go through a little door that led to the Box on the stage, for she had just been informed, by an aide de camp of the First Consul, that the pressure of affairs would not permit him to come. I felt, however, little enough at my ease, upon being placed in this conspicuous *loge*, though I contrived immediately to get into a corner the least in sight. Mdme. Campan's civility having given me a serious alarm, I earnestly pleaded with Mdme. d'Henin to represent to her my desire of continuing unnamed and unnoticed,—I mean publicly. Mdme. d'Henin complied, though rather reluctantly ; but I soon saw that Mdme. Campan, though she did not resist, received the request with a species of surprise somewhat bordering upon contempt. They have here no idea of a retired disposition such as mine. They think it impossible that any public distinction, if attended with approbation, can be painful and distressing. I however should have found them so in England—think then how much more so in a country of which I know the language so indifferently ! I mean with respect to speaking it.

The Geography had now given way to history, and the members of the Institut had notes presented to them, from which they were desired to examine the young students upon the building, the Monarchy, the Consulship and the Empire of Rome.

These members were almost inconceivably humane and delicate in their manner of making the enquiries, and turning them into fresh channels, when they discovered they had not been understood, or that their questions were too difficult or complicate; always beginning with " à présent, Mademoiselle, aurez vous la complaisance de nous dire comment—etc." and finishing with—" A merveille, Mademoiselle, il est impossible de mieux répondre."

After this, they were examined upon les belles lettres, et poésies ; and they each repeated some criticism from Laharpe, or some celebrated commentator, finishing with the recital of some poem.

No one here excelled the young Mdle. de Valence, who is very pretty, and has a physionomy promising talents and intelligence.

This was the conclusion of the examination.

It was followed by the selection of the claimants, and the distribution of the Prizes.

The first of these, I think, was for *Temper* ; The prize was a rose ; Mdme. Campan said she had taken the opinion of the whole school, both Masters, Teachers, and Scholars, and they had all joined in giving the palm for Sweetness of disposition to a young lady—whose name I cannot recollect—of only 7 or 8 years of age. She was summoned and told her happy lot, and received the Rose, with the most undisguised transport, jumping into the arms of Mdme. Campan to embrace and thank her, and then begging permission to descend to the audience that she might shew her rose to her Mama. This was readily granted, and the delighted little girl, flew on the wings of joy to her enraptured Parent. This was a very pleasant part of the ceremony, and I thought it a happy idea that general good conduct should take precedence of every accomplishment.

The other prizes, though less pretty, were more substantial ; they consisted of presents of Books, chosen and delivered by Mdme. Campan. The Masters of the Seminary decided to whom should be given those for writing, Musick, French, singing, Italian singing, Orthography, and Grammar. Geography, History and

recitation [1] were treated with greater dignity; the
merits of the several candidates were discussed by the
two members of the National Institute, who frequently
stood up, and declaimed aloud both upon the given
subject, and the performances of the young ladies;
always in a manner the most delicate for those who
were selected and the most soothing and encouraging
for those who failed : and the pupils were all ranged in
rows at the furthest end of the Salle, whence the successful were called by name, one at a time, to receive
their rewards. The summons was always answered with
a bound forward of the delighted person thus chosen,
who in taking, with a courtsie to the company, her book,
threw her arms round the neck of Mdme. Campan,
and gave and returned a warm embrace ; then again
courtsied to the company, and retired, with her trophy,
to her companions. The audience always applauded,
with violent clapping, every presentation. This was
animating ; yet rendered the examination rather too
much like some theatrical representation.

All the young ladies, however, were perfectly, and
even elegantly modest as well as graceful, in their
demeanour, delivering all they had to say unaffectedly
and gently, and seeming bent only upon their business,
not their observers. Two of them were so much frightened, that upon rising and attempting to answer the
questions put to them, they burst into tears, and were
forced to be allowed to re-seat themselves, though their
manner announced that their distress was the effect of
diffidence, not ignorance ; and the company felt this
so strongly, that none of the more successful were equally
applauded.

[1] Mademoiselle de Valence recited admirably the Ode of Rousseau to
Fortune. I was quite astonished to hear such hardy defiance of tyrants,
and of blood-thirsty victors pronounced in such an assembly. It did
high credit to Madame Campan that she ventured to instill such principles into her pupils : and, in truth, it reflected, though rather singularly, honour upon the First Consul that she did not fear ordering them
thus publicly to be declaimed.

During the latter part of the examination, the *recitation*, Mdme. Murat, the youngest sister of the premier Consul, came into our loge, attended by the tall handsome General her husband, General Valence, and various other officers. She is extremely handsome, in the Cleopatra style, with soft fine large languishing eyes, a fair complexion, an attractive smile, which rarely quitted her features, and a look of great good nature and softness, and very pleasure-loving eyes. Her dress was striking for elegant and becoming luxury, in the finest open worked muslin, with a veil put over one side of her head and hanging thence down to almost the train of her gown all of Brussels lace. I have never seen one so superb. She was extremely good-natured about the young ladies, joining with great vivacity in all the applause bestowed upon them. Mdme. Louis Bonaparte went still further, for she seemed to interest herself in all they did, as if she were a sister to every one of them. She bears the character of being a perfectly good young woman, without any species of art, coquetry, pride, or love of dissipation.

I was much surprised, just as the prizes were presenting, by seeing two ladies enter just opposite us, who were called *English*, but whose appearance was not what we should have chosen to denominate *national*. One was dressed extravagantly, in a most shewy, but not at all elegant manner. She was totally *passée*, yet had strong remains of great former beauty, but a look extremely hardy, almost to defiance ; the other was a great deal older, dressed like Mrs. Cole in the Minor, and having a not much better or more winning appearance. Mdme. Campan desired to know how they came in, and by what Tickets ? and a message came to say that la Margravine d'Anspach, happening to pass through St. Germain en laye, had heard at the auberge, of the Seminary and examination, and had therefore come to see it. Mdme. Campan seemed extremely surprised.

The comments I could make upon this establishment both in its favour and against it, must be sunk, from the

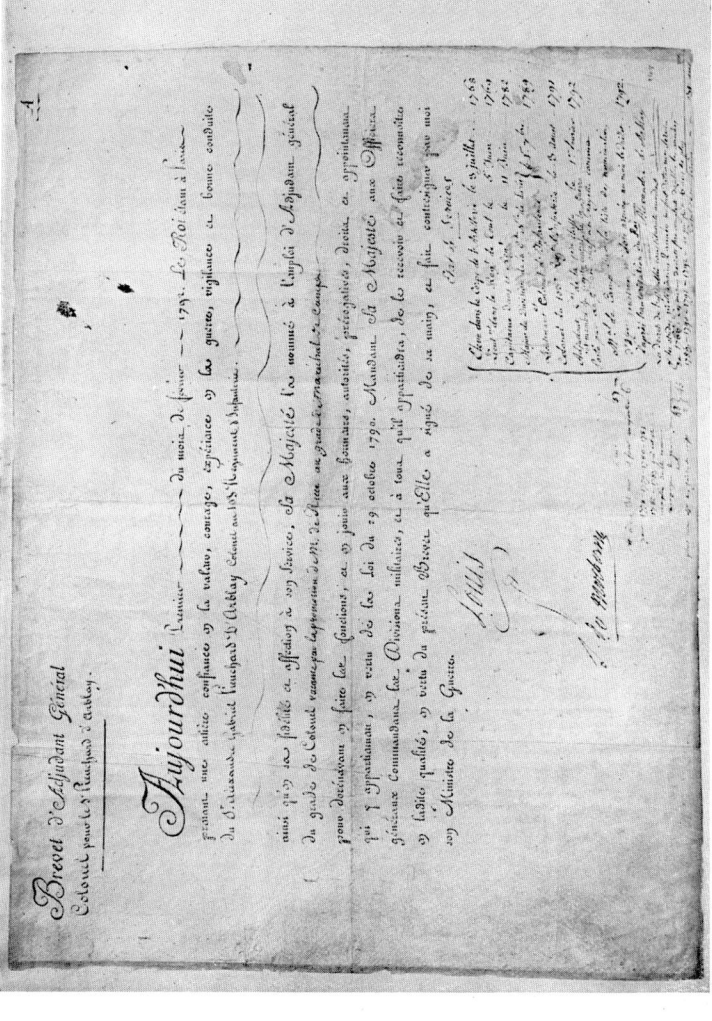

BREVET OF GENERAL D'ARBLAY.
From the original document.

enormous length of this letter, which I dare not augment. I must now only add, that the return of my sister Broome to Paris enables me to send this by her, to be delivered into the hands of Mr. Merry, whom she is to see for her passeport back, and that I fear I have made it tiresome, from a too great desire to make it clear and full.

Note in Madame D'Arblay's handwriting

In the fear that this account, although sent for England through the then British Minister, Mr. Merry, should miscarry, M. d'Arblay copied it, that it might be read to the Royal Personages for whom it was intended, on our return to England.

I had not room to add, that, while we were in the *loge* of Bonaparte, and before the arrival of the Murats, an English Map being prepared by one of the Pupils, Mdme. Campan looking full at me, begun a speech with saying that a most excellent judge of all that belonged to that country being then present, she should demand her pointed opinion of the merits of the *carte* . . . and she advanced with it to the *Loge* : but I was so intolerably averse to such a public display, that I sunk back instantly out of sight, behind Mdme. d'Henin ; who was obliged, though shrugging her shoulders with amazement and dissatisfaction, to plead for my alarm, and excuse my vanishing.

But when Madame Murat, afterwards Queen of Naples, and the Generals Murat, Valence, etc. entered, Mdme. d'Henin, unwilling either to take or give place to such a personage, retired to the back of the Loge herself : while I, curious to witness all that might pass, where I ran no risk of personal publicity, returned to my seat, and continued by the side of this destined Queen during the rest of the Examination ; flattering myself that, if I did wrong, in etiquette, it would only be imputed to English barbarism.

We were afterwards joined by the famous paintress

6

Madame Le Brun, whose picture of the unhappy and meritorious Queen of Prussia is one of the most interesting of Portraits, and was exhibited in the Grand Salon of Painting a few years afterwards.

At the conclusion, the assistant of Mdme. Campan desired to shew me the whole establishment, which indeed was elegantly and usefully and completely arranged. Madame Louis Bonaparte, afterwards Queen of Holland, met us in almost every room, running about as if still une *petite écolière*. Mr. Jerningham joined the Margravine of Anspach ; But, as soon as the whole ceremony was concluded, and we had completely viewed the premises and the Gardens, Madame d'Henin took M. d'Arblay and myself to the dwelling of Madame la Marechale de Beauvau, widow of the Marechal : and a widow so heart-broken, from the loss of a husband she adored, that she has renounced all society, and shut herself up in a small and insignificant house, at St. Germain en laye, that she may live only upon his remembrance ! To the ruin caused by the Revolution she was utterly indifferent, her own views, hopes, and cares in life having lost all object that made splendour, or even comfort, worth her regret. She had been, in the time of her too happy union with M. le Marechal, one of the most highly accomplished, highly gifted, and highly bred of women ; she was now very old, and—though I hate the word for such a woman,—very ugly ; but, as she had consented to receive us, at the request of la Princesse d'Henin, who was her niece, she displayed to us an elegance of politeness that soon wore away the ill impression made by the ever fastidious eye ; and though there was no thinking her handsome, one soon looked for and found something better than Beauty in the benevolence and the sense of her air and conversation. Madame d'Henin took me to her Bedchamber, to shew me the picture of the late Marechal,—the only thing of value his Widow has retained. This charming woman, —for such she proved,—in defiance of ugliness, age and unhappiness, kept us to dinner, and to spend the day, which turned out delightful for, once having suffered her seclusion to be broken in upon, she gave herself wholly up to affording us all the entertainment in her power ; and, by degrees, she enlivened not only into spirited and informing discourse, but into the most pleasing and attractive tones and manner of growing kindness. I regretted much that she did not live in Paris, for it was evident that she would have honoured me with the same social and partial goodness that made so great a part of my happiness in that Capital through her admirable niece, la Princesses d'Henin, her *spirituelle* Daughter in Law, la Princesses de Poix, and her very amiable petite niece, la Princesses de Beauvau. Madame d'Henin took us, in the evening, to see a small House in the Forest, which had formerly been inhabited by the Maréchal, as a spot for private retirement, in fine weather, with only her husband, or a very small party. They called it *une maison anglaise.* It was plain and simple and beautifully situated. I took leave of her with great regret which she appeared most conde- scendingly to reciprocate, saying to Madame d'Henin that if she could permit herself to love anyone again, she felt as if she should be tempted to take her English friend to her own heart. . . . Madame d'Henin was gratified ;—General D'Arblay's eyes had a proud lustre in them ; and to me this was a speech and a kindness to make the first feature and the first pleasure of the day.

We called, afterwards, at different houses, for Madame de Belloy, for M. Malhouet (who afterwards married that lady) and for the Chevalier Jerningham. And, upon our return to Paris, we had the great satisfaction to meet with M. de Lally Tolendahl just arrived from England, where he had lived in emigration many years. I had long and intimately had the real honour of knowing him : and my best Friend had been brought up with him at *le College d'Harcourt*, at Paris. A man of more worth and honour and patriotism I do not think exists, —for he still lives, now, in 1824, when I write this little addition to my Letter of 1803 : and for abilities, he is

generally called The Ciero (sic) of France. This title
he earned by his pious eloquence in redeeming the
character of his injured and sacrificed Father.

[Probably, *after* the letter to Mrs. Burney in the published Diary, i.e. V, p. 29.]

To Miss CAMBRIDGE. Passy. Death of Mr. CAM-
    BRIDGE and character; JOIGNY: LOUIS BUONA-
    PARTE; Troops met repairing from Joigny to join
    the invading army of England at Boulogne.

To Mademoiselle Cambridge

PASSY, *Novr.* 1802.

What kindness is yours, my dear, valuable friend, to
think of me again so soon at such a period! That you
should be sure of my deep interest in this awful event,
and in you, and its consequences, cannot surprise me, but
that you should expand your feelings so generously to
the care of mine, so immediately after your great personal trial, touches me extremely.[1]

Who indeed, if not I, can know how to appreciate
your loss. What a friend he was to me! for several
years of my life I owed many, very many of my most
pleasant hours to his society, which he bestowed upon
me with a partial kindness, nay I may say eagerness,

---

[1] This alludes to the death of Miss Cambridge's father, Richard Owen
Cambridge, Esq., author of *A History of India*, of *Martinus Scriblius the
Second*, of sundry gay pieces of poetry, and of many of the best papers
in *The World*. He was a man of excellent parts, and peculiar talents:
his understanding was as deep as his fancy was playful, and the solid worth
of his character equalled the rare entertainment of his conversation.
With him, and with Mrs. Delany, and with Dr. Johnson, I had the
high honour to become the reigning favourite of their latter days from
the time of the discovery of the authorship of Evelina and with all three,
I had the infinite happiness of being treated as their bosom friend and
confident to their last hours. What of pride, gratitude and joy did I
not owe to them! and what, in succession, of grief at their loss!

never to be rooted from my memory or my gratitude. . . .

. . . In the innumerable conversations with which he
indulged me he opened to me, not only most of his
intentions, but as far as subjects occurred, all his most
private opinions, both of persons and things ; inter-
spersing his admirable discourse with anecdotes not only
of his own life, but of almost all the persons with whom
either design or accident had led him to mix. What
a fund of delight and instruction, insensibly yet invariably mingled, did his society afford me ! and with what
partial sweetness did he accept from me the smallest
returns ! The day rarely passes, the week never, in
which I do not recollect with use as well as pleasure,
some notion, maxim, or counsel that dropt from his
lips. I lost him from the time I left my home for the
Q.H.'s, and it was one of the deprivations, exacted by
circumstances, which I always the most lamented. . . .

. . . Heaven rest his soul !—Amen ! How sweet to
hope it may already have met your loved sister's.

We are fixed at Passy, a village just out of Paris, for
the rest of our sojourn. We have but just come to it
from Joigny, where we spent 6 weeks, this last time,
with the dear and most excellent uncle and aunt of
M. d'Arblay. Worthier or more amiable people never
existed, nor can the fondest father more tenderly love
a son than this uncle loves his nephew. They would fain
have persuaded him to pass the winter, or rather, to *fix*
at Joigny ; but sundry reasons prevented his listening
to the first part of the request, and I need not tell you
what—or who operated against the second. You will
be glad for me, I am sure, that I shall not spend the
winter in Paris. Neither that nor London suits me for
long residence ; and my taste for the Country is happily
most compleatly participated in by my mate ; while
for our Boy it is truly and literally essential. We are so
near, however, to this famed and gay Capital, that with
the potent arm of my Knight errant, I can reach it in
an Hour, upon my own dear independent terms, i.e. feet.

While we were at Joigny, the youngest Brother of
the Premier Consul,[1] Colonel Louis Bonaparte, whose
regiment is quartered there made it a fortnight's visit,
and we had the pleasure of frequently seeing him.

You will not be sorry to hear that he was extremely
polite, nay flattering in his behaviour to M. d'Arblay,
nor that he desired in the most gratifying manner, to
have his English mate introduced to him, coming immediately himself to our residence for that purpose:
and neither you nor Sally,[2] will be very angry with him,
when I add that he was peculiarly kind to our little man
whom he noticed and caressed with striking distinction.
Alex was by no means insensible to this goodness. From
the moment he heard his name, he surveyed him with a
mixture of awe and curiosity very comical; and after
the Colonel's first caress, he flew, jumping, to me and
exclaimed " O Mama! I've a great secret to tell you!
Bonaparte's Brother has kissed me!—he has indeed!
But you must not tell it! for it's a great secret."—
" And why, my dear must not I tell it!"—" Because
Mama . . . for fear people should think I'm boasting."

This Colonel appears to be of a truly Gentlemanly
character, modest, sensible, reserved, and well bred;
generally silent, speaking only to the purpose, yet entirely
unassuming, decorous and gentle. He chose to be considered simply as the Commandant of his Regiment,
without seeming ever to recollect or ever to know his
peculiar claims of further distinction. I had much
conversation with him, during his short stay at Joigny,
for whereever I had the pleasure to meet with him, he
constantly, either before or after his card party, took a
seat by my side. I had great reason to regret his departure, for I was as much pleased with the good sense of
his discourse, as surprised by the graceful simplicity of
his manners, and gratified by his personal attentions.
He is but 23. . . .

N.B.—The following year, when we returned to make
our annual visit to our dear Uncle Bazille, we were met

[1] Afterwards King of Holland.   [2] Miss Sarah Baker.

by a troop of Horse about 10 miles from Joigny. Soon afterwards, we were accosted by one of the Officers, M. de Meulan, a gaily amiable man, of our intimate acquaintance ; and he informed us that the *Colonel Louis* was coming on, heading his Regiment, which was just obeying orders to repair to Boulogne, to join in the expedition then planned of invading England. I was so totally overset, overwhelmed with grief and alarm at this intelligence and at the melancholy circumstances of entering the Birth place of my beloved Husband at the moment it was being evacuated for so hostile and terrific a project against my own adored country, that I could not answer nor speak to M. de Meulan, nor yet hold up my head to look at the Colonel, (for only such he still was,) when, in passing us, he bowed, M. D'Arblay told me, with marked distinction. M. de Meulan had acquainted him who we were : and, indeed, he probably knew our Uncle's Calesh, which had been sent to meet us at Senlis. He did not, M. d'Arblay informed me, appear either surprized or hurt at my avoidance of his salutation : the idea of his Brother's infallibility in arms made him naturally surmize that such a *rencontre* must give rise to the most painful alarm ; and the general opinion that universal conquest was both the aim and the destiny of Buonaparte, must forcibly have explained both my depression, and my averseness to the sight of his Brother just accoutred for hostility, and heading a Regiment ordered forth to the Battles of Invasion. No one was more prone than myself to believe in the invulnerability of Great Britain ; but it was not upon that spot, and at that period that the menaced attack could be viewed with composure ; for upon that spot I had met with kindnesses, and formed connections, to make my Nation's enemies, there, be held amongst my dearest Friends : and at that period no news of combat ever reached my ears that did not resound with victory and Buonaparte as words so amalgamated as to have become inseparable. And, consequently, with all my proud reliance on England's ultimate success, I foresaw with horrour and affliction, the intervening ravages of war, the scenes of slaughter, the deluges of blood, the heart-rending loss of beloved individuals, which must accompany the Invasion, and precede the final evacuation of the Invaders. None of this, I thank God, happened, for Buonaparte while assaulting, with unbounded prowess, all other Nations, limitted his vengeance on Great Britain to simple threats.

To Miss Planta [see VI, p. 29] [1]

Account of *Joigny*, preceded by relating the purchase of a small estate at *Passy*; Narratory *eloge* of *Louis Bonaparte*, afterwards King of Holland. His character and exemplary conduct. *Made. de Souza*, niece of M. del Campo, and her reminiscence of our court. Made. de *Baufremont* and her chateau, daughters, and story. Made. de *Villeheurnois*, and *Sydney*, and *Spencer*.

Addressed to Miss Planta for the Queen and Princesses.

December 19, 1802.

[Rarely, indeed, my dear Miss Planta, have I received more pleasure than from your last most truly welcome letter with assurances so unspeakably seasonable] of the flourishing state of that noble oak and delicious garden in the prosperity of which my whole heart and soul are interested : little as is the credit which I give to common report, and uncertain as are my views or knowledge of newspaper anecdotes and assertions, there are yet some subjects as exquisitely tender, that we cannot rest, where a surmize is raised upon them, till we know all that is to be known. My kind Father, well aware of this had immediately caused a true relation to be sent to me of the matter to which I allude, and most fortu-

---

[1] The published version of this letter being compressed from the MS., a few words enclosed by square brackets are here included from it, for the sake of clearness.

nately it came to my quiet retirement before any other intelligence reached me. Nevertheless my joy on the arrival of your letter was inexpressible ; and none you have sent me have been so rapid in their journey ; a lacquey of the English Ambassador brought it and came the instant the dispatch was received. [I had it, here at Passy, the 5th day after its date. I thank you again and again,—but oh! how I thank God!]

The small house we inhabit in this village has kept us rigidly within its precincts since our return from Joigny, for we have entered it with the workmen who are making repairs which they promised should be finished in a week, but of which the superintendance still keeps us prisoners. It would be difficult, however, to find two persons, who with less murmuring could submit to such confinement, were that the only evil resulting from the procrastination ; but I much apprehend these tardy mecanics will put the philosophy of our purses into yet greater jeopardy than that of our persons. M. D'Arblay, nevertheless, finding all he formerly either possessed or expected lost, deems it essential to substantiate his right of claim to being a french citizen by making himself master of a small estate ; and this our present habitation was offered to him upon terms so seducingly reasonable, that you would rather laugh than be surprised at the purchase, were I to give you its history. The repairs, however, were not taken into the estimation, and I am terribly afraid they will not prove quite as risible! But they will secure us, we trust, a good Tenant, when we return to West Humble ; and they keep us, en attendant, in healthy air, with a small dwelling, English fashion, to ourselves, affording us a beautiful prospect from the banks of the Seine. And here let me mention that our cottage of Westhumble was let for the last four months to the Miss Rolles of Devonshire. It is now, I fear, again unoccupied.

Mr. D'A. always nourishes his hope of obtaining finally his so long expected *retraite*, for former services though the decision of his demand is still *ajournée*.

Quiet, however, and litteraly stationary as has been my residence at Passy, these last two months, the French newspapers, I am told, have all sent me to Bordeaux! . . . [VI, p. 29.—" Permit me now . . . gratifying to me," p. 30]. We have never seen Louis Bonaparte since we left Joigny, nor, indeed, anyone else, for we are truly as yet, shut up in our premises. . . .

[p. 32, Madame de Sousa one day showed me an urn dedicated to the memory of her first-born and early lost lamented daughter.] There was yet no inscription, and she was meditating where to find one that could bear being adapted to her peculiar and hard lot. Perhaps she led me to this melancholy spot with an idea that I might assist her researches ; but I was quite of opinion with M. D'Arblay, that what should be dictated by herself, and her own affection, in the simplest manner, would [most] conduce to soothe her design of demonstrating her maternal tenderness and regret. . . . [p. 32, Her remaining daughter, Madame de Listenois, is a very fine young woman] and the best lady Dancer, in a *ladylike* manner I have been in the way of seeing in this Country, where the ladies in general to my English eyes, foot it away with the graces, the agility and the intrepidity of opera *figurante*. But Madame de Listenois, with the form and air of a Nymph, and the attire which Vandyk would have liked to paint, has a decency in her look and demeanour that speak so forcibly in her favour, that they make one forget that her steps, motions, and appearance are theatrical ; and leave one only to admire them as light, graceful and picturesque. . . .

How thankful I am that the lovely and loved violet droops no longer ! That was most kindly inserted.— How I delighted to hear it ! Methought I smelt again all its sweetness.

You encourage me to write long letters, my dear Friend, and for that encouragement, and all else, receive the best thanks of your sincere, etc. . . .

F. D'A.

[Following the end of letter dated December 19, 1802, which reads—VI, p. 34.]

To Miss Planta, for Her Majesty, Queen Charlotte and the Princesses ; the infectious *La Grippe* at Paris ; in 1803 ; M. de *la Harpe* ; *Madame de Staël Holstein ; M. et Made. de la Fayette, La Grange* ; Mme. Charles de Maubourg; George et Virginie de La Fayette and Mdlle. de Tracy ; *Colonel Sebastiani ;* Alexandre ; *Lord Whitworth.*

To Miss Planta

For Her Majesty Queen Charlotte and their R.H. the Princesses Augusta, Eliza, Mary, Sophia, Amelia.

Passy, Rue Casse, No. 54.
March 18*th*, 1803.

It would be difficult to give you an idea of the eagerness with which I have received your letter, my dear Miss Planta, after so long a *famine* of such intelligence as is most precious to me : but when I came to that part where you mention the encouragement you are authorized to give me for writing long letters, and the hint that I am not forgotten by those for whom my heart beats in constant remembrance, I was melted quite to tears, and could not but wish I could have dried them at the feet of those for whom they were shed, but the more I see of the rest of the world, the more attached I feel myself to their rare—rare excellence. The thanks I know not how to express, their goodness will, I am sure, supply ; for while they deserve so much more gratitude than I can ever find means to offer, they expect little, and exact none. They are good, because it is right to be good and they are kind, because kindness is congenial to their nature. I am sure I need not say how great is my concern in your account of the ill effects of the cold winds to the most charming of plants and flowers, nor my joy that their, and our, prop escaped suffering by them. Here there has been a disorder the most pernicious, which has been called *le Grippe*, and which, though appearing but as a cold, has proved so frequently fatal, especially when joined or succeeding to any other complaint, that it has operated like a sort of plague, and the doors of Apothecaries shops have been crowded by buyers of drugs, with as much *monde* as if they were the entrances into public places ; and in the streets of Paris, there were scarcely more cabriolets than funerals. This is the account that has been brought to me ; for into Paris I have not once been since my residence at Passy. Early in the winter I caught a cold, which has not yet entirely left me, and it has only allowed me intervals of convalescence which have enabled me, much wrapt up, to walk sometimes in the Bois de Boulogne, which is very near us ; or upon the banks of the Seine. The purity of the air of this house saved all who steadily remained in it from this disorder and though M. D'Arblay from his occasional excursions to the Capitale, caught it, he had it so slightly, that it neither infected his family, nor lasted beyond a few days for himself. The person whom, in this recent mortality is regarded as the greatest public loss, is M. de La Harpe, who was esteemed the most correct writer of the french language remaining from the Voltaire school ; and he is the more to be regretted, as he had publicly renounced the irreligious doctrines of that sect.

It is so long now since I have been able to go out, or see anybody, from my tedious, though not dangerous confinement, that my only chance of getting rid of egotism in my letter, is by recollecting the names of those not yet mentioned with whom I had any intercourse before my Passy residence.

One of the first persons who was pleased to seek me upon my arrival was a lady with whom I had formed an intimate, though short-lived acquaintance in England, many years ago, while I was warm with admiration of her talents, and wholly uninformed of her character.

As, from Advice, I had latterly completely shunned her
in my own country though with infinite difficulty, from
her persevering pursuit, I had hoped her pride would
have made her distance me in my turn, upon my coming
hither : but, on the contrary, she was [so] eager to have me
acquainted that she impatiently expected to see me ;
and she sent me immediately a visiting ticket, with her
address, and inquiries after my health.   I was a good
deal distressed, from a real unwillingness to return
civility by offensive rudeness ; yet felt so great a repugnance to renewing an acquaintance I had so bitterly
regretted ever making, that I determined at least, to
leave the matter alone for a week, and then, without
calling, send my ticket in return.   This coldness, however, was insufficient ; she commissioned a lady whom
I frequently saw, to say to me, that though it was not
the custom for *les dames francaises* to make the first
visit, she would put by that *etiquette*, and come to me
directly, " if she were sure Madame D'arblay would give
her a kind reception."   The unexpected humility of
this message quite disconcerted me ; but I had at that
time an excuse only too good for declining to make any
direct answer ; my dear little boy was just beginning to
be ill of his first fever.   As soon as she heard of his
recovery, she wrote me the following note :—

" Je voudrais vous témoigner mon empressement,
Madame, et je crains d'etre indiscrete. J'éspere que
vous aurez le bonté de me faire dire quand vous serez,
remise des fatigues de votre voyage, pour que je puisse
avoir l'honneur de vous voir sans vous importuner."

I was now more disturbed than ever, being extremely
unwilling to make her an enemy, yet fixed to retreat
from any appearance of considering her as a friend.   We
consulted together, and Monsieur D'Arblay equally
anxious upon both these points, with myself, determined
that, in about 15 jours, I should call upon her, but
without any appointment ; and that, chez nous, she
should never be received.   He wrote for me the following
answer :—

" Madame D'Arblay ne peut qu'être infiniment flattée de l'extréme bonté de Madame la Baronne de Stael-Holstein. Elle aura l'honneur de se presenter chez Madame de S. H. aussitôt que possible."

Imagine my surprise when, after evasions so palpable, at the end of about a week, upon seeing and hearing nothing more of me, she came herself in person to me in la Rue de Miromenil.

I had already desired, should that happen, upon my first arrival, that the *portiere* would say I was not *visible*; this however did not suffice; she insisted that her name should be brought up, and begged that if I really could not receive her, Mr. D'Arblay would come down : I sent her word I was a mere *garde malade* to my boy, and could not see anybody; and Mr. D'Arblay, having no ambition to monopolize all the sallies these various provocations might draw forth, excused himself from descending. I can hardly tell you in what a tremor I presented myself, at last at the gate of her Hotel, nor my joy that she was really abroad : and the very next day she set off for her Father's house at Copet. And there, for my great good luck, she has continued ever since. But the business, all together, gave me a great deal of pain. I was kept however, the firmer, by having spoken upon my embarrassement to Mademoiselle de Mortemart, who, when I expressed my wish to avoid all renewal of acquaintance with her, on account of the terrible character she bore in England, answered : " It cannot be worse there than it is in France ! " How greatly is it to be lamented that such parts and talents should be bestowed where there are no principles ! and the more is it to be regretted, as she has qualities the most bewitching of kindness, generosity, and zeal, joined to almost every intellectual attribute, that can elevate a human being. Unrestrained passions, in short, are her bane ; for her Heart is as good as her head ; and she is so eminently agreeable and engaging, vivacious and clever, and possesses such a boundless fund of good humour, and such nearly matchless charms of conversation, that I can never cease regretting the ungrateful part I have seemed to act towards [her], though I was impelled to it by a belief it was indispensably right.

Another lady, one of a far different description, who almost as speedily, though far more gently, was so good as to find me upon my arrival, was Madame de la Fayette. She mounted up to our apartment, though almost lame, from the result of her long confinement in the dungeon at Olmutz, to invite me herself to spend a week at la Grange ; a chateau which has fallen to her from some relations since the general confiscation of all M. de Lafayette's property ; and as she insisted that we should take our little boy, then convalescent, the temptation was too great for resistance ; and for the time, it quite reinstated him. La Grange is a very antique Castle, in an airy, healthy, and pleasant, though not very picturesque country, only one room of which, an octogone, they have modernized. The more than unsullied, the exemplary character of Madame de la Fayette and which supported her blameless, and even honoured by all parties during the horrours of the Revolution, and amidst the bitterest ennemies as well as most enthousiastic friends of her husband, induced me to make this acquaintance without my usual shy reluctance ; and I found in her all I could expect of real and solid virtue. She is eminently pious, and her prayers and devotion to God are followed up by the most active and meritorious discharge of her conjugal, maternal, and filial duties ; for her Father, cy-devant Duc d'Ayen still living. She has singularly expressive eyes, but otherwise is far from handsome ; her manners are pleasing and amiable, and her mind is religiously humble. They live with the utmost simplicity and œconomy, have educated their children wholly themselves, keep no sort of equipage, dress in the plainest and cheapest style, and never come to Paris but upon business too important to be arranged by commission. M. de la F., who is extremely fond of agriculture, employs all his mornings in his Farm or Garden, and gives his evenings to his Family and books.

With all the various faults charged against him in public
life, his conduct in private can admit of but one description. In his own house he is all that is respectable
and amiable, fond, attentive, and instructive to his
children, active and zealous for his friends ; gentle and
equal with his servants and displaying, upon every occasion the tenderest gratitude to the wife, who followed
him to captivity, and to whom, from that period, he
became, by universal account, far more warmly and exclusively attached than he had ever been formerly ;
though her virtues and conduct had always been objects
to him of respect and esteem. Their eldest daughter
is about 23 and of a sensible, serious and estimable character. She is married to M. Charles de la Tour Maubourg, a young man who having no fortune, resides
with his wife and 2 little babies, at la Grange. Madame
de la Fayette told me a most affecting anecdote of the
filial devotion of Madame C. de Maubourg when she
was only 16. At that period her father was a captive at
Olmutz, and Madame de La Fayette was torn from her
family, and imprisoned by Robespierre. She languished
to follow and comfort and nurse her poor mother, whose
health was always very delicate, but knew not how to
travel, nor to whom to apply for protection. She grew
so very unhappy, that she determined in her sorrow, in
order to fulfil what she thought her first duty, to marry
their old Gardener, a working man of upwards seventy,
who she believed was low and poor enough to escape the
guillotine, and conduct her in safety to the prison : and
she had resolved, said Madame de Layfette, if she had
done it, to have him made a very good wife ; for she
would not break a vow once uttered for the universe.
Happily, however, the death of that monster, Robespierre, prevent this desperate resolution from taking
place ; and her mother was permitted to return to her
children, and take her Girls with her to share the dungeon of their father. The son, M. George La Fayette,
is a perfectly modest, unassuming and worthy young man.
He has been married, though but just 20, to Mademoi-

selle de Tracy, since our arrival; and as she has at present
no fortune, they, also, have appartments fitted up for
them in the attics of the chateau, which the young lady
is in a fair way of soon wanting to enlarge for a coming
Heir.   Mademoiselle Virginie de Lafayette, the youngest
Daughter is 19; but has so high a bloom upon a fair
complexion, that she hardly looks to be 15.   She has a
very good understanding, and a very distinguished air,
though she stoops, and, for France, has a very bad carriage; "How should it be otherwise?" said her
mother, to whom it was remarked by a friend, "elle a
été élevée dans les prisons!"

The family came to Paris about 6 weeks ago, to prepare for marrying M. G. La Fayette to Mlle. de Tracy;
when M. de Lf. during the severe frost, slipt down and
broke his thigh.   He has been extended ever since, by
a wooden machine, upon his Bed; and has suffered, and
is suffering, at times, the utmost torture; yet whether
he can ever perfectly recover the use of his limb is still
doubtful.   It is now forced down to its proper length
by the means of screws fastened to the wooden machine,
which encases it, in a manner that causes him excruciating pain.   His wife and children never quit him a
moment.   They are all at the house of Madame de
Tessé, who is sister to the duc d'Ayen and aunt to Madame
de Lafayette.

When we had finished our visit at la Grange, Madame
de Laf. et Melle. sa fille accompanied us to Paris, where
they had calls to see and prepare for Melle. de Tracy
whose marriage was then to take place in a few days.
We were all chearful in the route; but when we approached the Capital, Mde. de Laf. sunk into profound
silence and the most melancholy rumination; and as
we passed through the Barrière, her eyes were raised in
fervent prayer.   She soon after struggled to revive, but
her spirits returned no more.   A lady of the party gave
me a hint to make no enquiry, and informed me afterwards, that, at that very Barrière, this poor lady had
lost in one morning, her grandmother, her mother, the

Ds. de Ayen, and her favourite sister, la *Vesse.* de Noailles, by the Guillotine! She had mentioned to me herself this dreadful catastrophe, but not the spot on which it happened, in shedding a deluge of tears, while I was still at la Grange.

I must run away from these sad subjects.

And how can I do it more successfully than in reciting a speech which has been repeated to me of a certain bonny Duchess. She has a *loge* at the Opera house, in which she wished to receive only a select party. She called therefore, to the Box-opener and said : " *Ouvrier ! si vous laissez vener aucun personne dans mon boite, je vous chasse !* "

Last summer, we met with a gentleman who has since made no small noise in the world, Colonel Sebastiani. My little Alex was asked by some of the company, who understood English, to declaim in his own language. He chose a speech of Tom Thumb which I recollect he had once the happy fortune to recite within the fragrant scent of a sweet violet ; this speech demands a sword, and the little man strutted up to the Colonel, and made him a sign, for he could not then speak french, that he must disarm. The Colonel complied, and Alex spouted with great energy, and then pranced about with this unwieldy weapon, brandishing it one moment over his head, and the next tumbling with it between his legs ; he was so enamoured with it, that the Colonel, who could with difficulty recover it from him, said if he were so fond of warlike instruments, he would take him into his regiment. " Et vous irez avec moi," he added, " à Constantinople ? " " Qu'en dites vous ? " The child, when this was explained, very simply answered " Yes, if mama'll go." The Colonel could do no less than offer to take la Maman. What a pretty group such a trio would have made in such an expedition !

Of the same party was the good abbé Sicard, who was lately a victim to *la Gripe* ; He was the translator of Plutarch into french, and a writer upon Astronomy for youth, in verse, and other works for juvenile instruction.

He sat next *la maman*, and his plainness, quietness, and simplicity made her wish to see him again, which however she never did and much regrets his loss of this fatal infection.

The note with which I sent my last letter to Lord Whitworth procured me an answer not merely polite but kind, professing the most obliging readiness at any time, and on any occasion, to be of service to me. I regret excessively my distance from his chapel, though for this last winter, indeed, I must have refrained from going to it, had it been in the next street. I am reduced to reading the morning service of a sunday with my little boy, who I thank Heaven, notwithstanding his sword flourishes, has the happiest propensities for attending to and comprehending religious instructions. The Duchess of Dorset, I am told, has a plan, upon removing to her new Hotel, of having her seats in the chapel close to the door, so that as soon as the service is over, she may go away, she can see company, she says, afterwards in her drawing Room, but she shall avoid, by this retreat, what she greatly disapproves, being surrounded by discussions of Balls and Plays, immediatley upon the spot where she has heard divine service. She has the character of being strongly attached to her husband and children, fond of domestic life, and very seriously good ; Lord Witworth is very generally approved.

We have no news yet of *la retraite* ! But still cherish hopes, as none remains upon any other prospect !

Adieu, my dear Miss Plantan, your letter was delivered to me again in 5 days ! what a pleasure ! Believe me your ever obliged and effectionate Friend and servant

F. D'A-y.

M. D'Ar. presents his best compliments.
My boy is now in perfect health, I thank God.

[As the published Diaries contain no letters from F. B. to Dr. Burney in 1806 this properly concludes the record of her life in France.]

To. Dr. Burney. Account brief from 1802 to 1806.
Mousseau Passy.

To Dr. Burney [1]

October 5th, 1806.

Here, my dearest Father, ends all my old original
journal; various untoward circumstances impeded its
continuance at the time of its date (1802), and when the
rumours of war broke forth, I lost all spirit for my pen
in the excessive anxiety of my heart. I have kept,
however, pocket book *heads* of all I have seen or done,
which, should time and courage ever unite with opportunity, will still bring my days and my adventures, or,
observations, before the eyes of my dear Father. Meanwhile, I will give a brief history of the outline of our
lives, from the period of *May* 1802 to the present
moment, Oct. 1806. My excellent freind Madame
d'Henin, to our very great regret, quitted Paris for
Bordeaux, on a visit to her Ne[ph]hew, monsieur la tour-
du-pin, and his charming wife, who has been celebrated
by Mr. Delille in his poème de la pitié, and there Madame
d'Henin passed two years. A dreadful cough of our
ALEX drove us from Paris, in the beginning of summer,
to *Mousseau*, by and almost within the garden *ci-devant*
Orléans : which that name made me at first hate to
enter. It was not however, laid out by that baneful
wretch, but by a man of the tight [2] ; and beautiful it
is, in the Laylock season, beyond comparison, though
the prodigious preponderance of that lovely plant makes
its peculiar beauty, the excellence of only a week or two.
The walks, nevertheless, are always pretty, though not
always equally odoriferous ; and the seats are luxuriously
abondant and comfortable, though there are bridges
and queer buildings enough to content Mr. Dubster

---

[1] This letter was copied by Alexander when he was beginning to
write English with difficulty. His honoured father, fearing the original
might miscarry, thought fit to give him this task.

[2] The *Tight* was our way to denominate England, called the *tight
little Island* by Dibdin in a ballad.

himself. In this Garden we almost lived till Alex was
quite well. We then went to Joigny, whence Madame
Bazille, wife of Mr. D'Arblay's beloved maternal uncle,
with Madame Meignen, that uncle's only daughter,
had come to Paris immediately upon my arrival to
receive me into their family with the most affectionate,
flattering, and cordial kindness. Soon after our return
to our apartments at *Mousseau* we had the delight to see
our two *charlottes*, and to take them with us to the
vendanges at *Joigny*, where I had the happiness to
form a freindship, that proves delightfull to every moment of my life with Mr. Bazille, the excellent uncle so
deservedly dear to my better half. I have found him
a character of the very first merit, both in head, heart,
and manners. But I must leave him to another letter,
or I shall stand still at 1802. We staid about a fortnight at Joigny, after losing our two dear Charlottes
and then returned to the hotel marengo, rue de miromenil, where we had first begun our french residence
and thence we moved to Passy, where Mr. D'Arblay
purchased a small house, an up and down, queer, and
odd little building, in which we entered by the roof,
and of which we could only furnish the first floor; but
which had two or three magnificent views, from the
windows, and from a *Terrace* of near *four yards circum-*
ference, that was built up to our first floor from the
garden. Such as it was, we left it with infinite regret,
on account of its quiet, its prettyness, its neatness, and
beautifull views, rural walks and delicious prospects, and
its being our own, and only our own : but there were
objections to it on account of its distance from Paris,
that compelled the resignation when Mr. D'Arblay had
to attend his bureau during the winter. We passed
also, before this period, a week at la Grange, a chateau
of Madame Lafayette. Mr. La Fayette has not a foot
of land left. At Joigny, also, we repeatedly have passed
various weeks. Almost all the acquaintance that I
made upon my arrival, I have had the pleasure to keep
up, and some of them have become most kindly my

friends and afford me an infinite consolation, in my long
separation from those to whom I more natively and
originally belong. When my mind is not too much
oppressed by continual disappointment of my hopes of
peace, for enjoyment, I find great and true satisfaction
in the elegant society in which occasionally I mix.
Amiability, intelligence, gaiety, good humour and good
breeding, marke it in every instant ; and, though there
is a vivacity, which at times of discussion exalts itself
into even fiery dispute, it always stops short of quarrel,
of pettishness, or of reproach. Sarcasm never degene-
rates into sneer, nor energy into ill-nature. I don't
here, you will imagine, speak of *every day's* people, nor
of *every day's* society, which here, as every where also,
has its full share of petulance, contradiction, violence,
and personality.

[Letter from Alexander the younger to Mrs. Angerstein *née* Amelia Locke.]

January 26, Sunday, 1803.

My
Dear Amene I thank y very much for that kind
letter y have sent me : but what pleased me the most
to find that instead of saying *you and* in full, that you
made an abbreviation as y for *you*, & for *and*. but
my dear Amene I have not found y ungrateful at all :
on the contrary it is me that has been ungrateful ; but
I have only one excuse to make, that is that I have been
a good deal of time composing a book for my son, which
I hope will make y forgive me. This is the very first
time, in my whole life, that I have used a whole sheet
of paper ; but I am very sorry to say that I cannot
marry Caroline your daughter, because, do you know,
I'm engaged : so I hope you will forgive me for not
marrying your dear little Caroline whom I shall be very
glad to see. Tell me how John does, and Miss Angerstein ; And tell Mr. Boucherett that I should be very
glad to have a jack-ass to ride upon. I hope your

Caroline is well (that is Adrienne and Amelia) those two are my wifes. there is so much time that I have seen her, that I cannot tell you how she does. Mama has had a very long cold that a'nt yet over but a great deal better. I have seen the vandanges. You think perhaps that it is all done nailed up against a wall : but there your are mistaken for they tie them to a stick and they grow all round 'em in the middle of a field.

Mr. Locke said to Mama (a) that when grapes are ripe one can eat as much as one will without hurting themselves so I eat almost all that were ripe (b).

I have got an Uncle at Joigny named Bazille ; he always eat soup aux herbes, and I very fond of soup eat (1) (2) (3) (4) or 5, when I can get them, of plate and after that my second breakfast was boiled milk or sometimes milk and water when the milk is cold. Then, as I tell you mama puts hot water to it like at Westhumble. His wife Mrs. Bazille is my aunt you know (c). I am going to tell you something that will surpirze you very much. The daughter of my uncle is my cousin, or my cousin is my Uncle's daughter (d). Mrs. Locke said to Mama, in a letter, that you were making preparations of a letter, so the copy of writing was a letter from Amene is on the road ; so I flattered myself every day that it would come, I hope Mr. William Locke's son is well. Mrs. de la Chavagnac says that one day when Adrienne came to see us she heard that we were out. She enquired if I was there, and hearing not, she burst into tears. You will say, I fear, why do you tell me such bad news ? it is to let you know how affectionate her heart is. I don't know how Mr. de Narbone does, but some day or other and I will tell you when I see him, or when I write again which will not be long time.

Send my kindest love to Mr. and Mrs. Locke and Mr. Angerstein ; Mama and Papa both send their most

(a) When she was in England.
(b) Not all because mama Papa etc. had their share.
(c) A laugh !
(d) Another laugh !

affectionate love to you, and never will forget their old friend Amene.

Once more Adieu, Adieu, my dear Amene.

Pray send my love to Augusta and also to Mr. George Locke.

ENGLAND.

To MRS. ANGERSTEIN,
CUMBERLAND PLACE, LONDON.

[There is no evidence for the date of this letter, on the subject of which the Diary contains other comment.]

To *Mrs. Waddington*.[1] A brief account of the attachment and its discovery, of *Mrs. Thrale* with *Signor Piozzi*, etc.

What I see you wish me to write about is Mrs. Piozzi. Alas, my dear Mary, that to me is a melancholy subject, for though she was never a character approaching to any of these ideas of perfection my mind had formed, and which so few, like Mrs. Delany, Mrs. Locke, and my lost Angel, fulfilled ; yet with all her errors and excentricities about her, she had once a fond possession of my sincere and ardent friendship. And though she was always vain of her talents and proud of her pedigree, she was ever the first to laugh at her own vanity and to expose and mock her own pride, even while she cherished them. She was warm-hearted, generous, sweet-tempered and full of active zeal for her friends, and of fervent devotion in religion. She was replete with wit and pleasantry, and her powers of entertainment exceeded those of almost any woman I ever knew. But her manners were flaunting, her voice was loud, and she had no peace, and allowed none to others, but in the display of her talents. With draw-backs such (as) these to her better parts, you will not suppose I could ever have *chosen* her for a bosom friend,—yet being by her chosen as such she conceived for me so enthousiastic a regard, that it something nearly amounted to a species of idolatry.

[1] *Née* Port : grand-niece of Mrs. Delany.

She was never contented when I was out of her house ;
never happy when away from her sight.   All she did that
was singular, and had better have been left undone ; all
she said, that was strange, and had better have been
left unsaid ; she suffered me to point out, and with a
frankness the most extraordinary would acknowledge she
had been wrong, and make, if it were in her power,
reparation, either by some change of measures, or softening of speech.   Her whole conduct to me, during the
whole time of our intimacy, was of a nature the most
endearing that can be conceived ; but her marriage
annulled at once, the connexion.   She did not trust me
with her design, till she had bound herself to carry it
into execution.   Even then, it was accident brought it
forth, for she could not doubt my entire dislike of so
unaccountable a choice, nor my sincerity in speaking it.
It was from the Abbe Gerard's Synonimes that the discovery was made to me, and from the article *Songer,
rever, penser.*   But though the detection and its avowal
were subjects of severe grief of heart to me in those
days, when my feelings were so tenderly involved in hers
and her affairs, I did not dream of relinquishing our
friendship on that account.   She was not my ward ;
far otherwise, I had no right over her actions ; and
however ill advised and imprudent, and perhaps improper
her decision, it yet was not criminal.   I kept up therefore, the same connexion, and felt as much of the same
affection, as the change of esteem into pity could sustain :—but as various circumstances relative to her
children, which occurred, retarded her plan, and at
times made her seem to waver in its ultimate execution,
I scrupled not expressing my earnest wishes it might be
given up ; and oh ! what scenes followed !   Sometimes
I prevailed entirely :—then she repented her compliance
—then she repented her engagement, then her senses
seemed to fail her ;—then she raved—then she was seized
with a sort of stupor—then she used to fall suddenly
asleep, and talk aloud . . . frightful period !   I had no
peace nor rest.   If I conciliated for restoring her tran-

quillity, I felt as if accessory to what seemed to me a degradation of all sorts ; for Piozzi was yet more beneath her in understanding, and in mind, than in education and birth :—and if I opposed, in the hope to prevent, so ill-judged an alliance, the destruction of her health, or of her senses, menaced me with shortening or embittering her existence. Yet during all this time, her kindness, her sweetness, her fondness never wavered, never abated. Imagine therefore, my surprise when, upon her marriage actually taking place, she suddenly wrote me a letter of reproach for the want of cordiality in my congratulations !—!—as if a change from sincerity to hypocrisy ought not to have been as despicable to her as it would have been detestable in me ! I wrote her for my sole reply : " That I committed to Time and her own recollections my answer." She then sent me some very kind words, though very few, saying that she was at that moment setting off for Italy. I wrote an *immediate* promise to forget the only *un*kind words that had ever dropt from her, and added all that I thought most soothing ! but I have never heard from her since ! Whether as she was departing, my letter did not reach her, or whether she deemed our friendship a fitting sacrifice to offer up to her new engagements, I know not ; certainly as to *him* I never was his enemy : he was not in fault, and deserved not any blame. She was neither of an age nor a disposition to be seduced . . . though how she could so be bewitched, I have never been able to fathom. He was an itinerant musician, admirable in his profession, but without any other recommendation. And she cared not for music !—I have known nothing of her, except two or three accidental sights, since her marriage ; I hear from all quarters how much she is altered ; yet your account gave me real pain. How differently would you have described her in the days of her triumph and of Streatham !—I never without extreme reluctance enter upon a subject which calls forth so much regret. Dr. Johnson's opinion of her in those days did her but justice. I can only attribute all

I am told of her spirits and conduct, to a determination she has taken to hide her consciousness of her fall, by seeming content to let it pass, that she never held herself above her present circle.

BASTA!

May 3rd, 1818

[The published Diary for 1818 contains a narrative —dated November 17, 1819—of General D'Arblay's illness and death, one brief contemporary extract—VI, 370 for May 17 and other allusions on May 30 and the following days or weeks.]

This wretched day lost me the best—the tenderest— the sweetest—most amiable at once and most exemplary —and oh far most beloved of Husbands! Peace to his generous spirit! relief to his afflictions! Repose to his keen insupportable sufferings!—and oh Heaven! sweet Heaven! with the constant Hope of our Re-union may I be enabled to purify my soul and fortify my conduct for pursuing in the Right way that road that may lead. . . .

Alex took Sac*t*.

II
FRANCES BURNEY

Of the *Diary* and her two famous novels, it is not necessary to speak here. The pamphlet on *Emigrant Clergy* has considerable biographical interest as the only public expression of circumstances and events which occupied so much of her later years ; and were, moreover, entirely responsible for her happy marriage. *Camilla*, as elsewhere remarked, was the most complete expression of *sensibility*, the prevailing impulse of her own nature, she ever produced, and deserves far more attention than it has ever received.

The "Dedication" to *The Wanderer* expresses, more specifically than the often-quoted forewords to *Evelina*, her *theories* on fiction.

BRIEF REFLECTIONS RELATIVE TO THE EMIGRANT FRENCH CLERGY: Earnestly Submitted to the Humane Consideration of the Ladies of Great Britain. 1793.

Apology

However wide from the allotted boundaries and appointed province of Females may be all interference in public matters, even in the agitating season of general calamity, it does not thence follow that they are exempt from all public claims, or mere passive spectatresses of the moral as well as of the political œconomy of human life. The distinct ties of their prescriptive duties, which, pointed out by Nature, have been recognised by reason, and established by custom, remove, indeed, from their view and knowledge all materials for forming public characters. The privacy, therefore, of their lives is the dictate of common sense, stimulated by local discretion. But in the doctrine of morality the reverse is the case, and their feminine deficiencies are there changed into advantages : since the retirement, which divests them of practical skill for public purposes, guards them, at the same time, from the heart-hardening effects of general worldly commerce. It gives them leisure to reflect and to refine, not merely upon the virtues, but the pleasures of benevolence ; not only and abstractedly upon that sense of good and evil which is implanted in all, but feelingly, nay awefully, upon the woes they see, yet are spared ! It is here, then, in the cause of tenderness and humanity, they may come forth, without charge of presumption, or forfeiture of delicacy. Exertions here may be universal, without rivalry or impropriety ; the head may work, the hand may labour ; the heart may suggest, indiscriminately in all, in men without disdain, in women without a blush ; and however truly of the latter to withdraw from notice may be in general the first praise, in a service such as this, they may with yet more dignity come forward : for it is here that their purest principles, in union with their softest feelings, may blend immediate gratification with the most solemn future hopes.—And it is here, in full persuasion of sympathy as well as of pardon, that the author of these lines ventures to offer to her countrywomen a short exhortation in favour of the emigrant French Clergy.

Public Feelings

The astonishing period of political history upon which our days have fallen, robs all former times of wonder, wearies expectation, sickens even hope ! while the occurrences of every passing minute have such prevalence over our minds, that public affairs assume the interest of private feelings, affect domestic peace and occupy not merely the most retired part of mankind, but even mothers, wives, and children with solicitude irresistable.

Female Beneficence

No there is yet a resource ; a resource against which neither modesty nor equity plead ; a resource which, on the contrary, has every moral propensity, every divine obligation, in its favour : this resource is Female Beneficence. . . .

By addressing myself to females, I am far from inferring that charity is exclusively their praise ; no, it is a virtue as manly as it is gentle ; it is christian, in one word, and ought therefore to be universal. But the pressure of present need is so urgent, that the ladies who patronize this plan are content to spread it amongst their own sex, whose contributions, though smaller, may more conveniently be sudden, and whose demands for wealth being less serious, may render those contributions more general. . . .

Come forth, then, O ye Females, blest with affluence ! spare from your luxuries, diminish from your pleasures, solicit with your best powers ; and hold in heart and mind that, when the awful hour of your own dissolution arrives, the wide-opening portals of heaven may present to your view these venerable sires, as the precursors of your admission.

"CAMILLA"
A Family Scene

Repose is not more welcome to the worn and to the aged, to the sick and to the unhappy, than danger, difficulty, and toil to the young and adventurous. Danger they encounter but as the fore-runner of success ; difficulty as the spur of ingenuity ; and toil as the herald of honour. The experience which teaches the lesson of truth, and the blessings of tranquillity, comes not in the shape of warning nor of wisdom ; from such they turn aside, defying or disbelieving. 'Tis in the bitterness of personal proof alone, in suffering and in feeling, in erring and in repenting, that experience comes home with conviction, or impresses to any use.

In the bosom of her respectable family resided Camilla. Nature with a bounty the most profuse, had been lavish to her of attractions ; Fortune, with a moderation yet kinder, had placed her between luxury and indigence. Her abode was in the parsonage house of Etherington, beautifully situated in the unequal county of Hampshire, and in the vicinity of the varied landscapes of the New Forest. Her father the Rector, was the younger son of the house of Tyrold. The living, though not considerable, enabled its incumbent to attain every rational object of his modest and circumscribed wishes ; to bestow upon a deserving wife whatever her own forbearance declined not ; and to educate a lovely race of one son and three daughters, with that expansive propriety, which unites improvement for the future with present enjoyment.

In goodness of heart, and in principles of piety, this exemplary couple was bound to each other by the most perfect union of character, though in their tempers there was a contrast which had scarce the gradation of a single shade to smooth off its abrupt dissimilitude. Mr Tyrold, gentle with wisdom, and benign in virtue, saw with compassion all imperfections but his own, and there doubled the severity which to others he spared. Yet the mildness that urged him to pity blinded him not to approve ; his equity was unerring, though his judgment was indulgent. His partner had a firmness of mind which nothing could shake : calamity found her resolute ; even prosperity was powerless to lull her duties asleep. The exalted character of her husband was the pride of her existence, and the source of her happiness. He was not merely her standard of excellence, but of endurance, since her sense of his worth was the criterion for her opinion of all others. This instigated a spirit of comparison, which is almost always uncandid, and which here could rarely escape proving injurious. Such, at the very best, is the unskilfulness of our fallible nature, that even the noble principle which impels our love of right, misleads us but into new deviations, when its ambition presumes to point at perfection. In this instance, however, distinctness of disposition stifled not reciprocity of affection . . . that magnetic concentration of all marriage felicity ; . . . Mr Tyrold

sympathy

admired &

revered &

ever, distinctness of disposition stifled not reciprocity of affection----that magnetic concentration of all marriage felicity. Mr. Tyrold severed while he softened the rigid virtues of his wife, who adored while she fortified the melting humanity of her husband.

Thus, in an interchange of happiness the most deserved, and of parental occupations the most promising, passed the first married years of this blest and blessing pair. An event then came to pass extremely interesting at the moment, and yet more important in its consequences. This was the receipt of a letter from the elder brother of

to announce a design of removing

Mr. Tyrold, containing information that he meant to remove into Hampshire.

Sir Hugh Tyrold was a baronet, who resided upon the hereditary estate of the family in Yorkshire. He was many years older than Mr. Tyrold, who had never seen him since his marriage, religious duties,

 # concerns

prudence, and domestic affairs having from that period detained him at his benefice; while a passion for field sports had, with equal

since whose marriage the Bro- thers had never met, religious duties & domestic concerns having, from that period, detained the Rector at his benefice; while a passion for field sports had with e- qual constancy, kept the Baronet stationary.

-tionary at his sporting domain.

~~equal constancy, kept his brother sta-~~
~~tionary upon his own grounds.~~

The baronet began his letter with kind [Sir Hugh]
enquiries after the welfare of Mr. Tyrold
and his family, and then entered upon the
state of his own affairs, ~~briefly~~ narrating,
" ~~that~~ he had ~~lost his health, and, not~~ *copiously*
" knowing what to do with himself, had *the Gen hav-*
" resolved to change his habitation, and *well got hold*
" settle near his ~~relations—The~~ Cleves' *of his health*
" estate, which he heard was just by Ether- *he could not*
" ington, being then upon sale, he desired *mount his*
" his brother to make the purchase for *horse on...*
" him out of hand; and then to ~~prepare~~ *wind, not*
" Mrs. Tyrold, with whom he was yet un- *kill, and*
" acquainted, though he took it for *kind, and*
" granted she was a woman of great learn- *therefore,*
" ing, to receive a mere poor country *+*
" 'squire, who knew no more of hic, hæc, *I put in*
" hoc, than the ~~baby unborn. He begged~~ *a good*
" ~~him to provide a proper apartment for~~ *word for*
" their niece Indiana Lynmere, whom he *him to*
" should bring with him, and another for *man in*
" their nephew Clermont, who was to fol- *the Moon;*
" low at the next holidays; and not to *nor so*

he may be a very good Scholar, for "forget" *much nea...*
aught we can tell, the distance being *them, for*
so great, whatever our spyglasses may pretend to
the contrary, that we can be but poor
judges. He begged also, to have a proper
apartment provided for their niece

revered while he softened his wife, who adored while she fortified the melting humanity of her husband.

Thus, in an interchange of happiness the most deserved, and of parental occupations the most promising, passed the first married years of this blest and blessing pair.

A Character

Sir Hugh Tyrold inherited from his ancestors an unincumbered estate of £5000 per annum ; which he enjoyed with ease and affluence to himself, and disseminated with a good will so generous, that he appeared to think his personal prosperity, and that of all who surrounded him, bestowed but to be shared in common, rather from general right, than through his own dispensing bounty. His temper was unalterably sweet, and every thought of his breast was laid open to the world with an almost infantine artlessness. But his talents bore no proportion to the goodness of his heart, an insuperable want of quickness, and of application in his early days, having left him, at a later period, wholly uncultivated, and singularly self-formed.

The Heroine

Camilla was, in secret, the fondest hope of her mother, though the rigour of her justice scarce permitted the partiality to beat even in her own breast. Nor did the happy little person need the avowed distinction. The tide of youthful glee flowed jocund from her heart, and the transparency of her fine blue veins almost shewed the velocity of its current. Every look was a smile, every step was a spring, every thought was a hope, every feeling was joy ! and the early felicity of her mind was without alloy.

The Hero

Edgar Mandlebert was a young man who, if possessed neither of fortune nor its expectations, must from his person and his manners have been as attractive to the

young, as from his morals and his conduct to those of
riper years. His disposition was serious and meditative;
but liberal, open, and candid. He was observant of the
errors of others, and watched until he nearly eradicated
his own. But though with difficulty he bestowed admiration, he diffused, both in words and deeds, such
general amity and good will, that if the strictness of his
character inspired general respect, its virtues could no
less fail engaging the kinder mede of affections. When
to merit of a species so rare were added a fine estate
and a large independent fortune, it is not easy to decide
whether in prosperity or desert he was most distinguished.

IMPRUDENCE AND SUSPICION

Thus ended the long conflicts, doubts, suspences, and
sufferings of Edgar and Camilla; who, without one
inevitable calamity, one unavoidable distress, so nearly
fell the sacrifice to the two extremes of Imprudence and
Suspicion, to the natural heedlessness of youth unguided,
or to the acquired distrust of experience that had been
wounded. Edgar, by generous confidence, became the
repository of her every thought; and her friends read
her exquisite lot in a gaiety no longer to be feared: while,
faithful to his word, making Etherington, Cleves, and
Beech Park, his alternate dwellings, he rarely parted her
from the fond parents and enraptured Uncle. And
Dr Marchmont, as he saw the pure innocence, open
frankness, and spotless honour of her heart, found her
virtues, her errours, her facility, or her desperation,
but A PICTURE OF YOUTH; and regretting the false
light given by the spirit of comparison, in the hypo-
thesis which he had formed from individual experience,
acknowledged its injustice, and its arrogance. What, at
last, so diversified as man? What so little to be judged
by his fellow?

"THE WANDERER"
FROM "DEDICATION" TO DR. BURNEY

With regard to the very serious subject treated upon,

from time to time, in this work, some,—perhaps many
—may ask, Is a Novel the vehicle for such considerations ?
such discussions ? Permit me to answer ; whatever, in
illustrating the characters, manners or opinions of the
day, exhibits what is noxious or reprehensible, should
scrupulously be accompanied by what is salubrious, or
chastening. Not that poison ought to be infused merely
to display the virtues of an antidote ; but that, where
errour and mischief bask in the broad light of day,
truth ought not to be suffered to shrink timidly into the
shade.

Divest, for a moment, the title of Novel from its
stationary standard of insignificance, and say ! What is
the species of writing that offers fairer opportunities for
conveying useful precepts ? It is, or it ought to be, a
picture of supposed, but natural and probable human
existence. It holds, therefore, in its hands our best
affections ; it exercises our imaginations ; it points out
the path of honour ; and gives to juvenile credulity
knowledge of the world, without ruin, or repentance ;
and the lessons of experience, without its tears. And
is not a Novel, permit me, also, to ask, in common with
every other literary work, entitled to receive its stamp as
useful, mischievous or nugatory, from its execution ?
not necessarily, and in its changeless state, to be branded
as a mere vehicle for frivolous, or seductive amusement ?
If many may turn aside from all but mere entertainment presented under this form, many, also, may, un-
consciously, be allured by it unto reading the severest
truths, who would not even open any work of a graver
denomination. . . .

The power of prejudice annexed to nomenclature
is universal ; the same being who, unnamed, passes unnoticed, if preceded by the title of a hero, or a poten-
tate, catches every eye, and is pursued with clamorous
praize, or,—its common reverberator ;—abuse ; but in
nothing is the force of denomination more striking than
in the term Novel ; a species of writing which, though
never mentioned, even by its supporter, but with a

look that fears contempt, is not more rigidly excommuni-
cated from its appelation, in theory, than sought and
fostered from its attractions, in practice. . . .

The work which I here present to you may show in
the observations which it contains upon various characters,
ways, or eccentricities of human life, that an exteriour
the most frivolous may enwrap illustrations of conduct,
that the most rigid preceptor need not deem dangerous
to entrust to his pupils ; for, if what is inculcated is
right, it will not, I trust, be cast aside, merely because
so conveyed as not to be received as a task. On the
contrary, to make pleasant the path of propriety, is
snatching from evil its most alluring mode of ascendancy.
And your fortunate daughter, though past the period of
chusing to write, or desiring to read, a merely romantic
love-tale, or a story of improbable wonders, may still
hope to retain,—if she has ever posessed it,—the power
of interesting the affections, while still awake to them
herself, through the many much loved agents of sensibility, that still hold in their pristine energy her conjugal, maternal, fraternal, friendly, and,—dearest Sir,—
her filial feelings. . . .

In this country all sacred theories, far from being
either neglected, or derided, are become almost common
topics of common discourse ; and rather, perhaps, from
various sects, and diversified opinions, too familiarly
discussed, than defyingly set aside. But what I observed
in my long residence abroad, presented another picture ;
and its colours, not, indeed, with cementing harmony,
but to produce a striking contrast, have forcibly, though
not, I hope, glaringly tinted my pen. Nevertheless,
truth, and my own satisfaction, call upon me to mention,
that, in the circle to which, in Paris, I had the honour,
habitually, to belong, piety, generally, in practice as
well as in theory, held its just preeminence ; though
almost every other society, however cultured, brilliant,
and unaffectedly good, of which occasionally I heard, or
in which, incidentally I mixed, commonly considered
belief and bigotry as *synonymous* terms.

III

SUSAN BURNEY

(1755—1800)

SUSAN was not only the " peculiar darling of the whole house of Dr. Burney, as well as of his heart," but the dearest and closest comrade of Fanny in every thought and feeling of life ; as nearly every page of the well-known *Diary* declares, and these Letters even more intimately reveal.

They have no secrets on either side ; both always eager to hear and impart, with a thousand hints and understandings between the lines, that no man—not even the dear Father or brothers—could be expected to appreciate.

Fanny's journals and letters told much of the great world ; Susan's, equally vivid and detailed, more of home ; but—" from our earliest moments, we wanted nothing but each other. Joyfully as others were received by us—loved by us—all that was necessary to our happiness was fulfilled by our simple junction."

Even more, I think, than the authoress of *Evelina*, Susan herself personifies that shy, superior, refinement of taste and feeling, which their generation called " sensibility," a standard of Instinct they assume for themselves above that found or expected in average humanity. Susan describes herself as " an insipid person that likes everything " ; and believes her " heart to be ill furnished with bolts and bars "—at least she " never has a key " ; but there is far more spirit in the Letters than such words suggest. She certainly does not curb her wit towards those she scorns or dislikes ; though in part maybe, her gentler nature gave it less scope than her sister's.

In the *Early Diaries*, indeed, we saw them at times

recounting the same scenes, with equal vivacity, but there is here, at least, no evidence to support the conjecture of Mrs. Paine Ellis that, under similar conditions, Susan might have been as great an artist. The household subject-matter of these later Letters does not entirely account for their comparatively undramatic form. They are of great interest to us as intimate revelations of herself : transparently sincere, eagerly fond, and compact of generous, loyal affection. They reflect curious customs, and points of view, of her day and generation :—having the hair " papered " ; an opera-stage " filled with gentlemen perseveringly hissed by the gallery " ; and news of " an extraordinary man of Ayrshire, born and bred a *Ploughman*, who, tout en suivant la chance, has composed some pieces of poetry which, if situation be considered are wonderful, and even setting that aside seem the production of a real genius."

She brings her own charming children to life for us with much of Fanny's own genius for remembered dialogue ; she makes personalities of all the Lockes ; she comments with spirit on Fanny's news. But neither scene nor narrative is composed ; her phrasing is too often over-sweet ; her French idioms over-frequent ; and such barbarisms as " gentle-ized," " a wonderful flowerist," " martyrise," and " quietise " continually offend the ear.

The Letters cover two periods of great biographical interest. Those of the first " exercise book " begin in 1787—five years after her marriage, during the happy, and busy days of opening nursery life in a loving and united family group ; the daily intimacy already established with the wealthy and cultured, but cordially affectionate, neighbours at Norbury Park. There is abundant baby-talk,—amusing and charming scenes between the children at Mickleham and at " the Great House " ; gossip of neighbours ; and, above all, the strongest evidence of little Fanny and Norbury's devotion to their aunt—now at the " Queen's House," Windsor. This series carries us into 1789.

Before the second begins, the Émigrés have invaded
" Juniper Hall " ; Fanny has left the Court, met and
married General D'Arblay ; the little Alexander Charles
Louis Piochard, and Susan's youngest child William, are
now a few months old. The shadow on Susan's life,
though not yet clearly understood, seems hovering somewhere behind the actually more varied and lively scene.
The unsettled conditions in Ireland—threats of a French
invasion and rebellion among his fellow countrymen—
had already compelled Major Phillips to go over and
look after his estates. At some time for which we have
no letters, he had returned and taken Norbury with him
to Dublin. And now, in 1795, Susan is—temporarily
—settled in London, visiting her relations ; rejoicing in
occasional talks with the beloved Dr. Burney ; very
busy about practical help and suggestions for the publication of *Camilla* ; but with a heart ill at ease for the
absent child, haunted by continual dread of a summons
to banishment for herself.

Phillips once more returns, this time demanding that
she and her children should make their home in Ireland.
The sense of doom is already apparent. She slips away
at the last, not daring to face actual farewells ; and the
guarded allusions to her husband clearly reveal, without
stating, the tragic change in his feelings she had now to
face. He had, indeed, prepared some sort of a home
for her, inadequate enough ; but there are few more
pathetic records of a broken life, endured with courage
and forbearance, than the final letters which Fanny
preserved of these months.

Phillips had now, it seems, become totally careless
of appearances. " His pursuit "—of the charming and
beautiful Jane Brabazon—" is flagrant and his assiduity
unceasing." He is plainly determined, moreover, to
detach Norbury from his mother's love.

Susan is brief but explicit, and perfectly frank about
the scandal that is hidden from none of their friends ;
though, with a curiously instinctive self-confidence, she
immediately asserts her conviction that the lady is abso-

lutely indifferent and absolutely straight. They become, in fact, most intimate friends (not entirely without ill-natured comment of onlookers), and Susan's enthusiasm for her kindness and affection is at all times expressed without reserve. It next appears that Jane was privately engaged already ; and when she marries the Rev. Disney in 1798, Phillips becomes more sulky and disagreeable than ever ; until, once more, Susan surprisingly asserts herself, persuades him to call on " the bride," and—at least superficially—put an end to an impossible situation.

But, perhaps, the strangest factor of all in this peculiar triangle, is the attitude of twelve-year-old Norbury himself. Jane Brabazon had been always devoted to him, and talked much of his mother. He had, indeed, been affectionately welcomed by the whole clan. But it is he who most clearly warns Susan of certain subjects which are sure to put his father into a bad temper ; who frankly tells his father that she acts far more strictly in obedience to her conscience than he ; and who, finally, expresses—with almost uncanny intuition—the loyalty he contrives to maintain towards both.

Loving and liking, as he once explained to his baby brother, are quite different : " I like all sorts of people who seem good, but I can't love them all, and I love some people, that I don't like. *There is a person whom I dislike more than anybody I know in the world, yet I love him exceedingly*."

I wish there were more to say of Norbury than that he became a scholar of Trinity College, Dublin ; took " Orders " ; and died in 1814.

Susan had never been strong : the physical discom-fort and emotional strain could not be long upheld ; and she was dragged away at last—by protests from friends and relations, much as Fanny had been earlier dragged out of Court. She was allowed, finally, to bring Fanny and the little William back to England, managed to reach the old sailing and landing place for Irish ships, Park-gate, near Chester, where she was met by her brother Charles ; but died within a week.

This is the poignant tragedy in the Burney history; and for Molesworth Phillips himself, one must regret so dark a stain on a character which, though never quite in tune with the inner circle, had unquestionably many good and attractive traits. There was kinship with all the Burneys in the "raw youth" who "pawned his shirt to see Garrick" during a first visit to London; and the gallantry of his rescuing one of Cook's marines is beyond dispute. As a duellist he seems to have been at once a man and a gentleman. He was a sworn pal of the affectionate James, reached distinction in his profession, was elected to Johnson's Club, and—indeed —regarded as more presentable than James himself, among the friends of the fastidious Lockes.

Of his second marriage in 1800 with Ann Maturin (sister of Norbury's delightful tutor), their four children, and the first years after Susan's death, we have no record; but he reappears, as a widower, in old age, once more comrade with Admiral James, as the respected and loved friend of Charles Lamb, who calls him "the high-minded associate of Cook, the veteran Colonel, with his lusty heart still sending out cartels of defiance at old time." He was "among the little knot of whist-players, that used to assemble weekly at the Queen's Gate." In the gossiping Life of Nollekens it is said that "his venerable age is not beyond his politeness." He would tell stories of the great folk he had known in his youth, and the anecdote he once related of Madame de Staël's "manner in society," carries with it an unconscious tribute to his own natural tact. "He remembered she had a habit, while she discoursed, of taking a scrap of paper and a pair of scissors and snipping it to bits as an employment for her fingers: that once he observed her to be at a loss for this her usual mechanical resource and he quietly placed near her a back of a letter from his pocket: afterwards she earnestly thanked him for this timely supply of the means she desired as a needful aid to thought and speech." He died in 1832, aged seventy-seven.

Fanny Phillips (1782–1860) was a great favourite with her grandfather, whose house she kept for some time. She afterwards married a Mr. C. C. Raper ; and *their* daughter (Mrs. Minet Kingston) is said to have had more life and fun and *esprit* than any of them, though she was not so clever and well-read as the granddaughter of Charlotte, nor so brilliant in society as Sally Payne, James's daughter.

We hear no more of *William*, except that he died young.

It was to Susan that Madame de Staël addressed her pathetic parting from the English friends of Norbury Park :

" Douce image de Norbury, venez me rappeler qu'une félicité vive et pure peut exister sur la terre ? . . . . Dans cette retraite que la volonté des possesseurs rend obscure, que le jugement des hommes éclairés, que la reconnaissance de ceux qui suffrent doit illustrer, j'ai trouvé quelque tems un asyle loin des crimes de la France et des préjugés que l'horreur qu'ils doivent causer, inspirent à tous ceux qui n'ont pas la force de resister aux extrêmes contraires. Le respect, l'enthousiasme dont mon âme est remplie en contemplant l'ensemble des vertus morales et politiques qui constituent l'Angleterre. L'admiration d'un tel spectacle, le repos céleste qu'il me fesoit goûter : ces sentiments si doux et si necessaires après la tourmente de trois ans de révolution, s'unissent dans mon souvenir au délicieux séjour, aux respectables amis, près desquels je les ai éprouvés. Je les remercie de quatre mois de bonheur échappés au naufrage de la vie. Je les remercie de m'avoir aimés. . . . Lorsqu'un sentiment mélancolique porteroit à se lasser de combattre les injustes attaques des fureurs de l'esprit de parti, l'on se rattache à soi comme à l'objet de suffrages si puis. L'on se défend encore pour honorer ses amis."

William Locke (1732–1810) was a well-known amateur

artist and collector, who himself built the house so
affectionately described in these letters, and was universally recognised as deserving the character in which he
here appears.

The younger *William* (1767–1847) was a pupil of
Fuseli's, but remained, as one would expect from these
pages, an "amateur" artist to the end. Some of his
etchings and drawings, however, may be seen in the
print-room of the British Museum. He married the
daughter of "dog Jennings." His brother *Charles*
married Miss Ogilvie, daughter of the Duchess of
Leinster.

So many of her friends found William Locke in the
virtuous, but somewhat tiresome Edgar Mandelbert,
that "creature of accumulated punctilios," who spent
his "life in refining away his own happiness," that
we suspect Fanny must really have had the young artist
in view when drawing the hero of her *Camilla*. Young
Norbury saw the likeness, and also fancied that the
heroine's alarming mother was, at least in part, a picture
of Mrs. Locke.

There was a third *William* (1804–1832) distinguished
for his good looks, who combined the callings of life-
guardsman and amateur artist, published some illustrations to Byron, and was drowned in Lake Como, "in
sight of his bride."

Molesworth Phillip's father, John, was the natural son
of the first Viscount Molesworth, Baron Phillips. His
mother was a direct descendant of the first Lord Brabazon. His sister, Magdalene Dorothea, married one of
the Kiernans, frequently named in the Letters.

Like all Burney manuscripts, these were preserved,
partially cut up, and docketed by Madame D'Arblay,
who destroyed what she desired should not be seen by
other members of the family.

The earlier series were given by Mrs. Kingston,

Susan's granddaughter, to Henry Augustus Johnston, great-grandson of George Kiernan ; the later series were copied by his brother, Lieut.-Colonel George Hamilton Johnston, from the originals in the possession of the Rev. David Wauchope. Both Mr. Johnstons inserted numerous footnotes, elaborate genealogical trees of all the Phillips and Burney connections, with a large collection of newspaper cuttings, recording births, marriages, and death.

LETTER VII

March 25th, 1787.

Notwithstanding a most abominable propensity to indolence, and almost *distaste* that I have felt to journalising since our Friends have been with—or at least near my Fanny—write I will for you wish it. And what can be sweeter or more gratifying than the manner in which you receive and desire the continuance of my nothings ! It is true indeed that I have now less than ever to say—I have done nothing but play with my children, and work for them, and with a little reading and making music my time has always been completely filled up though to recount in what manner would not be very entertaining, unless you were the Describer. —From the time that I wrote to my dearest Fanny on the subject of my going to town, that idea had full possession of me and I do confess that when Phillips set out last Sunday, knowing that he would that evening meet at my sister B⁹ my Father—Mrs Lock and my Fanny—I felt myself more low spirited than I have been this many a day—My little Companions were of great use, as they always are on such occasions. Their innocent gaiety and total unconsciousness of evil, drive away all sorrowful recollections more effectually than the best reasoning or greatest efforts could do.—Monday—a dull day on which I knew I could receive no letter was wished for only that it might be over—but Tuesday to my no small disappointment the postman brought me nothing. —I thought this must be the effect of accident—and so indeed it was—for I ought that day to have received my Fanny's letter which had been missent, and did not arrive at me till two days after. I gave my Fanny a long lesson, and she was just gone out with Betty Parker and the little Boy, when I was surprised by a visitor— our dear James—I was sorry Phillips should be out of the way, but glad to see him at any time. He seemed better than when last here, and in spirits.—After dinner I walked with him and Fanny who gathered violets all the way, a country walk, and a most beautiful one: with sweet Norbury always in view—the White House appearing like the *Temple of Fame*, on a mountain almost inaccessible from its steepness, tho' not like that temple placed on a Rock of ice. The weather was so lovely that had the trees been more leafy I should have thought we were in June. James talked to me all the way of his studies. He is studying very hard, and all kinds of things at once—Law—Physic—Politics—and History— besides French, and Latin. He has set himself a task for a year I think, to read a certain number of pages a day. I believe he said a hundred on an average.—It keeps him in full employment which is always a good thing—but I think he is attempting too much at a time. We returned home glad of our tea, and after that and the little personages' departure, James read, and amused himself by playing and a little intermediate chat. I had had some little hope of Phillips' return, but no certainty, and he did not come. Wednesday Morning March 21st before we were seated at breakfast young Hoole was announced. James was much pleased to see him which made me the more so. He had breakfasted before 6 in the morning, and been part of the way to town with his Father, and was not sorry to join our party at our meal—which however James would scarce let him partake of, he attacked him with such eagerness first on Hogarth's Analysis of Beauty, which he had been reading here, and on matters of taste and the fine arts, and afterwards on politics. Mr Pitt, Mr Hastings etc. He can make nothing of me, for I hate useless arguments, when

neither party has a chance of convincing the other.—
So I never dispute with him—indifferent points I am
ready enough to give up, and where we differ in more
serious ones, I would rather laugh than argue—and at
Chessington his wife I fancy follows my course very
prudently, and nobody else can understand him—so
that when he meets a new person to whom he can unfold
his opinions (which are sometimes not quite so original
as he thinks them, and at others such as scarce anybody
but himself would support) his earnestness to talk, and
unwillingness to have done is really comic. Young
Hoole however and he seemed very good Friends, tho'
I believe the former might say to himself " Something
too much of this." They talked much of Cooper's poem
of the Task. I should like to see it. Does it deserve
the notice which seems to be taken of it ? I wish it
may—for except Dr Johnson's lives and two novels, I
do not recollect any super excellent thing that has been
published within my memory. The *death* of many
great men I can very well remember—but all the productions on which their fame was founded had appeared
I believe before I knew how to read—at least before I
got out of Goody Twoshoes—He went out of the room
for a few minutes, and young Hoole turned to seize the
opportunity to tell me he had seen Mr Young, and been
told by him that articles were absolutely drawn up for
the separation of himself and his wife, and they waited
only to hear from Mr Moxey Allen before they should
sign them. " But " said my Informer—" I do not
believe she will quit his house." Tho' all this was not
very *new* to me, I could not help shuddering at thoughts
of this dreadful connection, and James came in before
I could make any answer. Mr Hoole then changed the
subject. There seemed to me something a little *conscious* in his manner too—but perhaps there was not.
He had a funeral in the evening and could not stay
dinner, and James would not—so at one o'clock they
both left me together. Phillips returned in the evening,
and we had a long conversation upon the Sunday con-

cert etc—but he brought me no letters—I found he had almost promised for me to my sister, tho' I had begged him to make no engagement, as I was bent upon first hearing from my Fanny—and as he told me Mr Hawkins[1] was shortly coming to town and Nancy returning home, he wished me to hasten my visit. I went rather anxiously to bed—chagrined at having nothing to assist my determination and *much* chagrined at what the vexatious post was depriving me of. But the next morning—before Phillips came down, two letters were brought me—a paquet from my sweet Mrs Lock, and a precious letter from my dearest Fanny, whose hand-writing I was growing sick to see. I really began to feel myself *a person quite forgot*—Was it not a malicious accident that retarded two days my receiving this sweet letter, which you had already grieved to have lost a single post in sending ? The sight of it quite revived and the perusal [rejoiced] me.—One line determined my *wishes* with respect to the journey I had been so anxiously planning—for thro' all the delicate caution and kindness of my dearest Fanny, I saw what for her would be, and must be most desirable—Nothing *ne me tenoit au cœur* but our dearest Mrs Lock—but upon opening and reading her paquet, I found her earnestness that we should *spare the pleasure* of being near you together subsided ; and that her present earnest wishes were that her visit should be succeeded by mine—I believe I have already told you this was originally my own wish—going for so very short a time I felt that the less division of my inclinations there would be, where to bestow it the better, for my *own* sake. There will be always too much—For her too I foresaw, that from an excess of delicacy she would be greatly the loser, as I was sure she would study how to give up all her own opportunities of seeing you to me. So that this change of plan seemed to me every way for the best—but—all this but increased my difficulties—for I apprehended that *then or never*

---

[1] Rector of Halstead, Essex, who married Nancy, daughter of Richard Burney, of Worcester.

SUSAN BURNEY.
By Edward Burney.

according to Phillip's arrangements, by which he had
meant to gratify us *all* my purposed journey must take
place. However I will not dwell on all this further.
We had a long discussion upon the matter—I gave it
up to him—and then he determined that I should do
what seemed to me best for me—Mrs Lock and yourself. My journey must now take place after I am perfectly settled with my new nursery maid—but being in
view, I do not think its being deferred till a little interval
of time from your parting with our sweetest friend has
passed, will be amiss—but my Fanny must be sure to
let me know if any particular time would be best avoided,
or eminently desirable—and I would try to benefit by
the hint.—Oh how my Fanny's account of her reviving
spirits has revived me! Heaven be praised for it!
Upon leaving me James had said that if we would send
the Horse on Phillips' return he would come again
immediately—and accordingly we did so and he came
the next day. Friday March 23d: to dinner and slept
here that night—but as Phillips was going to town
again on Saturday this proved but a very short visit,
for he accompanied him on his little mare as far as
Epsom, Phillips on foot by his side; and thence walked
home. Whilst he was here, Fanny who is become a
great favourite with him, begged me to let her shew
him Aunt Fanny's box of bonbons, which is yet not
empty—he accepted a few from the little pleased girl,
and admired the *superscription* very much. In the
evening I had the comfort by return of Mr Lock's cart
to receive a few sweet lines from our dear Mrs Lock.
Did she tell you of Fanny's kissing the *violets* she sent
Thursday?—after the letter was gone "But Mama"
said she "I never have sent any violets to Aunt Fanny—
and I daresay she would like them—May I when you
write again?" I promised her she should.—My dearest
Mrs Lock's little letter gratified me very much. She
seems so pleased with the change of my plan—She gives
too most sweet accounts of our Fanny—How I rejoice
that you meet so often and so delightfully? Sunday

March 25th I ventured to take my little girl to church
for the first time—and you will think soon enough too
—but you would have been pleased to see how perfectly
raisonable and decorous the dear little thing was—how
attentive to imitate all my motions, sitting, kneeling, or
standing—and with what *reverential awe* she seemed
impressed—Mrs Barbauld's touching and admirable
hymns For Children, and a very well meant tho' not so
well executed little book, lent me by the dear girls at
Norbury, containing the *first principles of religion* for
young children had prepared her to enter this sacred
place of worship with sentiments as well fitted to it as
I believe infancy is capable of receiving.—She had long
been wishing to go and my promise of taking her had
filled her with joy—but nothing could be more composed nor better than her little deportment there. I
wished to make this trial when there should be only
herself and me, that her wonder at the new place, and
the entire novelty of it, and all the questions it was
likely to produce might be over before her young Friends
at Norbury might be of the party : who would have
been perhaps too much amused by any little error had
she made any, and by laughing or whispering have put
to flight those awful feelings which I was pleased to see
rising in her mind—at our return home she had a great
many of dear Aunt Fanny's bonbons, and was made the
happiest little creature in the world by my telling her
she had behaved like a *little Woman*—" What like such
a woman as you Mama ? like a—no, not an *old* woman
—but I mean a *great* woman—Mama you are not old
—only older than me, a great deal, else you could not
take care of me and of little Brother : and How much
older than you do you think I am Fanny ? " Why—
after a little hesitation—" I daresay Mama you are three
years older than me ? " I assured her I was. Once in
the evening I told her she made a sad noise. " Mama "
said she but very gravely, " I think it was like the people
when they were singing Psalms." Indeed it was not
much worse—however I did not encourage her to re-

peat this attempt. I found at our return home a letter
from our Aunt Nanny—She and Aunt Becky think
they have found out a cheap mode of conveyance here,
and will perhaps come soon to see us—I answered the
letter immediately : but could not *press* them to make
this fatiguing journey at present, as we could not possibly give them a bed—however I begged them to
consult only their own strength and feelings—and if
they *can* come, I certainly can*not* be otherwise than
much pleased to see them. My itty Nordia begins to
attempt saying everything he hears said. He is infinitely
more forward both in walking and in speech than Fanny
was—How do my dear Mama—and good by—and good
by Papa—and pitty teature, and I know not how many
more things he can say. Mr Williams' print which
hangs in our parlour he salutes every day by the name of
Billie, and Gan Papa's he is likewise very fond of but can
only say *A Papa*. . . . I must tell you that poor little
Fanny in reading Mrs Barbauld's account of a hare for
the first time to day—it being pursued by Huntsmen
and Hounds and at last torn to pieces, was so much
affected that the tears began to flow apace, and she
could not see to read on—Don't you think she will soon
deserve a Berquin ? I sent a letter to Esther by Phillips
to tell her I could not yet think of leaving home. . . .
Phillips returned yesterday evening, and brought me my
best loved Fanny's precious B— Shall I however give her
one caution ? 'Tis in future not to send such a paquet
by him, except *under cover* to Mrs Lock, and with some
pretext for its size—it is so likely to awaken a curiosity
very distressing to me that I need but hint at my objection.—Do not conclude from these words that I have
already *undergone* any distress—All has been managed
perfectly well without—but the pleasure he has had in
former journals, would make him ill bear being deprived
of the whole of even a letter, and naturally he must be
inquisitive when he sees such a paquet—Your *next* I
imagine I shall receive from sweet Mrs Lock—and after
that, I should wish them to pass first thro' her hands.

as she can make them arrive at me with the most perfect
snugitude, and the greatest speed—I have hastily read,
but will not attempt comments at present on this most
interesting and sweet B—as I am too much hurried—
Betty Parker's having been out all day, has given me very
little leisure, having been head nurse—an office I found
such, as to make me wonder she should be in so great
a hurry to cast it off—the dear children have been as
good and sweet as ever 15 months and four years old
could be—Whilst Nanny walked out with them in the
morning I was surprised and gladdened by the sight of
sweet Mrs Lock—I had hoped to have passed the evening at Norbury—but alas! their journey I found was
hastened—they go to morrow! She came loaded with
sweet flowers—and in return when we parted I trusted
her the dear B—which she is to send back packed up
with some music. When this is carried up to her—and
now my beloved Fanny it is so late I dare not add another
line—Heaven bless and preserve you? and may you
without disturbance, or disarrangement of any plan, or
any rule prescribed meet this dear Friend often and
sweetly during [her] short stay—tho' to me it will not
seem short. This sweet hope will be my solace during
her absence. Adieu, adieu and *good night* to my dear
and sweet sister!—10. o'clock Monday Night. I should
have told you Nordia was as sweet as he could be to dear
Mrs Lock this morning—and knew her and kissed her
and laughed at her, and made the best amends possible
for his little freak of sauciness when she last saw him
here—She will tell you how well He and Fanny look,
and are.—

MISS BURNEY.

LETTER VIII

April 18th, 1787.

. . . I finished my little pacquet of Journal to my Fanny
in a great hurry, and have scarce been out of that hurry
since. . . . The next day Thursday April 5th was the
day appointed for our sweet Friends return—but my joy

was moderated by considering from whence and from whom they came—particularly our dearest Mrs Lock, for whom I knew how to feel. At about 2 o'clock Abram announced " Mademoiselle Bristow et sa niece." I liked the appearance of my new maid very much— there is a look of softness and of sense in her eyes which makes her face very pleasing tho' not pretty—She reminds me a *little* of my Boulogne Friend Mademoiselle Belle—but she is not by any means *so* belle.—I found her Aunt wished her to sleep a night or two at Norbury to rest herself, and I was very well pleased she should do so on Betty Parker's account. They told me Mrs Lock etc were not expected till the evening, so that I was obliged to give up the hope of seeing them that day. My sweet friend wrote me half a dozen kind lines immediately on her arrival, and just as I was going to send off Abram with inquiries, a few minutes after Phillips returned, and you may think we did not much want topics for conversation that night. April 6th Good Friday—Against my inclination I missed church—Our dear little George brought me an invitation for the *day*, and as soon as the service was over, I set off with him. I should have taken my Fanny, but that she had the remains of a badish cold, and I feared her walking home in the evening. I was very sorry to leave the little good girl, who spent her time in but a melancholy way as I found afterwards, as Betty Parker left her alone in the nursery the whole evening!—We found only dear Mr Lock in the Picture Room, by whom I was most sweetly and affectionately received, and to see whom again almost *made me tender*—I heard his dearest Fredy was in—*Fanny's Room*—" You know where that is "—Helas oui, I could have said—I found the sweet soul in the midst of a confusion of arrangements —all of which were soon suspended by my appearance— so that I did her business a great deal of mischief—She and the dear little girls all looked pale—but only from the London air, and mode of life I found, and remains of colds, from which they are now quite free—Need I

tell you the subject of our discourse my Fanny? O,
it was a delightful one—and all I heard did *so* cheer and
comfort me! I was most happy too to see our sweet
Friend return so tranquilised, and to see that her sorrow
for what she had parted from had not incapacitated
her from every other enjoyment—in the midst of this
sweet discourse Mr Lock came up to us, and sat about a
quarter of an hour talking of Mr William and of you
alternately—and I think with equal interest—" I suppose (said he) Fredy has been telling you all about
Fanny "—all? cried she—no—nor half—we shall have
conversation for a week at least "—" Well at least you
have found time to tell her how well she looks—and
that she grows more and more used to her situation—
and that some of her extreme timidity is wearing off,
which will lessen many of the unpleasant parts of it—
a little courage in her situation is absolutely necessary
to prevent its being a constant wretchedness "—He then
went on speaking of your apartments—how much they
had seen of you, and how pleasantly—of the goodness
and attention of the L—s, in short of all those circumstances which he knew would give me most pleasure, and
then rising, " Well I'll go down again," said he, " now
I have seen a little of you—I am so glad to see you.
And you will be going soon—but we must see a great
deal of you first." I need not I think tell you how
deeply these kind words sunk in my heart—as well as
the kind tone of voice and manner in which they were
spoken—and when he was gone our sweet Mrs Lock
with a look full of that pleasure which she so highly
feels when she knows she is giving it said—" Oh he *does
love you dearly*—He wanted so much to see you—whenever our return home was mentioned, he always said
and then we shall see Mrs Phillips—that *sweet little
woman*." What delightful flattery was all this? But
it came from Mrs Lock, and so I cannot forbear repeating
it. I know my Fanny will be gratified almost as much
as I could be myself in hearing it. When our M^rs
Lock had done all she durst venture to begin that morning

we went down stairs where I saw two sweet heads of
Cipriani, which were in the number of [their] *purchases*
—they were quite new to me, not having even been
hung up at Norbury—One is a female head, which
would do for an Eloisa—the other an Angel's—which
Mrs Lock told me M^r L : had when they married, and
which had always been a great favourite with her—He
was writing—and Mrs L. had letters to write which she
began—" We do not use you very civilly "—said he
smiling—I think it is not very necessary to repeat my
answer. Just before dinner came Phillips, and M^rs L.
gave me her letter to you to add a few lines to, which
opportunity I was very glad of tho' I wrote in great
haste—I am now writing so likewise or I should not
have omitted telling you she had sent me your dear
little scrap, for which I have already thanked you, the
evening of her arrival—We had a sweet pleasant dinner
—and dear Mr Lock said " I rejoice we are met again "—
After it came the lovely Boy, whom I had before seen.
His cold had made him thin, but in all other respects
I think him improved—He is grown far more gentle
and tractable, and is a wonderful little creature in intelligence—He asked for all he wished as *a desert* as
clearly as Fanny could have done I think at 3 years old
—Mama told him that the Burnt almonds were not good
for him—" Are good," said he looking gravely at her—
" very nice " and then added " I want some very much
indeed." He would taste my toast and water, but soon
pushed it from him exclaiming " Oh-*too nasty* ! " Such
expressions sound very *curious* as Augusta says, in the
mouth of an Infant not yet 23 months old—but it is a
most extraordinary infant.—Our evening was all given
to conversation—and chiefly between sweet Mrs Lock
and myself—but I will not tell who nor what we talked
about—at parting it was agreed we should meet the
next evening—and so we did, and it was sweetly spent
—we had a little music—Sunday morning in their way
to church my sweet Mrs Lock and her dear little girls
stopped to tell me Mr Lock begged little Fanny might

accompany me to Norbury to dinner, and that the
chariot should bring her home as she had a cold—How
very kind ?—The dear little girl ran to embrace her
Friends one after the other with a warmth that gave
them much pleasure—and me, perhaps, more. They
came to us again after church, and my Nordia appeared
with much eclat, in spite of a cold he has lately had
from which his poor little nose has scarcely yet completely
recovered the disfigurement—Mrs Lock had most kindly
brought him a little flute, and Fanny some teathings,
and distributed her presents, and my little Fellow repeated all his little phrases—my dear Mama and my
good Papa—my pitty fitter—etc—but I was sorry to
find he was grown very shy since their long absence
during which he has scarce seen anybody but ourselves
—however the little girls were ready to devour him,
and my dear Mrs Lock was pleased with him and said
a great many sweet kind things—and after a long play
with him, we set off for Norbury with my Fanny who
se contenoit a peine, her delight was so excessive. Dear
Mr Lock seemed quite pleased to see her again, and after
dinner little Frederic was *enchanted* to meet her. I
visited Ma Bonne in the evening and heard the best
character of her that was possible. *Elle a été parfaite-
ment douce et caressante* toute la journée—pleine de joie,
et pourtant tranquile.''—Anne, our new nurse, went home
with her in the evening—as her staying so long at Norbury had seemed wished for I was rather pleased at it
on Betty Parker's account who certainly in her present
situation could not *wish* to see her settled here.—I cannot
help feeling sorry that poor Girl's Folly should have met
so immediate a punishment—However Bristow now
proposed her niece's return, and as it was not very
proper my dear Mrs Lock should keep one of my maids
for me, I approved of it very much.—In the evening we
had a little music, and looked over some of Mr William's
drawings, which his dear Father said after every absence
appeared to him more excellent than before—" but at
his return home " said he, " He will think of nobody

but Rubens—it will be all brilliant whites and reds—
He will want little Fanny to sit to him—her colouring
is very fine." They had been disappointed in their
hopes of hearing from him by that post, and when M^{rs}
Lock was away for a few minutes Mr L. said to me—
" That rogue William has not written from Dover—
tho' I gave him a model for a letter, that it might cost
him only 3 lines, to say he was well or otherwise—
When he arrived—and when he should sail—for my
part I know his aversion to writing to be such, and think
the chances of his being ill so few that I should not
have expected a line from him or required it—but his
Mother is very anxious "—I mentioned the post going
out in the middle of the day, and there being none of
a Saturday, to which this silence was probably owing—
Mr L. questioned us about the state of our House and
when we should paint it—when we went to town.—
" Ay," said he " when they get you, they'll keep you
there "—I thought he had meant the workmen at first,
and said that we had contrived to live in our House at
the worst, and therefore they could not now keep us
out of it—" but I mean your sisters " said he : " I wish
they may " said sweet Mrs Lock—" I wish them to do
it : But I do not," said He. Could I do otherwise
than thank them both ? Monday morning when I
went into the nursery I found my *two* attendants in
waiting. I hesitated a little which to employ for my
hair—but a kind of humanity I think, towards Betty,
determined me, and so I told the other her first employment must be to make acquaintance with Norbury,
who eyed her with great attention and some surprise,
and as if he would have said had he been able " *What is
the reason you stay here so long ?* "—I spent the whole
day at home. Tuesday it was suddenly determined that
we should *vacate* our Parlour, and remove for the present into one of the unfurnished rooms upstairs—but to
relieve you at once from uneasiness I must tell you it is
a perfectly dry and well aired room tho' it bears a wretched
appearance, half the old paper having been torn off by

the plaisterers in making a new ceiling, and it being impossible to put up a new one till the painters have done.   This employed me fully till the carriage came to take us to Mr Lock's, and occasioned my going alone, Phillips being yet very busy at home—I spent a sweet evening which did me good, and gave me an opportunity de me delasser which I should not have allowed myself to do had I been at home, all being yet in confusion— Wednesday morning : I was in the midst of dusting and new arranging my books etc. when the carriage stopped, and to our great *dismay* M^r and Mrs Lock came out of it—Phillips fled—and left me to make what sort of an appearance I could—Our dear visitors however joined with us in allowing it was better to submit to any temporary inconvenience than prolong the already tedious length of time spent in our repairs, and after having a little diverted themselves with our distress left us to go on with our business.   Thursday I thought Anne would wish to see her Aunt, and sent her and Betty with Nordia to Norbury—at their return I heard a shocking account of his misconduct.   He did not see the *Heads* of the House, who were out, but in Mrs Rich's room not choosing to be intimate with the dear little Frederic, my naughty boy gave him a *slap in the face* which quite scared him, and without making the least attempt at returning it he went away to his nurse, and said a *vedy naughty Boy come beat Feddy, and Feddy afaid of a naughty Boy*—After this very bad salutation however, Anne told me they grew very intimate and fond of one another—but I was very much vexed and scandalized at his naughtiness as well as surprised at the passive gentleness of the little Feddy—who not many months ago used to pinch and scratch everybody for his pastime, and even his greatest favourites.   It seemed as if the two Boys had changed characters—and indeed in some degree I think they have—Whether to save trouble Betty Parker has lately let him have wholly his own way, or from some other cause I know not, but my Nordia has lately not at all improved in

goodness—and his spirits are so excessively high that
makes him wild and turbulent, and sometimes most
comically naughty—for he enjoys his little mischief and
tricks, and laughs when he has done so *à gorge deployée*,
that it is almost impossible to see and hear him and not
laugh too—Even in the height of his more serious
naughtiness, and passion, nothing so easy as to convert
it into a violent fit of laughter—I never saw so merry a
little Fellow. however he has his passions, and fits of
wilfulness, which I never used to see a tendency to in
him, and Frederic's violence seems daily to abate, and
he becomes more soft and playful than I ever expected
him to be during his childhood. In the evening when
we went to Norbury I found Feddy in the Picture Room,
and told him I was sorry to hear such a naughty Boy
had been there in the morning—He looked very grave,
and shaking his little head said " a vedy, vedy naughty
Boy."—" What was it he did my little Frederic " said I
" tell me ?—What did he do ? "—" Scach a eyes out "
—said he looking fiercely. Mr Lock laughed with us
very much, and said " do you observe his piety—He
never did such a thing as fight or scratch in his life "—
" But he has left it off now," cries his dear Mother :
" No that he has not I can assure you " cries George much
louder—" I am sure he can scratch and pinch too very
well *Mrs Lock as I can witness* "—Friday we spent at
home—and Saturday evening again at dear Norbury—
Mr Lock had had an attack which threatened to be
serious, but thank Heaven has not proved so—he had
however a good deal of fever that evening, and seemed
so languid that it lowered me to see him—They had had
the satisfaction of hearing from Mr William who wrote
at Dunkerque instead of at Boulogne as he should have
done. Sunday morning I ventured to take my little
Fanny again to church—We went to Mr Lock's pew,
where he was not, but his Fredy, George and the sweet
girls, who were delighted to see little Fanny in this new
situation. I begged she might sit by me, and she behaved perfectly well I assure you—to the admiration of

all beholders—after church we accompanied our sweet
Mrs Lock etc to the kitchen garden, which was in beautiful order, and then examined all the poultry yards,
dairy etc of I believe the most complete Ferme in the
world. We then parted but not for very long—I brought
my Fanny home, and in a little stroll we took after dinner
with the little ones we met Ma Bonne and Augusta and
Amelia who were very much delighted at the rencounter
—Soon after this the carriage came to take us to Norbury, and we carried Fanny and Nordia part of the
way, who were then met by Anne who took them home
—the little Boy most reluctantly, who by no means
approved of changing his company or situation. We
found dear Mr Lock much better, and spent a sweet, quiet
evening. . . . I trust I shall soon hear from my dearest
Fanny—Our sweet Mrs Lock communicated the little
hasty scrap which we received most gladly last week—
I have scarce a minute more now, and that I must spend
in telling you we are all perfectly well, as well as all at
Norbury—Mrs Lock looks near ten years younger than
when she left the country, I believe from having given
up wearing a cloak. Augusta is recovering her complexion, and her *gaiety*, which had been much lowered
by leaving London, which begins to have nearly as
many charms in her eyes as formerly in those of poor
Bessey Burney? George is *Brilliant* in eyes, complexion
and spirits—I never saw him look better and am doubly
rejoiced at it as his two Brothers are absent. Fanny is
prating laughably enough to her doll. I hear her saying
" go in a corner and don't let me see any face of you—
you're so naughty you may *go and displease yourself*."
A poor little dead mouse that had been caught in a
Trap was shewn her this morning by her Papa—Nordia
trotted up to peep at it and cried out " *Pitty Feature* "
—" O Norbury cried the little Titter, you mustn't
have it for fear you should make it worse dead—but you
may *stroke it as many whiles* as you please."—Her lesson
to-day was of a little girl " who took great pleasure in
hurting anything that was less than herself "—" Mama "

cried she very innocently " what is that pleasure of hurting anything ? " But I must have done—Adieu adieu my ever dearest Fanny. Phillips has made me write you a lecture, which I think is worth considering of, about your new servant—I own I wish you may take his advice. Yours ever and ever! If there should be any change in the days you spend in London, pray let me know it ?—I must tell you I am very much pleased with all I have seen of my new nursery maid. The little Boy grows fond of her, and Betty's late neglect of him is rendered evident by his being more eager to go from Anne to the cook or the Housemaid than to her—I am I confess astonished at her insensibility respecting Him.

Letter XII

Mickleham,
Sunday, July 1st.

My last journal brought me up, I think, to last Wednesday—I had discovered that our dearest Mrs Lock was practising Mr Burney's sweet duet in A. with Augusta, and this morning prevailed upon her to let me hear them in it, the consequence of which was that I became *mistress*—for after hearing them once through it, I thought it would rather be treacherous than polite, only to tell them how well it went, and not the little errors, which acquainted so well as I am with it, could not but strike me at the first hearing—and our sweet friend, who is all humility upon the subject of her harpsichord playing, was even *delighted* to become my scholar. Only dear Augusta, who I found purposed playing it at Woodlands with eclat and who was perfectly well satisfied with it in its present state, was rather discomfited to find so much was to be *unlearned*, and so much remained yet to be done. Towards the end of our lesson Mr Lock came in, and did not seem displeased at finding how we were employed—He sat down to paint Lady Templetown's beautiful chimney piece—and we continued our occupation, tho' not without a little shame

and awkwardness on my part : when without any previous announce, a gentleman came in whom I had never
seen or scarce heard of, tho' by the freedom of his address
to Mʳ Lock, and Mʳˢ Lock's manner to him I immediately saw he was an intimate acquaintance. This was
Mʳ Minchin— a member of Parliament—at whose house
Mʳ Hinde passes a great part of his summers, and whom
I have heard *him* mention in conversation here, but
never imagined there was any acquaintance between
him and Mʳ Lock. " What are you alone " said Mʳ
Lock almost immediately on his entrance ? and upon
his answering in the affirmative " O Fye " said he again
—I afterwards heard that whilst you my dearest Fanny
were here the last time, this gentleman's wife and daughters were expected to the great mortification of our
dearest Mʳˢ Lock, who knows them but superficially
and who on that occasion quite dreaded their arrival.
Something then occasioned their visit to be deferred—
After this *O Fye*—not a word was said of his family but
as our lesson was completely interrupted, I soon took
an opportunity of sliding out of the room, and went
into my own where Augusta almost immediately followed me and insisted upon doing up my chignon,
which she did with as much adroitness as kindness and
good humour—She lamented warmly *that odious Mʳ
Minchin* being come whom she said she could not bear—
As she is generally rather pleased at *any* new visitor I
was rather surprised, particularly as he appeared to me
rather a fashionable, polite kind of man—but she soon
explained the cause of her aversion in a manner which
rather inclined me to share in it I confess—" Do you
know He never speaks to his wife—not one word—he
has made a vow of it I suppose, and never does utter
a syllable to her " : and do they live together ? : O dear
yes—they have been *here* together—and they were to
have come this summer only something has prevented
Mʳˢ Minchin—but when they were here, then one of
them had a bed up stairs and the other at the furthest
end of the house below stairs—and they never looked

at each other—yes—sometimes I have seen *him* look at her—so cross and ill natured ?—tho' you see he seems a very pleasant man to other people : and what can have occasioned such a dreadful breach ? " Oh I don't know—it has been so a great many years—Once when they lost one of their children he was prevailed upon to say a few words to poor Mrs Minchin—and one might have imagined that would quite have got over his shocking plan of never speaking to her—but he took it up after-wards again, and has never opened his lips to her since " —What a barbarous instance of insatiable revenge, and hardness of heart ?—Nobody it seems accuses Mrs Minchin of anything further than not having agreed with her husband in temper—such disagreements alone may I know make people wretched, and perhaps justify separation—but surely any separation is better and re-flects less dishonour on the parties than living together upon such unnatural and shocking terms—I suppose however their children prevent such a separation.— Whilst Augusta was talking our sweet friend came in lamenting our interruption—It was a sad change from Mr *Rust*, who had been expected and only prevented by the gout from coming—and I found Mr Minchin was to stay till Saturday, the day they were to go to Wood-lands—and we to return home. I was very much mortified at this. Mrs Lock told me he had been a very early acquaintance of Mr Lock's who met and travelled in company with him abroad, and who had in his youth received much civility from his family—and he has therefore that kind of regard for him that a very long acquaintance occasions. At dinner his conversa-tion was upon Parliamentary matters. He seems to me but a shallow man—very proud of having spoken upon such and such subjects *in the House*, and of having *abused* such and such men for an hour together :—I fancy neither his praise or his abuse has ever been of much effect. He is as strong *as he knows how to be* in the opposition, and Mr Lock said to me after he had left the room that he never entered upon politics with him, as their opinions were so entirely opposite that it became a very unpleasant conversation—however when Mr Minchin spoke of the probability of Charles Fox coming into place and power, Mr Lock could not forbear saying how unlikely he thought it and the reason why it was so —" I find all the people I speak to " said he " have a horror at the thoughts of such a thing—He is *fallen fallen fallen ?*—even the common people hold him in detestation." Mr Minchin heard patiently this attack upon *his dear Friend*—and I cannot but say I listened to it with some pleasure. Another favourite topic of Mr Minchin's was of sporting dogs and horses, which was very pleasant to Mr Lock—and discussion upon eating and the best manner of killing fish etc—tho' he seemed to me by no means an epicure—but talked upon these matters as being fashionable subjects of discourse—After dinner I went home to see my dear little ones whom I found perfectly well *helping to make hay*—I carried back some wild plants to our sweet friend which Fanny had assisted in gathering—Thursday she and Nordia came to me in the morning and after a duet lesson to my dear *Scolari*, I gave myself up to them till dinner, but on account of this disagreeable man, and further, as all the Miss Uptons dined with their young friends, I would not keep them to desert. Friday morning I went home to see them, and found Fanny with her good nurse Whitton, and her foster sister *Polly*, so very happy that I gave up my first design which was to have taken her back with me to Norbury, and left directions with Anne to bring her and Nordia after their dinner.—I then returned, and had a concluding *audience* of my two industrious dear scholars—the little ones came to say adieu to all their kind friends in the evening, and I accompanied them down to the bottom of the Hill in their way back, and then parted with my Fanny in great glee at hearing I should come home to *stay* the next day—I was vexed at that Mr Minchin's visit which led our dear Mr Lock always to talk on subjects which did not interest him, or to remain wholly silent. Saturday

MRS. LOCKE.
From the original.

morning we all wore the face of departure—our dear
friends I saw left their sweet home with a reluctance
which out of delicacy to those to whom they were going
they strove to conceal. Mr Lock questioned Phillips
and me repeatedly about our house, and charged us not
to sleep in it if the least ill smell from the paint should
remain in our bedroom. We gratefully promised him
in that case to return—Mr Minchin I should imagine
went away not unwillingly—at least Time had appeared
very frequently to hang heavy on his hands during his
little stay. He set out the first—then our dearest M^r
and Mrs Lock in the little phaeton, after a kind shake
of the hands from him, and most affectionate embrace
from her and last the dear girls and La Bonne in the
chaise—Amelia seemed ready to cry when she embraced
her little friends Miss Uptons and me, at going on this
party of pleasure and then threw her arms round poor
Bristow and Wells with an appearance of affection and
kindness that gave me as much pleasure to see as it could
to them to receive. She is a lovely little girl *de toutes
les facons*—I then sought the dear little Frederic who
was very unwilling that Ips should go away—we are
grown very great friends indeed—I then left this dear
but saddened house and returned to my dear children
whose little gladness at sight of me was the most refreshing thing possible for my spirits. I had much
business for that day and the following in resettling
myself at home—Sunday I took Fanny to visit sweet
Frederic, who was delighted to see us—at our return I
wrote to his dear Mother, and then told Fanny if she
would dictate a letter to you I would write it, as you
found her hand a little difficult to read—She assured
me repeatedly she would take great pains to *write her
very best*—however I at last prevailed upon her to tell
me what she would say. " But Mama I think if I write
to Aunt Fanny to come, she can't come unless the
Queen pleases or the King—and the Queen I'm afraid
won't let her come, for it is a great while since I wrote
to beg she would, and you know I wrote a great many

letters too—Mama : well my dear then what must we do ? Fanny. Why I suppose Mama was to write a letter to the King ? M : with all my heart—How will you begin. F. Why you must tell him that I want Aunt Fanny to come very much indeed and I am tired of waiting. M : yes but you must tell me to write as if you were writing yourself—When I write to M*rs* Lock I say *my dear M*rs* Lock*—or if I was to write to M*r* Hinde I should say *Sir*—and if to you *my dear little Fanny*—now how will you begin to the King ? F. Why what is his name Mama besides King ?—M. His name is George—and sometimes he is called George Rex. F. Oh—well Mama write *my dear King*. No you shouldn't laugh so Mama—say *my dear George Rex*. . . . What *does* make you laugh so Mama ? M. I laugh because people do not say *my dear* to the King—it is too familiar and not proper. F. Oh. Then I tell you what you shall say—" King George Rex, I am much obliged to the queen for letting Aunt Fanny come the last time to Norbury when we did not expect her : but I don't know what is the reason that she is so fond of her as not to let her come again when I asked her. So now I hope *you* will let her come to stay, and to sleep at Norbury, and to never go away as long as she lives, because I love her so much and Mama loves her so much too—I send my love to the queen and to Aunt Fanny and to the king. Adieu—I am."—Mama I could say I am your affectionate kind friend but I am afraid it would be too *familiar—then what shall I say ?* I was very unwilling to help her and at last she recollected having somewhere seen " I am your humble espectful servant Fanny Phillips." Now Mama may I write to Aunt Fanny ? yes my love—tell me what I shall say. My dearest Aunt Fanny. Mama has promised your dear little girl . . . (M. but who is that ?—F. Why that is me Mama ; you know Aunt Fanny calls me her dear little girl—) that as soon as our house is finished and painted, and don't smell of the paint, and is a pretty house like M*r* Lock's, to get a bed for dearest Aunt

Fanny, to sleep in here, at our house "—(Mama you
know you told me you would but do you think M^{rs}
Lock would be angry if Aunt Fanny was to come and
sleep here instead of at Norbury ?   M. No my love I
don't think she would be angry : But would she be
very sorry do you think : Why—I am afraid she would :
Well, but—if we were to ask her leave first : that would
certainly be very right—now what shall I say ?)—" I
send my love to you, and we will ask Mrs Lock's leave
when she comes home for you to come and live here—
I send you a kiss, and will give you a great many when
you come here, and hug you, and beg you if you please
to tell me a story. I think this paper is too dirty to
send a letter to you or to the king—but Mama is to
write it over again upon a clean sheet of paper to send
to Windsor, and she is to keep this to shew you when
you come here—Some days my dearest Aunt Fanny,
Anne says I have behaved quite good, like a woman,
when Mama was at Norbury. Papa desired her to go
and sleep there for a little while, but she stayed a great
many days—the House was very uncomfortable, and the
smell of the paint made Mama sick—but I liked it. Now
good by my dearest Aunt Fanny—
                I am your affectionate kind friend
                            FANNY PHILLIPS "

  Monday morning Phillips and I condemned ourselves
to go to pay visits. He had spent the preceding day at
Chesington where all were well, and my dear Father
was there—but only for a day or two. We were so
fortunate as to find nobody at home at Mr Talbot's
but stupified about ½ an hour with Mrs Rogers. We
then called at Lady Templetown's cottage and Miss Upton
received us very gracefully and prettily—We invited her
and her sister to tea the next evening. Tuesday morning
I called to see a Feddy—and wrote to his dear Mother,
and in the evening had the little Uptons, who were so
happy it was impossible to grudge the time given to them
—they are sensible and very well brought up children.

Wednesday I was busied at home. Thursday I again
visited sweet Frederic, and Friday morning early we
were awakened by a note from James to borrow the
horse, and pay us a visit. I rose and approved and was
very happy at seeing him arrive, tho' it was rather unluckily just the day of our sweet Friends returning home.
I wrote a welcoming and enclosed my dearest Fanny's
letter concerning her excellent Mrs Delany which was
a great comfort to Mrs Lock whom your first letter had
greatly alarmed, as it could not indeed fail of doing—
How grateful I feel that this sad alarm is over. I received a sweet answer from our sweet Friend and a
present of fruit, which as we had James could not but
be very acceptable. After dinner, and playing some time
with the children, we walked out, and returned to drink
tea on our little lawn—it was a beautiful evening—I
was sorry to hear of désagremens at Chesington, and that
M^rs H— had suffered herself to be led by Mrs Symmonds into giving a kind of affront to the Lady, the
consequence of which will probably be that my Father
will return to Chesington no more. James too has
highly resented it on my Father's account, and he had
quitted his home hoping not to return to it till M^rs
Symmonds should have decamped. Next morning James
induced Phillips to go and spend the day with the
Hooles, which I was very glad of, as I should be very
sorry to hurt or affront those good people. I was preparing with Fanny to go to Norbury when our dear
Mr Lock called in—He looked at and approved all our
rooms, and but that he saw by Fanny's gravity that
she did not enjoy *the* delay *of our visit* would I believe
have stayed longer—" but " said he, " it mortifies the
poor little girl—besides I keep you from Fredy, and she
is longing to see you"—So he would not be detained—
and we set off—and had a sweet meeting with our
dearest Mrs Lock. I spent the whole day there most
delightfully, and she accompanied me part of the way
home in the evening. Mr William had remained in
town—but was to come with Mr Charles that night—

the dear girls seemed not sorry they were come back and Augusta told me a great many laughable habits of M and Madame Hartsinck—they were expected and Miss Crokatt the next week. I was at home some time before my gentlemen returned. Sunday June 8th there was no church owing to Mr Filewood's being ill, so that I did not see any from dear Norbury—but Phillips went *to take leave* and carried Mrs Lock my alive to you which she was to enclose in her own. Mr Lock was riding out. Phillips went that afternoon to London, and is not yet returned—but the week has been sadly spent, and till to day I have not been able to attempt a word of Journal. John came into the room to me on Monday to say *Mr Lock was very ill*, and had sent for Mr Ansell —this he had heard in the village and I hoped it had not been true. However I felt very uneasy, and as James was with me and I could not go myself, sent off a note of inquiry instantly. I found by our sweet Friend's answer the account was but too true, and tho' she most kindly bid me not be uneasy, that she had sent to town for Dr Moore, I instantly determined to go and know particulars and see our dearest Mrs Lock— and James walked up the Hill with me. I rejoice every way that I did this for besides its being quite a necessary step for my own quiet, it soothed and something revived our dearest Mrs Lock. I found she had left Mr Lock at his earnest desire, to walk out : and tho' she would have taken me into the Picture Room, I persuaded her to go into the air, and upon a seat near the house she gave me an account of her alarm in which I need not tell you if I sympathised. He had returned ill from his ride the preceding day and complained of a great oppression on his stomach which in the evening deter- mined him to take an emetic—this was a terrible opera- tion to him without appearing to answer the end he desired, and his night was so feverish and bad that he did not object to Mrs Lock's sending for Mr Ansell— She told me that whilst he spoke to Mr Lock she ob- served that he looked very grave, and upon leaving the

room he beckoned her out of it. He then told her
He was very sorry to say Mr Lock was *very ill*—and that
*as he should extremely fear having so precious a life in his
hands*, if the medicine he was going to order did not
produce the effect for which it was meant, he should
advise that a Physician should be sent for the next day—
Judge of our sweet friend's sensations at hearing such a
speech. She says it made her feel *as if she had broken
all her bones and her heart with them*. He begged her
pardon over and over again. Whilst she thanked him
for the blow as soon as she could speak. He had something composed her afterwards by objecting to her
sending to any Physician that day, or at all if his medecine proved effectual—but when he had left her she could
not bear to delay this a moment, and sent off Thomas
for Dr Moore, whose coming she said could not alarm
Mr Lock as he had promised them a visit for some time.
I rejoiced that she had done so, and did not conceal it
from her—for tho' I hoped Mr Lock would not want
his assistance : to hear that he did not was quite necessary to compose our sweet Friend who was so justly
and cruelly alarmed—You will conceive easier than I
could tell you how it afflicted me to see her, and to hear
this account. In the midst of *such* an alarm I never
saw her more sweet more angelic—Deeply penetrated
with sorrow—yet enduring it with a patience and gentleness that was infinitely touching—Aaron returned
from Dorking with Mr Ansell's medecine whilst we
were together, which she went upstairs immediately
to administer. I followed her to the door—and had
the consolation of hearing her say I had cheered her,
and removed at least a part of the dejection which she
had felt ready to sink under. Indeed I did *sincerely*
hope Mr Ansell had been too hastily alarmed, and felt
certain he knew not to whom he was speaking when he
had so abruptly made her such a terrible speech—I had
determined to go again in the evening, and hear D^r
Moore's account but it turned out so very rainy it was
out of my power—however I had the unspeakable satis-

faction of receiving at night from our sweet friend a few lines, in which she told me Dr Moore saw nothing whatever alarming in Mr Lock's situation, and that he doubted not he would be quite well in a few days—and that she felt herself a different creature from what she had been in the morning—How I blessed Heaven!— Tuesday I sent early, and had a very comfortable account : —rain prevented my going out till after dinner. I then spent half an hour with our sweet Friend in your little green room most sweetly. O how happy it made me to see her dear countenance so serened—so cheerful! Whilst I was with her Dr Moore, who had been obliged in the morning to return to town came back, and I waited till he should have seen his patient to hear what he would say—I felt quite concerned and even lowered at this time that I could not like this odious Doctor better—His account was however very comfortable— but Wells told me in private, he had said in the morning to Braissam that Mr Lock had been very ill—and even dangerously—O this has been a blessed escape indeed ? —Being caught in the rain I got a sad cold in my face —however I would not let it detain me at home the next morning. Wednesday July 11th I found my sweet Mrs Lock in the highest spirits, and that all was going on as prosperously as could be wished, and returned home with the greatest mental comfort and satisfaction, which made me far the better endure my confinement since : for the pain in my face increased exceedingly by the wind, and I have not been able to leave my own room since that time—It is now Saturday July 14th— I have heard twice a day from our most kind and sweet friend, and in yesterday's note she says, " My Lock's account of his feelings is delightful—he feels such perfect ease and composure, and he says *a general renovation* " —James did not leave me till Thursday morning, and yesterday evening Phillips returned to me after having dined with him at Chesington.—He has brought me a pressing invitation to Titchfield Street from Betsey— and has promised for me that I shall accept it—but

my dearest Fanny will not be there next week—! I
shall be sadly mortified indeed to be there some days
yet not have a sight of you—but as my face is swelled
and will not render it prudent for me to move yet awhile
—and as I could not go easily and happily till our dearest
Mr Lock is so far recovered as that I may see him, and
leave his sweet wife perfectly easy and happy, I do
not think I *could* go till the middle of the next week—
and perhaps it may then be possible for me to catch
a glimpse of you in town the week after?—that would
be very sweet to me indeed—and certainly I will do
my best to obtain such a gratification. Esther and Mrs
B. are gone to Tunbridge with *Marianne* and Sophy,
and have placed their little Fanny at a school of Mr
Burnly's Mrs Castelfrake's. This occasions there being
room for us: were we to go whilst the dear Worcester
girls are in town. Lady Templetown returned to
Norbury Thursday evening: and this morning called
here. She is now gone to town, and Monday sets off
for Ireland. I was very sorry she could not remain a
little longer with our dearest Mrs Lock. Mr and Mrs
Hartsinck and Miss Crokatt defer their journey till Mr
Lock is better, which *I believe none at Norbury very
much regret*—Thursday evening, July 19th—I trust I
shall deliver this myself to my beloved Fanny, and time
presses so much that I shall scarce find wherewithal to
fill up the space since I last journalised—but all has gone
sweetly.—James returned to us Saturday, and stayed
very comfortably till Monday. Phillips went back to
London Tuesday, and Wednesday I spent the whole
day with our sweet Friends—and think of my surprise
and joy at seeing our dearest Mr Lock in the carriage to
fetch me?—Miss Crokatt was at Norbury.

LETTER XIII

MICKLEHAM, *Monday, Aug. 6th, '87.*

. . . . When we arrived within sight of Norbury, my
heart began to palpitate, and I already felt the near

approach to my children. I leave you to guess how I
felt on passing Mr Lock's farm, when I saw the dear little
souls, seated on the opposite bench, with Anne, waiting
for me ?—I started—exclaimed—and in a moment
stopped the carriage. Anne held up the little Boy,
who colouring as he spoke called out *a Mama*—and my
Fanny's face was crimsoned all over—I kissed them—not
half enough—but we were so stuffed up with boxes
we could not take in my poor little Patient Fanny—who
when she saw me take Nordia to sit on my lap, cried
out " I may run by the side of the carriage Mama,
mayn't I ? "—For the sake of this dear little soul, I
longed to be at home, tho' I had another little treasure
in my arms—who kept looking in my face with such
pleasure and surprise that it was very sweet to see him—
Both looked charmingly well too—and Norbury extraordinarily improved in many respects—*very* much grown,
and as if *touched* by my return, as *soft* and caressing and
serene as he could be. I found him wonderfully improved in his speech—able to say *everything*—and so
proud of his little acquirements ?—He made a speedy
acquaintance with Beckey, who is extremely fond of
children, and who was full of kindness and good nature
to both mine. My little Fanny kept pace with the
chaise, and met me as I alighted with her little affectionate embraces—Dinner waited, and with great *violence*
my poor Nordia was carried off—Fanny stayed by us,
tho' she had dined, and the Itty Boder was again
introduced to *a desert*—We took them with us out of
doors, and I shewed Beckey our garden and orchard—
but it was windy and cold, and my face not being easy
I could not venture walking, as I wished to have done,
in the park with her, but hoped I should be better able
the next day.—To my great mortification the upholsterer
who was to have brought us our spare room bed and
curtains and put them up whilst I was in town had
disappointed, so that of necessity Beckey slept with me
—and indeed the *distress* would have been much greater
had Betsey accepted my invitation and come with her

or even had Phillips accompanied us. We spent the
evening with the children till their bedtime, and after
it in mutual communications, and a little reading—I
found on my arrival two notes from our sweet Mrs Lock
to whom I wrote instantly how I was situated. I was
extremely vexed and concerned to receive an answer
from her, by which I found she was confined, and in a
good deal of pain with a cold and swelled face. I sympathised with her then in both—but much more the
following day, when I felt quite ill—It was a great
mortification to me on sweet Beckey's account, and a
great additional one that the weather was too bad to
admit of stirring out for anybody not quite well—I
could not therefore take her to church—After it we had
a visit from Augusta, Mr Charles, and Miss Angerstein,
who was at Norbury on a visit—and from them I heard
that *Amelia* had a sore throat of the *putrid* kind—that,
fortunately, (as it was merely accidental,) Mr Moore the
Surgeon was at Norbury on a visit, and had given orders
that none of her brothers and sisters should go near her
room. This was a sad account, and made me quite long
to see our sweet friend, and good fortune put it in my
power. The carriage waited at the door for my guests,
who, tho' it was very cold and threatened rain, declared
they would walk—upon this it occurred to me that as
Beckey could only spend that day with me, and I felt
unable from my cold to walk up the Hill, tho' I could
have managed to come down it, I had better make use
of the empty carriage, which accordingly I did, and
took Beckey that she might see the Room, whilst I
visited our sweet Friend—Everything prospered in this
undertaking—At her arrival, I conducted her myself
into the Painted Room, and having looked at it with
her a little time, was preparing to leave her to make
more minute observations whilst I sought for Mrs Lock,
when the door opened, and Mr Lock, who knew from
Augusta of our being there, entered—I was truly happy
to see him again, and to perceive that notwithstanding
his present anxiety he looked *considerably* better than

when I had left Mickleham—In the sweetest manner
imaginable he addressed Beckey, and undertook himself
to shew her the Room—He then made many kind inquiries about me—and about my dearest Fanny—Our
dearest Mrs Lock was with Amelia—but soon after I
heard her in the next room, and went in to speak to her.
I found her with her face exceedingly swelled, and very
anxious about her lovely girl—but notwithstanding, she
insisted upon seeing Beckey, and went into the Painted
room to invite her into the Picture room—I felt very
thankful to her for this sweetness, which gratified our
dear Beckey very much—When I rose to go, I found the
carriage had been kept in waiting for us. It rained so
there was no saying Nay—and my looks indeed rather
alarmed our kind Friends, who thought I was going to
be quite ill. Mrs Lock charged me to go home and nurse
for 3 days at least—I hoped at the time I should not
have been obliged to so much—but I *more* than obliged
her.—I was sorry Beckey should not have seen M^r
William, or George, both of whom I met when I first
went to speak to Mrs Lock, and who both looked *beautifully*, and gave me the most smiling reception—the
lovely little Amelia too she could not see—but a Feddy
accompanied us in the chaise part of the way up the
Hill in going, and looked charmingly.—Beckey left the
house much delighted by her little visit—and she seemed
to have pleased, as well as to be pleased, in so much that
I very much regretted the situation of things which
prevented our spending our evening there—Our dinner
was ready at our return, and after it the children found
us amusement till their bedtime. Beckey ne se lassoit pas
talking with Fanny, and kissing Norbury, who called her,
" *Dea Becca*," and was as sweet as he could be.—During
the evening I looked out some notes from Pacchierotti,
and other *little miscellanies*, [with] which we amused
ourselves very well till bedtime. Our dear Beckey was
early called for the stage the next morning, and had her
breakfast, tho' she would not suffer me to make it—at
7 she set off—I felt very thankful to her for her kind

little visit and only sorry the weather and my unwellness prevented my being able to make it pleasanter to her. When I rose I found a *robin* she had left behind her— not knowing how to convey it to *her*, I enclosed it under cover to Richard, who was at Farnham, with a few *explanatory lines.*—She and *Betsey* and *Edward* left London the following morning, and I have since received a very kind and affectionate letter from Betsey. The following week I was wholly confined by my obstinate swelled face and cold. I heard daily of sweet little Amelia, and our dear Mrs Lock, who recovered more speedily than I could have expected. Monday evening Mr William called with Mr Moore—they were scarce gone when my dear Phillips returned—the following days I was visited by Miss Angerstein Augusta, and Mr William who was their escort—and by dear Mr Lock. I lamented my confinement on account of the illness at Norbury—however the dear little girl continued to amend, and our sweet friend was able to pay *me* a visit on Friday morning. I had then a visitor—James—whose continued search for some habitation in our neighbour- hood, occasioned my seeing much more than usual of him—His visit kept me likewise from Norbury when I was well enough to go out—but I was glad to have him nevertheless—I had a short visit from all our kind friends after church the following Sunday, August 5th—and heard how busily Mrs Lock was preparing a *present de Fete* for our dearest Fanny—that evening M^{r} and Mrs Hartsinck arrived at Norbury, and Miss Crokatt, and Mrs Angerstein, and from that time I *less* lamented my want of power to be more there—Tuesday August 7th James went to see a house at Guildford, and as he pur- posed spending the day there, Phillips and I walked up the Hill. It was the first time of my going out since my bad cold : but the weather was very fine and I was even the better for the walk—I found my dearest Mrs Lock surrounded by a large party, among whom I had the pleasure of discovering the sweet little convalescente, Amelia—It was the first day of her dining down stairs,

and all her little friends, the Miss Uptons, were with
her. M^r and Mrs Hartsinck were riding out with M^r
Lock. Mrs Angerstein whom I had never seen was
with Mrs Lock, Miss Crokatt, and Miss Angerstein.
The former I should suspect to be near 50—She has
been handsome, and continues to *intend* being so—her
head dress, and indeed every other part of her dress
was perfectly in the same style as Miss Crockatt's—
if anything more showy—In her manner she is very
vulgar, which was what I expected—but she appears,
and is said to be perfectly good humoured—My dearest
Mrs Lock was so desirous of our staying, that tho' it had
been my intention to return home to dinner, I could not
say no—and after so long an absence, and so much illness,
it was so great a pleasure to me to be near her, that
notwithstanding her guests, I passed the day happily
and pleasantly. M^r and Mrs Hartsinck came in with
our dear Mr Lock just before dinner—He is a little man
who seems to be a very great F—l. I was near laughing
two or three times at his silly manner of playing with
Frederic : dancing him on his knee and singing to him
in a most ludicrous style, or hopping about the room
with the little sagacious child in his arms, who looked so
superior a being ?—of intellects already so much better
formed—who often eyed him with a kind of *stern surprise*, that was exceedingly comical—the more so as the
poor man never perceived it nor discovered how little
he entertained him.—Mrs H. is thinner than she was :
much the same in other respects—something less restless
and turbulent indeed—but en revanche quite fulsome
with fondness for her fond husband—there are most
curious scenes going on now and then as I am informed
by Augusta—but there was whispering and tendresse
enough going forwards when I was there to make everybody generally, afraid of looking their way. Tis most
abominable behaviour ?—and at Norbury too—that seat
of innocence and purity and pudens ! I expected James'
return in the evening, and would not stay tea—but he
did not come back to us till the next day—his search

had been unsuccessful—Saturday sweet George dined
with us, and was much diverted, tho' sometimes rather
honoured [sic] at James' abuse of the fine arts, green-
house plants etc—James on his side complains that he
is grown quite *effeminate with delicacy* and is quite
spoiled—I had a short visit after tea from La Bonne
and the two sweet girls—I was quite rejoiced to see
Amelia out again. Sunday 12ᵗʰ I went to church with
my little Fanny in my own pew, imagining Mʳ Lock's
would be full—but I met the young party coming from
it, and found the rest said prayers at home—Phillips
and I paid a long deferred visit to Mʳˢ Eckersall, and
James walked there with us. I had not seen her since
her having had the misfortune of losing her father, the
good Dʳ Wathen, who seems universally regretted.
She had a sister, Mʳˢ Wyse with her, and her husband—
they seem sensible people. The next morning Phillips
went with Mʳ William to see Mʳ Walpole's Collection,
and, by the latter's appointment, Mʳˢ Cambridge—I
had a very kind invitation at the same time to Twitnam,
and wrote a note of thanks by them to Mʳˢ Cambridge—
Mʳ William came here for my *tardy* Phillips, whilst we
were breakfasting—He stayed with James and me whilst
his companion got ready, and pleased James by his
manly air and behaviour—I know not what *he* thought
à son tour—but he was very well bred, and more conversable than usual—After they were gone, James set
out in the first stage for London, where he intended to
sleep, and I engaged myself to pass the evening at Norbury. Mʳ Lock after his evening's airing was so kind
as to call for me. I found he knew nothing of Mʳ
William's intention of sleeping out, and when I laughed
at his being in these matters like his companion, my
Phillips, Mʳ Lock said " at his age he must have his
liberty—and there is no more certain prevention of an
ill use being made of it, than the permitting it to be
wholly unrestrained. We make it a rule never to question him upon where he has been, or means to go—and
indeed he is so perfectly steady and thoughtful that

he requires no check ": "Oh no indeed " said I "He may I believe be trusted the world over "—but tho' I seriously thought this, I did not the less reverence the wisdom and resolution of this most admirable Father's conduct. As we approached the Farm, to my no small astonishment, I perceived James on foot, hurrying towards our home. I let down the glass to speak to him, and Mr Lock saying " Is it not your Brother," stopped the carriage—I found he had completed his business in London so early as to admit of his returning in a Leatherhead stage, and from that place he was walking towards our House ?—I was vexed at it, and wished to have returned with him. Mr Lock very sweetly asked him to accompany us up the Hill—but did not press upon his declining it, as he must imagine he would not have wished to go there so little equipped for visiting as he was. " Why then Mrs Phillips, you will wish to go home ? "—I said nothing—but James begged I would not, and Mr Lock saying 'twould be a sad disappointment to Fredy not to see me, added that I should have the carriage at 8 o'clock, when it might at the same time bring his girls home who were at the Cottage—I thanked him for his kind consideration, and giving James the key of tea and sugar, we parted—I was really vexed at this happening after so long an absence.—Our sweet friend received me with all her kindness—and was disappointed to find I should stay but an hour—on *that* account chiefly, I regretted it—for the party there was little to my taste—and I observed in Mrs Hartsinck such a jealous propensity to watching every word and look that passed between Mrs Lock and myself that it made me feel unpleasantly—My little visit was however very soon over—and I returned to my solitary James, who had amused himself with the fiddle after the children went to bed—He told me he should have followed me to Norbury but that he knew there was company there—I could not be sorry that he did not—The next day brought home my Phillips, and a very kind note in answer to mine from Mrs Cambridge. The following

Sunday 19th there was no church, and consequently I did not see our sweet friends. My visitor and the visitors at Norbury prevented Mrs Lock and myself from meeting. I should have regretted it at another time *much* more—Mr Lock made us a kind call that evening—and Mr Williams and Mr Charles.—The time for my dear Phillips' departure approached fast. It had long been in agitation but so often deferred, that I could not help secretly flattering myself it might not prove necessary. However he talked now of fixing his day—and Tuesday 21st brought him letters which finally decided him—I need not expatiate to my dearest Fanny upon the pain which this determination gave me —But for my children, I should have entreated to accompany him—but *He* wished me not to go on every account except his own, and indeed as we were situated, it would have been a very injudicious step—that same Tuesday Mr Hoole Senior called and stayed dinner. Wednesday we returned M^r and Mrs Talbot's visit which was of some standing, and called on the Rogers'— Thursday Morning 23rd August James left us for Chesington—promising to return *Saturday*, when he had some expectation that Mr *Hollamby*, an old shipmate he had met with at Guildford, would come here to dine with us. Phillips and I walked part of the way to Leatherhead with him—and returned to the sad employment of packing etc—But as he wished to visit dear Norbury again, I prepared myself to accompany him, and was nearly ready when *young* Mr Hoole arrived, whom I could never have been less happy to see—We were then obliged to give up going to Norbury, instead of which I sent a note there, and received a sweet answer from our kindest friend. This was a mortification, besides which we were under much inconvenience, being unable to make any arrangement or to pack up till 8 o'clock at night when our guest took leave—He would indeed have gone immediately on hearing Phillips' near departure, but as we were sure he must have been much too late for his own dinner we could not permit

MOLESWORTH PHILLIPS.
By A. Geddes.

but it was very unlucky—After he had left us we had
employment which kept us up till two in the morning—the next day. Friday August 24th soon after
breakfast, my dear Phillips left me. I passed an hour in
affliction, and the whole day in great sadness—from
which I yet scarce feel recovered—and having felt unable
to make memorandums, my journal is of necessity very
concise. The next day James came as he had promised
but no one met him—the weather was as bad as it could
be, and we drank tea by a fire and candles, which seemed
the setting in of winter—James left me early the next
morning Sunday 26th for Chesington, tho' too late for
me to go to church—I have not since seen him, but he
has promised me to bring his wife, child and nurse here
for a few days whenever he leaves Chesington, before he
fixes in any new place, as after that time it will probably
be even less convenient—After church M^r and M^{rs}
Lock called with their 3 sons, 2 daughters, Miss Upton,
Mrs Hartsinck and Miss Crokatt—I felt excessivly de-
pressed—but exerted myself as much as I was able to
receive this party—I found Mr Hinde was at Norbury,
and our dear Mrs Lock wished to take me there to
dinner—but excused me easily—for she saw I wished
to be excused. I received a sweet note from her afterwards, and wrote a part in her alive to my dearest Fanny
—Monday morning she had the sweetness, to come to
me for a couple of hours, whilst her party were airing,
and her tender sympathy and much loved society did
me real good, when we were thus *alone*—we read my
dearest Fanny's B. which was a sweet reviver. I had
read it long before to myself, but with her it was with
new pleasure.—She excused me from coming out again
that evening—but since that time I have not had an
evening to myself—and I have been so little fit for
company that had I thought only of my own indulgence,
I certainly should not have stirred from home. Tuesday
evening I spent at Norbury, and as it was George's last,
would not refuse playing on the organ—which as it
requires only slow pieces suited me very well, being

entirely out of practice. Wednesday I was obliged to spend the evening at Mrs Rogers', which was as dull as possible—Thursday morning I had a visit from M^r and Mrs Eckersall, and went in the evening to Norbury, where I again made music, and was honoured by Mr William's choosing and insisting upon *pumping* at the organ for me all the evening tho' his sisters sat idle by. He flatters me very much by his courtesy lately—and runs out regularly after supper since I have been there without my wonted companion, to seek for my cloak, and assist me in putting it on, and hand me to the carriage—these are really great favours from him, and I am not so proud as to deny that I am pleased by them. My dearest Mrs Lock so pressed me to go the next night, that having made a proviso to spend Saturday wholly at home I promised. By my desire the two dear girls came to me Friday (yesterday) afternoon to take a lesson again—they are to continue doing so regularly Tuesdays and Fridays, which are the evenings they always spend at the Cottage, where Augusta plays the part of *Mistress* to Miss Upton—When their lessons were over I left my dear children, whose bedtime it was, and walked to Norbury—My little affectionate Fanny accompanying me always to the garden gate, where she continues to stand till I am quite out of sight—this dear little girl had so lamented my going out every night, that had it been a great gratification to me, I should yet have wished to spend a night at home frequently on her account, not to mention my Nordia who, tho' less able to express himself, feels a great want of Mama near his bed time—but I had been so long, and so much away from Norbury, that when they knew it in my *power* to go as much as I pleased, I could not refuse. I worked for the fair quietly by our sweet friend that evening—and Saturday September 1st I spent still more quietly at home:—Sunday 2nd M^r and Mrs Hartsinck and Miss Crokatt left Norbury for Woodlands—but I hear they are to return at the Fair time next month. I took my Fanny to church, and after it, as I had promised, accom-

panied Mr William and Mr Charles, their sisters, and
the Miss Uptons to Norbury—My dear children with
Anne ran up the first hill with us, full of glee at being in
such a party, and cruelly disappointed not to go the
whole way—My Fanny indeed had not expected it,
and *commanded* herself—but poor Nordia could not
restrain his lamentations—Our kind friend *a son tour*
regretted extremely at our arrival that they had not
accompanied me—but I never would take them unless
expressly desired, and particularly upon a Sunday when
Lady Templeton's children are constantly there. My
dear Mrs Lock wished me to promise coming the next
day and bringing them to dine—but I could not spare
the whole day out again so soon, and therefore promised
them that gratification on Wednesday—Tuesday my
little scholars were to be with me, and I had asked Miss
Uptons to meet them at tea. Monday evening again I
spent at Norbury—and Tuesday morning I had the great
comfort of receiving a letter from my Phillips who
had not written to me since he left London the Tuesday
before—I found by his letter he was perfectly well and
in spirits, and within 40 miles when it was written of
Holyhead—he dated *Friday* from Conway, so that I
doubt not he was at Dublin the following Sunday,
tho' I have not yet had the satisfaction of being assured
of it. In his letter he repeats his regret at not having
been able to see you before his leaving England—He
went by Worcester, where my Uncle and little Charles
supped with him Tuesday night. He breakfasted with
them the following morning, and dined at Mrs Hawkins',
with all the family—He afterwards stopped at Shrewsbury, and dined or supped with Rebecca etc. By the
same post came my dearest Fanny's sweet letter to our
dear Mrs Lock—which was another delight to me—
In the afternoon Amelia and Augusta took their alternate
lessons, after which came Miss Uptons, with La Bonne,
and Mrs Beranger, their governess, a vulgar but good
humoured English woman, the widow of a Frenchman,
of whom I imagine she learned his languages which she

speaks fluently, tho' otherwise ill enough. My evening
was not unpleasantly spent, as the letters have already
raised my spirits and the dear girls seemed so happy and
made my children so, not to mention Lady Templetown's
little girls, who are very amiable and *perfectly* well behaved—*All* of them were *enchanted* with Nordia, who
was so full of glee and good humour, and seemed to
enjoy the young party so thoroughly that it was a great
treat to me to see them together, and Fanny de son
coté was a VERY good little girl—and pressed every body,
quite of her own accord, to eat some of her dear Aunt
Fanny's bonbons which had been given her for her good
behaviour in the morning. Wednesday morning—my
dear M^r and Mrs Lock stopped in the phaeton to tell
me they were going to pay visits and would call for me
on their return—but as Fanny had been promised a
dinner at Norbury, I sent Anne up with her and her
Brother before I was called for. Our sweet friends could
not stay at their first calling—but told me they had
now been able to settle the day for their purposed visit
to you. It was to be *Tuesday*, upon which morning
Mr Hinde leaves them. I was rejoiced to hear it would
be so soon—but what think you were my feelings when
my dearest Mrs Lock added " And we are in hopes my
dearest Mrs Phillips will be able to go with us . . . : with
you my dearest Mrs Lock . . . What—" how do you
mean, was my quick reply : " cannot you " : was the
answer in the sweet persuasive and kind voice you have
so often heard—" I hope she can " said dear Mr Lock
in his quiet but punctuating manner—I felt a very
pleasant *flutter* of spirits—but begged *not to be asked*—
it would be so difficult to me to refuse *such* a gratification, tho' I was sure it could not be done without too
much inconvenience to themselves, for the only idea I
had of the matter was that I should ride with them in
their chaise—" Oh, if that's all," said our sweet friend
smiling, and *colouring* with pleasure, " make yourself
quite easy, for there can be no inconvenience *whatever*
arising from it to us—nothing but added pleasure and

happiness: But Mr William . . . Does not he go ?—
yes surely—and it is for that reason we are the better
enabled to make this proposal to you as we shall take
two carriages—Amelia and Augusta occurred to me—
but I did not mention them—because I felt that this
kindness was made upon deliberation, unthought of,
much more unexpected by me. I could therefore only
endeavour to express my thanks, and give way to the
delight the very idea of such a journey could not but
give me, and our sweet friends, evidently very much
pleased, left me full of these sweet sensations, hoping
soon to be back from their visitationing to carry me to
Norbury. They were scarce driven from the door,
when an idea which saddened both my prospects and
feelings occurred—I have written lately so much out
of date and even without memorandums, that in *due*
place I forgot to mention a letter which I received from
the Lady, inviting me to spend a week at Chelsea, very
soon after Phillips had left me—*Nothing* but the fear of
disobliging my dear Father could have tempted me to
accept such an invitation a moment—and this fear was
overuled on the other hand by a certainty that if I went,
it would vex and even displease Phillips extremely—I
therefore after a little hesitation wrote word to the
Lady (which was then very true) that Norbury was very
indifferent with cutting his teeth, and that I could not
bring myself to leave him—expressing at the same time
an earnest desire to see my Father, and entreating him
if possible to bestow a week upon me *previous to his
Aylsham* journey *or after* it, with the Lady, Sally, and
Miss Young.—To this letter which is now of a week's
standing I have received no answer—but *if* my invitation should be accepted—what a mortification will it
not be, since it must happen precisely at the time that
our Friends go to Windsor, as my Father has settled to
go to Aylsham in the middle of this month !—It is every
way and how ever it may end, unfortunate, that this unexpected invitation should have been made [by] me now,
and forced from me all my objections against leaving

home . . . but I need not dwell on this, nor point it out
to my dearest Fanny—who will feel unassisted all that
I have to say.—The matter being uncertain, I was
tempted not to teize my dear Mrs Lock with mentioning it to her—but upon further reflection, that a *severe*
disappointment might be spared this kindest of friends
should I be prevented accompanying her, and that my
dearest Fanny might likewise not *hear* what was in agitation unless it were *happily* settled, I determined to tell
her precisely how I was situated. Accordingly when I
was called for, I did so,—and it has been a source of unpleasant perturbation ever since—Nothing can equal
the gentleness and kindness of this sweet and generous
Friend—When we arrived at Norbury, whilst Mrs Lock
settled her *Peaches* with La Bonne, I visited the nursery, to see Feddy and my children—I found Norbury
in the arms of Augusta, who was pointing out his blue
eyes and pink cheeks, and bright hair and *all his beauties*
with great warmth of admiration to Wells. Whilst
Feddy, tho' not in good humour, and *very* jealous of
him suffered Fanny to comb his hair, and tie his sash,
and make believe to dress him. His complaisance to her,
seems never to fail. It was a very pretty sight to see
them together—I then went down and settled M^{rs}
Lock's flowers—and whilst so employed Amelia came in
saying Frederick was so naughty, and so cross to poor
little dear Norbury, and took away all his boxes and playthings, and the other was *so* good and sweet etc etc.
I was sorry for these complaints—not merely that it
should be so, for these dear children will not be the
worse friends by and bye, but because it vexed our dear
Mrs Lock—besides I knew praise so accompanied would
not make my poor Nordia the greater favourite. After
dinner the little Heros came and Fanny their queen,
and there was much riotous play, with some naughtiness
on the part of Feddy, and the utmost glee on that of
Nordia—Fanny was very good—At coffee I proposed
carrying the two last to Anne, which Nordia opposed
by a very pathetic, " Ah no Mama—*Pay* Don't—" and

I was obliged to some coaxing and adroitness to deliver him to her without a burst of sorrow after all this joy. Frederic went out with Wells—and soon I accompanied Mr Lock and Mr Hinde into the Park—but the wind was extremely cold, and has given me a little return of my swelled face—When we came home I went upstairs again to see for my children, and was not sorry, as the night was so cold, to find they were already gone—But La Bonne and the two dear girls gave me a very good account of Fanny, and were unwearied in their praise of Norbury—" Avec tou: ce que ce petit mutin " (meaning Frederic) a pû faire, ceque auroit fait pleurer et en rager un autre enfant une centaine de fois, ce cher petit Norbury n'a jamais un moment perdu sa douceur, son egalité, et *son petit air mouton.*" When I came downstairs Feddy was at his supper—very comical at times—but full of little ill humours and whims—these indeed have lately been carried to such a height as to oblige his sweet and tender Mother to oppose him, which is ever most reluctantly done—He had cried that *whole* morning because she did not give up dressing herself to pay her visits—and all another because Mr Lock did not ride upon Jenny, as he had expected, and take him with him—Poor little Fellow ? with so much sense to be so little reasonable ?   Mr William was gone to Brighthelmstone ?—I was excessively surprised at hearing it, and not glad—He had been seduced there by Mr James Moore, the Surgeon—who, not I think very judiciously, has pressed him to making this excursion. I spent the evening in working for the Fair with Mrs Lock. Thursday Sept 6th I just saw our sweet friends a moment as they passed by to pay visits. They left a card for me at Mrs Tucker's. The Talbots have already returned my visit, when I was out—I am sorry they are so quick ?—and this morning came M^r and Mrs Eckersall and, what is much worse Mrs Rogers— Friday 7th I received a kind letter from Charlotte with a sad account of our dearest Esther, who has suffered dreadfully since she has been at Aylsham with the tooth-

ache, and been forced to having *two* drawn ?—Poor dear
souls ! as if she were not weakened and thin enough,
without the suffering and sleeplessness attendant on
this cruel malady !—She was thank Heaven, *much* better
when Charlotte wrote, and beginning to leave off her
wrappings. Mrs Lock called upon me to take me to
Mrs Majendie's—She was not at home—nor I *very*
sorry ? We then drove to Mickleham, where we wrote
a joint hasty letter to my dearest Fanny—I saw too my
dear ones, and Fanny was very kindly invited by M^rs
Lock—but as Amelia and Augusta would I knew be at
Miss Uptons with La Bonne, I did not accept the invitation for her dear little soul—sorry as I was to leave her,
I spent the rest of the day at Norbury—Saturday Sept 8th
No letter is yet come from Chelsea nor any from Dublin
—My whole leisure lately has been employed in writing
letters and journalising—yet have I in the latter employment missed many circumstances from hurry—One in
particular I must now tell you—One evening while the
Hartsincks were at Norbury when I went there to tea,
I met entering into Long-bury, a private walk down the
hill, that loving couple—we bowed and curtsied and I
proceeded. As I approached the House, I saw two
phaetons at the door, and a large party coming from it
who were making inquiries about the road, of Rich and
Wells who stood on the steps. I scarce knew how I
should make my way past—yet as I perceived I was seen,
could not retreat. Mr William stood smiling at his
bed room window, something diverted by my embarrass-
ment I believe—He bowed, and I went on, and upon
the steps saw a Lady who reminded me of somebody I
had before seen, but whom I did not perfectly recollect,
till being quite near her, she said " How do you do
Mrs Phillips "—with some surprise I saw it was Miss
Streatfield[1]—She begged to know how *Fanny* did—When
I had seen her—how she looked etc, and then told me *M^rs*

---

[1] Miss Streatfield was a very beautiful girl—a friend of the Thrales
(Fanny Burney's Early Diary).

Burney had been so good as to write her an account of
how happily *Dick* was going on in India—this always
a subject from which I feel inclined to shrink, I said
very little to, but that she was very good—a silence then
ensued—but she did not move to permit my going up
the steps, and I began a conversation with Feddy—in
this she joined, and lamented M^r and Mrs Lock's being
out, and Mr Hinde, whose *niece* she called herself—During
this conversation I saw there were two Ladies already
seated in one of the phaetons, and a clergyman whose
name I *suspected* I knew, who was going backwards and
forwards giving orders to the servants—there was likewise a young man on horseback.   After about ten minutes
of conversation with frequent pauses on each side, I
suppose the *S.S.* perceived her beau was in readiness,
tho' I did not, and, as if *studiously*, He never came our
way—but she then suddenly took leave, and hastened
away to the other phaeton in which in a moment I saw
her seated by—*Dr Vyse*.   I should not so boldly declare
the name from conjecture—but as soon as they were
gone, Rich begged to know who the young Lady was,
and said the servants had told her one of the gentlemen
was *Dr Vyse*—I hope they are going very soon to be
married.   As I found Mrs Lock was really out, I went
on in search of her, and met her with Miss Crokatt, and
Mr William, who had joined them, and who was curious
to hear who my acquaintance was—" She is *rather
pretty* is she not."—said he?   I said she *had* been exceedingly so—but she is indeed extremely passée.—I have
passed to day wholly at home, between writing to my
dearest Fanny, and playing with my children—not *all*
play however—for Fanny has her regular lesson of reading and working, and then of getting by heart—She
said to me just now—" Once Anne was reading a book
Mama—and it was a very shocking book—and Anne
cried a great deal—She was reading it in the spare room
Mama when you was at Windsor—It was something about
Cecilia—that was the name": "And how did you know
that Fanny?" "Why I heard in the book something

about that name—and Amelia has got a *doll* that is called Cecilia too." "Did you understand anything in the book Fanny ? " "No Mama," said she very innocently—" I believe it was not a book for such little girls as me to understand—but I knew it was SHOCKING because Anne cried so ": "And did Anne read it loud ? " "Yes Mama—to Nanny—Once Mama *I* cried you know when I was reading a book to you—about the poor little *Hare*." She has just asked me if I am writing to Aunt Fanny—" Then *pray* do thank her for the bonbons and let me kiss the letter a great many (Fanny's kiss) times, and tell her I will kiss her myself a great many times more when she comes back again to Norbury "—You will see my Fanny the place where the little mouth was pressed over and over again above—Here comes my Nordia fast asleep in Anne's arms—He will not say his prayers to night dear little love. But Anne has taught him to say them—and the other evening when he went up just as he was undressed He surprised me by running to the foot of the bed and kneeling down, and saying " Pay God bess Papa, Mama, Titter, Ganpapa, Uncles, Aunts, Anne, all good *Fends*, make Titter good girl— Norbudy good Boy "—and then he further surprised me and even affected me by adding " and pay God bess Papa and send him safe back "—I do not tell you this long prayer was *unprompted* by Anne—but the little soul *began* it alone, and said a great deal of it without help. This morning when Fanny came with great glee to tell me she had been quite a good girl when I was out yesterday, he ran up and looking laughing in my face said of his own accord—and " *Norbudy a good Boy*."—Its little talk is *very* sweet, and continually surprising me— When James was here, and I indulged him one morning by sitting him up at breakfast, he heard me beg his Papa to come, who was playing the fiddle with James, and he suddenly called out—" Come Papa—*Come Dem* "— and then hearing us laugh, as if to correct his *familiar* expression—" Come *Brother Dem* " said he—and after that time he never called James anything else than

Brother Dem—I have not time now for any of its little
diverting sayings—but I must tell you he is not only
a great musician, and has added to his stock of tunes
Osey Boys, which he calls *Frederick Lock's tune*, but is
a wonderful Flowerist, and surprises me by his observation and memory whenever we are in the garden, where
he knows the name of *every* flower—Ose, *Picks* that is
the Rose that *pricks*—Pinks, *Honeysuckle*—*teet pea*—lark-
spur—miniontett—Holly Hawk—*Lamander* (Lavender)—
China aster—*manigold* (marygold)—etc etc etc—what
he is once told he seems never to forget. Mr William
is one of his great admirers, and produced the other
night one of Fiamingo's most beautiful models as a
likeness of him. He is indeed—if a Mother's judgement may be taken, or if a Mother may take the
judgement of others to be sincere, one of the sweetest
children that can be met with—and it does *so* love
Mama, that my Fanny would best of all love him
for that, were she to see enough of him to know
him? Sunday morning Sept 9th No letter either from
Chelsea or my Phillips, which latter is a great disappointment to me—and indeed I had hoped I might have
received a rejection of my invitation from Chelsea which
would have removed every objection to the Windsor
journey: for which I shall however prepare with infinite
delight notwithstanding this untoward circumstance.
Will my Fanny have a B. for us?—a little one possibly
yet I seem not to deserve such a gratification having
never yet answered the last exquisite Partie—but I will
not meet my Fanny without so doing—How incomparable—how like something in one of her own excellent
novels is all the account of your French Clelia—My
dearest Fanny? to be so assailed?—the *Miss Borni-
coom to me arms*—and the embrassades—how they made
us laugh?—with so little encouragement, and to one of
character and manners so opposite to their own, it is
astonishing that such a scene could be so long sustained.
The sventurata Ivim is absolutely incorrigible, and acts
like an idiot—and Clelia seems a very extraordinary

character for one in *real life*—Her reciting her own history was most curious. Doubtless representing that and
herself as the counterpart of Rousseau's Julie—Her very
easy *communication* to two such new friends was certainly
very like that *truly* enchanting Julie—as much as *her*
St Preux resembles Rousseau ? in—*consoling himself with
an actress ?* It is all incomparably ridiculous—Her idea
of the *spectacles* and *gens celebus* of England too was excessively ludicrous, and I wonder not it so amused the
Major whom I cannot forbear pitying for being destined
to hear such narrations so rarely. We felt *outrée* at
the sventurata for besetting you with such extraordinary
indelicacy and even inhumanity about the dinner—it
filled us with concern and sorrow for the poor violet
who with such *infinite* difficulty must have sustained
such open and repeated attacks. Her behaviour too
concerning the *Baron* was most intolerable—but all that
related to her *Clelia* is so infinitely diverting, that were
we only to consult our own amusement we could not
bring ourselves so sincerely to rejoice that she has left
the kingdom and that our violet is relieved from her
fond and troublesome tenderness—As for the sventurata
nothing can keep *her* in order or conceal her intemperate
zeal—a great share of which I am tempted to suspect
must originate in vanity, and in a restless love of being
busy—I was much pleased at the judicious, sensible
answer of the Rose, upon her very improper application
to her—but all that lovely Rose says and does, seems to
be judicious and praiseworthy—the account of her Birth-
Day is sweet indeed *in all its parts*—The quietness of her
own behaviour, at the same time so free [from] *insensibility*, pleased me excessively. It was impossible not to
be pleased and amused with the sweet Daisy's innocent
speech about the violet's not *being fine too*, tho' I was
sorry that dear Violet should be abashed by the remark
—it was not lost on the Lawrel, who treasures up in his
mind I doubt not every word that sweet little creature
utters. I was glad he happened to see the Violet, in
her *gorgeous attire* afterwards. I was delighted to find her

in such favour with this sweet Daisy—and with her promising to *come and play with her*—and am very glad the
little Fork is so much honoured. Tis a lovely little
creature—How amiable and how charming the Rose's
interesting herself so much about the violet's placing
the *capette* where it was accustomed to be placed—and
her desire of Frisketta's fulfilling the hopes of the Ivy,
and the expectations that must be raised in every one
from her having such an example constantly before her
eyes, and such a tutress ? How do I wish that most
amiable and excellent woman could have seen her every
wish gratified in the purity of mind, constant propriety
of conduct, and tender gratitude of her once so promising charge ? but I fear that cannot be ?—This
Frisketta was possibly the Informer of the Honey suckle,
and, thro' her, of the Rose, in all that so surprised the
violet concerning herself, and the circumstances of her
illness—but I was very sorry that curious little conversation was so suddenly put a stop to—and I feel foolish
enough to be sorry the Rose should even *dislike* music
—yet it is not so *very* foolish—for of how great a pleasure is she from that circumstance deprived. The description of the Lady who *remembers nobody's face out of
sight*, diverted me very much—but I was sorry she interrupted the Ivy and Violet—What could the business
of so *very* private a nature between them, be ?—We felt
a little for the dear Violet's strangeness at the first tea
drinking in which she presided without another female,
and at the entrance of the Lawrel, finding only a *Trio*—
when I read his commendation of the *timely resignation*
of the Violet's successor, what must he think of the
Cerbera, thought I ?—and methought—I should not
be sorry had he *her* resignation to commend likewise—I
was glad the violet made so amusing an answer to the
Lawrel when he said she *must* have seen D—I like he
should be *encouraged* to talk to her—tho' he would I am
sure confound me more than all his Family—not from
awe—but from the fear of laughing or of being embarrassed by some very abrupt speech—We read with

great pleasure the account of the violet's being first
alone with the Magnolia—How many sweet instances
of kindness and amiable attention did the absence of
the Cerbera give occasion for—I was much diverted by
the *Wall flower* Lady breaking out about her, after
much edifying caution on both sides—" If he were not
so sick—and so CROSS " etc. Il Buono's superabundant
caution vexed us—but we joined in lamenting his loss
with the violet—it is indeed a great one—but was it not
a ridiculous treat the Cerbera found for him ? It
struck me as being so to ANY *man* but a Jeweller—Such
matters are dazzling enough and sufficiently delightful,
and interesting, generally to *women*—but to a gentleman . . . ?—we were provoked at that Cerbera's unexpected return . . . but much *more* so at the negligent
confidence of the violet's servant in *bringing " that man "*
—What a strange ridiculous scene it occasioned ?—I
was really very sorry for the poor man's mortification
and disappointment, particularly as he was *modest*, and
overset, by a mistake for which he was not accountable
—and the poor Violet ?—I am quite glad she parted with
that servant—What an abominable man ?—His im-
pertinence in the invitations to *tea* was quite intolerable
—no wonder the poor Col : was glum and offended—
We were very sorry the Partie ended here, without
saying whether in *future* the violet gained her point,
of being perfectly her own mistress to appear or not,
in the absence of the Cerbera, at tea time. It would be
a glorious privilege if attainable. All the interruptions
of the Cerbera, occasioning such sudden checks to the
most innocent gaiety or openness in conversation, do
so remind one of the Lady ? How hard that *two* such
should have been met by the Violet, and should have
successively overshadowed and excluded the sun from
this sweet flower. The first meeting of M^r and M^rs
S—— made us melancholy from the feelings of the violet
. . . Heaven be praised, I trust it is no longer so, nor
can ever be so again ? the power of making them this
invitation was sweetly given by the Magnolia—and the

manner of delivering the capette into the Violet's hands,
with such powers of using the superfluous room in it
for her own convenience, was so *kindly* attentive and
considerate ?—and how sweet the manner of sending
her to the Ivy's—etc etc etc.   I have indeed the
pleasure of recollecting having witnessed many things
very like all these instances of sweet condescension.   We
must thank the Violet particularly for the sweet representation given us of the interesting little scene which
passed in her presence between the Lawrel and Magnolia
—it pleases one extremely to see marks of such sweet
and sincere attachment between *any two*, united as
these are—but even particularly when so exalted by
situation.   All the violet says of the Magnolia's *extraordinary* clearness and soundness of judgement etc.
would have struck me as being true even from the
little I had the happiness of seeing of her—but how
admirably it is said ?   " In *her* sagacity seems *intuitively*
to *supply the place of experience*"—etc etc I could
have cried at the stanzas about the *great coat* being
so buried alive ?—Why—why were they not shewn ?—
since they were so readily and hastily penned.   Why
did not that dear violet the same evening lay them
on the toilette ?—It is too vexatious—you must however make her shew them to *me*.   I do entreat to
have them with the next *partie*—and I will faithfully
promise not, without leave, to make any copy. . . . Pray
do lecture her never to do another time as she did this—
The magnolia must have thought it almost cross of her,
so to neglect her desire.—I must now thank you a thousand and thousand times for this sweet Partie, which
has given me most true delight—but shall I not shortly
be able to thank my Fanny *de vive voix* ?   Heaven be
praised, I trust I shall—Ah my dearest Fanny ?—what
an unexpected happiness ?—Our sweet friends have been
here this morning—Dr. Moore and his sons are at Norbury, and I was glad to be excused, and stay at home to
write to you and play with my children.—To morrow
will be given to packing and arrangements—I have

written to my dear Father. Adieu, adieu my beloved Fanny till Tuesday ?

MICKLEHAM,
Sunday evening, Sept. 9th, '87.

LETTER XIX

11 *Oct.* 1787

Monday Octr 8th the morning was fine and we took a sweet walk, in which I was pleased at the appearance of *perfect amity* as my dear Fanny expresses it, I observed in James and his wife—She has of him the highest opinion —her *nature* I am convinced is not tender—however she is very desirous it should appear so—and the attempt is certainly laudable, tho' for her sake as much as James' I wish there were more warmth of heart—Our children were delightful together—Fanny's perfect goodness in giving up everything to either of the little ones of her own accord was very sweet—Nordia acted the same part *nearly* as virtuously towards *Pitty ittle Kitty*, as he always called her—He would never suffer anybody to say she *cried*—but always said " No no—Kitty *won't* ky—*Kitty be a goo Boy !* "—The little Kitty meanwhile rolled on the carpet with a thousand comical little *affected* airs— 'tis a whimsical sweet little thing, and I verily think will have a great deal of sense—I can scarce tell whether James seemed fondest of his own babe or of my children. Nordia is in as high favour with him as ever, and *Unken Dem* no less a favourite with Nordia.—In playing with a little smelling bottle this evening he broke the cork— " Oh that was very naughty " said Mama :—Nordia who is always grieved and sometimes *au desespoir* to be told he is naughty, repeatedly said in a pathetic voice— " No no—Norbudy goo boy "—But was'nt Norbury naughty to break the cork ? " No Mama," and raising his voice with a degree of spirit that was comical, added— " Cork naughty—Cork boke—Naughty Cork ! "—It was impossible to hear this accusation and defence of himself without laughing—Tuesday Oct 9th brought me a letter

BABY NORBURY.
By Edward Burney.

from our dear Father, and a very kind one—but positively declining any more visits for this year, and expressing an earnest desire that I would peep upon him
at least, at Chelsea—My heart yearned instantly to
accept this proposition—but the next day sweet M^{rs}
Delany was expected—and to remain till Saturday—
and by a letter the same post brought me from my dear
Phillips, I had reason to expect his return in above a
week or ten days from that time. I knew not therefore
what to do—and as James advised me *not to go*, I determined to defer my answer for a day or two at least.
He was to leave me the next morning—and I had agreed
to accompany him to Leatherhead Fair with Fanny,
and to have John to walk back with me—had I had no
hope of seeing Mrs Delany—he and his could not have
prolonged their stay further, as they were on the point
of leaving Chesington, and had all their packings and
arrangements to make. Our day was quietly and pleasantly spent. I had offered my dearest Mrs Lock that
Anne should accompany her aunt Mrs Bristow, to assist
at the Fair, which offer was very sweetly accepted—I
therefore rose very early on the day appointed—Wed-
nesday Octr 10th in order to have from her the little
assistance I require, and to take charge of Nordia, and of
Fanny, who was delighted at being *dressed by Mama*—
I hurried away Anne as fast as I could, and as it began
to rain sent her with an umbrella to meet the carriage
at the Farm which was to carry her, her Aunt, and the
Fairings. But alas all this was in vain !—to my very
great concern the rain fell with increasing violence, and
most unremitting constancy the whole morning—the
whole day—My accompanying James and his wife as I
had wished and intended was wholly out of the question,
as had his chaise been *large* enough for us all, and I had
had a carriage to return in, it would have been impossible to have walked down the fair when there. I was
on my own account vexed the more at this as my guests
had prevented my visiting Norbury, and seeing the usual
exhibition of sweet things the day before the sale—but

this was a small concern compared to that I felt for our dear benevolent friend.—Soon after breakfast our James took a most affectionate leave of me—and his wife a very kind one—the little baby set out well, tho' I felt some anxiety about her, and for them all indeed at their undertaking a journey over such roads in such weather. —Our disappointment in not seeing sweet Mrs Delany I need not discant upon—it was quite a melancholy day—and at one o'clock Anne returned home with an account that Bristow was not to go to the Fair, which literally was not kept that day by any of the people who had brought their goods to Leatherhead—judging they must not only be vainly exposed but spoiled.

Letter XXII

Sunday, Novr 4th, 87.

I had written myself almost blind Wednesday when I sent my dearest Fanny my paquet, which I have just had the satisfaction of hearing she has safely received. I hear too that another parcel is going to her, and must send a *mite* in continuation. I walked up to Norbury between my two dear little ones Thursday morning— the weather was like May, and my little companions were in the highest health and glee—My spirits however were a little checked by finding our sweet friend on the point of setting out to pay visits with Mr Lock—and her disappointment doubled my own—particularly as I was in such daily expectation of my Phillips' return that I could not comply with her wish that I should stay till she came back and spend the day. Mr William was employed about his drawing—but laid down his pencil to take Norbury on his knee—and examine him, which he did very good humouredly and even kindly—When he had set him down again, " Norbury would make a *very* pretty love," said he, " with his fine hair and a pair of white wings."—Presently Feddy came down—and it was then not without *great* difficulty that I could get away —the dear little boy almost with tears in his eyes, begged

so hard that *Fannu* should stay with him to dinner—
Meanwhile my poor Fanny bore *her* disappointment
very patiently and sweetly—for had not Mrs Lock been
going out I had meant to have stayed whilst she dined
with the young party—but the pleasure of another walk
with Mama seemed to make her amends, and she danced
and bounded by my side all the way home, and Nordia
tho' growing very tired held fast my other hand, and
answered Anne always with " *No* tanky " when she
proposed to carry him. My evening produced nothing
—the next morning I had a kind and comfortable letter
from my Traveller, who had been visiting Dr Priestly,
to whom Mr Kirwan gave him a letter of recommendation, and Warwick Castle. I had a note of inquiry
from my sweet Mrs Lock, and heard that Lady Templetown and her little ones were gone to London for the
winter—I was sorry not to have seen them before they
went. The evening was so *very* dreadful a one, that as
Phillips travelled on horseback I had not a chance of
seeing him—and found afterwards that the weather
alone detained him, for he was within ten miles of me
when the violent storm arose—He did not pass through
London—but not being aware of this I concluded
yesterday I should certainly not see him till night—so
Fanny was sitting quietly at her lesson as usual when
behold—the door opened, and an exclamation and shriek
declared *Papa*—He looks quite well, and is so thank
Heaven and sends my Fanny his very kind love—I despatched news of his arrival to my ever kind and sympa-
thising friend who has just been here from church
with her sweet girls and Mr William, all congratulating
(me with) eyes and with voice in the sweetest and most
expressive manner.—My Fanny is quite happy in Papa's
return, who has loaded her with little presents—but
Norbury's remembrance of him and fondness is quite
surprising—He would not come from his Papa yesterday even to *me* who was never refused before, and who
now joyed in *being* refused—" No *tanky* Mama " he
said—" Papa caddy Norbudy "—He brought him all

his little playthings, and told him the history that belonged to them all—who gave, and who broke, and who should mend them—but here is a Papa who will not let me write a word more, so Heaven bless my dearest Fanny—I shall long to hear from you when you have read my last pacquet—I had a letter from Marianne this morning—Our dear Esther has the rheumatism sadly in her head still—

Miss Burney,
Queen's Lodge,
Windsor.

Letter XXIII

Nov. 1787

My Folio sheet letter I think brought me up to the 11th of this month tho' in some respects I am well aware my former journal has been written with a brevity which only extreme hurry could have occasioned— particularly concerning the exquisite little ballad, and my Fanny's most sweet and admirable letters relative to the affair which till that long letter had been despatched so very much engrossed all our thoughts—I was then confined by a violent swelled face, and continued so the two following days, receiving continually kind notes of inquiry from our dearest Mrs Lock—Phillips was still in London. My little companions were my resources, as I suffered no violent pain, except during the nights, so that their playfulness amused me and sweetened my confinement—but Nordia was very much displeased by my dress, and seeing me so wrapped up cried out—" *Mama old Woman* " to my great diversion —" Mama—put a pitty bonnet on "—not being able to succeed in this request, he repeated his complaint of my being *an old woman* afterwards to his nurse from whom he learned a new phrase—for the next morning he said to me with great gravity " Mama *not old woman* —*old Lady* Mama ! "—Wednesday Morning 14th I had resolution sufficient to send for Mr Ansell to draw my tooth which was not at all decayed, but had been loosened

by the drawing of the other, and under it an abscess
had been formed which rendered it quite necessary to
be taken out. Poor little Fanny made me many questions concerning the operation—but ended with saying
with great energy " I *can't* be in the room Mama when
Mr Ansell comes—that I am *sure* I can't." " What !—
not if you can be of some use to me my dear Fanny ? "
"Yes Mama . . . but I think I am too little to be of any
use, and if you are frightened I am sure I shall be much
worse—and I am afraid Mama it would make me quite
shriek out "—I need not tell you the consent I gave
her to leave me—indeed I would not have had the poor
little thing with me to have saved another tooth. The
moment therefore Mr Ansell was announced I hurried
her away—and composed myself as well as I was able
for the terrible operation—which he performed very
safely tho' not without occasioning considerable pain—
I was scarcely recovered from it when Mr Lock's carriage
stopped at the door. Our sweet friend was in it and
had brought her lovely boy with her to see me—It was
very unlucky just then as I was hardly able to speak,
and it would certainly have been best for me not to
attempt it—but I most regretted my inability to entertain the dear little Feddy, whose visit, tho' then unexpected I had frequently solicited—Our sweet and considerate friend however sent him up into the nursery to
my little ones, who were preparing to pay a visit to
Norbury, and then undertook *tous les frais de la conversation*. . . . My dearest Mrs Lock, finding my little
ones were going to Norbury insisted on carrying them in
the carriage with her and her Feddy—and I was then too
helpless to oppose her, tho' very much afraid it would
prove a very laborious task—At their return home however Fanny told me they had been *all* VERY good—and
that at first Mrs Lock placed Frederic on the seat by
her, and Nordia on her lap—but then Frederic wanted
to be on her lap too—and so Mrs Lock took them *both*
—but they did not quarrel at *all*—only *kissed one another
every now and then*—This *very* good account was

afterwards confirmed to me by our dear Mrs Lock—
who said her little journey was quite *pleasant*.—M^r
William called in for a moment to know how I did, and
was very good naturedly concerned to see the state I
was in—He paid me little visits of inquiry every morning for 2 days more, which were very kindly taken. My
dearest Mrs Lock told me *M^r* Lock had intended accompanying her to see me that morning, but had been
stopped by the arrival of Mr Uredale Price—I could
not then regret it, as I was so little fit for conversation.
. . . . The next day I had another visit from Mr Lock—
I had that morning a letter from Phillips which led me
to expect him that day, and a *very* sweet one from my
beloved Fanny, which touched me very much for her,
and her venerable and most excellent friend!—My
wanderer returned to me to dinner—and brought me
the pleasant intelligence that he had seen my dearest
Fanny—and delivered to me her sweet pacquet in the
evening when his trunk was unpacked. I should otherwise have acknowledged the receipt of it instantly, as
there was no post the next day—but I got it too late—
Another little letter arrived Saturday morning 17th to
inquire after the *caps*—both were answered by Sunday's
post. I was put into a terrible fright this day for my
sweet boy—His Father, who loves him beyond all
things I believe was the cause—and the *sufferer* at the
same time, as he was excessively alarmed—In the midst
of a violent romp he unfortunately hurt the poor little
thing's arm so severely that he screamed out, and could
not bear to move it, or have it touched—and—we feared
it had been *put out*, as it is called—I cannot forbear
mentioning it, tho' thank God our alarm was not of above
two hours duration, that I may tell you how like a little
angel it behaved—the pain at first seemed excessive,
but the moment it had recovered a little it bid me " put
a little *'matum* on it "—remembering some *pomade
divine* which had been rubbed a few days before on a
bruise he had received. "Where my sweet love—
where—is it *here* you are hurt ? " " Oh *pay* don't—

Mama—*pay* don't hurt Norbury," cried the little sweet soul with tears running down its cheeks, the moment its arm was touched—but presently after, as I had got him in an easy position on my lap, its little face grew composed, and looking up at me, remembering my late swelled face, he cried out in the kindest voice you can conceive " *How is your Pace (face) Mama?* "—and then gently stroking it with his *well* arm. " Mama's bell (well) now—Mama got on a Pitty cap "—an effort made by Phillips who was anxious to know whether any serious mischief was done renewed his pain, which seemed almost agonizing—He suffered it however with a patience and sweetness that would have affected I believe any indifferent person—I need not tell you how it affected *me*—his poor Father too was shocked and terrified excessively—and touched too, at observing the sweet child, even when tortured by his moving about his arm, seemed sensible that he *intended* not to hurt him, and kissed and clung about him the moment he desisted—At length, wearied by the pain, and the tears it had occasioned, it sunk gently to sleep in my arms : and I was able to lay him down on a bed in the next room, which Phillips opened for me without waking him— Here I continued watching the little sweet soul, as long as his Father would let me, who feared my catching cold—but when I left him it was only for the adjoining apartment, where I could hear him even breathe—He had a sleep of above an hour, during which we were in a state of most anxious apprehension—but on his awakening it was most sweetly dispelled, as except at first being moved, the pain from the little strain he had received seemed no longer felt. He permitted us then to undress him, and with all his usual animation and spirits enjoyed being rid of the encumbrance of his clothes, and told us Norbudy was a *Dolly (Jolly) Bacchus* now remembering Unken Dames having called him so once. What a blessed relief was this !—and how gratefully delighted did I not feel the whole evening after it ! . . .

Norbury has learned a little phrase from his Papa with which he daily accosts him—" pray Cousin Edward [1] *paint my portrait.*" Cousin Edward always answers that he wishes he could—and does indeed seem to have a great inclination to do it, tho' he says *nothing less than Rubens should attempt it* !—My Fanny has her share of kindness, tho' not of notice, as she behaves very quietly and well, and consequently does not put herself in the way so much as the little Rantipole—and Edward is too modest to seek even a baby—Tuesday Dec[r] 4th Phillips met Feddy with M[rs] Wells in our neighbourhood, and seizing upon him brought him in to the great delight of myself and Nordia, as well as Fanny, who was at her lesson—All lessons were now laid aside and our little People as happy as possible—Nordia giving the visitor all his playthings and imitating Fanny in all the caresses she bestowed—In the midst of all this arrived my sweet Friend, who was surprised, and not *much* displeased at seeing whom we had got with us—Mais helas ?—at her appearance the pacific dispositions of our Feddy were at an end—Nordia, who is *extremely* fond of M[rs] Lowock ran to her expecting her usual kind notice, which was not withheld, but this produced a furious outcry in a Feddy, who considered himself as rightful owner of her caresses and love, and notwithstanding all the measures the Mamas took to keep peace, it was not to be obtained—tho' I must say Nordia behaved like a little angel, giving up to and even caressing the little *Lyon* whenever it was not raving, and not suspecting himself to be the cause of his change of humour—Feddy meanwhile snatched everything from him, which tho' with surprise and gravity he bore with patience till a new little watering pot he had just obtained was likewise seized upon, on which he made a little struggle, and burst into tears : and I then, not liking to see him oppressed when he had been so good, interfered as did M[rs] Lock, and carried him off *with the watering pot* to his friend the

[1] Edward Burney was amongst the earliest students of the Royal Academy (F. Burney's Early Diary).

Cook, who is always rejoiced to receive him. Feddy
then, finding the field his own, was willing to go into the
nursery with Fanny to Anne—and then our dear M^rs^
Lock and I had about a quarter of an hour's quiet talk—
My cold was so much better that I promised to go to
Norbury the next evening, with Phillips, and my *Guest*.
When Mr Lock came Phillips brought in Edward, whom
he addressed very politely and even kindly—the little
ones soon came in, who had been with Anne visiting our
Mare, the two boys with each a twig of box in their
hands—this was not long considered as a mere ornament
by Feddy, who seeing Nordia run to his Mama, gave him
a stroke with it—this Nordia who now conceived Feddy's
intention of insulting him returned—I interfered—but
Mr Lock, laughing very much begged I would let him
defend himself—and was extremely diverted to see
Nordia preparing to *box*, as his Father had taught him
—but perceiving Feddy aiming a very hard blow, he
was afraid my little one would have the worst of it, and
to prevent mischief, as well as discourage fighting, I
turned Nordia to Mr Lock, and bid him shew *him* how
well he could box—this was productive of immediate
good humour—a little touch from Mr Lock, which
tickled him, made him burst into laughter, and M^r^
Lock himself was not a little diverted by his attempts.
—Wednesday morning 5th while Fanny was at her lesson
Mr William called—He has been every day since, tho'
I have not always seen him, as he pays his visit in the
drawing room to Edward, whom I believe he likes very
much. I had then *a visite decongé* from Mrs Rogers and
her niece who are now gone to town—While they were
here came our dear Mr Lock, whom I lamented to receive in such company—In the evening I went with
Edward and Phillips to Norbury—My dearest Mrs Lock
whom I have not seen *at her home* for ten days received
me with open arms—Miss Crokatt in her *best* manner—
and the dear girls most affectionately—I rejoiced to
see Amelia look as sweetly as ever. Mr William took
charge of Edward, who seemed much pleased with his

evening—A little cut on my finger made me escape a persecution about playing—for as I scarce know 3 *tunes* that Edward has not been used to hearing performed incomparably in T. street, I am very glad to keep quiet in that way—We had an *operation* to be performed in our kitchen Friday, which made it impossible for us to *cook*—and therefore by Phillips' desire I was obliged to *beg to be invited to dinner*—the proposal was most sweetly accepted, and our dear Mrs Lock assured Phillips this was the *improvement* most to her taste that he had yet made. We spent Thursday at home, and Friday Dec 7th went to a late dinner at Norbury—Mr Lock was in particular spirits, and kept Edward on the laugh the whole day, tho' that was I believe the only way in which his voice was heard. A Feddy was very droll and amusing after dinner, and seeing Augusta sitting on a chair Mr Lock had left at desert, with a very comical little action told her to *go off from Papa's chair*, adding with vehemence "I am *socked* (*shocked*) *of you Augusta !* "—When we went into the Picture Room, he came to me to hear more stories about Fanny and Nordia and played with me till his supper came after which very reluctantly he was carried off to bed.—We had a pleasant, quiet evening —and I promised to spend this evening with them again, Sunday Decr 9th. Yesterday was passed alone, except a little visit from Mr Lock, and one from his son. The former has been here this morning, and looked at the tablet Edward is about in the drawing room—it is a copy from a Basso Relievo of Fiamingo's, representing a number of children surrounding a goat, who is frightened by a mask held by one of them, and endeavouring to make his escape—Mr Lock seemed very much pleased by it, and said he saw only one thing he should wish altered, which was an error in the model itself whence Edward had copied it. He advised him here to depart from the original, and to take that part from our Norbury—it was in the position of one of the arms—Edward took the hint with his usual modesty, and very thankfully. Mr Lock brought Fanny a present

from Feddy for her and Nordia—I told him Feddy
seemed determined to lessen her exaggeration, when she
had said a few days ago that Frederic now sent her some
present EVERY *day*—She had at that time received twice
a present of some plums from him at the distance of
about a week—I told Mr Lock that she was much distressed for something to send him in return—" Send
him your love Fanny "—said he " that will be the
best present you can make."—" But I should like to
send him something *real*," said she very innocently—
Mr Lock smiling assured her her love was all he would
wish for. Since he has been gone Nordia has been here
to receive his share, which he has endeavoured to make
us all partake of—and being distressed that Edward
would not take any of it, to relieve him from the innocent little persecutor I bid him give some to his little
Parson, a droll little figure which I bought for him in
town—Away he ran contented to find somebody that
would eat with him—but in a minute he was at my side
again to say—" *Open a little Parton's mouse Mama ?* "—
Fanny has been descanting on the goodness and kindness of dear Mrs Lock—" but Mama " she says Isn't my
nurse Whitton very good too ? " Yes my dear—very
good. Because when I said she was very good, and
that Mrs Lock was very good, Anne said she was not
NEAR so good as Mrs Lock—and that she *could not* be
so good." " And what did you say Fanny ? " " Why
Mama I said that Nurse Whitton was not so *Powerful*—
but that I thought she might be as *good*—because she
did all the good she could." This was a little stroke
of morality and reasoning I did not expect, and pleased
me very much—I preached upon her text a little while,
and gave it my *sanction*, and the little girl was quite
pleased to find her nurse might be possibly as good as
Mrs Lock, tho' she had it not in her power to bestow
as much—I explained to her Anne's meaning too as well
as I could. She is now learning a hymn of Mrs Barbauld's in which there is an address to a *negro woman*—this
raised much curiosity, which as well as I could I sought

to satisfy, and just now after our morning prayers, (for
the day was rainy and would not permit our going to
church) "Mama," said she, "I said something new in my
prayers last night . . . it was nothing *naughty*." "What
was it Fanny?" "Why Mama—I *prayed for all the poor
negroes*." . . . She is beginning to learn French tout
doucement, at the rate of about half a dozen words a day.
—Sunday Dec 16ᵗʰ I have just finished my alive to my
Fanny and a letter to Esther, and shall now steal a little
time for journalising—Just before dinner last Sunday
Fanny came eagerly to ask if she had not some of Aunt
Fanny's bon bons left—" because Mama you have often
told me those are *quite really my own*—So I think I
might send some of them to Frederic."—I approved of
this notion, and the box was produced, which as the
stock is now but small, has not been much seen of late.
She divided the little quantity in it, giving me one half
of it for Frederic—I made up a little *cornet* of white
paper and put them up for him, repaying amply her
generosity by telling her I was sure he would be very
much pleased with the present. "And can't poor little
Norbury send him something too Mama?" "My love
you know he has nothing of his own to send—but perhaps he will spare some of his raisins at desert." "O—I
daresay he will—because you know Mama he always
wants to give me a great many—and perhaps it may
teach Frederic not to be so jealous when he sees how
good little Norbury is."—Accordingly after dinner
Nordia had his share of the cake, and was told who it
came from—I then asked him what he would send to
Frederic. He immediately broke the cake in two, and
putting half in my hand—"Dare (there)"—he said—"*at
por pedigik*." I explained to him that he must not send
back his own present—and asked if he would not give
something else—He understood my question perfectly,
and put in my hand at least half the plums that had been
given him, and saw me put them up in a paper for
Pedigik. I carried these little presents in the evening
but a Feddy was gone to bed—so I had not the satis-

faction of delivering them, but left them with his dear Mother for him—Edward accompanied us and seemed much pleased with his evening, looking over prints with M͏ʳ William, M͏ʳ Charles, and sometimes M͏ʳ Lock who however seemed to me not in spirits, and did not look well. . . .

Friday morning I had the happiness of spending by appointment at dear Norbury with our sweet friend and M͏ʳ Lock—I found both, tho' yet weak, in other respects well, and in sweet spirits. I carried my dear ones with me, as I knew I should be home to dinner, and could bring them back in the carriage, and nothing could exceed *their* delight unless it was the dear Augusta's and Amelia's at sight of them. I had not meant that they should make their appearance below stairs, at least till I should be taking leave. However I had scarce been seated 10 minutes when Augusta rushed into the room with Nordia in her arms, whom she tossed about as if one of her dolls, tho' he is no very *inconsiderable* little person now either in size or weight—" *Do, look* at *this* BEAUTY—this *sweet love*," was exclaimed by her, and echoed by Amelia, who followed close with Fanny— " 'Tis a beautiful little creature," said our dear M͏ʳ Lock—" He is one of the very finest boys I ever saw in my life ?—his *colouring* is one of the sweetest things that can be conceived—the hair—eyes and complexion, so vivid tho' so delicate, and in such *perfect harmony*." Do you wonder my Fanny that to *you*, who cannot see my little darling whilst he merits such a panegyric, I should find myself unable to resist repeating it ?—I think you will not—and that you will even like to hear it. I foresee that two years hence this loveliness will be at an end, even if the small pox does not prove cruel— and I foresee it tho' not without *some* regret, with far less than I should feel were it a *little girl*—I still hope the countenance will ever remain open, honest, and sweet and, barring any terrible *accident*, he will be healthy, strong, robust—Is there not there enough amply to content *me* ?—At present excepting our *brother Richard*—I think I have not seen a more lovely *fair* boy—His hair is of exactly the same beautiful tint —but is by no means equal in *luxuriance*—We cannot boast of such *magnificent* lovely curls, tho' there is a general and very fine *wave* in his hair, and when *this* comparison is not made it seems as beautiful as one can easily conceive. His complexion, eyes, and teeth, would I think bear the comparison with Richard's—and his features and the form of the face are at present *very* pretty—tho' I do not expect these to be *lastingly* so.— I have let my pen run on in all this because I know my beloved Fanny will like to picture to herself what is a part of her Susan—tho' it is a specimen so fair, that she never can cease wondering how she came by it—I remember almost the last words that poor Cipriani spoke to me, the night before my Nordia so unexpectedly made his appearance, were, to bid one not look at some gigantic and furious figures which he was then drawing— "*you should look at that fine Boy* Mrs Phillips" said he pointing to Algardi's—Had he lived till now he would have thought I had profited from his advice ?—We cannot persuade Edward to take his portrait, tho' he is amongst his *warmest* admirers—for that very reason I believe amongst others—for no pencil but *Rubens's* he continually says could do justice to his colouring—and that could a *cast* of his little figure be made it would be *inestimable*. He is indeed so excessively active, that it would be difficult to gain a likeness but from *memory* of him, which is yet a greater obstacle to getting a resemblance of him—but I cannot help wishing it, as a little *memorandum* to us of what he is now. "But" methinks I hear you say, "does my Fanny improve ? How is she ? " I wish I could give such a description of her as I have of Nordia—but he has indeed at present *all* the advantage in point of beauty—Fanny retains her glowing complexion, and innocent, good humoured countenance, her comprehension enlarges daily, and her heart is as susceptible, affectionate, and warm as it well can be—She is a dear little companion to me, and will

I trust prove an excellent good girl—Her faults, unlike those of Frisketta, rise all to view, and shew themselves *most* to strangers—but I think the deeper one sees into her, the more *elle* est APPROFONDUÈ, the better she will always be found—She requires however a good deal of attention, unless at times when we live quite alone, and then very little will do—but she would, if left to herself—be subject to a great many little affectations, and her manners would not be such as I should wish them—quiet, retenuê, and simple—at 5 years old such an account may seem absurd—however the seeds of our good and ill qualities bring forth early fruits from which the future may frequently be foreseen or at least conjectured, tho' care and cultivation if well directed, may improve the bad, and preserve the good—In my little girl there is the promise of so much goodness, truth, affection, and tenderness, that it will be well worth the pains of eradicating, if it be *possible*, her little faults and failings—I therefore shall never be discouraged in the attempt nor hopeless of success—but to return to my visit, after this long digression—As soon as I could, fearing the noise would be too much for Mr Lock, I sent my little personages away, who were escorted back by their sweet kind friends—I had then some quiet, comfortable talk with our dear Mrs Lock—chiefly of my dearest Fanny and the Qu : s desire of receiving another lesson, which seems really to have gratified M^r L : very much—you can conceive how delighted his sweet Fredy must be, tho' the *season* is not just what we should have desired.—I stayed till near 4 and then brought away my little ones and returned to Edward. Saturday was spent wholly alone—but in the evening I had a letter from my dearest Mrs Lock telling me George had brought her from town, which he had visited with his brother William to see two plays, a paquet for me from my Fanny, which she waited for a safe conveyance to send me—I spent the evening partly in *longing* for it—tho' as Edward passes his time with me from dinner till bedtime, I could only have *looked* at it, and not read it—But this morning it was brought me by my dear little friend George in his way to church. . . .

Sunday, January 20th.—I am much in arrears to my Fanny—My vagabond returned to us to dinner Wednesday the 9th and made our party a little louder and more merry—tho' we had not indeed been *dull*, nor spent our time heavily in his absence—Edward does not shew himself insensible to the affectionate regard and esteem felt for him by us both—and I have great pleasure in observing him to be more gayly open and confidential in society with either of us whether apart or together, than I have ever seen him before—or heard of his being save—formerly, with *you*—and with his younger brothers and sisters.—He is a sweet young man—and I am persuaded, notwithstanding his apparent shyness and too great reserve, formed for domestic happiness and comfort—I see in him so many excellencies, that I cannot forbear forming a hundred wild wishes for his future situation—*wild* because improbable to happen not to say impossible—I must tell you how his time is *allotted* here—Phillips has rather corrupted him by keeping him up late, and being so lazy himself in the morning, so that our breakfast never *begins* till between ten and eleven—Edward however comparatively speaking rises early, and goes to his painting in the drawing room, till he receives a summons from me, or my little Fanny, to tea and cocoa—the first of which he partakes with me—and the second with Phillips—who if he *resists* fails not to say " *consider how thin you are?* "—With this argument he loads him at every meal with all kinds of things—and if *laughter* can fatten, should the provisions fail of their effect, Edward will certainly benefit by his residence with us—He has the highest goust for Phillips's comical buffoonery and humour which puts him quite off his guard, and makes him laugh as loud and as heartily as Mr Burney—Our breakfast is commonly very gay, and Nordia has his share generally in making it so—Edward is grown *excessively* fond of him, and manifests that fondness not merely by playing with him as long as

DRAWINGS
FOR ILLUSTRATION.
By Edward Burney.

I permit after every meal but by expressions of love and
admiration, and by caresses—They are grown the closest
of friends ; and in order that my little personage may
not take up a most unreasonable share of Edward's time,
I am obliged to invent methods and amusements to
induce him to give him his liberty after every breakfast
and every desert. Fanny has her share of kind attention, and amuses him I see very much by her innocent
little talk whenever she is heard.—Our breakfast over,
Edward escapes into his drawing room as soon as he can,
and there, except by occasional visits from Phillips, he
continues uninterruptedly working till about two, when
I am the bearer of chocolate, or sandwiches, or something, and take my share with him, and see how he goes
on. We then part again till dinner at ½ past four—We
have it so late that he may make as much use of the
light as possible—but from that time we continue *en
sociète* till bedtime. My Fanny always dines with me
—Nordia comes in at desert with a curious little bow,
and rushes forward to " *May* own Mama "—He cannot pronounce our i or y—but gives it the sound that
foreigners do—Mr William observing it, said it was the
effect of *his delicate ear*, which could not bear so barbarous
a pronunciation of that letter, as we alone of all European nations make use of ?—When my Nordia has had
his desert, and visited Papa for the share which he likes
to give him, he comes back to me to wash his hands—
" Norbudy won't dirty Cousin *Edarde's* pitty *kean coat* "—
a maxim always repeated upon these occasions and
always applauded by Mama—He then flies to Cousin
Edarde, who receives him with open arms, and gives
him many a *stolen* kiss—for he scarce caresses even *him*
with confidence—then Nordia bids him take down the
Faddle, and " *Norbudy* take the *Bow*, and Cousin Edarde
make Norbudy pay *Marlbone* "—this Cousin Edarde
accordingly does, and he calls for all his tunes, which I
think now amount to eight, and *would* continue thus
employing and employed three hours I believe, were I
not to relieve poor Edward's arm and ears—the next

13

operation is to take him on a little stool, which he calls
his *caddage* (carriage), to visit Mrs Lock—" Coashman "
—he says "you must go up the Hill "—He then pre-
tends to admire the pitty ba lambs etc—and diverted
us very much the other day by adding, " Dare the *box
trees*—and Dare the walnut trees "—remembering I
suppose my having pointed them out to Fanny when
we last rode in a party up to Norbury.—When Edward
takes him to the corner where he says Mrs Lock lives,
he stops, and Nordia enquires most affectionately how
all the family does, and kisses "*may dear* Mittes Lock"
—and *Amelia*, and Augusta, and Ma Bonne etc etc—
then *sings them a song*, and says good bye, and Edward
resumes his Jaunt, till at last Mama is obliged to interfere, and relieve him by entering the lists as Play Fellow
herself, in which capacity she is ever very kindly received.
Edward then draws till tea, and my little Fellow is at
that time carried off—at these hours Edward works
generally for himself, and his work does not interrupt
conversation, when Phillips does not persecute me to
play—We do not apply to Edward for music commonly
till after supper—and then he is grown very good—He
has an excellent ear, and memory, and taste, and has
given me I believe a dozen sweet bits of Pleyell's at least.
—But to go back to my dear Phillips' return. He
brought me a most welcome account of my Fanny's
health and looks. I could not but be sorry that Edward
missed you the evening you spent in Titchfield Street.
—I had a little sketch to shew him of my Nordia which
I had persuaded Edward to take the evening before when
he was brought in sleeping—this evening we gained
another, and have at length wrought from him a promise
to attempt him on canvas—*sleeping*—for awake, it must
be chiefly a work of memory, as it is impossible to fix
him in a position three moments together—this is a
loss—as he is much prettiest awake, when his features
are animated and his bright blue eyes open—but I
rejoice to have something of him in any way—and still
more in the hope of its inducing Edward to take up

painting again—in the course of the following evenings
he took several sweet sketches—Saturday I had a visit
from Mrs Eckersall, and Sunday young Mr Hoole came
to us to dinner—He was very conversable and entertaining—but his presence immediately seemed to have
placed a padlock on the tongue of Edward—What pity
it is *who speaks so well* should ever be silenced!—I heard
a very good account of my sister's little girls from him,
and as Phillips I found was engaged to a *concert* in Titchfield Street for the next Wednesday and would be kept
on business near a week longer in town, I expressed
my wishes to Mrs S. Hoole that my little nieces might
be *dropped here* on their way home and spend a little
time with me, which in her absence I could manage
perfectly.—After he had left us, my little love was
brought in sleeping, and I gained that evening I think,
the sweetest sketch that had yet been made, tho Edward
insists on it he made him look very *morose* in it.   I wish
I could shew it my Fanny!—The next morning Monday
January 14th I was preparing for breakfast, but my
idle mate yet in bed, when George arrived, to whom he
had promised his *mare*—He was going on a hunting party
with his brother William—who—strange to say?—has
lately taken an unaccountable fancy to this am . . . I
do not love to use so pleasant a word as *amusement*!—
Our dear Mr Lock who so detests these sports, cannot
be pleased—and that makes me doubly the reverse when
I hear, or think of this new pursuit—He will not however oppose—Concluding I doubt not, and *justly* in all
probability, that his son will soon be surfeited if the
reins are left in his own hands—but the vexation is that
he has infected his brother Charles, who during the 4
Holy days allowed him at Xmas was daily lamenting the
weather which prevented him from hunting?—George
too is *initiated*—Tho' he assures Phillips and me solemnly
he *does not at all like* it, and only goes because his brother
William desired it—Their party on the present occasion
was of about a *dozen Farmers*, who had requested M^r
William to join them!—All the *good* that has, or I think

that *could* accrue from this amusement is that it has
given rise to a few very spirited and clever sketches of
hunters and huntsmen, which is I hope *some* compensa-
tion to Mr Lock. Mr William has taken a good deal
of pains to induce Phillips to join him on these excursions, but, to my great satisfaction without any effect—
not *wholly*, tho' in part, from disliking the pursuit—
but he feels that it must be an unpleasant one to his
dear and incomparable Father, and therefore he has not
only declined, but freely enough enlarged on his want
of relish for it. The mare however was lent to George,
who wished for it—and who, very fortunately had not
much reason to repent of having her, tho' he had some
—for she grew so unruly and wild in the chase that he
could not manage her, and she was with difficulty
stopped in her career by the party, who were alarmed a
good deal for him—How frightened should I have been
had I heard of it at the moment it happened! We had
but just breakfasted, and repaired to our several occupations when Mr Hoole Senr arrived—intending good
naturedly to settle in the most convenient manner the
little girls purposed visit to Mickleham—It was arranged
for the following Thursday, and that they should stay
till the Tuesday after, at which time Phillips purposed
to be at home again. I carried Mr Hoole into Edward's
room, as he wished to see his work, and there they took
some chocolate together—We soon were carried to the
window by hearing a cry of hounds—and found the
cause was the poor little hare which had been the object
of the pursuit, had been driven into the river and at
that part of it which separates our meadow from the
Park. Phillips immediately ran out to join the hunters,
and soon after returned with Mr William, who seemed
a little *ashamed* of the conclusion of their expedition and
better pleased to talk upon other subjects—He seemed
to like all Edward had been doing since his last visit
extremely—and Phillips shewed him the sketches he had
made from our sweet boy, and the promise we had
extorted that he would attempt him upon canvas—M^r

William who was much pleased with the sketches very
kindly offered him immediately an *eysel*—and all the
colours, brushes etc that he could want. The eysel
and canvas were all with which he was not already
prepared : but that he might have the precise size that
he wanted Mr William proposed that he should walk
to Norbury with him and choose it for himself—his
horse he had already sent home—We pressed Edward
to this being very desirous of fixing him to his promise,
and as he could not but be gratified by Mr William's
good natured kindness, he did not resist, and they set
out together—Mr Hoole in the meantime had taken
leave—Edward was not long absent—he returned full
of the kindness of Mr William who had insisted upon
assisting him with so many things that he [and] our
man could scarcely bring them at once. I need not tell
my dearest Fanny how much I was pleased at all this,
nor how delighted at the thoughts of the picture I
should get—and that not merely—no, nor really not
more than *half* for my own sake—but from the hope
of its encouraging Edward in resuming portrait painting,
which Mr Lock most kindly and strenuously had advised
us to persuade him not to give up—in the evening we
sent for the canvas, eysel, etc—and I had a sweet note
from our dearest Mrs Lock who wished to have seen us
the next evening but Phillips was to go early to town
on the Wednesday and had so much business previously
to arrange that we could not—At breakfast Tuesday
morning January 15th Edward and I, as it often happened,
met before Phillips was ready. I had a letter from
Esther lamenting Edward's absence and how much he
would be wanted at their concert—this made me not
only *wish* that he should not miss it, since I was sure it
would give him much pleasure, as well as that he would
be of great use, but even press him to accompany Phillips
—He professed no desire at all to go—unless I could—
and with all his delicacy and gentleness, expressed so
persuasively his wishes that I *could*, and *the happiness
it would be to all the party* if I did—that I do confess

I never *for a party of pleasure*, as the going for a *concert* must have seemed, longed more—I could not but be gratified neither by the pains Edward took, and had Phillips been there to second him I don't know how I should have resisted—but—that was not the case, and with the utmost openness I confessed to him that were the expense indifferent to me, nothing would have prevented my taking a peep at all my dear friends upon this tempting occasion—the openness I used towards him pleased tho' it silenced him—and Phillips coming into the room, I read him our Esther's letter, and expressed my wishes that Edward and he could shew themselves at her concert the next night together—this he seconded so strenuously that—at length Edward was persuaded so all thoughts of our having a sitting of our little boy till after his return was cast aside—In the morning he gave himself up to his painting, and the evening we were all employed in packing, with the addition on my part of many letters to write and bills to settle.—The first plan had been for Phillips to ride —but the chaise had rather tired his mare—and at length it was determined that he and his companion would *walk*—the day proved the best calculated possible for such an expedition—and after breakfast my two gentlemen set out—Edward promising to return on Friday, tho' I charged him not if either pleasure or business should interfere—Phillips I was not to expect 'till the following Tuesday.—I had promised my dear Mrs Lock to spend the evening with her this Wednesday January 16th as I did not expect our little nieces till the next morning—but my travellers were but just departed when a note came from our sweet friend to beg we might make a *whole* holyday of it after our long separation—I could not resist—and a most sweet day it proved to me—All this delightful family were well—full of spirits—and of kindness and affection for your Susan— I had an opportunity of reading a little of my last new paquet, concerning the mysterious mother, to Mrs Lock, but *very* little—and the evening was chiefly given

to music—At parting our dearest Mrs Lock begged to
know if, it would be quite *unreasonable* to beg me to
come the next day! I expected the little girls. . . .
" O—then, we are not to see you of an age again I
suppose ? " said dear Mrs Lock—so I promised for
Saturday, when I expected Edward would accompany
me.—Thursday January 17th.—Our little nieces,
Fanny and Sophy, arrived early with the two Mr Hooles
in a post chaise—the Elder was going on to London,
and was soon stopped for by the stage—Mr J. Hoole
stayed with us to breakfast, and the greatest part of the
morning in very sensible and entertaining discourse,
which was not interrupted by the little ones, as I had
appropriated a neighbouring room with a fire, and the
whole large collection of Fanny's playthings, for their
sole use.—Norbury I scarce need tell you was never
trusted of this party ; it would have been much too
dangerous for him, and he would have been a great
annoyance in their plays—Fanny's delight was *excessive*
—and she was an admirable little playmate for them—
perfectly comprehending all their intentions, and submitting implicitly to whatever they ordained—I paid
occasional visits, to watch the fire—but they were very
good, and no mischief whatever was done, tho' they
were full of spirits and delight at having a room, so
furnished with toys to themselves—You will perhaps
wonder to hear Fanny should possess so large a collection—I contrary to my usual custom increased it exceedingly in our visit to the good old woman at Chertsey
—and all our Norbury friends have at different times
largely contributed—and, as Nordia is at present a very
destructive little personage, Fanny even *solicits* to have
all her *best* playthings taken under my care and only
given out on particular occasions—by this means her
store is in good order, and continues to increase. The
little girls in their visit en passant to Abinger had
appeared to me very much improved—I think they are
so—tho' in a less degree than I had then hoped—your
name sake—is not very like you in manners—or any-

thing else—tho' indeed she is a shrewd sensible little
girl, with a retentive memory, and a desire of improvement—but she is still very rude, seems by nature uncivil
and wants softness not only in manners, but I think in
temper for she is generally harsh and overbearing to
Sophy, who I think, as I always thought is much the
most interesting and pleasing of the two—there is a
forwardness, and conceit too in her that I am sorry to
see—and which perhaps might have been checked, had
it struck her dear parents as it does me, tho' now I
believe it would be too late—I was surprised however
by the proficiency she has made in her French since she
went to school she speaks it tolerably, and understands
it really extremely well—Sophy too gets on in this and
other accomplishments—She has I think very quick
parts, and having been less praised, is wholly free from
affectation or arrogance—and there is a kind of naiveté
and constant *gaieté de cœur* about her, that will make
her I believe everywhere the favourite—I was very happy
in having them at this time, as, had they been troublesome, which indeed they were not, I alone should have
been the sufferer—and my Fanny's delight was no inconsiderable one to me—they too seemed to enjoy
themselves very much—and in the evenings I gave myself up to them—they were best pleased in having their
room to themselves in the morning and Fanny was
almost wholly excused, as the time was to be so short,
from all her lessons, during their stay.   Friday 18th we
had *not* the hoped for pleasure of seeing Edward return
—I had a letter from my Captain promising him the
next day—This was a busy one to my Fanny ?—Saturday
however did not bring him, much to the disappointment
of little Sophy, who seems an affectionate little thing
and very fond of him, and myself—in the evening very
near their bedtime I went according to promise to
Norbury, where I had a most sweet evening—a great
deal of it was given up to music, and Augusta burst
forth into an exclamation that she was *glad Mr Edward
Burney did not come* because if he had I would not have

played—this little speech to which a kind laughing assent was given, made me *internally* resolve not to suffer my own repugnance to performing before him to be the means of making him an unwelcome guest—I therefore determined *not* to refuse to play when next we should be there together—My sweet Mrs Lock wished to tempt me for the next evening but I would not leave my little girls so soon again, as I had hitherto *supped* with them, which was a kind of frolic they liked very much, and which I could not give them if I went out at night, however late—Augusta and Amelia very sweetly charged me with many kind messages to them—Sunday morning 20th I sent Sophy and Fanny to church with Anne, and stayed at home with little Fanny, who had a cold, so that I did not venture to take her—My dear little friend George called after the service, which was the last time I saw him, as he returned to Cheam the following day—We had no Edward and I began to think Phillips must have persuaded him to remain in town till he should return himself the 22nd. The next day Monday January 21st was little Fanny's birthday—and Fanny and I made our offerings to her on the occasion, not forgetting little Sophy—to whom Fanny gave one of the most valuable of her playthings with at least as much joy as she had expressed some time ago on receiving it herself—All the dear little girls were I believe perfectly happy—christened a wax doll of Fanny's, which had received no name since Mr William gave it her, and had a *christening cake* etc etc on the occasion— A little before dinner I had a visit from Mr S. Hoole, who accepted my invitation to stay, tho' I had no gentlemen to assist in amusing him. I brought in the little girls to him, having first begged them not to forget to ask after their good friend Mrs Hoole, which they would otherwise certainly have done. Children really require to be taught thankfulness and gratitude—these little girls, tho' certainly born with good dispositions, have not the least idea of their obligations even to those who *load* them with favours and caresses—At Abinger the

whole family had exhausted themselves in kind endeavours to make them happy—but when brought here
they required me to tell them even to say *good bye* to
Mr Hoole when he left them, and expressed neither
pleasure nor gratitude for anything that had been done
for them, tho' I took frequent occasions to point out
how much I thought them obliged to Mr S. Hoole they
were perfectly easy, not to say *saucy*—but he took it all
with the utmost good humour, and being fond of children and by nature indulgent was neither disconcerted
nor displeased by their little airs. We had dined, and
were beginning our desert—My Nordia as usual on my
lap, when the door opened, and a *cri de joie* from Sophy
and me proclaimed Edward—I believe he was not
rejoiced at seeing a visitor with us, yet with all his
modesty, and respectful manner, his eyes looked a little
the brighter for the expressions of joy which his appearance occasioned—I could not make him suffer me to
order up dinner for him, as he insisted he had dined,
tho' I dare say merely on *bread cheese* on the road—but
as Mr Hoole was with us, I would not embarrass him by
persisting too long, and he joined forces with us at desert
—Norbury could scarce eat his from his eagerness to
ask him to take the *faddle doune* and *pay Marlbone*—but
recollecting that when Mr S. Hoole dined here one
Sunday, he had been referred to *him* when he asked
Cousin Edarde to play, he went up to him, and said
"Mitter Hoole do ou pease Marlbone?" "What Sir?"
said Mr Hoole "do ou pease Cousin Edarde may pay
Marlbone? This explanation being perfectly comprehended, and the request made from Mr Hoole, who was
much diverted by the application, Cousin Edarde with
his accustomed complaisance took his little friend on
his knee, and played to him till coffee was brought, and
I was obliged to make him over to Anne.—Edward then
told me he had brought a little parcel for me *from Miss
Fanny*—and expressed his surprise that it was not arrived
—He had walked, and sent it by the stage—I was very
uneasy about it—but as it was in a parcel with *all* his

things quieted myself as well as I could and next morning
it arrived—Mr S. Hoole stayed till near the children's
bedtime—The next morning Tuesday 22nd we parted
with them—I should have been glad to keep them a
little longer, as I found Phillips would not come till
Thursday—but as my sister expected them, and it would
have been too late to let her know the change we could
not—To soften the stroke to my Fanny I gave her a
whole Holyday, and all the indulgences in my power—
the little girls went off gaily and well, tho' perfectly
happy in the visit they had made—and the next day I
had the satisfaction of hearing they returned safe and
well home by a sweet letter from my sister. The dear
Paquet arrived safely this morning—it had by accident
been left at the Mickleham Inn instead of our house—
I wrote instantly to my dearest Fanny, and Mrs Lock
added a half, and told me Lady Templetown, who with
Mrs Egerton was then with her, would carry it to town
the next day, which would be as quick as the post, and
send it on to Windsor. How sorry was I when I heard
how much anxious time was spent by my dearest Fanny
before this letter reached her? My little boy *slept*
for his picture that morning for the first time—it was a
very short nap—yet I was delighted with the head
sketched out in it by Edward. I wrote I believe *meanwhile* to my Fanny, her parcel being yet unopened—It
remained not so however till night—tho' I could but
peep—as Edward was with me from dinner time and here
I must rest in my Journal—as, by the present opportunity—in which indeed I cannot rejoice—I shall have
time to add no more. Edward's long stay in town
had been owing to some business which unexpectedly
occurred to him—Betsey and Richard I found did not
pass again thro' town in their way to Worcester from
Farnham where they were detained till the very last
moment—Adieu and Heaven bless you ever my sweet
Fanny—I am sorry I cannot get nearer to the present
date—for this is three weeks back—but I find it will
be impossible as I must write many letters by Edward,

and scarce any time remains. All have been perfectly well, and very happy *during* these last 3 weeks—All are so now—Once more adieu and Heaven bless my beloved sister !—

SECOND SERIES

a Lundi DE CHELSEA,

[1795].

A present l'addresse plus particulièrement ma chere Fanny—and first let me tell you I rejoice, and so does my Father that the work is of the same [kind] as Cecilia— My dear Father wishes you were not "immovable as to the title—he says that [what] you first gave him of *youth* or *domestic details* did not seem to promise what he rejoices that you now allow, nor what he remembers to have formerly read of the work." I write my Fanny from his own lips whilst he is most hastily dressing to go out. He bids me say he is quite against your keeping the copyright—that it must be a great number of years before in a subscription so numerous as he hopes yours will be you c^d be indemnified for the expenses of printing advertising etc etc—that if you print for yourself you will be called upon for ready money, and for sums which to you will seem enormous—that you will be obliged *to an eternal application to your Friends for transacting your business* and that the various troubles it will create will occupy all those thoughts wch sh^d be bestowed on your work—My Father sees no objection to giving the power of signing receipts to Mr Payne—but declines doing it himself—I very much wish the same power to be freely offered to James, who says he can insure 40 or 50 persons subscribing to himself, (his club friends) who otherwise would wait for the book when it can be had at a circulating library. "I must write in all civility" (says my Father) "to Mr Cadell, tell me what I may say." This page was written under the *dictation* of our dearest Father—I must hasten my end alone—and say (tho' this he did not *bid* me say) that his positive opinion is that you w^d do best, everything considered, to accept freely and handsomely Payne's offer, which he thinks of better and better, on considering it deeper, and comparing with the successes of others—this is his sincere opinion and from all I can gather it is likewise mine. For himself he will certainly give his opinion when called on by you, but he says he cannot act either wth James or Charles and I might add that I am sure he c^d not be prevailed on to become a leader in the business himself. Remember my Fanny I am ever a willing *courier* but you have but to think what I am to see how ill fitted for negociating any money matters or wth men of business. I only can engage to deliver messages, ask questions and so on. I have written in a cruel hurry—10,000 loves to d^r Norbury. My Father is as unable to understand the Tableau Approximatif as myself. The proposals have already been in some of the newspapers.

Saturday, A. D'Arblay, Esq., Bookham, near Leatherhead, Surrey.

St. James' Street,
Wed^y June 24 [1795].

I could not have been easy without sooner thanking my Fanny, and my kind Brother for their dear long letter, had I not written the same day on which I received it to Norbury : and my letters there are to Bookham likewise—Since that time the fatigue and agitation of the last fortnight has been a little more felt by me than before—I concluded my week Saturday by visiting our two dear sisters, and was cheared by the sight of Charlotte and her sweet children, and not less so by that of our Esther, who looks better than when I was last in town, and who *whilst we were together* agreed that we might pass for two of the most " Contentes personnes " in the world ?—Yet dear soul, she is worn and hippish enough and declares herself weary of all that is to be found in this nether world—She did not wait for my information wth respect to your promised work my Fanny, wch however I told her you had commissioned

me with kindest loves to give her—She almost instantly
began speaking of it wth much rejoicing, and had heard
the particulars from Marianne, who is still residing at
Chelsea, and wrote them to her Mother—that dear girl
and Sarah had both expressed themselves *rapturously*
on the subject when I first saw them the day after my
arrival. Charlotte was likewise preinformed of your
plan, tho' I do not now recollect by whom—and in high
spirits and expectations from it—before I quit the subject let me tell my Fanny, if James has not (who has
adopted a disappointing way of writing and sending
his letters off to you from some coffee house by w^{ch}
means I neither see nor can add a line to them) that
Mr Payne will certainly undertake the advertising
properly for you if you wish it—but James seems doubtful whether my Father may not have undertaken this
business, and two cannot be employed about it—Let
me name another thing—in y^r proposals I s^{hd} think to
say a novel would be more unexceptionable and more
certain to attract than *a new work*—My Fanny will consult
Mr Lock upon this—here I find all around me of my
opinion—I find too (and I imagine my Father has told it
you) that Mrs Crewe is for *a guinea* subscription *in all* but
to be p^d at once—My Father—Mother—James etc think
the subscription at a guinea w^d fill infinitely quicker than
at a guinea and half—for my part, I confess I think the
same, tho' I shall *begrudge* your *six* volumes at this price
excessively, unless they are small—my Father and James
have I imagine written so largely on all this that I shall
now have done, trusting my dearest Fanny will weigh
all, consider all—and determine upon whatever is wisest
and best. I am writing miserably, wth 2 or 3 conversations going on among the children, M^{rs} B—and one
of the maids—but I shall be too dissatisfied if to morrow's
post sh^d escape me—Our Esther shewed me on Saturday a very long letter from her Fanny, full of minute
details—all of them promising more comfort and good
than could reasonably have been hoped for in her situation—she writes in revived spirits, and indeed it w^d be

strange if she were not touched as well as cheared by
the considerate and amicable attentions shewn her
where she is, but particularly by Lady Beverley and her
eldest daughter Lady Charlotte Percy, whom she says
she can only compare to Miss Amelia Lock for sweetness and perfection. Sunday and Monday I sh^d be
tempted to pass over in my account to my dear Brother
and Sister—but it is best to be sincere, and besides—
on Tuesday I had a message from our beloved Friends
who wished me to have breakfasted wth them this morn^g
and grievous as it was to me, it proved impossible—and
of this you will hear—but you must hear at the same
time my Fanny that since yesterday I have been amend-
ing—and that this eve^g I am almost well—I have had
a good deal of fever—but if I have a tolerable night and
the weather is not very perverse, I think I shall be
quite able to see our dearest Mrs Lock to morrow—I
find she remains in town till twelve—Charlotte has
deferred her Margate journey, and waits for warmer
weather—She drank tea here yesterday—to-day I have
seen Mrs Dickens, who behaved in the handsomest manner
possible, and indeed very pleasantly ;—and our Esther
has dined here. Dear James is full of kindness and
cordiality even encreasing I think daily—Mrs B. has
been very perfectly obliging too—and I really believe
is not dissatisfied with her guests—She is very good to
both the children and Martin and Willy scuffle and romp
without quarrelling—Willy's manners alas are not likely
to be much improved by his original little companion
—but at present—to see him joyous and happy nearly
contents me—he thinks poor little boy he is here on a
visit, and came to me yesterday to ask in a low voice
when we were *to go home* ?—I should like to write a
few lines to my kind Brother—and to thank him for his
touching letter—I don't know whether his English does
not make it the more so—but I must finish this sad
scrawl which I have written at many different times,
and he must take hasty but very heartfelt thanks from
me—Pray tell him I am not inclined to dispute the *degree*

of his affection—I am very well aware how much greater
it is than I deserve—but if I had not some loved friends
so very good to me, what sh^d I do ? surely I then *must*
sink—I feel pleased that he likes to look at the engravings.   Shall I tell you what the morning's dawn first
presents to my view ?   dearest Mrs Lock's portrait—this
is at the foot of my bed, beneath it hangs Cecilia—and
when I turn to the side opposite the light, I see my
Norbury.   I had this morning a letter from that dear
darling—full of kind affection—he says he is quite glad
Aunt D'Arblay and his Uncle, and cousin Alexander are
so well, and *so pretty* (all 3 of you he means no doubt)
he is very sorry his dear wife, and all her family have
been ill—*I am sure* he says, *they w^d if I was*—the place
looks very pretty he says now the leaves are out and
adds " *I am sure Norbury must* "—He wishes dear boy
I c^d *come* and see his garden.   How kindly my Brother
hastened to execute all my commissions—his acc^t of
his visit to Mrs Arnold is capital—I hope you read of
the ugly dame etc ?—He is very good to take care of the
poor rose tree—if it recovers I shall owe it to him.—On
Saturday I am to go to my dearest Father's—he talks of
a *month* my Fanny—the 18th of July will therefore be
impossible.   I w^d fain be wth you on the 28th cannot
our sweet Babe's *half fete* be the 18th *Augt* since so kindly
you have deferred it—I sh^d have been much pleased
to have seen the good nurse again—Adieu adieu my
Fanny—take your little niece's affec^{te} love and kiss again
for me our Alexander.   I beg to have little Cecilia's
letter and dialogue if possible by return of post—direct
to Chelsea if your please—*M^{rs} D'Arblay, Bookham,
Surrey.* (Thursday morn^g I have had a quiet night
my Fanny, but the weather has been such as not only
to render it out of my power to see our dearest Friends
but even to send the children with this letter and a
few lines to Mrs Lock.   Give my tenderest love when
you see her.   I assure you I have nothing remaining of
my late unwellness but a little degree of weakness once
more adieu.

NORBURY AND FANNY PHILLIPS.
By Edward Burney.

JAMES STREET,
Friday, July 3ᵈ [1795].

I must heartily thank my Fanny for her kind letter,
and answer it at more leisure. I will only say I rejoice
in the news of Mʳ George's having got the Mickleham
living—and that all relating to the marriage goes on so
happily. The state of *your* affairs my Fanny wᵗʰ regard
to the new work, gives me great delight, and I must
add much anxiety—I perceive that 3 persons all loving
you, and desirous of forwarding your interests make
nevertheless three not very good counsellors, because
no conciliation seems obtainable from them, and their
opinions on many important points are *far as the poles
asunder*—I should hesitate greatly in determining you
to which to adhere; lest future circumstances shᵈ prove
you to be a loser by following my opinion—however,
since at a distance it is impossible for you to guess the
kind of difficulties that arise, I wish to give you the
best idea of them that I can—Our good Carlos met me
yesterday at James'—He is so sanguine, and so determined in his opinion and at the same time so active and
so zealous, that in listening to him I confess I could not
but wish the whole matter might be thrown into his
hands without reserve—I felt this whilst we were alone
—but when we were joined by James and Mʳˢ B—I
perceived the former was so *much* hurt by a supposition
that a better offer than Mʳ Payne's was in the least
likely to be made, and that his wife was so much offended
at the idea of a meeting between her Brother and the
other booksellers in wᶜʰ the *highest bidder* was to prevail
(this was Charles' proposal) that I felt much staggered.
Mʳ Payne's proposal seems to me really a liberal one—
he is a particularly honest, fair dealing man—if any
agreement is entered into with him there is a greater
certainty both from his general character and from
his connection with our family of its being unequivocally and honourably fulfilled than can be expected
from any other Bookseller, and at least to give him
no dissatisfaction is highly to be desired—Now our

14

Charles' intentions, if he has power given him to do as he pleases will infallibly I perceive occasion a defection on the part of Mr Payne, whose pride his sister will interest in the matter, and James I am sorry to say is likely to take the affair up as an offence to himself. I am obliged to write hastily—and perhaps *too* openly my Fanny—but it is cruel to me to have such thoughts and conceal them from you till the moment that decides the business is past. Charles' temper is such, that, tho' he now declares *all* to be wrong, and opposes every idea of my Father and of James, I am convinced he will take no lasting, nor even a momentary offence if your want of reliance on his success, or your fear of dissatisfying others, or a different opinion of your own determines you on declining his very brotherly and zealous offers —this is a real comfort—Now he may be *too* sanguine in the matter—and if he is trusted, he may perhaps affront the persons in question, who are all so much connected wth one another, that the declaration of one of the 3 that they declined treating further if angrily given, might perhaps induce the others to make a similar declaration—and Booksellers of less eminence and wealth will not be able to make proposals equally advantageous —All this I venture to throw out my Fanny to you, as I sh^d if we were together, depending upon it that you will see the real motive that prompts me to say whatever occurs to me on the subject—pleasant or unpleasant. With respect to my Father, I believe he will acquiesce wth pretty nearly equal readiness either with James's or Charles's opinions—but he shrinks from the idea of taking *any* active part—and the other two wish each to have the *whole* regulation to himself or to have nothing at all to do with it. I cannot tell you how vexed I am to give you this unpleasant statement, nor how vexed I have been in my visits to James yesterday and to day. however I believed it must be to *me* that at present you must apply for commissions—I have already been to Mr Payne with 260 receipts, which he desired to keep, they are in 3 papers from no 41 to 100 f^m 101 *to* 200 and

f^{m} 201 to 300—the following 40 numbers my Father has
kept for himself and Mrs Crewe, with whom he dines
to day—the first 40 were not in the parcel you sent us
and I suppose were taken out by Mrs Lock before they
came to us—in all we received 360 by various ill luck we
never got them till late yesterday evening—they were
sent to James' immediately where I found them when
I called at about 10 o'clock to day. After a long unpleasant discourse between him, our dear Father and
myself Mrs B. putting in a word from time to time, *I*
proposed being agent with Mr Payne—and having received my Father's willing leave, and James' tacit acquiescence I set out to him—He very readily and wth
his usual civility answered my queries—and undertook
the proposals being immediately advertised in the best
newspapers, and the distribution of the 260 receipts
to his colleagues, in equal numbers—When those were
gone he said he thought it w^{d} be best for the booksellers
when called upon to sign their own names adding for
F D'Arblay, a mode he thought preferable to their
being sent ready signed. This I passed over without
discussion and believe there w^{d} be no occasion to object
to Mr Payne's having the power given him—but that
may be settled some time hence. I enquired of him
if there were any particular kind of book for Ladies
who took in subscriptions—he believed not he told me
but supposed a neat memorandum book w^{d} be perfectly
proper. He made no enquiries and of course I said
nothing of his proposal—James now says there is no
necessity for you to answer it instantly, since the booksellers have not written to yourself—Chas advises against
any answer till after Xmas—and my Father thinks if
you were at present to accede to any proposal w^{ch}
might occasion it to get abroad that you had parted with
the copy right, it might probably lessen the zeal of the
public in subscribing, from an idea that the benefit w^{d}
not be yours but the booksellers. James this morning
has two or 3 times declared his wish that you w^{d} *keep
the copyright*—but whether this w^{d} be his cool and last-

ing opinion, or only the effect of present pique, I am quite unable to say—however to suspend your decision I believe may be the wisest thing to do and give *least* dissatisfaction, for to give none when 3 persons all give different counsel is alas impossible. Before any absolute agreement c^d be made your Triumvirate however are unanimous in declaring that the bookseller or booksellers who may be dealt with (I understand Payne, Robinson and Cadell have agreed to go together in the business if you accept them and this by the way alone would preclude our Charles' plan of setting them upon bidding *against one another*) must be told whether your new work is of the same nature as that of Cecilia—this enquiry has already been made to those who c^d not answer it, both by Mr Payne and Mr Robinson.—My d^r Father charged me to urge you to weave into one story of interest and length what you had yet to write— he thinks y^r book consists of *detached* stories, and that the Public are all longing for and the booksellers depending on another Evelina or Cecilia—as Mr Payne (whether you print for yourself or sell the copy right) stands foremost amongst y^r booksellers, and is willing to take on himself any trouble that may result from it, my Father and James both wish you in future to address yourself directly to him when you have directions to give—but sh^d this be disagreeable to you, whilst I am here let me be your Mercury, and I promise to do the best I can in executing yr commission as I know Mr Payne and have now been once, the awkwardness that might belong to it is at an end. Chas being at Greenwich renders it out of his power—moreover he is going Monday to Margate—God bless you my Fanny and my dear Brother and your little love—I write this from our Charlotte's, and the sound of the bell w^d oblige me to stop even if I had more paper. Mind my d^r Father and Chas are very kind ? [So is] our James whom I cannot find the one [way now] to satisfy—how sorry I am for the [worry] to you.

M^{rs} D'Arblay, Bookham, near Leatherhead, Surrey.

My dearest Fanny I rejoice to hear of your good intentions in the writing way—pray send me word in your
next to our dear Susan whether you ever rec^d a letter
I sent you 6 weeks ago with the acc^{ts} in it.—How is
my d^r Godson in *caps*?   I have found two or 3 of
Clements, wch are much at his service.   Send me word
if they will be useful—I will not fill the paper on acc^t
of our dear Susan, so adieu my dearest Fanny.   My
love to my Bro^r d'Arblay, and kiss my dear godson for
y^{rs} ever and ever most truly,

C. F.

CHELSEA,
Sunday night, everybody gone to bed [1795].

I was not disappointed in my hopes of finding a
letter from dear Bookham at my arrival here, which
was not till eve^g yesterday—I thank my Fanny for so
speedily complying with my desire in returning sweet
little Cecilia's extraordinary performance, which her
dear Mother was anxious to possess again, and I have
sent it her—I have scarce been able to find time for
writing a most hasty scrap to our Mrs Lock since my
arrival here—and now I must, if at all, write equally hastily
of you—to you both my dear and kind correspondents—
It vexed me *additionally* that I was not able to see sweet
Mrs Lock, because I foresaw it w^d mortify, and create
anxiety in *you* my Fanny—but be assured that all my
complaints have left me after a week of suffering, for
on Friday I was ill again.   I seem to have thrown them
compleatly off, and since yesterday I have had neither
head ache nor toothache, nor any other bodily ache—
the happiness of being under my Father's roof, revived
by the sunshine of his kindness and delighted by his
uncommonly excellent spirits and good looks is not lost
on me either, believe me—I hope my politics will not
end in lessening my favour with him dear soul—but
they stand sadly in my way—I w^d not presume to argue
against his principles—but I confess it has given me
2 or 3 times such a pang to hear Individuals mentioned

with contempt and sometimes execration whom I have
never thought of but to respect and admire them, that
I tremble lest my constancy s^{hd} forsake me sooner or
later, and my resolution of listening to what I cannot
help hearing in *silence*, be quite too severe an exertion—
Don't let this frighten you however—the individuals I
mean are persons I never had the pleasure or sorrow
of knowing tho' I feel so much interested for their characters, and have sincerely deplored their fate—Nobody
has tried me by an attack upon our Friends—and they
may as well not, car pour le coup de n'y tiendrois pas.
But let me talk of your *new work* my Fanny—I cannot
say I compleatly enter into your objections to the *word
novel*—Evelina and Cecilia alone w^d ennoble it in *my*
mind I confess, even had there never existed a Richardson or a Cervantes, or a Le Sage or a . . . At least half
a dozen more, to whom the world is indebted for reading the most universally delightful of any that can be
named, and which these writers have agreed to entitle
novels—however I am glad the word is avoided since you
dislike it, tho' I believe associated with your name it
w^d give only ideas of delight to everybody else. My
Father says he will write my dear one and will give
me none of his messages, tho' most gladly I would have
undertaken their delivery—Mr Payne undertakes the
advertisements and James wants you to be in town—
but I take it for granted you will wish to avoid a journey
now, tho' you w^d find all very conveniently prepared
for you at our dear Brother's, Beds, bureaus etc etc—
I trust my Fanny I *shall* get to you on the eve^g of the
27th of July. Did you imagine I had not recollected
what was the 28th when I before mentioned being that
day with you? it will be a particular gratification to
me—but *I* shall beg to have the Parlour bed for me and
little Fanny, and take a room at the Inn for Susan and
my Willie—*or* my two children and Susan sh^d sleep in
the Parlour and I on sofa wch indeed w^d be the bed
I sh^d choose in preference to all the others. I positively
will not have my Brother's room—and my Fanny will

accept of me and mine as our kind and excellent James
does I am sure—She is too good, and too considerate,
and too affectionate not to agree readily to this, as
otherwise I sh^d certainly be forced to make a *very* short
stay tho' I now look forward wth joy to a considerable
one—It is very late my dear Brother, and I must only
say once thank you for your kind English—*sermon*—is it
not a little so ?—but that once is truly from my heart.
I beg you to observe that I write in good spirits, and
that I do not mean that affection and kind reasoning
should *always* be lost upon me—Pray continue to write
me long letters—Our Fanny must now scarce allow
herself two lines to a *correspondent*—I shall be in a fever
for her to advance in her great work—I might however
ask of *her* methinks to kiss my sweet *half* Godson for me
but if you think it will take her too much off, pray
undertake the commission for her—Adieu, adieu—Did
I tell you my little Fanny was very much delighted and
touched by y^r kind letter.

M^rs D'Arblay, Bookham, Leatherhead, Surrey.

Wed^y morn^g, March 9th [1796].

It is a very unusual thing to me to hesitate whether to
begin on a long sheet of paper if I have one within my
reach when I sit down to write to my dearest of Bookham or of Norbury—but I have a vile cold and stupifying
headache which together would have deterred me from
attempting to write at all to day were I not practically
urged to it by a letter I have just received from my M^rs
Locke after so long a silence as began to make me feel
uncomfortable The day after I last wrote to you and
returned M de Narbonne's very interesting and charming
letter, I received a long and most kind one from my
brother d'Arblay—I was I confess disappointed at the
impossibility he tells me of, that Camilla should be
finished before our dearest Friends come to town—however—I did not hesitate in determining to be present at
the reading promised to our sweet Mrs Lock but I

expected to hear when her journey was absolutely fixed to take place, before I determined my own time of departure, or even named it here, which I yet have not done—To day my Mrs Lock bids me hasten—but still does not name her own time of quitting Norbury, and I think the more of that precious commodity is granted to my Fanny the longer and more liberal will be the treat she proposes to us. It will be impossible for me likewise without occasioning a good deal of disappointment to leave town till *the end of next week* —Mr Brabazon is to dine with us on tuesday—and thursday *or* Friday our Charlotte has a dance, where my Fanny would be miserable not to be, and where I confess I should be uncomfortable and disatisfied to send her without me—she is so young—so untaught—so inexperienced, and the idea of appearing and dancing before a number of strangers is so new to her—I forget whether I have told you she has been taking lessons some weeks—but still—nous ne sommes pas trop habiles—I have been secretly vexed enough at this unseasonable engagement—however our dearest Friends certainly do not purpose coming to town till after Passion week, and therefore I still hope I shall arrive to you in good time on *Saturday the* 19th and that my own Fanny will kindly arrange *the time and place* of the reading previous to my arrival—for I would wish not a moment to be lost when I am with you—As I shall leave my children behind, I cannot think comfortably of a long absence from them—and my Fanny must allow for and forgive my weakness on this point— After all, I have lost another post, by a succession of callers—the last of whom were dear Marianne and Sophy, who seldom come to us, and who have spent [the] day here—I am grieved that my poor Brother se ressente encore de son accident—il est bien bon—trop bon et trop aimable d'm'avoir ecrite une aussi longue et charmante lettre quant il avoue ne pouvoir copier de suite —Il le remercie de tout ce qu'il me dit—sans pourtant avoir sur ma conscience d'avoir *calomniée* quelqu'un

comme il m'en accuse. Je suis un peu etonné de ce que
M. Lock n'ai pas eu de reponse de M de N—et quelque
fois, comme il ne homme ni sa lettre ni la mienne dans
ce qu'il ecrit a Bookham je ne peux pas me defendre d'un
soupçon qu'il y a en encore une lettre de perdue !—Cela
ne vous semble s'il pas au moins probable Je remets au
promene où Je vous verrai de parles surtout ce qu'il
nous mande, et sur le plaisir et la consolation que
J'éprouve en songeant aux resources et aux esperances
qui lui restent. Mon cher Frere a bien raison c'était
le c^{te} Chas^s de Dumas que Je rencontre chez la P^{sse}
Je ne sçais pas comment j'ai fait cette faute là—pour le
Chevalier, j'ai bien en entendre que c'était *de Penâtes*
mais il y avait beaucoup de bruit autour de moi—et il
se peut bien que Je me sois mepris—I am very glad
Charles has been with you—and have been *extremely*
pleased wth Mrs Schwellenburgh's letter, tho' my dear
Father seems to doubt so much being intended by it
as my Fanny seems to understand, and he says M^{rs}
Boscawen shares his doubts. Our good Miss Cambridge
seems to have none whatever, and has written me a few
affectionate lines written with great warmth and delight
upon the subject—Let me now my dearest tell you I
earnestly wish you or my Brother to write to Mr Shirley
concerning the money he ought to pay—[It is] too useless to apply to the Major, who may perhaps [refuse]
to speak to him on the subject—James is of the same
opinion as myself, and thinks you sh^d lose [no time] in
making this direct application. I have already told you
any letter to him will be forwarded, directed to him
(the Revd Walter Shirley) at Mr Kiernan's, Henry Street,
Dublin—Have the kindness to give this bit to our M^{rs}
L—It is indeed quite true that to me it has seemed an
age my own sweet Friend since we have exchanged
anything—but I believe my last was a very long letter,
and I *hope* it was received. I have had a tiresome cold,
wch tho' I have not been wholly confined by it, has made
me feverish and weak, and unable to use the time I have
spent at home in any very comfortable manner—even

in scribbling to my own dearest Friends—I am very
very sorry your dear head and eyes have suffered—pray
nurse them—sorry too for your sweet daughter Cecilia—
What a mortification and disappointment—My Willy's
cold is almost gone—only *almost,* but he looks as rosy
and merry as ever—Fanny has her share too. What a
happiness and a wonder at once is dearest Mr Lock's
ability to ride in the Phaeton now *the winter is* come.
I will certainly call as soon as in my power on M^e
Dusaussoy. I have some long sad accounts to give to
my beloved Friend—but cannot enter on them at present—I need not I imagine say I mean emigré accounts—
I refer my Mrs Lock to what I have written to our
Fanny for all that relates to our approaching meeting
etc etc. Heaven bless her and all Hers. 1000 loves.

I am sorry to send you this hasty stupid letter—but
to morrow I may possibly be prevented from writing to
you at all. Last Wed^y our Charlotte had a little
dancing party. Thursday I saw la P^sse et M de Lally
in Edgware Road where James accomp^d me—Called on
Me de Chavagnac—on Esther and dined at Chelsea—
where amendment is very slow. Friday I did my best to
nurse at home and rec^d M de Chavagnac, and in the
eve^g poor good Mr Clarke to tea—Saturday, tho' really
ill, I was carried out by some business wch has given me
pleasure—Mrs Wall takes little Mlle Gourdeau, and I
visited her Mother with Me de Maurville who spent
yesterday morning wth me, and told me many things
I must repeat to you and our Mrs Lock sad as they
are when I see you, or can write more at leisure—Sunday I again nursed at home—Monday I did a *great* deal
—having the carriage—called on the good de Landelles
—wth them on Me de Boisvouvray—on Me de Thieny
who rec^d very gratefully my Mrs Locke's present—I
c^d not before obtain her direction—and last on M^e
de Ternay, for whom, and her family (in wch I *include*
the good Femme de chambre) I feel more and more
deeply interested—I lament quite truly the immense
distance at wch we are placed from each other—I ended

my day at Chelsea—our dearest Father is a little rheumatic—the Invalide not much better than she was—Sarah well, and pleasant—these are mere *hints* of my employments—I shall hope I give you another time [the particulars] Heaven bless you both and the sweet Darling. Pray answer. Thursday morning. My Fanny has just had a very kind letter and send 1000 thanks —I am very sorry my long silence [has] created anxiety but I had been daily hoping for news from Norbury Park and had but *just* sent away a letter to Bookham when my Brother's was brought me—I am vexed that no time is yet named for our Friends journey to town, and for the impediments to my removal next week— Yet I think myself sure that Norbury Park will not be abandoned during Passion week.

M^rs D'Arblay, Leatherhead, Surrey.

CHELSEA,
Sunday, July —, 96.

I am sorry my own dearest Fanny it was impossible for me to write yesterday—My Father had carried me to Town before the Post came in, and we returned too late to save that which went out—so I found your letter, and your notion that we should meet to morrow—which alas cannot be—too late to spare a useless expectation—if possible will be with you on Thursday—but I have scarce a hope sooner—I am vexed particularly on account of our invaluables at Norbury—otherwise our dearest Father is so exquisitely kind—I scarce should know how to resist his desire of keeping me. Moreover the reading of Camilla with him is an enjoyment of the *highest* sort, and it goes hard with me to relinquish it—he is *delightfully* enthusiastic—and for myself I am perpetually discovering new beauties, and sh^d be too happy if I c^d find terms to express the emotions of EXQUISITE pleasure and of admiration with which I am alternately filled—I was not in many places aware of the wonderful skill with which the story is conducted at my first read-

ing so that I am now making new and delightful discoveries continually—and the incomparable simplicity
of dear Sir Hugh—the perfection of Edgar, the charm
of that darling Camilla and all that most touched or
most highly amused me in the first perusal, at the least
lose nothing in the repetition, tho' the first forcible
impression made on my mind is still so fresh—I scarce
know how to tear myself away from the subject to talk
to you of anything else—but I must—for our niece
Fanny [1] (who is properly bewitched herself, and to
whom therefore I can talk with unrepressed animation)
is here to spend the day, and to morrow I shall have
1000 employments for every hour. I hope our sweet
Alexander will have got rid of his teizing rash when I
return—I shall be quite sorry to have him seen disad-
vantageously by Miss Cambridge and Miss Baker—Why
do they come to you now. My dear Father is quite
disappointed at the delay of y^r Windsor account—for
heaven's sake make haste and let him have it. I have
not uttered *one word* relative to what passed there—but
my Father, who has refrained from asking questions
that he might hear all from yourself, will be really
mortified if you keep him longer in suspense—if you
have the *power* therefore let him forthwith have a new
sheet. I am very sorry to have missed James—and fear
I shall not see him here for he was not come yesterday.
I will do all that is possible with respect to the books,
M de Chavagnac's journey being again delayed—I must
try to see him and his amiable wife once more—I thank
my brother for copying our Charles's opinion, which
is such as I should have expected and very satisfactory
—poor Esther is quite ill with the toothache—I have
had a few lines from her with a few words on the " wonderful beauties " of Camilla—as soon as she is a little
easy she means to write to you—I have got for M
d'Arblay a little parcel from Windsor, containing I am
persuaded his watch—and two other small parcels w^{ch}
look like proofs—and the first book from hence, all

[1] Daughter of Ch. Rousseau and Esther.

which I shall bring to you—but I have heard nothing of the Taylor—if I had known his direction and what was to be paid I w^d have tried to call upon him—if anything can be done by me pray let me know—pray tell my sweet Mrs Locke how grieved I am not to be able to welcome her first return, and 10co tenderest loves to her and hers. Monday morn^g I am now without a hope of seeing you till thursday eve^g. I trust no contrariétés will deprive me of that joy then. I take it for granted you have heard nothing of my Willy since I left you—if I had foreseen this delay I should have desired Susan to have written—in a fatiguing hurry I must only add Heaven bless you my Fanny and give my kind love to my Brothers.

> *M^{rs} D'Arblay, Bookham, Leatherhead, Surrey.*

> *Tuesday, July 19th*, Chelsea, 96.

Your young namesake and I were near an hour waiting at the Inn yesterday, and I was quite sorry dear M d'Arblay c^d not guess it, and write his letter to the *Tailleur* and tell me what I was to pay the Gentleman out of the £10.—and that I sh^d unnecessarily have hurried from you and the darling little boy, whose sweetness at our parting makes me yet tender to recollect—We were fortunate in passengers—they were more than decent—our journey was without crosses or accidents of any kind, and we arrived a full hour before the dinner time at Chelsea, warmly greeted, and even *too* warmly by the *Patient,* who tells me her agitation was too much for her—I little foresaw such an honour w^d ever have been mine when we so vainly struggled not to *dis*satisfy in days of yore hopeless of doing more—I found a letter had just been sent off to me wth a renewal of invitation, wch letter may keep till I see dear Bookham again if my dearest Fanny has not already sent it off—I had been but a few moments surrounded by the family party, when our dearest Father asked me if I suspected the scheme he had in view for me ? I was fain to confess not having the gift of divination, and perhaps you will not readily imagine his idea. "Why then, my dear Susey, as I suppose like myself that you have yet only *gobbled* the *Cam*, from eagerness in the story, I want to begin it over again, and that you and I sh^d read aloud alternately—everybody being agreeable." The proposal absolutely enchanted me—and we have done scarce anything since but read and talk over the dearest of books—of which fortunately the Patient (how happy and just is that title) is so really fond, that we meet with no rubs and excite no soft melancholy in pursuing this delectable occupation—How do I wish you were in some snug corner, and c^d hear the laughs, the exclamations of how *well* that is said ? how deeply that is considered ? how sweet—how comic—how keen how delightfully described etc etc etc wch are breaking forth continually around.—My tongue here is *rengagged* [sic], and my dearest Father's pleasure is so delicious to behold, that my own seems almost doubled by it—With all this we have yet read slowly, and are only past the *studies of a grown gentleman*—I foresee I shall not compleat this lecture here : but shall be content to read the last volume in coy upon my dear Bookham tree, where I trust I may uninterruptedly give myself wholly up to it—This morn^g the Patient having been, as she says, too much exhilerated by the exquisite joy of seeing me ? ? c^d not get up to breakfast—and my dearest Father is going out, and dines out—so there's an end of my hopes of proceeding for to day—but he has just been writing a letter to Charles at the Isle of Wight, wch he suffered me to read. The first page is on some Homerical business, in consequence of a letter my Father had from a Dr Osborne who much respects Charles's erudition, and wishes to consult him but he c^d not turn over the leaf without speaking of our new acquisition in the Family—and tho' most of the things he says concerning it have already been written to yourself, I could not help wishing you c^d see what our dearest Father has written to Carlos, from whom by the way he has heard

nothing since his travels began—I began with expressing
tout simplement this wish—it was first treated laugh-
ingly as nonsense, but just now the letter was again
put in my hands to do what I w^d with—it is therefore
that I have began one to my dearest Fanny in so great
a hurry—and so now to transcribing—"What think
you all of your little niece and kinswoman Camilla ?
she soon fastened upon me, and with the partial fondness
of an old Grandfather I doat upon her so much that I
think of nothing else night or day. Besides the story
entertainment there is here and there better writing
and deeper thinking than in either of her former novels
—less oppressive distress than in the last volume of
Cecilia, and a wider and deeper reach in the knowledge
of the world and of the human heart—the moral tendencies are so numerous, delicate and free from severity
and cant, that the work seems to me the best and most
impressive system of female education that I have ever
seen—Sir Hugh is a delightful and perfectly original
book character—everybody must love him through all
his deficiencies of knowledge and intellect. M^r and
Mrs Tyrold are as perfect in their situation as humanity
will allow—Edgar is a handsome likeness of William
Locke, and sufficiently punished for his too fastidious
system of ideal perfection." (Dear Edgar ? he w^d
never have been too fastidious but for M le Docteur
Marchmont—this is only an aside of mine—you must
excuse) " Lionel certainly deserved to be hanged and
Clermont to have been punished for his extravagance,
insolence and *imperence*, and Dubster is a vulgar and
detestable animal—but not out of nature—his language
is not his only merit—his sordid ideas are truely those
of a low tradesman—there may perhaps be a little too
much of him and of Mrs Mittew for squeamish stomachs,
or those who read novels only for the love stories they
contain ; but the mixture of characters, for the sake of
contrast, is here as necessary as shade in painting or dis-
cord in music—Miss Maryland—the amiable Miss
Maryland will be doated upon by all young readers ?

tho' your niece Fanny B. writes to Sarah that this lady is ' just what I shall be myself twenty years hence and *I hate her accordingly*'—Mrs Alberry is a compleat saucy fine Lady—with wit and knowledge of the world, yet free from vice—the Baronet is an improvement upon Meadows—with yet more affectation but more sense . . . and what say you to the nothingness and insipidity of the beauty of Indiana ? the goodness of heart of Eugenia ? and the delightful sprightliness, impudence and innocence of little Camilla ?—the character given of her in childhood by her mother M^{rs} d'Arblay is exquisite." Our dearest Father after laughing at himself for complaining of want of leisure yet reading and rereading, and commenting thus long on a romance, says " but tho' Sall has dubbed me Dr Orkborne for making dinner wait etc and Dr Orkborne never reads novels, I sh^d think Dr Marchmont likely to be pleased with the *picture of youth* ; and that you wth all y^r *learning* have more of the latter than the former in y^r composition." Adieu my dearest dear—The nosegay was faded but still sweet when we arrived yesterday, and rec^d very graciously—1000 loves are sent to my Brother d'A.—and to you—Kiss my little cherub for me—I hope not to stay from him long enough to be forgotten—Heaven bless you—I put the [letter to] Mr Payne instantly to the post. Your 2nd Windsor acct has been greedily swallowed. My Father begs you to attend to his cravings for the 3^d etc. The D^{ss} of Newcastle's guinea is received—My Father has not a doubt of L^y Harrington's.

M^{rs} D'Arblay, Bookham, Leatherhead, Surrey.

Wednesday, 31st August 96.

I cannot help feeling very anxious my dearest Fanny lest a parcel I sent you last Saturday by the Guildford stage should not have been delivered it is booked however at Charing Cross—but if you should not have received it, I must entreat you to write me a line

immediately that I may enquire after it. I must hastily
tell you what has passed since I last wrote—The Major
wrote to me from Buxton no doubt to prepare me for
not seeing my poor Norbury—and yet a lingering hope
remained—that a wish might exist for once to surprise
me delightfully—I acknowledged it scarce to myself—
but c^d not crush it—Saturday eve^s however on returning home with Fanny from Mad^e de Chavagnac's I
heard the Major was arrived, and that he was alone—
finding me absent he was gone out in the expectation
of meeting with me. I was not sorry to have thus
a little while alone to subdue an excess of chagrin
before our meeting. He says he *wished* to bring me
Norbury—but he was out of town on a visit to his
niece Mrs Bunbury and Mr Maturin thought he would
lose ground by such long holidays. He had heard so
much of the growth of Fanny and Willy that he expected to see them yet taller and more stout—au reste—
all is smooth my dearest Fanny—I have fears—but have
hopes likewise—a desire of travelling back *en famille*
has been manifested, but not quite openly declared—
and something even in his own mind seems to balance
the wish—I cannot enter into details—my heart is too
unquiet—but thank Heaven I have none at present
very alarming or very bad to give—and you will I am
sure rejoice to hear our kind and excellent James is
returned from Norfolk—he waited not indeed to hear
of Ph's arrival—a very sad business hastened him, which
relates to our dear Charlotte. Mr Robt Francis Jun
is a Bankrupt and has disappeared—a considerable sum
(upwards of £1000) had been lent him of the 3 children's
fortunes, and it is yet uncertain whether, or in what
degree the Father (M^r R Francis of Ailsham) may be
responsible—at all events it is a very unfortunate circumstance, and must be much regretted by Charlotte—
She came from Richmond to meet James Monday eve^s
and dined with us yesterday—her sweet little girl is
better, but still far from well—dear Charlotte looks
well, and gives a pretty good account of our sister B

15

and a very good one of all hers—I accomp^d Phillips
yesterday to Titchfield Street—and was able to deliver
unheard by any but Edward your and my brother
d'Arblay's kind invitation ; he received it very smilingly,
but I could only beg him to *think of it*—it was not in
my power to talk it over with him—I have had another
sweet letter from our beloved Mrs Locke wth very good
accounts of health.—She says her hearers were *delighted*
with the fifth volume of Camilla. William she says was
particularly struck, and even beg^d her to tell you the
excess of his admiration. " I have scarce ever heard
him express so much " says our Mrs Locke—" You
know he is not demonstratif." (*No address nor postmark.*)

Friday ½ past two Octr 21st [1796].

Not till this morning have I been able to conclude
and send a letter to our darling Friend my own Fanny,
and another to my Father—We travel very slowly, scarcely
more than two stages in a day, and consequently spend a
considerable part of our time at Inns—Yet I have but few
moments for writing, as the little gig generally follows us
very closely.   I should however have sent you a very short
letter sooner, but that I am impressed with an expression
in your last dear one to me, when you say the hearing
Friday was fixed for our departure had *cost you a pang.*   I
wished the news of our being upon our way to be softened
by its coming to you thro' the medium of our ange amie,
and I could not bear the intelligence sh^d first be conveyed
to you by seeing a distant post mark on my letter—How
anxiously shall I wish for news of you and of Norbury
Park when I reach Dublin—Yet in the haste of concluding to our Mrs Locke I forgot to mention where I
should entreat you to direct to me.   At Geo : Kiernan's
Esqre Henry St., Dublin—I shall hope to find a consoling
union letter on my arrival—We proceed so leisurely
that I am sure there will be time for it to arrive before
us.   May you be able to tell me sincerely that you are
well, Your lovely boy blooming, and my dear Brother

free from colds rheumatisms, or any complaint that can
interfere with his present pursuit—I think of your building, and of the situation *of Camilla Cottage* continually
—the thought of your having this occupation and the
train of ideas it produces are dear and consolatory—tell
me if you have changed the spot, and in that case try
to describe it to me—I saw some sweet spots in Berkshire that reminded me of the view you w^d have if you
built where you intended—tho' I looked in vain for anything approaching to our incomparable Norbury hills
in beauty—Friday was the last day that I spent at Chelsea—Saturday our dearest Father called on me, and
we parted expecting to meet again in a day or two—
Phillips was so uncertain to the last minute and when
going is in question so given to delay that I really thought
we might yet pass many days in James Street, tho'
every preparation I c^d make was already made—Sunday
I had the comfort of seeing our two dear sisters—Esther
and Charlotte, they spent the whole day wth me, and
Mr Burney joined us in the eve^g. The Major dined at
Mr FitzGerald's. I felt deeply saddened when they
left me—tho' still by no means without expectation
that in a day or two we might meet again—Monday
however Phillips declared we sh^d go—he went out for
an hour, and stayed about 4—it was therefore late when
we set out—but the weather was unusually beautiful—
a few minutes before we quitted James St I rec^d a kind
note of enquiry from our dearest Father wth a melancholy acct of my Mother, wch did not contribute to
make me set out heroically. What sh^d I have done
had any dear sister been near ? My Mrs Locke who is
another, and how precious a sister—our dearest James
was truly kind, and affectionate—but—it is easier to
subdue one's feelings in his presence than in that of
some others—I am anxious to hear my Mother is better
—it w^d be cruel to me to think I had left my dearest
Father at the eve of meeting a severe shock, which no
length of preparation will prevent his suffering from
deeply—I think the poor soul was materially worse than

I had before seen her when I last quitted her 3 days before my dear Father's account of her encreased sufferings and danger. I can hear nothing of this till I reach Dublin. Monday Bridgenorth. I find it inconceivably difficult to write my Fanny tho' we often do not go above 22 miles a day and consequently live much at Inns—but the gig sets out and arrives so nearly at the same time with us that I have no time to spare from those immediately about me—le temps n'est pas mauvais —Nous avons des broisellards mais nous n'avons pas eu d'orages. I was not quite free from cold at setting out. But the weather generally has been so favourable that I have gained one day what I lost another—in short my colds have not been violent, and our method of proceeding is too leisurely to fatigue *bodily*—neither does it otherwise for my most pleasant time is whilst we are in motion—We have passed thro' some delightful [scenes] and I never see a pretty spot wth indifference. My mind too travels back to where I quitted you my dearest and nos anges de Norbury—I shall hasten this to you, and endeavour to write again if only a few lines before we embark to our Mrs Locke—W^{th} a thousand things to say c^{d} I write in quiet, I can only add blessings and loves on you and yours.

M^{rs} d'Arblay, Bookham, Leatherhead, Surrey.

(This address was erased and at Dr Burney's Chelsea Middlesex substituted with the endorsement " paid at Bookham." The postmark is Bridgenorth.)

Monday, Octr 31st between 3 and 4. –96.

Safe landed at Dublin will I know suffice to my beloved Fanny and my Mrs Locke sh^{d} it not be possible for me to say more—We have had a tedious passage of above one and forty hours, and I am yet wondering to find myself alive to tell it. We embarked Saturday eve^{g} at 9. o'clock, and were not landed here till after two this afternoon—

The first moment I c^d hold my pen and find my crumpled paper, wch I had in readiness, I began two letters— one to my dearest Father, and the other *this present*— the Major is gone to enquire where Mr Kiernan has taken our lodgings, and is to bring me—My Norbury! —we are waiting at the Marine Hotel, which stands on the Quay, where we landed. I sent my last to my Mrs Locke, which was finished at Gwindy in the desolate Isle of Anglesea, from Holyhead, hoping the news of my landing might arrive to you only a day later— but alas our dreadful long passage will render it much longer—at least two I fear—I did not forget the laudanum and coffee for myself and party—but alas—half an hour after we were in the packet I was seized wth that dreadful sickness wch no other sickness can equal, and suffered in an encreasing degree till we reached shore—Never able to take anything whatever the whole time, and what is much more extraordinary poor Susan, my poor little girl, and even Willy were all so sick that except a dish of tea and a biscuit they refused all kind of nourish- ment, tho' the Major had laid in a sufficient sea store, and the passengers were good natured and liberal in offers of supply. Susan was nearly as ill as myself, and poor Fanny part of the time suffered severely, which I had not expected—My Willy's sickness was that of a child—soon over—yet never sufficiently so for him to wish to eat anything—he bore the inconvenience wth extraordinary patience dear fellow—making no outcries or even complaints—had our passage been from Park- gate with this unfavourable westerly wind we sh^d have been *three days longer* everybody tells us—and I think such a passage must have carried me at least to a final one—how wonderful that after such suffering a little weakness and qualmishness should alone remain—Why does not my Norbury come—yet I am glad to have nearly finished a letter to my dearest Father, and written thus much to my Fanny and all my beloved Friends around her : whilst I have the power—when that dear child comes I can only add a concluding line—and if he is much longer I find I must hasten this away not to lose the mail—perhaps I shall have a letter from my Fanny, or my Mrs Locke, or both from Mr Kiernan's—what a comfort that will be. Except the wind during our passage all has been fortunate during our journey—the weather invariably fine—no rain except on one day, and not the shadow of an unpleasant accident. You will guess the great pleasure it gave me to see Bessy and Mrs Sandford in Worcester—not to mention Richard, who is most comfortably situated there, and of whom I heard an *excellent* account, and Mr Sandford who is an uncommonly pleasant man—I was so happy to see his sweet wife so well bestowed—they have a very pretty house on the banks of the Severn, near the new bridge, and the Malvern Hills full in sight—My Fanny may perhaps be curious to know something more of our Avebury visit—Sir A. Williamson sent at last a satisfactory answer to Phillips, wth a draft for the money owing—but he had already determined to carry us there and our dear James from a wild notion of possible chances, Sir Adam having now no nearer relation living than Phillips, strongly advised his introducing his children—As I know Sir Adam long ago had decided to leave his fortune to his wife's nieces, who are pretty amiable girls, now living with him, this notion seems to me a mere chimera—however as the visit was so insisted upon I am not sorry it has been made—we were very cordially received and treated—it was lamentably dull, except for the amusement given us by a monkey, 2 parroquets and 3 puppies. One line more to say my Norbury is with me in sweet looks and seeming to me to deserve the acct given me of him by Mr Wall—I will write soon again, and am a little disappointed at finding no letter from you or my Mrs Locke. Pray write My kindest tenderest love to her and all Norbury and the sweet baby—

M^{rs} d'Arblay, Bookham, Leatherhead, Surrey, England.
(Postmark Ireland.)

Monday 7ᵗʰ Nov –96.

HENRY ST DUBLIN.—I can scarce persuade myself
it is but a week since I arrived here and sent a letter
to my beloved Fanny—that letter can but just now
be received, and I find you and my Mʳˢ Locke have
determined not to direct to me here till you have
heard of my arrival—so I must have patience—but the
time is dismally long since I have heard from you—It
is true that last tuesday two franks came to me from
dear James, enclosing amongst other papers for the
Major, a letter from my Brother d'Arblay, and one from
my Mʳˢ Locke—but both these had been directed to
James Street where I was concluded to be when they
were written—they were joyfully received by me, but
I require more recent news, and particularly wish to
know you are all easy wᵗʰ respect to my journey. I
shall not make a long reply to my kind Brother, who has
doubtless long ago heard from James an explanation
of his disappointment wᵗʰ respect to the books he wanted
—I imagine James never recᵈ his letter. I at least never
heard of it. Mᵉ de Montrond's direction was *Kings
Mead* Bath, as I doubt not my Mʳˢ Locke remembers
—thank him for me for his dear letter, as I now thank
you for the dear lines you added to it. My Mʳˢ Locke's
letter is of a day later—tell that dearest Friend I believe
my envoy to her came very safe in the old silk bag—one
of the brown paper parcels contained letters etc to be
added to the stock you keep of mine, the other the
french Evelina and Cecilia wᵗʰ a petition respecting
them to my Brother—the music book and letter wᵗʰ
the change out of a guinea and half I had recᵈ for Cowthorne were all I believe sent to my Mʳˢ Locke—I had
paid 6 shillings to the de la Landelles for two pair of
garters, and a shilling charged by Cowthorne for his
catalogue—his subscription was a guinea—As I may
not for some days be able to write another letter I mention this wᶜʰ you will tell my sweet Friend, and that
certainly Mad de Mansigny must have two pair of
sheets—I am quite grateful to hear of a coat for good

Me de la Landelle—his direction is No 11 Portland Street near Poland St, Soho—he and his daughters w^d be very glad I am sure to hear of my safe arrival—As soon as I have an opportunity I will write—but my difficulty to write even to you at present is very great—My Mrs Locke's is an exquisitely sweet letter, and I am longing to write to her every day. I hope her cold has long since quitted her, and rejoice in the good accounts of our dearest Mr Locke. My Fanny has been sadly occupied since I left her—I was very much affected, tho' not much surprised when I heard she was able so to hasten to our beloved Father—dearest M d'Arblay—I love him for so readily parting with you, and wth you wth so large a portion of comfort. I want to know that the sweet baby has not suffered by your absence—that you left my dearest Father composed and that you are restored to your dear tranquil home, and little darling, and his dear Father!—a letter from our dearest Father brought me the news [1] wch I had apprehended w^d soon arrive when I quitted him, and it is the only letter I have had directed to me here—I rec^d it the night of my arrival—but not till after I had sealed and sent away one to Chelsea and another to you, wch I earnestly hope were not long in their passage—I am obliged to hasten at present and cannot give you any minute details, or write wth any comfortable feeling of leisure —but I sh^d be sorry to lose another day without sending you some account of our Norbury—that darling child is improved in some respects, and I think injured in none since I parted from him and I feel unspeakably grateful in telling you this, which except to myself will give to no one I am sure more comfort and happiness than to you—but you will have *sympathies* in your feelings—I am sure of my Mrs Locke, my Amelia, my kind Brother—and indeed of the kind satisfaction of every individual belonging to the dearest family in the world—in what I have said however I speak confidentially —With no view of boasting of my dear Boy—who retains

[1] Death of Mrs. Burney.

many of his little idle tricks, and whom I do not mean
to represent as *a model of perfection*—but his heart is
warm, affectionate, tender as it used to be—and *à
l'exterieur* he has rather gained than lost—He is extremely
grown—not merely encreased in height, but propor-
tionably in breadth—his face has more plumpness than
it had, and he has generally more colour—his features
are not changed but enlarged, and his countenance
what it used to be—in his manners he is certainly improved—he is less restless, and very gentle—in the
excellent Family where he is a perfect harmony reigns,
and Norbury whose temper is naturally sweet has nothing to ruffle it, so that he seems and has the character
given him from the whole house of being mildness itself.
Monday night—I fear I must lose another post—I have
just rec^d a dear letter from Esther which will enable me
wth something less anxiety to wait till I hear from you—
What a touching pleasure it has given me !—I will give
you a short journal of this week my Fanny—I had
almost filled my letters to you and my Father at the
Marine Hotel where we landed when the Major came
back without Norbury whom he had not found at M^rs
Cartland's—he was gone out wth her younger son, but
was expected home to dinner, and his good Mrs Cartland insisted on our all coming to her to meet him—my
earnest wish was to drive to the lodgings taken for us
by Mr Kiernan—and to see my Norbury alone—this
however was not to be—and we arrived between 4 and
5 at Mrs Cartland's—she rec^d us most hospitably, and
her 4 daughters seemed all curious to see Norbury's
mother—It is a fine family and appears a remarkably
affectionate one—there are 3 sons—the eldest is settled
at some distance from Dublin—Mr Henry Maturin
Norbury's Master is only 3 or 4 and twenty, and already
a fellow of the college, and there is a son of about 17
whose name ? is Cartland, by a 2nd marriage—I will
tell you more of them another time, but I will not defer
saying that I very much like the Family, and am *more*
than satisfied with the manner in wch my Norbury is

treated—they are all evidently extremely fond of him : yet
not willing to spoil him, or to pass over anything he says
or does amiss. He had returned shortly after his Papa
was gone and was in an extasy of joy I was told at hearing
we were arrived, and so eager to meet us Mrs Cartland
had permitted her son George to set out wth him for the
Marine Hotel, in the way to wch we had missed. I had
however not long to wait—but wished there had been
no witnesses as I really was quite unable to repress a deluge of tears, and scarcely c^d support myself when I
felt him in my arms—the dearest boy kissed my neck,
my shoulders, my gown, my arms, murmuring kind words
of joy and fondness in great emotion—and all the good
and amiable females gently glided out of the room—
the Major was gone with the luggage to our lodgings
and I had not yet seen Mr Maturin. I had the relief
and happiness of passing 5 or 6 minutes wth only my
Norbury and his Brother and sister before the Major's
return. Judge if they were precious to me. I was
then presented to Mr Maturin—and spent a few hours
very sweetly, and with as little restraint as possible before
observers so perfectly new to me—but I saw they entered
into my feelings, and that they were happy in the happiness of Norbury—I left him as late as on Willy's account
I could, and the next day we dined together wth M^{rs}
Kiernan who is a very good and amiable woman—I am
very much pleased with her and her children—Wed^y
was spent in the same manner. Thursday I dined at
Mrs Cartland's with 2 or 3 fellows of the College, and
a Miss Smith who boards there—Friday the 4th we
dined there again in order to see a good procession in
honour of the day, the Ld Lieutenant, the Chancellor
wth his magnificent english coach, the Lord Mayor of
Dublin in one made to imitate it etc etc. Saturday I
had the indulgence of having my Norbury to dine at
our lodgings, and this was my happiest day—Sunday alas
—I dined at Dr Purcell's—he is the Dr Warren of this
place his wife a sister of Mr John Fitzgerald's—a kind of
would-be fine Lady very little to my taste—however

Norbury dined there with me and to day Monday I have been returning visits, and dining at *Drumcondra,* Mrs Kiernan's country house—My Norbury has just quitted me, as I now must you my dearest—I am really quite well—recovered from my fatigue, and have got rid of a violent cough I had on the way, bless and preserve you.

M^{rs} d'Arblay, Bookham, Leatherhead, Surry, England.

Monday night Novr 14th from BELCOTTON.

Time passes heavily with me my beloved Friends—and if all were gay around me, so it must pass whilst I obtain no letters—I sometimes fear mine to you may have been lost—but this can scarcely have happened to all, and this will be the fourth I shall have sent to Bookham and Norbury, and the 8th I have addressed to England since I landed the 31st October—a week ago I had the consolation of receiving a dear letter from Esther, with the most comfortable account of my dearest Father that I could hope for—I have lived on this letter ever since—but when it was written you had not any of you rec^d news of our arrival in this land, and I shall feel internally disturbed and anxious till I know you are all so far easy about me—I was suddenly called upon *to fill up a letter* that was going to Norbury Park a day or two before I quitted Dublin. My Mrs Locke will have conceived that this letter could not be quite as unconstrained as those she is accustomed to receive from her faithful Philly—however it contained only truths very honestly told, tho' other truths might perhaps have been added had the letter not been liable to pass thro' the inquisition before it c^d reach her—She will likewise guess that I sh^d not have *chosen* the very moment I had finished a letter to my dearest Fanny for writing to her, so that both letters must have arrived the same day—I certainly sh^d have preferred giving these notices of my existence at a little distance, since I cannot write when and as often as I wish. I have been in so perpetual a hurry since my arrival that I scarce know what I have written

to my most dear Friends—but I do not think I have
mentioned to my Fanny that I had seen our old Friends,
late *Miss Kirwans*, and that their Father, who is as
singular in his appearance and manners as ever, made
me two very long morning visits, and seemed really
much pleased to see me—he spoke in high praise of
Camilla, and said it was in *everybody's* hands here,
and *universally* liked—that your work in behalf of the
emigrant clergy had gained you in Ireland the greatest
respect and admiration, and that it had procured many
friends to the unhappy men for whom it was written
among those who had originally been very unjustly
prejudiced against them—To all this I listened wth
pleasure—but I c^d scarcely help smiling when he communicated to me his earnest desire that you w^d write
a pamphlet in defence of . . . *the Empress of Russia*, who
he assured me had been grossly calumniated and libelled
in this country—he s^d he w^d furnish materials for her
exculpation, and be answerable for the facts he sh^d
bring forward.—When I assured him you w^d have insuperable objections to writing on any political subject,
he asked me if M d'Arblay might not be engaged to
undertake a work of this kind, which would undoubtedly
procure him *a handsome pension from the Empress* etc.
I made a similar reply for my dear Brother to that I had
made for you—at least I ventured to declare, I was con-
vinced he w^d not write on any subject with wch he did not
feel himself well acquainted whatever respect he might
be willing to pay Mr Kirwan, who was so ready to pledge
himself for the truth of the facts he meant to provide
him with—he was fain to be content with this answer
—only lamenting that so great a woman sh^d not find a
worthy defender.   His daughter Mrs Hill lives ten miles
from Dublin but comes there frequently to see her
Father, and hastened to me the moment she heard of
my arrival—her countenance spoke so much affection,
such warmth of heart and shewed marks of such tender
emotion, that the pleasure I rec^d from her visit was
extremely great—Since I left you all, I have felt nothing

approaching to it except when my Norbury has been
near me—she is an uncommonly good and charming
woman I thank God she is happy too—her husband is
attached to her as she merits that he should be, and
she has a girl and two boys who are the pride and delight
of her heart. I c^d see her but once, my engagements
(some of wch were very worthless and compleatly uninteresting) being numerous, and her stay in Dublin
limited. Neither her husband nor children were with
her—but whenever I go to Dublin I shall have the happiness of seeing her, as she has promised to meet me at
any time I may give her notice and pressed me to spend
some time at her house wch possibly I may do—she
enquired minutely after Esther, Charlotte, and tho'
with less intimacy wth great interest after you and your
little darling—her sister Mrs Barnewall came to me as
soon as she heard of my arrival and I returned her visit,
but we met but once—she too shewed great kindness
and affection—her husband tho' of an Irish family (he
is nephew and reputed heir to Lord Trimblestone) spent
all his life in france till driven from it by the Revolution—
he speaks English tolerably and is a well bred young man
—they have a very fine boy of about half a year old of
wch both seem very fond—I have already told my dearest
friends how pleased I have been with my Norbury's Tutor,
and the Family he lives with—they are amiable and
pleasant people, and Mr Maturin I believe one of the
best young men in the world—very pious—but mild
and untinctured with fanaticism—his religion will do
nothing but good to Norbury, who is not at all inclined
to become Methodistical. You will be likewise pleased
to hear that all Mr Kiernan's Family have shewn me
every mark in their power of distinguished regard, and
even of a quickly growing affection—I owe much of this
perhaps to the impression made in my favour by my
niece Augusta Kiernan whom you remember at Mickleham and who there so soon attached herself to me, and
as it has proved so durably. The day of my arrival I
have told you I dined at Mrs Cartland's—I came home

to our lodgings, at about 8, and was seeing and assisting in putting Willy to bed, when a young person I did not immediately recollect entered the room, and coming forward as if to embrace me, stopt short, her eyes filling fast with tears, and as if struck by the surprise momentarily expressed in my countenance. "Don't you know me—Don't you know Augusta," was all she c^d say—my answer you will imagine—indeed I was really touched by her kind warmth and tenderness of heart—I heard after her first emotion was over that her Mother, whose health does not allow of her sleeping in town or scarcely spending 2 hours at a time there, was come to Dublin on purpose to see me, and presently Mr Kiernan appeared —of him I will content myself wth saying he was uniformly and really good naturedly attentive to me during my stay in Dublin—I believe him to be a good hearted man—tho' a Fanatic and possessed of esprit extrêmement borné—consequently full of prejudice and intolerance —as our lodgings were only a few doors removed from his house, and I found Mrs Kiernan only waited to hear she sh^d not disturb me, to come, I determined to go directly to her—My young friend Augusta was enchanted at my making this proposal, and Mr Kiernan seemed gratified by it—Mrs Kiernan is still a pretty woman, tho' too fat, and in ill health—she has a good deal of resemblance of Mrs Shirley, but seems to me to have some advantages over her late sister, who tho' she had excellent qualities had many little weaknesses which Mrs Kiernan seems to me free from—She rec^d me with cordiality and was unintermitting in her kindness and attentions, and [every] time we met impressed [me] with more affection for me—I really feel grateful for her kindness—Mr Kiernan's sister who lives with them and is I imagine about 8 or 9 ? and twenty seems an excellent woman—with a most obliging disposition and a heart that appears to overflow with benevolence and affection—I owe to her a hundred little kindnesses and such is the tenderness of her disposition that latterly she c^d not mention my leaving Dublin without her eyes filling with tears—Harriet, the eldest daughter, is very pretty, not above 15—a pattern of goodness and simplicity, and at the same time very ingenious, and desirous of information—Since Miss Shirley brought her an account of the Fair at Leatherhead, all her leisure moments have been bestowed on works such as she heard were there disposed of, wch she has obtained a milliner in Dublin to expose at her window and sell for her she appropriates the money rec^d to the Poor— Miss Kiernan, her good aunt, who privately told me this, says she has already had the happiness of clothing many poor families by the works of her hands—I think my Mrs Locke will feel some pleasure in hearing of this trait—my Friend Augusta is a less elegant workwoman —but does all the good she can, and almost daily visits a school of poor children in her neighbourhood, whom she assists in teaching, and to whom she is of more use than the Mistress—She is two months younger than Fanny but considerably larger and more formed—The 3^d girl Selina seems very good, but less distinguished than the others—the 4th Sophia has a charming countenance and manners—She is just the age of dear little Charlotte Francis, and has some resemblance of her, wch added to my partial liking of her—I must tell you that she too grew passionately fond of me—George is a year older than Willy—he is a pretty boy, and seems very affectionate, as indeed the whole family appear to be—the youngest, Matilda, is a fine fat baby of about three years old—if you imagine that Somebody is *outrée* at these fine names you are not much mistaken—he says " they can never *come to good with such names as those.*" I have got much to say of my darling Norbury—but it must be in a future letter—I am to have him with me for a week in next month—As yet (at least till this eve^g when a ball at Drogheda has *entrainé* my usual companion) I have had not a moment of leisure and c^d scarce have enjoyed him had he been with me. We have been here since Friday—Our unfinished cottage is in itself less uncomfortable than I expected, and will probably every day be something better—I shall not

attempt to describe it—but for your comfort will say
that our sitting room is warm, and that the situation is
s^d to be very healthy. I have only had slight colds, and
all around me are well—Ma pauvre petite commence
à se faire un peu à sa destinée, et devient moins triste—
Ma bonne Susanne aussi, et sa santé Dieu mercé se ré-
tablit. Willy n'est pas trop content de notre chateau—
Mais s'amuse beaucoup à suivre les chevaux etc. le
temps est quelquefois assez mauvais, mais nous n'avons
pas eu de grands orages et à l'heure qu'il est tout est
tranquille—before I conclude wth my most affect^{te} love
to my dear Brother, our sweet Mrs Locke and all hers,
I shall entreat you to request that dear Angel to desire
her servant to call at Susan's sister's, *Mrs Newton*, the
first time he goes to Dorking, and to let her know Susan
is quite well—and means [to write] her a long letter
soon—at present the poor girl has really no time if she
is not the best creature in the world I know not comment
elle

Adieu adieu my [love] kiss for me our baby. I viens
de recevoir votre cher lettre du 7 Nov—Milles graces.
J'ecrivir bientot à l'autre ange—

M^{rs} d'Arblay, Bookham, Leatherhead, Surrey. (*Postmark Ireland.*)

BELCOTTON *Wed^y Nov* 23, '6.

I have already sealed a letter to my dearest Fanny which
was only withheld till I sh^d have a safe opportunity of
sending it, when one from her was delivered me enclosing
my sweet Friend's kind and precious lines—What a relief,
what a consolation did it prove to me—I fain w^d have
begun another letter instantly in answer to you both—but
opportunities for writing are rare, and the claims many
—of the former I lose none that I can obtain to
remove the solicitude of some one who loves me, and
to entitle myself to the hope of hearing in return. I
have just sent a letter to my dearest Father for whom
I have been very anxious—and not causelessly as the
sadness of one I rec^d from him yesterday makes me but

MRS. DELANY
AT COURT AND AMONG THE WITS

Mrs. Delany at Work. By Lady Catherine Hanmer

"*I have heard Burke say that Mrs. Delany was the highest bred woman in the world, and the woman of fashion of all ages.*"—*Dr. Johnson.*

Edited and with an Introduction
by R. BRIMLEY JOHNSON

Demy 8vo. Cloth, gilt, with sixteen full-page illustrations and a coloured frontispiece. 16s. net

THE autobiography and letters of Mrs. Delany tell a story of profound human interest, covering eighty-five years of an active and distinguished life. They reveal an unique personality of great charm and strength, who has also something to tell us about all the great men and women of that extraordinarily interesting period—the eighteenth century, from its dawn to its close.

Mrs. Delany absorbed everything with which she came in contact, commenting upon all with eager interest, quick wit, and, to those deserving it, with a ready though kindly gift for caricature. The style of her personal letters is seldom formal or self-conscious, for these are not characteristics of the woman herself :—

> " *The curly-murly fashion of the hair is not much worn now. The town is mussy, though very full.*"

> " *Sure the women were never so audacious as they are now. This may well be called the brazen age . . . . The men are odd, fantastic things.*"

Or, again, was brevity in a friendly letter ever excused in so sprightly, yet sincere, a confession :—

> " *I can write no longer, my ink is a puddle, my pen a skewer, my head stupid, but my heart—ever yours.*"

She has also a delightful habit of referring to her friends by apt pet-names. Thus Henry Hervey is " Apollo's Imp," Mrs. Laroche is " Chatter-chops," Grace, Countess Granville " The Dragon," the Duke of Portland " Sweet William " or " True Blue," and Mrs. Edward Montagu the famous Queen of the Blue-Stockings, " Fidget."

Mr. Brimley Johnson in his brilliant Introduction describes her artistic activities quite as fully and vividly as he portrays her success as a grande-dame. For under the veneer of eighteenth century propriety, Mrs. Delany was essentially temperamental. Her work as an artist was praised by Walpole in " Anecdotes of Painting " and admired for its harmony and brilliance by Sir Joshua Reynolds.

There are examples of every medium in her paintings or drawing ; crayons, pastels, sepias, oils, pen and ink. Her shell-mosaics have been described as like " carving " or " Irish Stitch," and a white-tiffany handkerchief was compared to " an etching in colours on a white ground." Mr. Brimley Johnson points out the real merit in her work—especially in the famous " Flora," now in the British Museum—and comments upon the fact that the colour-schemes she employed were often in advance of her times.

But apart from the series of illustrations (many of them reproduced by the courtesy of Lord and Lady Treowen), the charm of this book must rest with the woman herself and the circle of distinguished friends she gathered around her ; especially perhaps, Lord Lands-downe, the Hamiltons, the Granvilles, the Duchess of Queensberry, and the Duke and Duchess of Portland. Other features of interest are her characteristic essay on " Propriety," and some occasional verses, of which the following, written in her eighty-fifth year, is typical :—

> Allons, M'amselle, votre reverence,
> Hold yourself straight—mind time when
>   you dance,
> Sink gracefully—and bound with ease ;
> (No affectation, if you please;)
> The polish of the person, and the mind
> Is gentleness, with spirit join'd,
> Your task perform'd—then curtsy low,
> And Mr. French will say—Bravo !
> Your busyness done, and you at ease,
> To take your game at Spilakees. . . .

The historical value of the volume depends largely upon Mrs. Delany's intimacy with the King and Queen. In her later days George III gave her a house at Windsor and a pension of £300 a year, " which Queen Charlotte brought to her every six months in a pocket-book that it might escape the tax-collector."

London : Stanley Paul & Co., Ltd., 8 Endsleigh Gardens

too sure. I was very grateful to my Fanny for all the details she gives me concerning him and the late melancholy scene, in which Heaven be praised, she was suffered to assist and console him—but—I shall never cease to regret that at such a period I should have been separated from him—This moment a darling letter is brought me from the sweetest of Friends, with six lines from my beloved Fanny—and I am alone—and I have read it without interruption and been permitted to enjoy all its deliciousness—save the moments I have spent with my Norbury I have not had so soothing a pleasure since I quitted you—Your letter carries me to the paradise that contains you—I see you all—I enter into all your sweet and benevolent occupations—I almost hear you— Can I ever thank you sufficiently for such delight—Yet is it not wholly unmixed, for nothing must be so I imagine under the sun—it is grievous that you should so suffer by the rheumatism—and if we were a little nearer I think I must grogner at you for your *indiscreet* amusements, when dear naughty person, you confess you had such warnings given you—I know by whom— and indeed lament for him as much as for your dear self all the suffering that has ensued—Heaven send the mustard medecine may be efficacious and that I may be able to rejoice in your health as I do in the blessed account you give me of dearest Mrs Locke's—Every line of your letter is most sweet and interesting to me, and how good you are to indulge me by writing so small, and by the cross lines, which are in your hand perfectly clear—a thousand thousand thanks—I am glad poor Alfonse has had the happiness of spending so much time at dear Norbury, particularly as he grew in y^r esteem and did not prove a weight on anybody—I wish his Mother could be gratified by hearing of this visit and that he left you all pleased with him—but I fear no such happy tydings reach her where she is and as you do not mention it, I take it for granted that he has had no letter from her, nor from Switzerland, which is very sad and very strange—the *breastplate* wch defended him

16

is indeed an affecting circumstance—I sh^d wish her to hear of it—tho' perhaps not till she sees him, for such a terrible history w^d leave too painful an impression on her mind whilst he is absent from her. I received only yesterday the dear Princess' letter—she does not give me her direction, wch I entreat to have from my sweet friend—it pains me to be dilatory, or to seem so in answering one whose kindness I so highly prize—if any chance occasions Mrs Locke to write to her before it is in my power to exculpate myself, I shall beg her to account for my not writing—her date is f^m *Norbury Park*. Having an opportunity of conveying some letters free to *Dublin*, I have already fulfilled promises reluctantly given tho' I felt the kindness that compelled me to make them, of writing to three of my good and affectionate foreign friends—Mad^e de Maurville, to whom I mentioned my ignorance of the dear Princess' direction, Mad^e de Ternay, and Mlle de la Landelle—having written to Me de Maurville increases my anxiety to write to the Princess, tho' it is not possible she sh^d suspect any preference, and she is indeed superior to unjust suspicions of any sort. It was an affecting pleasure to me to hear of her visit to Norbury, and the details my beloved Friend gives me relating to it, and to M de Lally's pladoyer are delicious. I am proud for him of dearest Mr Locke's expression that he *envied his pillow*, for I really love at least as much as I admire him—and it pleases me extremely that he sh^d be loved at Norbury Park—I feel what a gratification this visit must have proved to him and the excellent and charming Princess—they indeed (to borrow my Mrs Locke's expression wch I shall use more justly) are *worthy to rehearse* Norbury and its Possessors—I am glad poor M de Chavagnac was indulged with a few days, and delighted by the improvements of his fortunate little Adrienne. My Mrs Locke will tell me when she hears he has had news of his wife, for whom I am sincerely interested—I am glad he knows of my arrival in this land, for I believe in his kind interest and regard—You are very dear to tell me you

sent a good paquet to the de la Landelles, and I must
thank you for it, sweetest Friend, and wish I had your
little fingers to kiss on the occasion—Heaven bless you
for your never failing beneficence! I feel sure that
you have had the goodness to let Thomas call on Susan's
sister at Dorking to make her easy wth respect to her
arrival—This excellent creature is even a greater treasure to me than I expected to find her—I c^d fill all my
paper with details of her various useful services—but
none that I owe her can give me more pleasure than
to perceive that her situation here notwithstanding
many (very many alas) desagrements and hardships, is
less unpleasant to her than she supposed she sh^d find it—
She is very much with me, and almost constantly within
hearing, as the kitchen immediately joins our parlour,
and upstairs she sleeps in a long narrow room, within
our bedroom, with the two children—I have so sincere
a regard, indeed I may say affection for her, and she is
so constantly unobtrusive, modest and quiet, that it is
never a constraint to me to have her in my room, and
often a real comfort—She aids me too in the exertions
I make to recover a little chearfulness. I feel such a
desire to sweeten the sacrifice she has made me in coming
hither, such an interest in whatever may soften her
situation, and revive her, that in her presence I not
only try to appear, but really find myself less sad—how
much do I not owe her? and how touching it is to me
to see that a few moments alone wth me, when I can
shew my encreased regard and confidence in her seems
to compensate all the unpleasantnesses she has to undergo,
and to give her new life and courage—having s^d thus
much, let me for the comfort of my dearest Norbury
and Bookham sisters add, that the impatience and the
roughness she meets with at *some* times, and the total want
of consideration at *all*, are beyond what c^d easily be
imagined, her patience forbearance, and the real use
she is of by performing a thousand disagreeable offices
which were never before expected from her are not wholly
unfelt, and I have the consolation of perceiving that she

is risen in favour, tho' care is taken not to spoil her by expressing too much—Whilst I am yet on this subject I am tempted to tell my Mrs Locke that the poor soul sprained her right arm long ago, wch has occasioned her a good deal of pain from time to time—and lately perhaps by making too much use of it she has felt this sprain very severely—I have made her bind her wrist round wth ribband, but if my Mrs Locke knows of any simple remedy within my reach I shall be very thankful—her arm is weaker and rather swelled—I will beg no excuse for writing so much on this subject—Do I not too well know the exquisite kindness of my beloved Friend which renders everything interesting that can affect those she loves? My Mrs Locke must heed her dreams no more. She will perceive by the openness wth wch I write that without supernatural aid she will not be left in ignorance about me. The M. was a little disappointed by dearest Mrs Locke's answer—but not much, as I find he by no means [admires Miss] Angerstein—but he was flattered by y^r conclusions respecting Belcotton, the more as you are not very likely to see it. Alas! I could not wish you [to] even were I destined here to vegetate for life I think. This was the only part of my sweet Friend's letter that I read—I was called on for no more—nor have I been to read aloud more than 3 letters since I quitted England, 2 of these were my dear Father's— The 3^d was from *la Princesse*—being in french you may imagine how edifying a hearing it must have proved— this intelligence may perhaps interest our Fanny—and obtain me unconstrained letters. I must hasten this away as it is friday and no post leaves Drogheda to morrow —I have written *a baton rompu* as I could find ten minutes, and sometimes am obliged to keep a letter by me many days till I meet an opportunity by wch I can trust it. Shall I tell you anything of Belcotton? I think I will not, for it is not comfortable—and *entre nous* can *never* be elegant—but it is the passion of its Master, and I w^d not for the world he sh^d suppose that I w^d publish my objections to it. I make none to anything

Heaven knows but I cannot so belie my conscience
as to admire, wch is sometimes required—the parlour
since there has been a door to it, for there was none for
a week after our arrival, is warm—wch certainly is a first
rate consideration and a very fortunate one for me—
it is convenient enough too, has 2 little closets, some
shelves in a recess for books, and the walls tho' neither
painted nor papered are adorned with some precious
drawings—I am almost ashamed to say how difficult it
is to me to look at them with pleasure here, tho' in
themselves they are delightful—the room meant for a
drawing room, but in wch we sleep till another is finished,
is large and lofty—but very dark as is the parlour, having
only one window, and that small—the kitchen is really
convenient tho' small—besides these, and the children's
room, there are 3 rooms upstairs and one below which
except papering are finished—The country around is
flat, and I think very dreary—some little hills appear
at a distance, 3 spires and the *sea* which is a grand object,
but one which by no means raises my spirits to behold
—it is at about a mile and half distant from us—We
have a garden at present in great disorder, and the house
is almost surrounded by barns and outhouses, where
blacksmiths and carpenters are continually at work—
Our nearest neighbours are the Brabazons who are above
a mile off—We have indeed a few wretched cabins much
nearer one of wch is in sight from the window of the
room where I write. this acc^t is too true to be very
comfortable—but I think it will be some comfort to my
sisters to be assured I write to them so undisguisedly—
—all these particulars are for them alone and their
beloved mates—I particularly wish nothing may tran-
spire that I say of Belcotton, except that it is yet in an
unfinished state 1000,000,000, loves to all yours—
individually—I can only name my [Fanny] for want of
paper—Heaven bless, bless and preserve you. My Norbury is not to be with me till a fortnight hence, indeed
we have not yet a bed for him dearest boy. Fanny and
Willy have colds and I—but really not material ones

wch astonishes me as much as it will please my Mrs Locke and our Fanny—it is an almost inconceivable thing the state of the house considered. the weather is by no means bad.

Mrs Locke, Norbury Park, Leatherhead, Surry, England.

BELCOTTON *Nov '96.*

I am truly rejoiced in what you say of Sarah, and very earnestly hope you will find cause to approve and love her more and more—Richard no doubt has been written to and she will now I hope take up that correspondence— I think it happy on her account and on some others that Mrs Meeke had quitted the kingdom before this event, particularly as the poor soul by no means seemed to regret her departure, tho' it took place very lately and when she c^{d} have little hope of prolonged existence— Your six lines at the beginning of our Mrs Locke's letter of the 16th were very sweet it revives me to hear that anything you receive from me can give you such pleasure and comfort. I am almost afraid nevertheless I may have s^{d} too much of my satisfaction at my Norbury's appearance. You who know what my thoughts and feelings were respecting him may perhaps have con- cluded more than I intended from the word *improved*— in manners he is however certainly, and I think in person he has yet lost nothing, and in size and height has considerably gained—of his scholarship I cannot judge —but Mr Maturin seems contented wth his progress, and 2 or 3 other persons of the college speak of him as being very forward for his age. All the Miss Maturins tell me he is the sweetest tempered creature in the world —but I perceive he has yet a few *whines*—perhaps he may not fulfil my dearest Fanny's expectations in many points—but as with all my love for him I never expected him to grow up a Prodigy, I sh^{d} be ungrateful and disin- genuous not to own that as far as I have had opportunity to observe or judge him he has exceeded my hopes—I do not mean the hopes I might have formed had we never been separated, and had it been possible for me to give him such a Tutor as I sh^d have chosen . . . but in that case my expectations w^d probably have led me too far and might have occasioned me some disappointment. I have—(*The continuation has been cut off*) —Camilla with me—Somebody had lent it to Mrs Cartland who was charmed [, she told] me but she c^d keep it so short a time that even her daughters had not been able to read it. I was very glad afterwards that the Major (whose 4 sets arrived so late that Ld Charlemont had already procured himself a copy, so that he returned him his guinea) made Miss Maturins a present of the Book—I believe he might have studied a month and not have found anything by wch he c^d so much have obliged them—This was only two days before I quitted Dublin—the Morn^g we set out my Norbury breakfasted with me, and told me he had at his leisure time read almost to the end of the second volume "and have you been much amused?" "Oh Mama *exquisitely* —I think it beautiful?" This was at a moment that we c^d converse unnoticed—the dear little fellow alas is but too well aware that many subjects dear to him and to [me] are liable to objection elsewhere—his caution and foresight surprised me frequently, tho' the very eve^g of my arrival I perceived that the impression made on his mind before we were separated was indelibly fixed. I told my Fanny we arrived at Mrs Cartland's to a late dinner—the dear boy nestled himself in between me and his sister and the M. being on the opposite side of the table, wch was large and filled with this numerous family (there are 4 daughters and two sons at home) was occupied by those on each side of him—Norbury so situated and his mind filled wth tender emotions, was less guarded than he used to be formerly, or than he became afterwards when more composed, and excited painful yet mixed feeling in me wch you will easily conceive—he expressed great pleasure in hearing Susan was come over wth me, and was almost glad that the dinner sh^d be over that he might go and welcome her— All the desert given him he privately slipt into his little

pockets to carry her—" poor good Susan " cried he, in
a tone of affection and tenderness—" you did not say
in your letter " (I had written to him on the road) " she
was with you my dear Mama—and it quite affected me
—I thought her friends perhaps had persuaded her not
to come with you—or " (hesitating and lowering his
voice) " perhaps that Papa might not let her—I did
not think it her choice, because I am sure she loves my
dear Mama too well to bear to leave her—tho'—indeed
—it was very good—very affectionate—really quite
extraordinary of her, poor creature, considering . . .
that shocking affair which—I shall never forget ! !—A
little while after, when a Miss Smith, who boards w^th
Mrs Cartland but who was out that day was mentioned
as being very partial to Norbury " you love her very
much too " s^d I, " do you not "=ye-s I *like* her s^d
Norbury—" it is not as I love THESE *people*," glancing
his eye round at the Miss Maturins, for that is as if they
were my sisters—" but I like her very well "—I expressed
my delight in seeing him, so happily situated " I am
indeed very happy here my dearest Mama—and now—
I have you ! This family (he added) is always as you
see now—here are no violent passions and rages—My
poor dear Mama (his eyes filling wth tears) such as I
hope never to see again, and which give me such pain
to think of,"—amongst various recollections he spoke
to me of his good Nanny Richbill—and of his *poor
Salloo*, and asked me how she came to leave me as she
loved me *and all of us* so much—" Was it Papa who
forced her away ? "—" hush my Norbury " s^d I gently—
he lowered his voice, but s^d " it is very odd—for I thought
he liked her particularly much "—In speaking of Belcotton " you will find it a shocking place my poor dear
Mama " s^d he refraining wth difficulty from laughing
—" but whatever you think of it . . . let me beg you not
to say one word, because that is one of the things Papa
cannot *bear*." Nothing as I have found could be more
judicious than this caution—and I have not failed to
observe it—but you may imagine the effect all this had

on me so immediately on my arrival—I saw the dear
boy scarce ever alone—We dined every day at M^r
Kiernan's when not engaged elsewhere, except one—
tho' I was so situated that I c^d with propriety and ease
have excused myself, it was impossible to gain a respite
even for 3 days without an insistancy on my part w^{ch}
would have produced tremendous tempests, reproaches
of affectation and hypocrisy were liberally bestowed—
Nothing was granted to sorrow, tho' indeed I felt a
great deal for my dearest Father ; for peace sake, tho'
wth great internal reluctance, I therefore submitted.
The single day we dined at home my Norbury was with
me—but there was not more opportunity of conversing
quietly, nor indeed so much as when we met in other
places—the dear little boy became quite low spirited at
it towards the end of the evening, and took a moment
when he c^d speak unheard to say " even when I come to
you at Belcotton I am afraid we shall not be comfortable my dear Mama—there will be such confusion and
noise and hurrying us all about. . . . Perhaps then, you
do not wish to come my Norbury ? " — Oh Mama he
exclaimed in a reproachful [tone] of voice " how can you
say such a thing—if I was to be [there] and you too my
dearest Mama, and we c^d never speak to one another
only sit in a little corner and see you, I sh^d wish to come
more than anything in the world, to be in the same
room and just to look at you." My Fanny is almost
the only one to whom I c^d write this—but I feel that
these traits will interest her, and it relieves and soothes
my own mind to communicate where so it will be felt
whatever so nearly touches me—I don't know whether
I have yet mentioned a circumstance wch is less pleasant
to me than these I have related in Norbury—he has the
accent of the country not more strongly than I expected
—but he has it—and blunders in the words would and
should now and then, tho' Mr Maturin is very attentive
to avoid this error himself, and I have heard him set
Norbury right in it—I am sorry—but it is impossible
to wonder—the other two children will I fear soon have

absolute *brogues*, and I begin to be persuaded I shall not
escape it myself—Fanny's was observable before we
had been 3 days in Dublin—Willy's not so soon—but he
is now making a quick progress. I do what I can to stop
it—but you will all of you laugh at us all. . . . Would
that the time were come ? We met several times at
Mᵣˢ Cartland's a M Ganzelle, who teaches her daughters
and Norbury french—he is going to publish a journal,
and since our arrival here has favoured me wᵗʰ sending
2 little books containing his Prospectus that I may obtain
him subscriptions and requested thro' Norbury's means
that I wᵈ write to Madᵉ d'Arblay recommending this
work and requesting her interest—Norbury tells me he
begs *me to send him the letter to you wᶜʰ he will enclose
in a frank wᵗʰ one of his books of proposals.* I have answered and my greatest concern was for my poor Norbury, who will be shocked at my declining the Commissions and who will be under the necessity of giving
M. Ganzelle this disappointment, if such it can be—
had the subscription been like poor Mᵣ Clarke's of three
shillings I cᵈ not perhaps have been so *discouraging*—but
it is of *two guineas*—it is impossible it can ever answer as
french is in this country far less generally understood
than in England—At Mᵣ Brabazon's not one of the family
can read it. My Fanny and my Mᵣˢ Locke may perhaps
wish to hear how I like this house. Mᵣ Brabazon is
friendly and so good a young man that I like and esteem
him very much—his Lady is polite, but rather insipid,
and not likely to be pleased or to please in this country
as her manners are cold and reserved—She plays the
piano forte exceedingly well wᵗʰ a correctness unusual in
dilettantes, and her choice of music is good—this will
be a resource when conversation fails, and my Mᵣˢ Locke
will be pleased to hear such a one exists. Miss Jane
Brabazon christened by Norbury *Jane*pany, has spent
almost all her life at Rath tho' her father is settled at
Drogheda—but on the death of her Mother her education was undertaken by her two aunts, Mᵣ Brabazon's
Mother who has been dead about two years, and his

Father's sister Mrs Ann Brabazon who resided with
them. Mrs Ann who is I am told an excellent old
Lady, and who has established a school in imitation of
our Mrs Locke in the village remained in the house till
Mr Brabazon brought over his wife—She then preferred
settling herself at Drogheda, and Miss Jane is gone to
keep the house of one of her brothers—her Father has
married a 2nd wife wch renders his own undesirable—
She is about 5 miles from us but often at Rath. I wish
she were there always—her affection for Norbury prepared me to feel some for her, and it is by no means her
only claim, for she is sensible, modest, well informed,
obliging, and moreover earnestly desirous of being useful
in every way possible to her, to *Norbury's Mama*, as she
generally calls me—wth a thousand more things to say
my paper warns me to conclude—let me my dearest
Fanny have some particulars of our Alexander in return
for my Norburiana, and some of y^r building—and at
what depth you have obtained water at last—I have not
told you I believe how infinitely useful your dear pocket
book was to me on the road—and how touched I was by
the dear lines written in it which I never discovered till
I was at Belcotton not having filled more than the first
leaf of the memorandum paper before—it is a precious
thing to me. I have not told you neither that I wrote
on my arrival to Mrs Wall, and had a very kind answer
with a piece of intelligence wch much surprised me—
What will you say when you hear Mr Wall is married ?
I believe this event took place the day I arrived in
Dublin—it was I find suddenly concluded, and his
Mother seems not without anxiety tho' she says she c^d
make no objections—and that her son had been unhappy [and] was restless—and perhaps a little hasty—
She writes very unreservedly as you will perceive by
what I have s^d. Heaven bless bless bless you Kindest
love to my brother and to all the choir of angels at Norbury—pray write whenever you can—
    M^rs d'Arblay Bookham, Leatherhead, Surry. (Close
    to the address is the date, Nov 28–96.)

BELCOTTON FORLORN HOUSE *Dec* 30th 96.

What a time has passed since I last wrote to my
beloved Fanny, to whom I now write in sorrow—for
I have this morning parted with my Norbury.
Instead of one week promised me by his kind tutor,
near 3 have been accorded, but his lengthened visit,
tho it resigned me to his departure as being best
for himself, has not much contributed to blunt the
pain of losing him—he has been the life of the house
ever since he came to us, and notwithstanding the
addition of trouble he occasioned poor Susan, she is
almost as morose as I am at his being gone from
us—even Willy looks grave, judge if his sister is gay—
Norbury's wonderful spirits, and *never failing* good
humour have been of real use in restoring *her* to her
native chearfulness—her disgust at this journey and all
the circumstances attending it, had very much affected
her, and made her quite unlike herself—I owe to my
dear Boy, who never seemed quite so fond of her before,
the revival of her spirits and return of her placid and
pleasant temper. As for himself every day seemed but
to augment his delight and enjoyment in being with us,
and it is a great proof of the singular happiness that is
his at Mrs Cartland's that he sh^d have thought with
pleasure of seeing her and her family again even in the
midst of his regret at leaving Belcotton—Indeed we have
been far from the enjoyment of unmixed pleasure—At
his arrival, and for near a week after, we had the most
unpleasant weather imaginable, and a continual threat
of hurricanes, which affect him excessively as well as me—
On other occasions and indeed when it was apparently
fair, I was obliged to remain duo below stairs, working
or reading newspapers or agricultural tracts aloud,
whilst the 3 dear children were driven upstairs, and my
sole consolation in submitting to this penance at a time
when the mere sight of my Norbury or sound of his
voice would have been a joy to me, was reflecting that in
my room wch is the largest in the house, and where there
is a constant fire, he and his sister and brother could

be quiet and enjoy some comfort—By degrees the extreme storminess of the weather abated, and from time to time there has been sunshine, so that the conclusion of my dear one's visit has been pleasanter than its commencement. Yet he s^d to me last night " if it were not for you Mama I sh^d think Belcotton an odious uncomfortable place—at Dawson St there are no disturbances and I love all the family, and they all love me—I am always quiet there and contented . . . but lowering his voice I am HAPPIER here—because I am with you." This written seems a [trifle] but the expression wth which it was spoken rendered it very touching. Clear sighted as is this dear little soul, I am at once gratified and surprised in observing the real affection he has for le Temps —I have seen it in a hundred little instances wch w^d be too long to relate, and wch taken separately w^d perhaps appear trivial—but I must mention two wch occurred in the course of yesterday—Speaking of Willy whom he thinks very [charming] and sensible, and who diverts him exceedingly and who notwithstanding many ruptures loves him passionately, and is extremely loved by him, he exclaimed he was sure he would be very like le Temps when he was a man—"Why he is so even already he is so busy, and so bustling, and so *active*, and so *clever*, and so loved, and so *good humoured* and so passionate ! " There was a favourable mixture in these epithets wch as they were I am sure sincerely made use of, struck me—sometime after the two Boys were playing by the side of the fire, and I employed wth Fanny at the other end of the room—but in the midst of my conversation with her I was caught by Norbury's telling his brother he liked one of the workmen he had named to him very much, but did not love him—" but why not love him "—says Willy—" Ah because that is quite another thing—I like all sort of people that seem good, but I can't love them all—and I love some people that I don't like. There is a person (he continued, rather to himself than to Willy, who was standing before him whilst he mended his whips) whom I *dis*like more than

anybody I know in the world—yet I *love* him exceedingly—After Mama and Fanny I love him . . . and then
you my dear Willy." . . . I perceived he thought himself
unheard except by Willy, whom he justly concluded c^d
not understand him, and as Fanny really was not listening, I did not undeceive him wth respect to myself—
How this dear boy absorbs me! You will surely be
astonished to read this much and not find the word invasion, nor anything resembling alarm Heaven grant
you may not be suffering any for me and mine my
beloved Fanny. I hope you have heard from Chelsea
where I wrote hoping to quiet my dearest Father's fears
as far as we ourselves were concerned almost as soon as
the fearful tydings from Cork reached me—As it was
really out of my power on that day to write more than
the one hasty letter I sent to Chelsea, I entreated that
its contents might be immediately communicated to
my 3 dear sisters, and in naming *you* I know our blessed
adopted sister would be included. Since that time we
have gained no new intelligence that c^d be depended
upon, wch together wth the approaching departure of
my Norbury deterred me from (the otherwise difficult
enterprise of) writing. At this moment by the accts
from the Dublin and Drogheda newspapers it seems
doubtful whether it is a French fleet that is seen off
Bantry, where no Troops are known to have landed—
It is supposed possible to be our *own* fleet—however I
do not quite credit these flattering reports—but hope
we may rely on the loyalty and spirit of the people in
and about Cork, and on the firmness of the Troops in
which case we may not unreasonably hope no landing
will be effected—We passed our Christmas Day not only
quietly, but something better, our Norbury being with
us wch was a pleasure we had not looked forward to and
it we owed to a visit paid us 2 days before by Mr Maturin,
who was so well contented wth his application (for he
has many tasks to get thro' every day under his ancien
Schoolmistress) that he s^d he perceived he might be
trusted here yet another week without impeding his

progress. Monday 26th we expected Mr Harry Brabazon to dinner : he is a cousin of Mr Brabazon of Rath,
a good humoured young man, brother to *Miss Jane*, to
whom I am not quite sure I have yet introduced you,
but whom I must en passant tell you I like, and . . .
almost love, as to be sincere she seems to love not only
Norbury but his Mother—We waited late and then rec^d
a few lines f^m Mr Brabazon saying a particular circumstance had obliged Harry to go to Drogheda, and that
he earnestly beg^d the Major to come to Rath. I write
to you with abominable incoherence at stolen half
moments, or I sh^d have told you the Major after an
attempt at *raising* a corps of Yeomanry here, has joined
Mr Brabazon's of Rath who had secured all the persons
who c^d be confided in within many miles of us—On
Christmas day they all wore their uniforms, and I concluded the business Mr B. wished to speak of to the
Major related to this Corps. I was not therefore
uneasy tho' he returned very late—at near one in the
morning—wch as he says whenever he goes to Rath is
not indeed much before his customary hour. On
arriving however he told me news had reached M^r B.
of the descent of the French on our coast near Cork—
that he was in great alarm, and dubious whether he s^d
not remove his wife (who is with child) to Dublin as a
place more secure sh^d any great evil await us. I need
not tell you I had no very refreshing sleep that night—
but indeed no painful idea so frequently recurred as
that of the shock and alarm that w^d probably be felt
for me by my dear Father, you, and a few more most
dearly loved persons—Tuesday [my] occupation was
to write to Chelsea—Mr Maturin, who arrived early
brought such accounts as were believed in Dublin
the day before—the alarm reached that place as you will
see by the newspapers in the eve^g of Christmas Day,
and all the regular Troops were ordered to march, some
within ten minutes of receiving the order for Cork, and
Bantry Bay—the same operations took place in the
middle of the night at Drogheda, on the news being

received—I looked forwards to the arrival of the newspapers yesterday wth great anxiety: we are indebted
to Mr Kiernan for them, and sometimes have a Drogheda paper from Mr Brabazon—they came—but contained no certain accounts whatever—many contradictory and vague ones—but these gave me some pleasure
by persuading me that the landing had not been effected
—happily the people in the south are s^d to be very loyal
and well disposed—c^d this attack have been made to the
northward of us, there w^d have been great and various
reasons for terror. Since I have been writing a letter
is come from Mr Kiernan he says "It is a fact that the
French are in Bantry Bay—their troops amount to
2500. a Lieutenant with 6 men were driven on shore
in a small boat and have been taken prisoners—they are
now in the Castle." He says the general alarm is much
abated since it has been known that no landing had
been made, or as yet attempted, and a strong hope pre-
vails that they will be surrounded by our own Fleet
whilst yet in the Bay—Our situation compared to that
of the greatest part of Ireland is even enviable my
dearest Fanny, and tho' I am neither so thoughtless nor
so insensible as to be unmoved by the calamities wth
which the country is threatened, any danger to ourselves seems at least *distant*—I shall long to hear from
you all, and to know you have not suffered an alarm
much greater than ours—I have been very anxious to
keep off any seizure of terror from poor Susan and the
children and have succeeded—the M. acknowledges no
alarm and sings and dances—upon all that I feel I am
silent, and indeed tho' deeply impressed and very solicitous, I am not terrified—poor Mrs Wall's situation must
I fear be very unpleasant, but I earnestly hope she will
be soon relieved from her apprehension—I have only
thro' sweet Amelia acknowledged the two last dear
letters I have had from Norbury and Bookham—I sh^d
wish to answer them minutely, but I see it will be impossible. I will try however not to be long without
writing to our beloved Mrs Locke, and en attendant I

entreat you to say for me all that is most tenderly
affectionate—I am longing to hear she has succeeded
perfectly in making a nurse of her sweet daughter, and
that all there prospers. I hope her rheumatism may
not have been encreased by change of house—dearest
soul! how kindly she thinks of all that can give me
most comfort and happiness by her constant and chearing
accounts of the health of all hers—dearest Mr Locke's
—*yours* my Fanny, and your lovely little Alexander's.
When you talk to him of Mama Pilly does he solemnly
exclaim " A.W. . . dawn." . . . I hope you are at Chelsea my dearest—it does me good to think our beloved
Father should have you and this little love and its dear
Papa, to whom give my very affectionate love and thanks
for his four lines, which I loved very much and have
wth the rest of the letter kept to myself, tho' I believe
he did not think only of me whilst he was writing—I
was touched and delighted by the accts of M de Lally's
plaidoyer, and of his visit, and that of the dear Princesse
whose constant goodness and kindness penetrates me—
What a pleasure it w^d have been to see her here if—if
if! but alas those ifs are irremoveable—how angelic is
what you tell me of the conduct of nos Anges towards
the little Adrienne's Father. Heaven bless and reward
them—My kindest most tenderly affect^te love to them
all and pray confide in our sweet Amelia whatever you
can of my letters—I know my Fanny will judge for me
with a delicacy as scrupulous as she w^d for herself, and
give her therefore carte blanche, and I know too the
sincere affection and interest that sweetest girl feels for
all that relates to me. My good Susan's arm is better.
She is much gratified by hearing she has been so distinguished in y^r letters, and begs me to present her duty
and many thanks to you, our Mrs Locke and M d'Arblay
—I wish it were possible to hear how the Dorking sister
does, and to let her know Susan is well. Perhaps my
Mrs Locke w^d some time commission Thomas to call
—perhaps even, if he ever goes to Dorking, my dear
Brother w^d have that kindness—I am grieved for poor

17

Alfonse and his Mother—I am grieved too (for that word does not express too much) at a later interference of our brother James—Kindly intended no doubt towards the M—I can scarcely say towards *us*, as he knows my repugnance to such a measure—My dearest Fanny cannot but guess to what I allude, and if she judges of my feelings by what her own w^d be under the same circumstances she will not need to be told to what a degree the new formed arrangement concerns, mortifies and chagrins me—Tell my dear Brother. Monday morn^g I was interrupted and cannot recollect what I was going to say but know it related to my chagrin concerning poor (name erased) My dearest souls! at this time to encrease your expenses—and that it sh^d be [forced on] when so much is wasted, thrown away—lost by whims and unprofitable projects, it goes to my heart —the M. in his answer to James who wrote to him not me on the subject desired all might continue as before— but I apprehend it was then too late to change the plan entered in as he says by you, dear Charles and himself. I feel as if I wanted to ask your pardon and my brother's for this business my Fanny tho' Heaven knows I believe it concerns me more than anybody. Adieu ever most dear. Sh^d this meet you at Chelsea say 1000 loves and duties for me and tell our dearest Father news is arrived of the French having quitted Bantry. Heaven bless you my dearest

Monday 2nd January.

M^rs d'Arblay at Dr Burney's Chelsea College Middlesex. (Redirected to Bookham.)

Sunday morn^g J^an 15th 1797.

Once more let me begin a letter to my sisters without anxiety or self reproach—All I have written since my almost 3 weeks indulgence with my Norbury have had an unpleasant proportion of those ingredients, notwithstanding the full confidence I felt in the considerate kindness of my beloved correspondents—but I feared they w^d become uneasy—and they have been a little so, which I find rather difficult to forgive myself for—My Fanny (my Fanny of this place) is gone to church with her Papa, except during a hard frost the roads are impassible on foot for women who like us are encumbered with shoes and stockings and the distance is above two miles—except on Xmas day we have therefore never been able to go to church en famille—Fanny and I take it in turn to go in the gig, which is low and I believe not likely to be overset— I must likewise add that the novelty of driving being over our Guide goes very quietly, and unlike his former manner—the church is neat and warm, containing about 5 large pews for the gentlemen's families about, (amongst wch are Mr Brabazon's, an uncle of his who resides at Caresetown [written Cussetown] and ours) and 6 or 7 others for the farmers and poor people—The clergyman is a well looking young man but a wretched preacher, with a vile pronunciation tho' no considerable brogue—I believe I have already told you we are upon a dead flat, with scarce a tree to be seen, except a few (I am told some thousands but they are so small and scattered they look no better than those of our old neighbour Mr Rogers on the Downs) wch have been planted by the Major—On one side of us at a distance of 3 miles we see the spire of Ballymaglan [Ballymakenny] Church, and beyond it some gentle eminences which are perfectly bare, (and therefore I suppose) called mountains by the Major, who but that it seriously chagrines me sometimes, I sh^d think *comically* enamoured of this place—On another side we have a view of the Boyne; and beyond the town of Termonfecan in wch stands our church, we see the sea. I have not yet made my peace with it, and cannot look that way without sadness, tho it is the only object worth looking at around us! —Belcotton at a little distance looks like an Irish village —a village not of comfortable neat cottages, but of *cabins*—the House itself is formed of two of these cabins wch the Major found standing together: and 3 or 4

lesser ones which were detached he has connected, and
transformed into stables, store houses and workshops
—amongst the latter are a Carpenter's and a Blacksmith
shop compleat—these face the *front* of the house, in a
Inner circle—but the front contains only an entrance—
No windows, and has a very curious appearance. two
little rooms (the first of w^(ch) wholly unfinished, contains
the staircase, and may be dignified with the name of a
Hall) must be passed thro' before you reach our parlour
—this is a long rather narrow room, not ugly in its form,
and fortunately warm—it contains two little closets,
a recess with 5 shelves for books, and the bare walls
w^(ch) cannot be papered or painted till spring, are ornamented w^(th) sweet drawings w^(ch), like the unfriendly
element that separates me from you, tho' not from quite
the same cause, sadden, instead of delighting me as
they were wont! they seem out of their place, as I do
myself . . . but to proceed—I have told you this room
is warm—I wish I c^d tell you it was light—for my eyes
have already very much suffered by its darkness—it contains only one long narrow window, which is placed so
high that unless when standing up and close to it the
sky alone can be discerned from it—close to this room
w^(th) a window of the same kind looking the same way
(that is to the back of the house, whence we have a view
of *Ballymaglan* [Ballymakenny] spire etc.) is the kitchen
w^(ch) tho' small is very convenient, and thanks to my good
Susan always clean and tidy—then there is a Skullery
w^(ch) has a window that in the summer time may be
pleasant as it looks into the garden, a large piece of
ground containing some trees a little taller than I was
going to say Willy—but to be scrupulously just I believe
I may say than *me*, w^(th) gooseberry bushes and vegetables
w^(ch) at least will be green—it is on the north side of the
house—there is to be likewise a dairy w^(ch) is not yet
floored, and there is already a door into the court yard
where stands a pump etc and w^(ch) leads into the afore
mentioned *garden*. We have a very tidy little Pantry,
and a long room on the other side of the house, w^(ch)

is chearful when there is any sun, and wch had it a fire
place I sh^d prefer to the parlour—this looks south towards Termonfecan Church, and the sea—We distin-
guish vessels upon it (sometimes very large ones pass)
wth great ease—the distance indeed is said to be less than
two miles from us—Now I am to carry you upstairs
—but the stair case is to be altered—at present one room
leads to all the others—this when finished will be a good
bedroom—it is over the kitchen, and has a fireplace—
but at present is a mere receptacle for trunks and boxes—
On the right hand side there are two doors the first
leads into a bed room for a servant—very dark, and
wch ne *conviendrait* pas to our spoilt and happy people of
England—I sh^d never then have had courage to propose
such a bedroom, even if I had had the inclination—but
here—after visiting two or three of the *cabins* I could
enter it to sleep in myself, and think I was luxuriously
treated—further on thro' a little passage wth shelves on
each side, is another room that is appropriated to my
Norbury—it is over the skullery and looks into the
garden—Opposite to the door of this room is that
which leads into mine and which the M. sometimes
talks of converting into a *drawing room*—this is a large
room—it is over the parlour, but not narrow, as it likewise stretches over both the passage rooms—but here
likewise there is a short allowance of light—One only
narrow window, so that it is literally true that in these
dark days I am in the middle of the day either perished
by sitting close to the window, or reduced to work,
read, or write by *firelight*. this is by far the most
serious complaint I have to make of the house—At the
end of our large bedroom, opposite the entrance, is a
long narrow, but light and chearful room looking towards
the sea—this contains two beds, and my Fanny and
Willy, and their good and careful Susan sleep here.
You will be immediately struck with the inconvenience
of this room being thro' ours—but notwithstanding the
obvious objections you will perhaps guess there may be
some advantages in their being so near—and indeed it

is a real comfort to me—I have now given my Fanny,
not very clearly I fear tho' very minutely, the plan of
Belcotton—I had not intended to bestow so much
paper upon it, tho' I have indeed nothing gayer to talk
about that relates to *myself*—But to your dear self I
have never yet spoke my thanks for your Chelsea sweet
letters. I rec^d the first immediately after sending a
long one to you, and was most happy in hearing your
acc^t of our dearest Father's mended spirits, and quite
soothed by thinking you were together. I trusted that
my letter concerning our late terrible tho' short alarm
might have reached you nearly as soon as Government
information—at least I was comforted by your being
at such a time with my Father, and how pleased that
he should have your sweet darling with him. I thank
you sincerely for having at last given me a little account
of him—I see and hear his *Fo it eag*—I wish I could hear
too his *Dea-Gan-papa*—bless him! pray kiss him and
say it is for me once a day at least. I w^d wish my name
at least to be familiar to him—My Brother will now and
then perhaps relieve you from this commission—Your
account of dear Sally's improvement gave me the truest
pleasure, and all the family details I owe you were most
interesting. I am sorry—and disappointed rather, that
our Esther is not more frequently at Chelsea—in the
first week you were there you tell me you saw her but
once, and that once was at her own home. I think she
has great powers of chearing and soothing our dearest
Father and I lament they sh^d not oftener be together.
I am glad and not surprised that our James is so happy
and so busy with his babsy—I wish dear Charles' holyday may have been chearfully and pleasantly spent.

(No address. A fragment endorsed by M^rs d'Arblay
"No I Description of Belcotton.")

BELCOTTON, *March* 24th *Friday.* 1797.
I have scarce recovered sight my Fanny, for your most
touching letter nearly blinded me—yet I must un-

burthen my heart by instantly writing you my tenderest, warmest congratulations tho' it may be hastily—Notwithstanding all my apprehensions of being unfairly dealt by in these days of my exile, from too great solicitude to spare me, I feel I sh^d be too ungrateful were I not to thank you for having concealed yr intention of inoculating our little darling, and saved me the knowledge of his and *your* sufferings whilst they lasted, for the anxiety w^d have been trebled by the distance wch separates us. Never was there a more sweetly interesting account than that you have given me—it enables me to see our little heroic darling, holding voluntarily his little arms to the lancet—bless him! That I could have seen him with real eyes! Yet I had rather see him now, with the *triple associations* you tell me of on his dear nose. I am persuaded from yr account, wch I have read over again since I began this letter, that he will not be the least marked, and that your heroism and his Papa's in being willing to relinquish all his beauty, will be rewarded by your seeing him more flourishing and vigorous than ever. I sh^d almost be ready to quarrel wth Mr Ansell for poisoning *both* his arms and *studying* to infect his pure blood, wch probably increased his suffering considerably, but that since wth all he c^d do only one pustule rose *in order* to use your term, you might otherwise perhaps have doubted his having really had this most tremendous distemper—What a relief— What a joy to my dearest Fanny and her *True* Partner, that it is past? O God be praised! I do assure you I scarce know an event that c^d so have filled me wth grateful joy, my own darlings being all safe—Now too that my removal makes me I think more greedy of good for my beloved Fanny, and for all my most cherished Beloveds—I think I can less than ever endure to hear of their meeting wth any sorrows or misfortunes—I think too, tho' it sh^d be but to such as you that I say it, for there seems too strong a portion of presumption in the confession,—but I feel as if you had a sort of *claim* on Fortune for new blessings now that you have not yr

poor Susan to soothe and console, and—sometimes—
to be soothed and comforted by—Let me then hope
that all concurs in compleating y^r present happiness my
dearest—that you may not yourself have been too severely
shaken—for your darling I perceive has suffered a great
deal, and I know how exquisitely you have felt all his
pain and uneasiness—that his dear Father, my kind,
excellent Brother, is not any longer martyrised by his
rheumatism, wch I find by my Mrs Locke's account has
been very severe, tho' neither of you speak much of it.
What upon Earth can be more touching than the offer
—the promise made you by that dear generous Brother
of bringing you to me were any severe illness to seize
me! I cannot tell you, yet I should be sorry you did
not conceive, how deeply it has penetrated me—Tell
him so—repeat it to him—embrace him for yourself, and
for me my dearest—tell yourself I often seek refuge from
my own pains and weariness in times of trouble, by
reflecting on your rare as it is well merited lot—nothing
can be more soothing to my spirit, no, not even the
praises that reach me of my absent darling, and the
fond hopes of him I sometimes admit—but you require
on *my* part, a promise, an engagement—it w^d be painful
to me to resist anything so urgently demanded—
depend therefore on my sincerity in all points relative
to health—indeed on all whatever—and on my acquiescence. I do not indeed expect to be very *hasty* in calling you hither my dear one—My health has been surprisingly good since I have been here, for the illness of
wch you, dearest and tenderest Friends have thought so
much, was short, at least all that was not mere weakness
and depression. With respect to my *Fevers*, the thoughts
of wch alarm you, I think you may become perfectly
easy—My constitution is certainly altered within some
years, and I think there is now scarce an inflammatory
particle in it—I may have *feverettes*, but shall I dare
say have no more furious high fevers—This winter too,
I have in an extraordinary manner escaped Cough—
I had a very severe one on the road, but I have had only

slight ones since I landed—perhaps I owe this to the sea
passage—and in part I doubt not to my having *kept
the house* nearly entirely since I came to Belcotton—for
were I much exposed to the air of this land I do not
imagine it would treat me better than that of dear good
England used to do

(No address—Endorsed by M^rs d'Arblay " Alex's
Inoculation " " No. 2.")

Jan 5th 1798.

I feel as if I sh^d like to fill half a quire of paper
with thanks alone for your last truly delicious paquet
my beloved Friends. I scarce know to which of my
kind Trio I ought first to address myself, for altho'
our sweetest Mrs Locke has confined herself to an
enveloppe, every line she has written is precious and
chearing, and before I rec^d *this* paquet I felt deeply in
her debt, my last to her having been so short and so
shabby—my kind indulgent Brother has on his part
made the best possible amends for his long silence, and
I know si Je m'y laissais aller, my poor solitary sheet of
paper would but too soon be filled only in answering
his magnificent sized folio—this makes me afraid to begin
with him, for my heart would smite me too severely if
I deferred telling my beloved Fanny the really exquisite
pleasure I received from her letter—the account of the
removal is delicious—I should never be tired of reading
it, and dearest Mr Locke's visits and smiling benediction !
and his and our Amelia at his side—blessed souls ! viewing everything with interest and kind and tender sympathy and joy—and the sweet spot, wch is impressed in
my memory as perfectly as Norbury itself or Mickleham
—and the dear house, w^ch, thanks to the excellent archi-
tect, I am now quite well acquainted with—and then
our darling prancing from room to room on his wooden
steed—and your own and my Brother's laughable dis-
tresses, and joyous feelings in the midst of them, what
a picture of delight it presents ! My Fanny who is
grateful for all her blessings as if she deserved not one

of them, must be grateful *over again* for my sake, and for the good they do to me.—In despite of the assessed Taxes and other evils, I feel a sweet confidence in the permanent enjoyment this dear new habitation will be to you, and that you will never regret what you have sacrificed to possess it—Such a dwelling with little more than bread and water w^d seem paradise to me—I need not say I mean a dwelling so placed—so surrounded and so inhabited—such long explanations are not quite necessary to you—Thursday 18th Jan^y—All good and pleasure attend the Queen upon it—the foregoing was written my Fanny almost as soon as I rec^d y^r last dear paquet, wch was not till the 4th of this month tho y^r last date was the 17th Decr. We have since been all laid up with colds, save my *great Fanny*—who is more invulnerable than ever—Susan's share made me most uneasy, who would not be dissuaded from waiting on me as if she had had nothing the matter with her—there can scarcely be a better soul—in the midst of all this I was called upon for my part of a letter to our dearest Friends, since the departure of which I have felt less anxious at retarding the concluding my present Folio, wch I wished to do, till I could *bona fide* assure you the household was in a convalescent state, as is now the case. I long to know our Mrs Locke is once more free from rheumatism and cold—it is a grievance to me to think of her having been so cruelly long confined—the history of my Brother's indiscretions, in despite of his too severe punishment, I found incomparably comic—I think he has no luck in dogs—is the Barbette still guardian to the coal hole ? It was at *Court* that I feared he c^d not attend you, not to West humble where I did not imagine you w^d go without him—I had concluded y^r visit w^d be made to Windsor. I lament anew your losing the dear P^sse and M de Lally—it is particularly sweet and affects me to hear of her continued partial and precious kindness for me—indeed not many persons exist whose affection I value as I do hers, or which so nearly touches me—This leads me irresistibly to speak

of a new claimant, against whom my Fanny admonishes
me *not to shut my heart.* I believe it is ill furnished
with bolts and bars, and that I never had a key—at least
I have never been long able to resist loving those who
have loved me, and who have seemed to deserve it, and
to say the truth I have not often had cause to repent
my facility in this respect—To explain what seems to
have raised your curiosity wth respect to Jany paney w^d
require a long letter and is an embarrassing history to
give . . . however—I sh^d surely tell it my dearest Fanny
were I by her side, and I will therefore not resist an
enquiry to which I have myself given rise—in saying
this, I comprise not only my Brother but *nos anges*—
You may perhaps recollect my telling you of a hint I
rec^d fm James before my journey hither had been insisted upon—We had rec^d in James Street a young sea-
man (Miss Brabazon's youngest brother) recommended
by the M. with whom he had been living for some
months at Rath. This young man, probably without
disguising it gave James the idea that his sister was too
much noticed by the M. that her Family thought it
foolish and were a little embarrassed by it—Some months
after I rec^d an urgent letter f^m the Major to induce me
to join him—in short he arrived, and you know the event
—but tho' he mentioned to me his family and acquaintance who were all desirous of my arrival here, I never
heard the name of Miss B. till I met with my Norbury,
who spoke to me of her as of the person I should best
love in Ireland—We arrived at Belcotton on a Friday
evening—the next morning Fanny was suddenly desired
to get ready for a ride in the gig and (privately) to dress
herself as well as she c^d. On my making a slight representation, as I really wanted her and tho^t it too early
to begin visiting, I was told she sh^d only be taken an
airing—just to the seaside—and she went. At her
return, very late, she told me she had been introduced
to Miss Brabazon, who was at her Brother's house, w^ch
stands close to the banks of the sea—and that she thought
Papa would never come away. The next day I went to

church, where we have a seat of our own—but as I
knew it not, I c^d only follow the M. up the aisle—he
opened the door of a pew, where I was a little surprised
at seeing a Lady and Gent^n already placed—but as the
service was already begun no introduction or explanation
c^d take place—I soon found I was in the pew of M^r
Brabazon of Rath, who was then wth his wife at Dublin
—that the gent^n was his cousin Harry of Seafield, and
the Lady his sister, by whom from time to time, tho'
with great modesty, I perceived myself viewed in stolen
glances with something like particular interest—tho' my
feelings perhaps did not wholly correspond wth those of
my fair observer, I saw her I believe without prejudice
—and will now introduce her to you—She is tall—with
perhaps something more than the right degree of embon-
point, and I think rather too large—but well made, with
a good carriage, a great modesty of deportment—a very
fair and brilliant complexion, uncommonly white, small
teeth, fine fair hair, without one bad, tho' perhaps without one perfect feature, and blue eyes to which I did not
at first do justice—but wch I have since found capable
of conveying the sweetest expressions—As soon as the
service was over I endeavoured to apologise for my
sudden and undesigned intrusion, and was answered
wth more than *politeness*, wth empressement—the next
day she called on me with her Brother, and pressed a
thousand offers of assistance wth great sweetness—seemed
shocked and uneasy at the unfinished state of the house,
and surprised me by breaking out into exclamations
upon the thoughtlessness of the M—" I assure you " s^d
she " *the whole country is in arms* against him for bringing
you at such a season of the year to such an unfinished
place as this—and now I have seen it I shall not be
able to say a word in his defence "—presently after she
supposed he w^d not be in a hurry to shew himself at
Drogheda adding that he was not at all *popular* just then
—she spoke of Norbury with the tenderest affection and
interest : s^d he had been *her child* whilst at Rath, in
consideration of wch she hoped I w^d not consider her

as a new acquaintance, for she had been so much in the
habit of conversing with him about his absent Mama,
that she felt as if she had intimately known me for near
two years—She then entered into many details concerning him—told me, laughing, how his Papa's handwriting
used to puzzle him " do Janey Paney," he used to say
to me when he was quite in despair, " pray read this
letter for me, for I cannot make out a word "—" but
when " (added she) " a letter used to arrive from *you*, I
would see the colour mount into his cheeks, and often,
his eyes fill with tears, and he used to shut himself up
to read it, and then said never a word—till *by degrees*,
some parts used to come forth—dear little boy—it
shewed such true love ! " Such was the opening of our
acquaintance and soon after I met her at Rath—and once,
I visited her at Seafield, feeling at every visit an increase
of bien veillance towards her, and at once struck and
affected by the whole of her manner towards me, which
expressed nearly all that can be imagined of solicitude,
respect, and tenderness. She spent great part of the
winter at a Friend's 50 or 60 miles distant—during this
time I rec^d two very sweet letters from her, and she
met me at her return like *a bosom friend*—with a warmth
and sensibility so evidently genuine that I could not
but be touched by them—She was indefatigably zealous
in seeking for me whatever she tho^t w^d prove a comfort
or an advantage at Belcotton—finding I loved flowers,
she continually brought or sent me such regales as I
was least proof against—for all others I did my utmost,
tho' not successfully, to repress : again every newspaper
I have seen this year has been conveyed to me by her
and on taking leave of me to accompany a sick friend to
Cheltenham, a confidence she placed in me further
advanced and seemed to confirm our *liaison*—of this (if it
does not tire you) in another letter. I know not how to
conclude all I have to say in wch I am *personally* interested
in my present sheet. Since her return from England
we have not met very often—but on her part it has
always been with a kind of idolizing fondness—an ex-

pression wch to you may be ventured without seeming
ridiculous, and wch you will not suspect to originate
simply in my own vanity—but this, tho' I certainly
am not insensible to it, is not her greatest charm in my
eyes—I find that kind of congeniality in our feelings
which perhaps forms the surest basis of durable friendship—She interests me, to say beyond any person I have
seen in this country, were but little, but indeed beyond
most people I have ever met with—her sensibility, and
caressing manners where she loves, for they are not such
to *all*, are touching—Add to these irresistable attractions
a very lively understanding, self improved ; that conversation never flags with her tho' she is not a great
talker—that she is compleatly free from all affectations
—that her nature is at once open and modest—her principles pure ; and even strict, and her benevolence such
as might render her worthy of a place even at Norbury.
She is I find adored in the village, and her good works
seem all she is solicitous of hiding—Her modest firmness
I am convinced has awed the M. from anything like open
declarations, or rather from *any* declarations save of
friendly regard—but this can certainly be known only
by themselves, and in the meanwhile his pursuit of her
is flagrant and his assiduity unceasing. I am but too well
persuaded these have been very generally remarked,
and you will not require now to conceive the *drawbacks*
at which I hinted. I am far enough removed from a
jealous wife by my nature, and circumstances have rendered any tendencies of that kind for many years impossible—yet it w^d be as repugnant to my feelings as
to every idea I have of rectitude to submit to being
considered as *la complaisante de mon Mari* in such a
situation—I sh^d be in the present case doubly wounded
by such a suggestion, because it w^d be as injurious to
an amiable and innocent girl as it w^d be offensive to
myself, and I have once or twice feared it from the
littleness of Mrs Brab^n and her malignity towards Jane,
who is supported by her own conscious rectitude and by
the idea that no one *could* suspect, or would dare to

accuse her—but I am aware that her extreme anxiety
about me, my health, and all that concerns me ; her
solicitude to obtain whatever she thinks w^d amuse or be
a comfort to me, may be maliciously interpreted—and
were it in her *power* to be continually at Belcotton, as
I am sure she would if that were the case, the good
natured world w^d probably not consider M^{rs} P as the
only attraction. Such thoughts you may believe must
have given me various subjects of inquietude—however . . . I feel so convinced of the blamelessness of one
Party, that long before I rec^d my Fanny's advice I have
given up any wish to resist the impulse which led me
to love her, and had determined to manifest as far as
I am able the justice my heart does her—My drawbacks
however end not here—for I am become an object of
jealousy ; and the acquaintance between us wch at
first was desired, is become a cause of suspicion, and
every means employed to interrupt it—Nothing can
be less acceptable than the expression of her unbounded
regard, wch in our short acquaintance, (the circumstances of which indeed have been peculiar) resembles
that of my most partial friends—her nature is not merely
tenderly affectionate, but in a high degree susceptible
and enthusiastic—and if she conceives that, however
innocently on her part, but for her I sh^d be more valued
and happier, the soft and peculiar interest she feels for
me is natural—I have frequently seen tears start in her
eyes at receiving an expression of affection from me
—but I must now turn to some other subject—I must
assure my Fanny very great care is taken of me, tho' I
do not pretend to take all the merit to *myself*—but poor
Susan is never so happy as in tending and *cottering*
me as much as she is able ; and I do *try* to sleep with
all my power, and I am very thankful when I succeed—
I have not left untried all you propose—but *en fait de
vers*, one poem constantly forces itself on my recollection nearly to the exclusion of every other—the Hymn
to Adversity—I think I *feel the iron hand scourge*—and
the train of thoughts which follow are not friendly to

rest—but believe me even in my worst nights, I always calm myself as well and as speedily as I can—and when such soothing attempts are not impossible, I try to beguile the time wth happier recollections than the last year has afforded ; and now I often view my Fanny at her *new* beloved home, wth her dear Partner and their darling—and then turn to Norbury, and I think myself amidst you all—I must leave much unsaid that I sh^{d} like to say—but I must repeat that Susan and I have now only slight remains of our colds—all else well—I am *myself* very much in arrears concerning my Norbury. I know not when I may have him here again dear boy— he writes often however and is well, and with some of the kindest persons in the world—some other time I must write to you a little about my Willy—Heaven preserve you my dearest—say for me love things to nos anges and let me hear again f^{m} you as soon as possible. 1000 thanks for y^{r} account of y^{r} London journey, and as many for all you tell me of my good Susan's sister—which gave *me* great relief, as I was uneasy about her, and was a great comfort to her. She is very grateful to you for it.

M^{rs} D'Arblay, West Humble, Leatherhead, Surrey.
(Endorsed extraordinary History of Miss B. or Janey Paney No. 3.)

Tuesday June 26th DUBLIN 1798.

At length I have received a letter to myself my beloved Fanny, but if it restored and touched and delighted, it grieved me too—that I could not at once fly to your affectionate arms and prove to you, my excellent brother, and our Esther, how fully sensible I am of your precious love, and of the heartfelt sincerity of your generous offers, pained me unspeakably—it required many hours to bring me back to perfectly reasonable considerations, such as, however gloomy and depressing are most necessary to support me in the situation in which I am placed—I have a world of interests to weigh for others, which must be opposed to my own gratification and even to the exquisitely tender and generous wishes of my beloved Friends—were the decision in my own hands my first prayer would be for strength of mind to forget myself, and to discern the course by the pursuit of which the least injury would be done to others—Such a decision it is impossible for me to make—but it still behoves me to resign myself to that which may be determined for me sh^d it be opposite to all that my heart impels me to wish—I have copied and sent to the M. who continues in D^n a great part of my dearest Fanny's letter, and my Brother's of the 20th of June—to it I have subjoined such motives as—*perhaps* may induce him to agree to the temporary absence of his Family—but to press, to urge strenuously any action must ultimately fall heavily on those I love—or indeed on those for whom personally I have no regard—w^d be so repugnant to my feelings, that not even my darling sisters solicitude c^d impel me to it. It is impossible for me to say how many days I may wait his answer, nor how vague and unsatisfactory it may be—he has now had my dear James' letter a week who with the generous kindness that is a part of his nature, and which his sisters have so repeatedly experienced, begs us to *draw on him* for any sum that may be necessary for our journey—I have beg^d him to write to this dear kind James and to let me conclude the letter—but I have yet had no answer—God knows my dearest Fanny it w^d hurt me grievously to have this proposal accepted and that *so* to come to you must embitter what under usual circumstances w^d be the happiest event of my life—I am under most painful anxiety concerning the £100 you and my Brother d'Arblay with a liberality so much too great offer—I have written to request an explanation and to that likewise have yet had no answer :

I have had the envelope written by our sweet Mrs Locke the 22nd and a letter you had bid me expect of the 20th of June—you are too sweet—too tender—too exquisitely kind to me my beloved Fanny—you make it

18

too difficult to resist listening to you and to my own
heart wholly—too hard a trial not to forget many many
serious duties—but I must repeat to you the decision
rests not with me—

[His] death, probable approach of certain ruin—the
great *im*probability in any case of his being able to replace
any fresh sum that he might borrow—Does my dearest
Fanny conceive my whole soul does not shrink from
calling upon our James, or my other brother, d'Arblay
—and herself—no my best and kindest—If I am unhappy, I w^d not be forced into becoming voluntarily
despicable—Times may be fairer—We shall meet in a
happier manner I trust—and the joy of such a meeting
not be poisoned as it w^d be now—Meanwhile let me
assure you there is *nothing* to apprehend for our personal
safety—this terrible struggle may yet, and I fear will
be prolonged—but situated as we are, to mourn for the
innumerable but *distant* victims is all we have to endure.
At Belcotton all continues as tranquil as when we left
it, and I c^d almost regret our precipitate departure
from it—the fears of my dear absent Friends have however been lessened by this measure as well as those of
my kind Jane, whose apprehensions overpowered her
judgment and whose solicitude for me resembles only
my beloved sisters—I know she w^d have been wretched
when she left that part of the country, had she not
succeeded in occasioning my removal from it—She has
now acquired more courage and better hopes—the great
number of English troops that have landed, have revived and comforted even the most timid. Lord Cornwallis is looked up to with confidence, and tho' perfect
tranquility may be distant, a state of open rebellion it
is thought by the most reasonable persons I have met
with, will soon be at an end—I am so continually interrupted that it becomes difficult to me to write with any
coherence. The sight and hearing of my Norbury is
a comfort and a joy to me—my other two dear children,
and my good Susan it is comfortable to have always at
hand in this agitating period—and I meet with every

attention every mark of kindness that can be imagined from every individual of the excellent Family I am in, and from all the good Kiernans whom I often see—but a little undisturbed quiet—a little *silence*—some moments when all exertion may cease, and when even my most melancholy feelings may be indulged, for these I often sigh in vain—yet I have not often in my life needed such refreshment more.

The anxiety of my darling sisters—of my best loved Friends—but most *your* anxiety my Fanny sits heavily at my heart—in what I have written I have said but a small part of the cruel impediments to a journey which w^d restore me to you—new ones are for ever occurring, and for ever presenting themselves to my thoughts— Many of these without great length I know not how to explain to you, and some are too painful to mention. Do not let me however alarm you—the difficulties are all of a pecuniary nature—if our property in Louth sh^d not eventually suffer by the civil war, and the poor M could be new moulded—I might yet hope that the self denial I am willing to practice, and the sacrifices to which I w^d submit, in time might clear him, and relieve my mind from a burthen which the consciousness of not having voluntarily contributed to creating can scarce make supportable.

My kind Jane travelled to Dublin with us—and tho' we are at opposite ends of the town, neither the distance, heat of the weather, confusion of the times, or claims of her other friends, have prevented her from coming to me every day save one since I have been here— She is a wonderful creature to me—the enthusiastic warmth of her Friendships, her zealous activity in promoting whatever she conceives can serve or give one comfort, her tender and never failing attentions and the partiality of her fondness are such, that I can only compare her to—our Esther—our Mrs Locke—our lovely Amelia—or, to say all that *can* be said, to yourself—and this upon so short a knowledge, and in a country where I expected neither to interest or be interested by one

single individual, save the few persons in it I had known
and loved in England. I consider it as a species of
miracle that has been worked in my favour—unmerited
but not unfelt. The hopes of this dear girl when
we arrived in Dublin were that 3 or 4 days later we
might sail together for England ! she had just received
a sum of money with which all the expenses of the
journey were to be defrayed—her supplications to me
to listen to this scheme were such that one might have
imagined yourself had inspired her—Since affairs have
appeared less alarming, her friends have interfered in
persuading her to defer at least the emigration she medi-
tates. Some circumstances relative to her fortune
render this not only prudential but necessary—yet this
has by no means abated the earnestness of her desire
that I and the children sh^d be removed from this kingdom, and I never had such supplications to resist as hers
have been that I w^d take from her the means of making
the journey—I have been necessitated to use every
argument of defence, and at the same time to soothe and
console her for the firmness of my resolution.

You may perhaps be curious to hear some new
details concerning le Temps—Since I first opened to
you on a particular subject many have been the mortifications endured on one part, and the struggles on the other
to resist expressing without reserve a disgust and resentment wch if a little more unequivocally manifested must
have produced an open breach—the motives for this
discretion your own kindness will present to you—it
was clearly perceived that a rupture with one individual
of the Family must produce a cessation of all intercourse
with the rest—My business has been to soften sensations
of anger and indignation on the part of l'amie—and to
check the suspicions and jealousy wch in a great measure
gave rise to them in le Temps—At present a great coldness subsists on both sides, tho' flowing from very different causes, and as deep and as fixed in the female as
it is superficial in the other. How grievous it is to me
that I should have lost so many of y^r letters my beloved

Fanny! I trust to my Fanny for giving such news of us as she can make most comfortable to our beloved Father and to Esther, James, and nos anges in particular— My kindest love to our affect^te Charles when you write and to dear Charlotte. Kiss the darling Alexander for me, and give my love most sincere and most affect^te to his dear Father

> M^rs d'Arblay, Westhumble, near Dorking, Surry—(7
> passages in this letter have been erased by
> M^rs d'Arblay, who endorsed it thus: "Exquisite
> forbearing virtue with exquisite disinterested and
> touching fondness—Exquisite piety virtue and
> pious fortitude") "No. 4."

July 30th 1798 Dublin.

In the midst of the most harassing uncertainty and uneasiness on my own account my dearest Fanny, I find myself continually exclaiming—"encore si ce n'était que pour moi!" I give you the phrase in the language in which it presents itself to me. It was well indeed if my precious and too tender Friends could escape participating the anxiety and suspense I endure and which then w^d less agitate and afflict me—but it is vain to prolong my silence in hopes of sparing you, since the letters sent two days ago to my Brothers will perhaps lead you to draw false conclusions, and may embitter a disappointment to wch I look forwards without being able to prepare myself for it, tho' great and many w^d be the drawbacks to me were I to escape it—I will not enumerate these—to some my dearest Fanny w^d be insensible except in as much as they affected *my* mind—and amongst the others there is one on wch I will not now enter—I must present it to my beloved Friends if I am *not* to see them. For then it may avail something to them to know it. You will have perceived by my last letter to our Esther that when I wrote it I was nearly in despair since that time my hopes of being reunited to you all have been revived, but never steadily enjoyed—Your Frank my dearest wth our Mrs Locke's kind words and my Brother's affectionate remonstrances came to me on tuesday—how greatly I was touched by them, how penetrated by your excessive urgency I could not tell you, and I am persuaded I need not—the same morning, quite unexpectedly, the M. arrived from Drogheda. He had been one of a detachment employed in guarding the Speaker to Town, and *was* to have returned the next day—however he found *every* day so much business that it was with difficulty he c^d leave Dublin at the end of a week—He is but just gone—and he has left me as uncertain of my destination for the next three months, as I can possibly be of what it may prove at the end of 3, or as many more years as you please—The poor M's indecision on the present occasion I compassionate, tho' it grieves and harasses me in many ways, and even w^d do so for his sake alone—

I must myself have ended the conflict by a voluntary and decided sacrifice—there is so much to be said on this subject, that I sh^d not fear my kind Brother's remonstrances if I were able to answer them—but to do that w^d require a folio, and I must therefore wait till it may be de vive voix—the M. spent near a week here, and when we were alone c^d only talk of—la luie et le beau temps—all my endeavours to lead to what most nearly concerned me—*us* I might say, were ineffectual—and when I was desired to *begin* letters to my Brothers James and Charles, I knew not what to say, nor c^d obtain one word from the M. by wch I c^d infer what might be his secret and ultimate determination—I was therefore compelled to express nothing beyond my truly grateful feelings to these excellent Brothers, and at length the M. concluded the letters—for a short time I judged from his words that I was to see you my beloved Friends—however I was not allowed to remain possessed with this idea even an hour—everything has since been contradictory, and the M. left me to return to Drogheda two days ago, as I have already told you. Compleatly at a loss as to his intentions, and consequently unable to make up my mind in as much as might be in my power to my destiny whatever it may prove—I must now wait till I hear from him—and perhaps may hear from him without being better informed than at this moment—it is therefore that I must write to my dearest Fanny, since even this unsatisfactory account may be preferable to utter silence, and at least in some degree prevent her suffering too severe a disappointment in preparing her to expect it—I write in the midst of interruptions—My room being of course the resort of all the dear children when I am able to retire to it, wch is by no means so frequently as I wish—the Family is so large, and so kind, and so sociable, that I am for ever detained by one or another, not to mention Janey paney's daily visits, and some other claims—it is to these circumstances that my dearest Fanny must attribute the want of clearness she may perceive in what I write, and not indeed to these alone, for my mind is in a very confused state, and I am aware that there are many important things that I ought to tell you which do not occur whilst I am writing—

I wish to write to my dearest Father—but till something is positively settled respecting us I am forced to be silent—I depend on you my Fanny for explaining this a little to him, and I know you will communicate whatever will most interest our Esther, James etc. to them. Tell my Mrs Locke I do not write to her because this suspensive state nearly incapacitates me—and because all that is addressed to Westhumble will I know not be long in reaching Norbury Park—tell her every line of her dear letter went to my heart—how well she knows its feelings! After what I have already said I think I need not *answer* many parts of my beloved Fanny's letter nor of my Brother's—they will see that I do *not* resist the efforts which their almost unparallelled generous love has prompted them to make ; and that if I do not share with them all the comforts of their dear house, I am not with held by such ideas or such feelings as they have suggested—there are parts of y^r letter wch made me smile thro' the tears of tender and grateful admiration that they forced from me—but I will not

discuss them, and tell you *I* am *not* Mrs *Delany*, nor my
Fanny the D^{ss} of Portland that Mrs Delany had neither
a husband nor a child—that the D^{ss} in the midst of
affluence and prosperity ? c^{d} in no way so highly have
enjoyed the blessings of—as—I will not proceed—My
Fanny must be sure that my love at least not
less towards her and towards her beloved partner than
was that of her incomparable Friend for the D^{ss} of
Portland, and that trust in your perfect affection, and
a confidence the steadiest, the most invariable, and the
sweetest in all that relates to you both, in all that regards *yourselves*, y^{r} characters, your inmost hearts, can
rise no higher.   In speaking of the
kind *cabal* of wch I am the unworthy object, explain these
words to me, " one who for particular reasons appears
not is *à la tete* and ought to be." I do not require the
particular reasons, but wish for the name wch may be
safely given when you write again thus—*the person whose
name you require is*—etc.   Je devrais vous
repondre à vous mon aimable Frere, du moins sur un mot
de votre lettre qui m'a fait de la peine—Je vous proteste
que fut elle encore *Miss Burney* les sentimens que J'ai
éprouvé et que J'éprouve auraient été juste ce qu'ils
sont sur toutes les propositions que cette sœur cherie
m'a faite. Il vous jure que quand vous seriez né mon
Frère il me serait impossible de me fier plus que Je ne
le fais sur vous, et que J'ai même le bonheur de croise
pleinement a votre tendre amitié—Je n'admet point du
tout que vous valez mieux que moi en *amitié*—peut ètre
en serez vous convaincu un jour, et de la façon dont
vous l'entendez—mais en attendant, croyez m'en sur
ma parole que Je vous donne de bien bon cœur en bien
mauvais francais Je ne sçais plus comment m'expliquer
du tout. Je vous remercie d'aimer ma nouvelle amie
qui m'aime bien comme une ancienne—Elle is réellement
inconceivable à mon egard, et Je me sçais un peu bon grè
de l'impression qu'elle a faite sur votre esprit et celui
de notre Fanny. My head is confused and I am unwilling to keep my letter yet another post—Dublin is

very quiet, there has been no attempt at tumult since I have been in it notwithstanding the executions which are daily going on, and wch at first created a good deal of alarm, and notwithstanding that the city has almost been surrounded by Rebels, who have fled and concealed themselves on the approach of the military in the mountains—the vigilance of Government and the activity of the yeomanry have been admirable. I have had a very kind letter f^m Miss Wall, and a very pleasant one filled with accounts of Westhumble and of Norbury Park—how good you are

> M^{rs} d'Arblay—Westhumble, Dorking, Surrey—(endorsed " No 5." 5 passages have been erased).

Saturday, Septth. 8, 1798.

My beloved Fanny must have received two letters from me since hers of the 29th was sent, the last of which since the Invasion—a subsequent letter to my dearest Father, and one of a yet later date to our Esther must I trust have softened your apprehensions my too kind and too anxious sister—Since that last, near a week has elapsed without bringing me one word of intelligence, and we know here no more of the Invaders, or of Ld Cornwallis and his army than if we were in America—this seems to me incomprehensible, and will probably appear yet more so to you—An Officer of the Dumfrieshire Militia or Fencibles now stationed in Drogheda was here yesterday, and said no news whatever have been rec^d there since Sunday from Ld Cornwallis, tho' it was concluded some action must have taken place. Unconfirmed accounts of Admiral Nelson and Buonoparte were all he had to bring wch very little satisfied me, for I am as you will imagine very anxious for news and the ignorance we are in is as unpleasant as extraordinary—Meanwhile my own dearest Fanny we have great great cause to be grateful for our present secure and undisturbed existence in this country—the people around us work on tranquilly, and shew no alarm except when they conceive we are likely to leave them—

so little is known about the Invasion that they conclude
the French to have been *all killed*, and they seem perfectly content with the supposition—While all continues in this state, it w^d be difficult to convince one
more candid than the M. that our situation is dangerous,
or a removal requisite—the alarm of my Friends is a
subject of derision, and complaints or remonstrances
are worse than useless, as they irritate, and produce fits
of outrage and phrenzy the mere apprehension of w^ch
is an evil amongst the most difficult to support. It is
in many ways painful to me to tell you this my Fanny,
who seem yet unconscious how impracticable a being
we have to encounter—but it is necessary to spare you
the torment of unsatisfied expectation and of hopes
which arise only to be blighted—Your anxiety—our
Esther's—your precious letters and my Mrs Locke's have
urged me to go much further than any personal feelings
c^d have done, tho' with a hopelessness of success that
redoubled the difficulty of the attempt. It is past, and
I have only to commit myself to Providence, and the
chance of such circumstances arising as Time may give
birth to—Would to Heaven my dearest Fanny c^d with
any degree of composure resign herself to a destiny
wch it is vain to resist, and share with me an humble
trust in Providence which shields me from such terrors
as times like these might otherwise create. If I cease
to struggle do not impute my seeming passiveness to
an Insensibility that w^d be odious, but to a too certain
conviction of the uselessness of effort : and be not dissatisfied if under such circumstances y^r poor Susan can
derive some degree of support from the idea that her
duty, strictly speaking, is more compleatly fulfilled by
relinquishing this journey with all its soothing and
delicious temptations, than it c^d have been by accom-
plishing it thro' so many obstacles, and by a *compelled*
acquiescence if any c^d have been obtained. To quit
this country in its present state without *all* my children
would be wretched—My dearest Fanny could not wish
it for me—and were I now to come it w^d be without

Norbury, as his Father tho' he sometimes amuses him-
self wth saying we are to go wth the first vessel that sails
from Drogheda always accompanies this declaration
with expressions of satisfaction that NORBURY, *who is
not afraid,* and *for whom there is no cause to fear, will
continue in this kingdom*—Let me however tell my dearest
Fanny that were danger to *approach* us, I feel persuaded
this point w^d be given up, and that the M. w^d send us
all away together, tho' at present not choosing to part
with *any of us,* he is aware that by detaining Norbury he
effectually checks the attempts I might continue to
make were I not so withheld—O my dear Fanny!—
What w^d have become of me had my poor boy been
already at Rathmelton? Since this letter was begun I
have obtained news. Ld Cornwallis is at Carrick on
Shannon—the French have eluded pursuit thus far, and
overcome such opposition as has been made them—but
it seems almost impossible that shortly they sh^d escape
being surrounded. Apprehending the approach of the
Lord Lieutenant they quitted Castlebar, and proceeded
northward to Foxford—thence to Coloony, Drumahair
and Manor Hamilton in Leitrim—so far the acc^{ts} are
official—but they are reported to have proceeded as far
as to *Cavan*—and it is said they mean to push on to
Dublin—but this is almost incredible, or if it can be
credited it is impossible to doubt their immediate defeat
—Sometimes I wish my Norbury were with me in this
obscure quiet corner—at others I conceive his present
situation to be as secure as any can be in this country—
Mrs Brabazon is wonderfully phlegmatic—W^d you
believe it, she is purposing to inoculate her two babies
at this period, one of whom an infant of 4 months, the
other not 16 months old, because it is *a good season of
the year*—She is at Rath where her husband spends all
the time he can be away from his corps which is at
Drogheda—the M. has continued to be hitherto very
little with it—indeed everything is so quiet as not to
render great exertions necessary and the Harvest requires
him at home. Tuesday 11th I have had more than my

usual hindrances in writing this time my dearest, for the
rainy weather has kept *all* the Family within almost
constantly, but now I am not sorry for the delay as I
have just rec^d most excellent news from my dear Janey
Paney wch tho' I am sure it will reach you before this
letter I like you sh^d hear likewise from me—God be
praised your alarm f^m the Invasion will now close, and
God be praised the mischief had not time to spread
wider—May this unsuccessful effort be the last! Genl
Lake came up wth the French on Saturday at a place
called Ruskey Bridge in Longford, and totally defeated
them. [They] have *surrendered at discretion*, a great
number of the Rebels who had joined them [were]
killed or taken prisoners—No officer of ours except
General Cradock who is . . . . In two days more, so rapid
was their march the French might have been in Dublin,
a considerable body of Rebels from Kildare and Wicklow
were advancing fast to join them—These have been dispersed or put to the sword, for several actions have taken
place within a few days—Jane writes me word that L^d
Fitzwilliam had arrived in Dublin on Sunday—but upon
hearing the French were defeated, he s^d he w^d not fight
against the Irish—and immediately returned. I trust
there will shortly be no need for anyone to fight against
the Irish, and that this blow will be decisive. " How I
long for M^{rs} d'Arblay to hear all this " says my dst
Janey paney—" I have a great mind to write it to her
myself and to assure her her dear sister is yet alive—but
if it must be you that give her this intelligence, say a
word for your J. P. who is so grateful for being thought
of wth such unmerited kindness, and who longs to send
her love, but that it w^d be too great a liberty, tho' no
other phrase so well accords with her feelings "—were
I not cruelly pressed for time, as there is an immediate
opportunity of sending this I have something to tell
you of this sweet girl which deeply interests me—it
shall be for my next letter—and will not my Fanny
explain her enigma to me when she answers this ? I
understand the initials in the corner, and long for an

explanation—write between hooks [thus] my dearest. In all probability even that precaution will be unnecessary, but with it there is perfect security—the answer to my query in the name of our Father [padre] filled my eyes wth tears and my heart wth tender gratitude—I had wished—but scarcely hoped for that name—because . . . you will discover wherefore—and it w^d be difficult and long to write it—Heaven bless him ! Our dear Charles is very kind—pray thank him most affectionately for me—I have heard from Esther and have ever since been painfully occupied in thinking of her—dearest soul—You do not mention the martyrdom she has been suffering, and perhaps scarcely knew it when you wrote. I trust I shall not be much longer without having some account of her from herself—and my Fanny when she writes will tell me how she is—She was in a state not only of terrible pain but of alarm for what might be the cause of it when she wrote to me, having already parted with a tooth without being relieved. Thanking Mrs Locke for her sweet kind lines—I hope soon to have more and many details of her and hers—how good you are in calling on Susan's sister—that faithful soul is infinitely gratified by y^r kindness in this particular—I must must have done, wch I hate—for I have not named y^r captivating little darling, tho' the little traits this letter of y^{rs} contains of him have touched and enchanted me as I cannot describe—sweet little soul ! I must thank you for so bringing him before me—I see him so clearly, so well—yet alas—very insufficiently—Adieu adieu dearest—let our Father know you have heard fm me since the good news, and our Esther in particular—I am sure you will name me as I wish to all ours when you can—loves 1000 to Norbury Park, and to my dear kind Brother. I am very well—quite well my Fanny —the dear children so. My Willy an old man to morrow it will be his birth day—Is not the project a literary one my dearest ? explain more if it does not quite go against you and pray write soon

M^{rs} d'Arblay, Westhumble, Dorking, Surry.

Tuesday, Oct. 9ᵗʰ, 1798.

The same day on which I had sent an answer to a most touchingly kind letter from our beloved Father, and by the return of the same messenger, I received my Mʳˢ Locke's Frank with her and my dearest Fanny's letters—These have been ever since uppermost in my thoughts, but not a moment till the present one have I found in which I cᵈ venture to commit to paper one of the thousand feelings to which they have given rise—Ah my dearest Fanny! if distant from me you can ever wonder that I should not in defiance of possible consequences and of every obstacle the most ingenious tyranny can supply, fly to my incomparable and never more beloved Friends, how wᵈ that feeling be increased were it possible for you, unseen and unsuspected, once to become a witness of *ma triste vie!* of all the variety of sorrows and mortifications wᶜʰ in endless succession chase each other—of all the emotions of alarm, of Indignation, of disdain—of the distaste—the disgust that every day renews—Would I could boast of that *determined Philosophy of acquiescence* you say you regret to have *broken in upon*—but I fear I am destined to endless conflicts—conflicts I wished to conceal from you, because I thought the knowledge of them wᵈ but augment your disappointment; not to wish myself restored to you, to wish it most *ardently*, wᵈ be impossible to me—that wish alone is sufficient to delude me into listening to false hopes wᶜʰ serve only to embitter my regret in their failure. I strive to submit patiently—not from *determined philosophy*, but because what I endure appears to me inevitable—or avoidable only by a mode of action wᶜʰ my best friends could not wish me to pursue, and wᶜʰ wᵈ in the end render me more hopelessly wretched than now—but in ceasing to combat I don't cease to suffer, and tho' I may assume an appearance of calmness my mind is not the less perturbed—the destination of my poor Norbury has operated in checking my earnestness to return to England from time to time, and constantly and powerfully whilst the country seemed in danger fm the rebellion, and since fᵐ Invasion

—but as apprehensions of the kind have subsided, my heart has again yearned to be restored to my Father, my Sisters, my beloved Friends, and every little ray of hope has revived me, and every change caused me new agitation—When despairing of success I have sought to resign myself—as a *duty*—and to strengthen my mind by such considerations as reason c^d suggest to me—I have endeavoured to forget myself, and to find consolation in thinking that for many others it might be best I sh^d be condemned to remaining here—It w^d be endless, by letter at least to develop fully all that has been passing in my mind—but one support of my constancy has failed—and my eyes fill, and my heart overflows wth tenderness when it recurs to me—and it is perpetually recurring that our Father wishes for me—for *Himself* wishes it—for his *own* comfort and consolation—[not] simply from compassionate and tender feelings for mine ! Ah my dearest Fanny this exceeds all I had an idea of —it drives from my mind every wish but that of being at his feet—in his arms—I feel as if I c^d willingly sacrifice one of my own to be allowed to be with him—those words you repeat that he *sighs for an answer from Ireland* that may *comfortably form his new establishment,* melt me penetrate me—are never out of my mind—fill it at once wth joy and sorrow, tho' both of the softest kind—I had already answered his dear letter—tenderly and gratefully—but without conceiving half I owed this beloved Parent—but if I had—my task w^d have been yet more painful and my trial greater—before you receive this letter, doubtless my dearest Fanny you will have heard wth what shocking—what inconceivable levity the first application was answered—an application wch all circumstances considered must have touched any— save the one person to whom it was addressed—how much such a return hurt and afflicted me it is needless to say —but c^d I have conceived it w^d have cost my Father a *personal* disappointment I sh^d have felt inconsolable—I have been interrupted, and have so many things to say I must check my pen that the most essential may not remain unsaid. " You w^d *take no one's place in pre-siding*," says my dearest Fanny—is there any signification in those words that require explanation—to *preside* is you know not amongst things *essential to my happiness* —but where is Sarah going—for what time ? and Mrs Rishton—my dear Father's letter gives me no particulars —With respect to the money which I rejoice you have rec^d f^m Ireland, let it not lie useless for me my dar-ling—and my kindest of Brothers—Sh^d ever the M^s *veto* be withdrawn, I w^d not scruple, if necessary, to call on you or James for assistance, but meanwhile it will occa-sion a new uneasiness to my mind to imagine you are suffering a large sum of money to lie useless on my account—I am very very earnest in my wishes on this subject my dearest Fanny, and if I urge you no further it is because my paper fills so fast—but let me hope to be understood, and that what I have already s^d may suffice—I rec^d long ago a letter wch comforted me greatly from our dearest Esther, to whom I mean very soon to write—and I will not be long neither without thanking our beloved Mrs Locke for her sweet letter and affecting communications—how touching is the account you give me of Mrs Charles ! how I pity the Duchess ! she sh^d methinks have been spared a new sorrow when bowed down by a calamity so dreadful as that which has fallen upon her—My Mrs Locke will I fear feel but too severe a pang in the separation alone from her loved son and all his—but I hope too, she will be reconciled to an event wch in every point of view save the distancing him from his Family is so highly desirable—a thousand thousand tender wishes give her from her and your Susan. I long at once to congratulate and to condole with her—To morrow will be Leatherhead Fair day, and we shall all be praying for good weather—how kind in that sweet soul to find time for writing to me in the midst of all her hurries and disturbances ? I hope the Fair may be particularly fortunate not only for the usual motives of wishing it, but because I know it will chear her—I had not an idea you had a shilling of mine my

Fanny, but since you have—I sh^d be pleased if I c^d
obtain from the Fair some little offering for my dear
Janey paney—The Time of choice will be past when
this reaches you but as she is so simple that I know she
w^d best like something fabricated by myself, if I c^d have
materials for a letter case, wth the chevrils (and even the
needle to work them wth) whenever an opportunity of
sending them occurs, it w^d gratify me particularly—and
this reminds me of a parcel sweet Amelia sent lately to
Norbury—les annales de la vertu wch I think an excellent
work for him, and the sweetest kind letter you can conceive—I hope she has had his answer, which was (as usual)
scribbled in great haste, for no letter can be otherwise
written in this house—You will know before this reaches
you that Mr Maturin's Friends being happily for me
of temper more anxious than the M^s, have prevailed
upon him to delay establishing himself in the North—
his neighbourhood however continues quiet so I must
prepare myself I imagine for my Norbury's travelling
thither shortly ! I shall at least see him first again and
I hope keep him a little while—his stay here the last time
was prolonged to a fortnight. The reason of his not
going to see Dominic w^d be difficult to give—it had
been even solicited wth earnestness, and at *first* promised by the M : Mrs Browne offered to send her
carriage wth Col Brown's valet, a servant deconfiance,
40 miles of the road to meet him—but this proposal
was written by Mr Gabriel Maturin (Dominic's Tutor,
and the intimate acquaintance of the M) who suddenly
professed himself much offended that Mrs Brown had
not written it *herself*, and without apology, declared
Norbury sh^d not go—the consequence of this was a disappointment to the two boys, and that Mrs Browne
was affronted. You know that on the breaking out of
the rebellion she was amongst the earliest fugitives wth
her Family—I believe they are all still at Beaumauris.
Mrs Cartland has written me word she had rec^d a very
polite letter from M. d'Arblay, wth a postscript from
you of which she was not a little proud—I am writing

19

very incoherently—I have not time to *arrange* my
subjects—there is one my Fanny is desirous to hear
of wch I sh^d be sorry not to have room for—my Jane—
and there is one mentioned in her letter of which I hope
to know more. You have then at length heard again
from M de N. that his letter should be *triste et noir*
does not surprise me—Nor can I wonder at the feelings
expressed by Mr Locke—but I am concerned at both.
My dear Brother is very kind in designing to transcribe
this letter for me—or at least a part of it—I wish to hear
all it contains—to know where the writer is—He does
not I conclude mention M de F—but poor Ferdinand
is I am sure a still faithful and I hope a useful Friend—
I much wish this good man may receive my Brother's
letter to him—How cruel it is that he should still be
deprived of the means of corresponding with his excellent Uncle! but I must quit this to speak of my young
Friend. When in Dublin she frequently wished to introduce me to an old Lady, a relation of her mother,
whose memory she reverences and almost idolizes, who
was she told me a *second* Mother to her—She spoke
not only of her but of her children wth great warmth
of affection, and s^d they had spent a great part of their
Infancy and childhood together like Brothers and Sisters
—this old Lady, a Mrs Disney, lived in my neighbourhood, and I often saw my Janey escorted home by one
of her sons in the evening (no one was suffered to be out
after nine o'clock at night) the first time I saw him I
was struck with his countenance, I perceived he eyed me
with attention, and a desire of liking me, wch I knew to
whom to attribute. My liking of him was more in-
voluntary I thought he had the pleasantest face, the
most agreeable expression in it of sense and *bienveillance* I
had seen in one of his sex since I left dear England—I
mentioned this to my Jane, who was not a little pleased,
but who spoke of him and his merits so unaffectedly,
that I had not an idea they were *peculiarly* interesting
to her—He is not an elder Brother, and I knew his
fortune was small—he is a clergyman, and his living

unhappily near Kilcullen, where one of the first battles was fought, wch place he was compelled to leave, and from whence he will *this* year at least probably obtain no part of his income—these circumstances distanced from me the idea of any connection, wch something in his manner w^d otherwise have raised in me—for as he accompanied her home whenever she had spent the day with his Mother, I saw him very frequently, and saw that he seemed to cherish the arm he held under his wth irrepressible fondness—I quite compassionated him, for I was persuaded he was compleatly won and devoted to my Jane—and nothing seemed more natural—However a few days before I quitted Dublin, this dear Girl wth a good deal of embarasment, confessed she had something to communicate to me—and I found that my conjectures were perfectly justified wth respect to the feelings of Mr Disney, but that my commiseration might be spared—for my Jane was insensible neither to his worth nor to his attachment—and tho' her fortune is small, and his very inconsiderable, the Mother and whole Family so justly prize her in herself, that they have been unanimous in wishing the connection to take place—the Eldest Brother to render it possible has in the most generous manner almost forced his acceptance of an estate wch brings in above 100 a year, wch will make their income very comfortable—and the marriage will probably take place in less than a month—It so happened that I never saw him after I rec^d this confession, but many friendly messages have passed between us— My Janey is but just now come into the country—I saw her kind face since this letter was begun this morning, and shall again embrace her to morrow previous to her return to Dublin, where she will remain till the ceremony takes place—where her place of residence will be I know not—but not here alas—she will be removed far from me—but I shall know her happy, and that will be a blessing to me—I have always been dissatisfied, and at times even afflicted at her situation in her own Family, where her merit has never been felt but to be envied—

She will be delighted wth your lines my Fanny w^{ch}
to morrow I mean to let her hear—to-day I had of her
but a glimpse—W^{th} respect to the M. for a great while
past her manner has been more and more mortifying—
She however made use of every means, even those of
solicitation, to induce him to take some measures of
safety for me and the children from the commencement
of the Rebellion till my final disappointment in Dublin
—this stroke was quite too much for her, and produced,
not an absolute quarrel, because the M. wished to pass
it off as a jest, but the keenest reproaches from her, and
the most mortifying that c^{d} be uttered—He was not
insensible to this—but ignorant of her situation, trusted
that her affection for me w^{d} bring her to Belcotton, and
that every ill impression w^{d} soon be effaced—they have
not since met—and the M. has here learnt that soon she
will bear another name—I was not wth him when this
news reached him—but guessed he had heard it by his
manner—his great pleasure now is to represent her as
being completely *passée—too old for her husband*, whom
he is so good as to pronounce *a Fool*, etc. etc.—he is now
at Castle Bellingham, and stays for a Fair held there
to morrow, wch has enabled me to write thus much of a
history I wished to give you—let me, if you *can* have
your *court* history my dear one—Alas how long may it
be ere verbal communications become possible ?—I am
peculiarly desirous of having all that relates to sweet
Alexander's appearance and behaviour—I am sorry he
is not *fatter*—a little darling—but glad that he grows,
and whatever you tell me of him interests me most
particularly. I must briefly answer your questions relative to Fanny—She is much grown every way—her face
still as infantine as when you saw her, but her person
that of a young woman, and certainly rather too large—
She holds herself however something better than before
we went to Dublin—She preserves her bloom—but is
sadly tanned—Belcotton is not a place to encrease
delicacy, and the M. perseveres in not choosing she sh^{d}
wear gloves, a veil, or even a bonnet when he can prevent

it—in her manner she is I think not much changed since
you saw her—She is good humoured, pleasant, and has
I think acquired no affectations—Willy is sometimes an
amusing little Buffoon—but his passion for mimicry
is not advantageous here—his brogue, and the manner
he affects will shock you whenever you see him—I have
not room for details—else I might give some that w^d
divert you. My good Susan is greatly gratified by the
kind things s^d of her—to tell them her is the best return
I can make for her faithful service, and the pleasure she
receives from them she well deserves—She begs me to
give her humble duty and thanks to you and my dearest
Mrs Locke. Mrs Brabazon inoculated her two infants
last Saturday—She is indeed anxiously phlegmatic—
Mrs Hill was gone into the country before I quitted
Dublin and I know her direction—however [it is safe] to
direct to her at her Father's. He is recovered—My
kindest respects and love to dearest Mr Locke and remember me to the dear Girls most affectionately pray. I
told you I believe I had heard f^m Miss Wall and how
mortified she and her Mother were at Mrs Dickens'
perseverance—What noble news is come at last from
Admiral Nelson but what a desperate conflict and how
hardly earned a victory ? We have had illuminations
here as well as in Dublin. Adieu adieu most dear one.
Kiss for me Alexander and give 1000 loves to his dear
Father

> *M^{rs} d'Arblay, Westhumble, Dorking, Surry*—(endorsed
> by M^{rs} d'Arblay " Exemplary sweetness and forti-
> tude and tender friendship with the admirable
> Mrs Disney then Miss Jane Brabazon) " No 7."

BELCOTTON—*Jan* 5th 1799.

My dearest Fanny's, my Mrs Locke's precious paquet
ought to have reached me I believe only a day or two
after I had sent a letter to that last named beloved Friend
—but it chanced that no one was sent to the post office
for many days, so that altho' the Frank is dated the 20th I
did not receive it till the last day of December. I thought

it arrived then to reconcile me a little at parting with that
—iniquitous year, which by its succession of baleful events
makes me wish and pray the remembrance of it might never
more recur to me.   Yet from 98 I must date the happiness
of one sweet Friend—my Janey's—and that at least I
would not forget.   The next morning I wrote to our loved
Father—it was long since I had heard from him or had
courage to write—I have been happier since that letter
went, and did not reproach myself for not giving the
first moments I could so employ to my Fanny, notwithstanding her urgent request and solicitude because my
letter to N Park, and another to our Esther must have
tranquilized her with regard to my health ; and unless
to remove immediate anxiety I could not bear to send
hasty and short scrawls in return for such rich and
precious paquets as those of my darling Friends—I know
that not only Norbury Park and Westhumble are one
but that our Esther communicates to you the chief
contents of my letters, and when they have been some
time gone, it frequently happens to me to think I have
written to you what has been addressed to her—however
in all that wch materially interests you, I know it is the
same thing—Do not be afraid of my deceiving you upon
the subject of health my dearest. I know the importance
it is of to you to be convinced of my *integrity* in this
respect, and you may depend upon my sincerity although
I cannot forbear smiling when you seem almost to
expect, and almost to require that I sh^d *send for you*
on the appearance of *a feverish cold*—dearest, dearest
soul. If Belcotton were not guarded by a kind of
Cerberus, subject to such malignant damps, such un-
genial and inclement weather perhaps you w^d do indiscreetly to trust so much to my forbearance, and so to
tempt me—lest however you sh^d imagine I may have
suffered from any uncommon severity of the season
I must hasten to assure you it has been calmer, more
temperate, and less changeable a great deal than usual
for a good while past—I am not you well know a profound *Philosopher*, and yet I not only experience an

amendment in the climate, but trust it may in some degree be permanent, because I think I have discovered some of the causes to which it may be attributed—Thus much for my Fanny's satisfaction, and now for my own let me mention the treasures of my paquet—her dear letter—my M[rs] Locke's, my Amelia's the 5th sheet of the charming journal—the kindest of all Transcribers' promise of restoring to me its commencement—the dear little lock of hair, which it delighted and comforted me to receive—and the sketches, which are *lovely*—That dear little darling Alexander—how sweetly they bring him before my eyes! but how they make me long anew to behold the lovely little model, and to caress, and to half devour him—not that I think I sh[d] play the cannibal if I were to see him neither—I feel that I sh[d] approach him with great gentleness and precaution that I might not be repulsed—it is cruel to be cut off thus from the knowledge of his infantine years—I regret it as I remember I used my beloved Fanny's courtly but cloistered state when my little Norbury seemed in my eyes to be every hour gaining some new charm, and when, sure of her participation in my pleasure, I wished her to see every motion and listen to every word he uttered—One w[d] fain on such occasions retard the progress of Time : but 'tis an obstinate monster, that will neither slacken his pace nor mend it at our pleasure— Acquit me (at least till I write again to Norbury Park) in some degree to our darling Amelia—embrace for her *Mama Petty* who inasmuch as she can be proud of what she does not merit feels most proud of still retaining that title from *her* how I thank her—how I love her— you *can* and I must thank you too, my dearest for procuring me so speedily the lock for which I petitioned, and which consoles me for what I lost—her letter is full of *honied words* and melted me as I read it—I had thought it long since I had had a line from her dear hand, and tho' I know her heart and can never doubt her invariable sweetness and goodness, I think from time to time I require the support of her touching assur-

ances of unabated affection—My Norbury shall receive
the sketch when I can obtain a sure conveyance, tho' I
shall feel miserly in parting with it, and a little dread
his indiscreet raptures, for he will be wanting to shew
it all the world—All the world of Fanet is not indeed
very considerable—I am much vexed that his letter
was lost—it was sent by Post and I directed it myself,
so that to what its failure has been owing I cannot tell
—like your *invaluable* paquet I suppose it must have
been destroyed in some stol'n mail—*Many* have been
seized since the *troubles* here were at the eve of beginning. Friday Jany 11th this letter has been long begun,
and when I shall be able to conclude it I know not—but
I am not so anxious as common, since I am sure you
must have been relieved from y^r kind fears about me
before I received your paquet—We celebrated à notre
facon the birth day of l'ange gardien de Norbury, the
sixth—it is a blessed day—and having done what I could
towards rejoicing my young ones not forgetting good
Susan, I solaced my own self by reading over some of
the dear letters I received from N. Park and Bookham
when I first arrived here—I exhibited too my Amelia's
cuttings of her little niece and our darling, and the sketches
were again produced—Whilst I am speaking of birth
days you do not suppose our Alexander was forgotten—
but I felt melancholy in recollecting he was four years
of age—quite old!—I long to know news has been received of the arrival of Mr Charles and his lovely family—
I hope he got over by degrees that wretched sea sickness,
and that sweet Mrs Charles c^d receive some assistance
from the nurses—What a blessing that she sh^d have been
enabled to supply their places. I quite *look up to her*
with admiration when I think of it, and of what w^d
have been my own helpless incapacity under the same
circumstances—but seriously, I hope the necessity of
making such exertions may have been of use in restoring
her in some measure to her natural state by dissipating
afflicting recollections, and more forcibly impressing her
with a sense of her own importance to her sweet children

and their Father. Are Lady Lucy and Lady Sophia
always with the Duchess ? and is Miss Ogilvie's health
restored ?—Give my Mrs Locke my tenderest thanks
for all the sweet and interesting details of her dear
letter, and the delightful extracts from M de Lally. I
hope not to be very long without writing to her, and to
our Esther I must write almost immediately—I had
from her a long confidential letter at the same time wth
your paquet—both arrived so seasonably qu'il n'en a
pas été question du tout—I continue moreover unmolested with respect to my letters, which I tell you that
you may not be discouraged in writing à cœur ouvert—
I entreat you to tell me faithfully if this large sheet pays
double ? it is my only one alas—but if it is not over
charged, I may possibly be able to obtain a fresh supply
when I see my Janey—but that I fear will not be yet—
I have had a sweet letter, and account of her happiness,
wch she ventured to send me notwithstanding Cerberic
fears being strongly upon her—their first evening reading in her new establishment at Naas has been *Camilla,*
wch never was so compleatly enjoyed she says—" Never
were love scenes so sweetly so delicately depicted—yet
my dear M^{rs} d'Arblay puts me in a fever every evening
by the ingenuity wth which she has taught Edgar and
Camilla alternately to torment themselves and each
other—She afterwards mentions with the tenderest
gratitude the manner in wch you have written of her in
some passages, I pleased myself with transcribing—" You
have made Robert quite proud," she says " but do not
think I shall so soon become so for do I not know that
when M^{rs} d'Arblay so expresses herself, it is not me,
but only *your* Janey Paney that she has an idea of "
What she writes of Camilla reminds me of Norbury's
passion for that work, wch tho' when he was last here he
had met a new flame in the *Sentimental Journey* wch had
fallen in his way, was not at all abated—he has many
parts of it by heart and frequently broke out wth little
phrases such as these " *Camilla blushing yet smiling* denied the charge "—that scene was one of his darling

favourites—and Edgar *reading the prayers*, and most of all Camilla *seeing her Mother standing at the foot of her bed* which scene has occasioned him great emotion I found—Pray Mama he once gravely asked me, "is not Edgar Mandlebert like Mr William?" Mrs Tyrold he said a few times made him think of Mrs Locke—but he found out she was not so soft, so tender as his beloved foster mother, of whom he retains the most perfect remembrance, and once when we were speaking of handsome persons he almost surprised me by saying " I think Mrs Locke *the most beautiful woman in the world*." You will understand the cause of my surprise and Fanny *spoke* it " Oh " cried he " I know Amelia is the sweetest creature that ever *was*, and *should think so if she was not pretty at all*—but you do'nt suppose because of what I said of Mrs Locke that I have forgot that Amelia is *exquisitely* beautiful too " in corroboration of this assertion he added that Mama thought Mr Locke, " *certainly* " the best and sweetest of men—yet he did not for that conclude she did not think " *Grandpapa eminent for his goodness and wisdom*," and " *love him better than anybody* " —this past a good while ago, and I hesitated a little whether to *record* it in the annales of my Norbury—but you will find in it his old style of reasoning—He was *burning* to read Evelina and Cecilia, and it w^d have been a great delight to me to have read them to him—but the fear of losing those dear books deter'd me from bringing them hither, and my own Camilla is I believe at Westhumble—the M. gave away his, and w^d have done the same wth the other works had they been here—Did you not hear from Chelsea long ago how Norbury taught Willy to exclaim " Lauk! says Mr Dubster— Mrs Mitton—save Miss Dennel—help us cries Sir Hugh " the words sounded the more ridiculous from passing thro' Willy's mouth, who repeated them with many comical gesticulations and changes of voice—You call upon me for some traits of this little person—who is an original—and if his Papa did not spoil him w^d be— not all I c^d wish—but a great deal nearer it—he is a

dear little soul with all his imperfections and [shows] his
affection for *all Mama's Friends* and *takes their part* in a
very comic way when they fall under censure—The other
day the M. told him *Madame sh⁴ go to England* and he
and Jenny (Fanny's old name) sh⁴ stay wᵗʰ him. " But
Papa," answered he after a little very grave consideration,
" people will say its a wickedness of you not to go with
your wife—and I am sure all our Friends will *hate* you
for not keeping your word—and you know we were
only to be here a year at any rate "—his eloquent little
harangue did not anger but divert, indeed he is become
so great a favourite, and everybody says he is so wonderfully like his Father, that whatever he says succeeds—
This favour is not however always shewn in the most
gratifying manner, and the poor little Fellow is generally tormented most when played with, as you may
gather from the following little speech, made wᵗʰ a
deeply heightened colour, and the utmost gravity after
escaping from the *caresses* of his Father, who was only
playing with him—" Papa—I would have you *leave off*
those tricks of biting and pinching—because else, when
people grow up not to be children they never will come to
see you I assure you, so you had best leave it off *now* I
think "—His brogue is undescribable—but if I c⁴ recollect
them I w⁴ give you some of his blunders—the bigness
for instance he calls the *bigny* and the *muchny,* and has
coined a number of other such words—and when we
were speaking of a storm we had this summer in Dublin
he exclaimed " Mama heard three great thunders that
day and there wasn't one lightening." Upon something
he s⁴ wᶜʰ I cannot remember, his Papa asked why he said
that—" Because it came into my head—and who put
it in your head ? I don't know—I suppose God Almighty
—and how did he put it in your head ?—I can't tell
nor you can't neither Papa—you can't tell a great many
things that God Almighty does in Heaven—its *impossible* to say that "—presently after he added with great
gravity " God Almighty has such power that he could
fell us down without a push"—Not long ago he laughed

to himself upon his Papa's saying I had no conscience—
—"What do you laugh at Sir" he was asked a little
sternly—"because I think she has—I think Mama has
a great *deal* of conscience"—and softening his voice he
added very gently "*rather a little more than you have
Papa*" the M only laughed but presently asked him
what conscience was "Why when we do wrong our
conscience makes us sorry for it" "so Mama has more conscience than I have, because she does wrong the oftenest?"
"No I didn't say that—but if she does wrong *in an accident* she is very sorry" and am I not sorry too when I
do wrong *in an accident*? "no Papa" (laughing) "nor
not sorry neither when—when—when" "How, little
villain?" Here the argument ended without another
word but in a loud fit of laughing on both sides—I know
that the sensation which these little traits will produce
in dearest Fanny will not be an unmixed pleasure, tho'
I think they will amuse her, and our darling Friend—
and if . . . my Amelia w^d like to hear them or any parts
of my letters it w^d much gratify me they sh^d be communicated to her since I cannot regularly nor often
write to her, and unless from the wish of sparing her
tender mind unnecessary pain, there is scarce a confidence
I w^d not place in her—it is the only testimony I can
give of my true and grateful affection—I hope she does
not still suffer by the pain in her face she caught on her
journey from Lincolnshire—pray let me hear—what a
precious blessing it is to me to hear such accounts of
dearest Mr Locke's health! it is one *unspeakable*—but
with many things to add, notwithstanding this long
bavardages my conscience smites me for not having said
a little more of the 5th *sheet* and that amiable lovely
P^{ss}—how much I admired with you her manner of
speaking to Miss Farren and Miss Wallis—her kind desire
of recommending P^e Edwarde by the trait she told of
him, in wch the sensibility he shewed at the pain he had
given more than made amends for his etourderie—etc.
etc., nor how amused I was by her simile of a toad in
the hole—the *noble sirloin* in a *paltry batter pudding*—

and by her eagerness to desire her Brothers to *shut the door
after them*—It was a most gratifying conversation—But
how curious and unexpected the discourse about Chesington, and our dear good Kitty Cooke! I c^d not forbear
laughing as I read it, and at his R. H's formal *Madam*
etc. tho I really felt uneasy for the sensations you must
have experienced whilst the discourse lasted and was
relieved that the P^{ss} asked no questions—I shall rejoice
to have a continuation, and wish I c^d have more at once,
wch you will say is very greedy—but you must at least
own that if I return you homely fare, I give you as much
of it as I am able, and that in despite of the most *retarding* wretched pens that ever were written with—Have
you heard of Mr Shirley—I believe he grows more and
more stupid and absorbed, and I am told he never writes
to any of his family—unhappily Mr G. M's account of
the bad state of finances in this country is I fear but
too just—how glad I sh^d be if this business of yrs was
terminated—Adieu my dearest: we are well—the
weather far from bad—My account from Fanet good
and recent—Give 1000 loves for me at N. P. to my dear
Brother Alexander and kisses to *Alex^r the young*—I w^d
not be so rude as to say the little, yet in this I expose
myself to a cavil; ever ever your S. E. P. My good
Fanny's affec^{te} love and kindest wishes must not always
be [forgotten] it is not her fault; How kind of sweet
Mrs Locke to send a [message] to Mrs Newton's, Susan
is truly grateful for this and for every mention made of
her sister in yr dear letters—I think I ought to be doubly
so. The under written is for dear Charlotte whose
direction I don't know.

> *M^{rs} d'Arblay, West humble, Dorking, Surry.* (Re-
> directed "Gone to Doctor Burney's Chelsea
> College." Endorsed by M^{rs} d'Arblay "No 9"
> " I cannot bring myself to part with this tenderly
> beautiful letter! May it devolve to the hands of
> a tender daughter in law who will prize such an
> acquaintance with the most loved incomparable
> Aunt of my Alexander. F. d'A.")

BELCOTTON, *Sunday, Oct* 20*th* 99.

My dearest, dearest Fanny, my kind and excellent
Brother—your letter has gone to my very heart, and there
the impression will remain whilst I draw my breath—Yet
what is there of zealous and generous affection that ought
from you to surprise me—and *surprise* indeed is not the
right word—but it touches me past expression—You have
been only too hasty dearest souls—the money will not I
trust be wanted, and it concerns me greatly it sh^d be prematurely drawn from the funds, if ever, for me—yet
should it be required, I accept, with the tenderest love,
the loan, and I think Phillips would not forbid me—he
says she must write to you himself—but before he begins,
I must tell you it is in *England* we must meet, where only
some strange fatality can now prevent my being in about
a month—not earlier my dearest—but November is as
good a season as the present, and often milder—I am
making arrangements for warm clothing for the journey,
and carefully endeavouring to strengthen myself—Since
I last wrote to Amelia I have certainly been gradually
mending—but you must not alarm yourself if I own I
have yet some complaints wch must be overcome before
I set out—they are not dangerous, but might become
so by a long journey and w^d be inconvenient and painful
—I entreat you to thank my dear Charles for me—I beg
you to say to our loved Father the things you will feel
and know I wish to have said till I can write to him
myself—and let dear Esther know I have had her kind
letter, to which the purport of this must for the present
serve as a reply, for my nervous complaints render much
writing difficult to me, and some times scarcely possible
—I will not attempt now entering on many parts of your
dear letter, nor do more than thank you for a very charming paquet which was contained in our dearest Mrs Locke's
last frank—1000 loves to her, dearest Mr Locke—our
lovely Bride, and all that beloved and unmatchable Family
—and now let me embrace you both, and Alexander too,
and Heaven preserve and bless you my kind beloveds—

(*No address. Endorsed by M^{rs} d'Arblay " No 13 ".*)

I owe you my Fanny I know not how many letters—I think—but am not sure I acknowledged the receipt of our beloved Friend's first frank to Mrs Cartland, wch followed me to Belcotton, the date was the 16th Nov—if I did not, thank that most precious of Friends for me, and beg her to thank our darling for her sweet letter from Wellingham, and next—pray thank your own dear self—Yesterday my Norbury brought me the unexpected blessing of another letter—it is such a joy to see your dear handwriting—yet I ought to be travelling on and I am with-held—that dear Mr Kiernan will not he says let me risk the being stop^t on the road if he can help it—Our Esther to whom I sent a letter the eve^g I arrived here will have acquainted you of the time we arrived in this place. The Kiernans procured us the same lodgings we had on our first arrival, wch are excellent, but terribly dear wch is a great grievance to me—but they conceive anything less good w^d not be *worthy to receive me* dear souls and in all other things contrive to spare us every possible expense—send me jellies, Beef tea, blanc mange and twenty things besides, and the dear girls Harriet, and Augusta (who is indeed one of the most affectionate, kind hearted creatures I ever met with) empty their pockets I believe daily in my service in search of light rolls, or cakes that they say are better for me than bread—I really half long that Augusta were my *child*—if she were I sh^d be contented with the portion of love she shews me—She is greatly gratified by your remembrance. The morning after my arrival dear Mr Kiernan whose kindness and affection has quite won my heart, was too anxious to be satisfied without bringing me Dr Purcell—he is by many reckoned the first physician in Ireland—he did not consult me, as he knew I sh^d oppose this measure—He examined me wth great attention, and consulted afterwards wth Mr Kiernan, and has been here twice since—Mr Kiernan whose house is only a few doors below ours generally looks in *three times a day*—Judge if I am well attended—

I am better to day than I have been yet—on my arrival
I was overpowered by fatigue, and have been tried by
a medecine wch to me proved a severe one—but to day
I am far more comfortable, and want to talk about sailing—Mr Kiernan at first pronounced that he w^d not
let me stir for a *month*—but on hearing Charles' kind
offer, said that made a material difference, and that *on
condition I accepted it*, he would suffer me to go in half
that time, or possibly less, if nothing new occurred—if
therefore it will not interfere with dear Charles's Christmas excursion, pray write him word I shall gratefully
accept his offered carriage, and as soon as landed will
write him word where we are, and our route—the M.
is so uncertain nothing can be determined on till the
last moment, but at any rate, 'till I am actually in England I c^d not bear the carriage sh^d be put in motion for
me—I think we can avoid missing by regularly enquiring
and giving the direction to our inn, as soon as we arrive,
at the post office in every post town and the coachman
must do the same. I shall probably go very slowly the
first two or three days—Let me now thank my own M^{rs}
Locke and my Fanny for the sweetness of their ready
acquiescence in my views—For many reasons I can be
nowhere so well as at my beloved Father's at least till
the M is returned to Ireland—My Fanny the same—
Willy he will do what he chooses with—dear little Boy
it pains me to think how long he has been neglected, and
the disadvantage to wch you will all see him—his Father
does his best to spoil him, and I am no longer able to
present antidotes—Do not my beloved talk of W
Humble as a possible dwelling for us, even at a distant
period—there is a terrible jealousy of my happiness
existing, wch must be guarded against—I believe the
thought of Norbury Park w^d not be tolerated were it
not deemed an *honour*. By no means dearest stir from
y^r dear home till you hear we are arrived—our motions
must be so slow, and sh^d I not be well so uncertain, it
w^d be grievous to lose a day or an hour of you by your
coming prematurely—beg y^r little cherub to continue

remembering me in his *orisons* bless him—how I shall delight to see him!—Do not be uneasy at my ill writing —I have a bad pen—but if I did not hurry could write as well as usual—but I have so many kind enquiries succeeding each other, I have really no time for writing. —My dear Mrs Disney spent the morning with me—the third time of her coming since my arrival—Mrs Hill is out of town, and I fear I have little chance of seeing her —but I have written to her—My Norbury begins to fear he shall go to Fanet before I am gone—but I hope it will not be so—Adieu my darling. My letter is *circular*, and within a week I will write again. I trust to you to say all that is kind, tender, grateful for me at N Park —Chelsea—and to your dear invaluable mate

> *M^rs d'Arblay, West-humble, Dorking, Surry.* (Endorsed by M^rs d'Arblay " No 14 "—" The last letter written immediately to myself from Ireland by my adored sister Susanna—one only was added f^m Park Gate!" "My last letter from fatal Ireland!!! Mrs Disney, Cartland, Kierneys [*sic*] Harriet ∿ AUGUSTA ∿ ")

IV

DR. BURNEY

(Born : Raven Street, Shrewsbury, April 12, 1726.
Died : at Chelsea, April 12, 1814.)

DR. BURNEY'S was probably the most remarkable and
energetic personality of an almost innumerable and
phenomenally active clan. Those were the days of
patronage, before Johnson had flung the " noble lord "
out of Grub Street, and young Burney's chance came
when the elegant Fulke Greville asked a " professional "
acquaintance " if he knew of any young musician who
was fit company for a gentleman "—clearly expecting
that no such phenomenon could actually exist.

Surprise hurried them into intimacy, the " gentleman " proved liberal, in a " vortex of dissipation," among
other diversions at Newmarket and its " noble quadru-
peds, whose rival swiftness made running seem a flight,
and that flight an airy game or gambol, of some fabled
animal of elastic grace and celerity." In due course,
Burney assisted his patron through " the customary
routine of matrimonial elopers," and when his own
" breast had been penetrated " by " one of those same
blissful or baneful darts," was imperiously bidden to
marry at once.

What followed, however, Burney won for himself ; by
dogged industry, an insatiable curiosity for facts, and a
personal charm few even desired to resist. Like all true
" professionals," he was a born entertainer to mankind,
with a *flair* for talent whose service it quickly became
his to command : a genial showman who pulled the
strings that Society might meet Genius in the " freedom " of Bohemia.

Few of his own folk ever quite grew up ; and it was

in part the untiring eagerness with which he pursued
art and enjoyed it to the end, that drew so many and
varied temperaments to his side. His enthusiasm for
Great People—of birth or intellect—was always a child's
ardour ; though clothed at times, one must acknowledge,
in the words and bearing of a snob—fruits of self-educated provincialism, like the desire after " good " marriages for his daughters, and the stiff morality that
forbade Fanny herself to make a friend of Madame de
Staël.

Amidst a family of inveterate scribblers, he was surely
the most voluminous of them all ; incredibly copious
with the pen, though he never mastered his native
language and was always an amateur of style.   His verse is
fluent and mediocre, his translated drama, *The Cunning
Man*, shows some stage-craft but no distinction ; his
reams of prose attained the limit of verbosity in undisguised Johnsonese.   But his worst habit in writing,
which persists in Fanny herself, in Susan, Charlotte, and
all the family, was a passion for hybrid phrasing, and the
pseudo-wit of made-up words.   They were too impatient of solid culture to acquire sound literary taste,
and twisted words as a naughty child might, in half-
conscious imitation of their foreign friends' broken
English.

Yet something always shows through of the man himself, constantly vital and alert ; and when we read of
Sterne as " a man who chooses to walk about the world
with a cambric handkerchief always in his hand," we
must recognise and admire a too-seldom-used power of
expression.

He was finally the loving, if sometimes tiresome and
unpractical, patriarch to his brilliant, super-sensitive,
and emotional daughters and sons.   Fanny's devotion
to her father and her father's memory was a lifelong
passion ; " sweet " Susan idolised him with more quiet,
but no more moderate, intensity—so that none so willing
or fit as her only daughter to tend the old man's last years ;
Esther was proud and glad to be the *pièce de résistance*

at his "harmonical coteries," whether intimate or official, drawing her cousin-husband into the stock "caste"; the reverend scholar, Dr. Charles, jun., played librarian or amanuensis as one honoured by the task. The "journal" of Worcester cousins duly records each "literary performance of his celebrated pen."

This was not a tyrant, an egotist, or a fool; but a great and good man.

AN ESSAY TOWARDS A HISTORY OF THE PRINCIPAL COMETS THAT HAVE APPEARED SINCE 1742: WITH A LETTER UPON COMETS TO A LADY BY THE LATE M. DE MAUPERTUIS [TRANSLATED BY ESTHER SLEEPE, MRS. BURNEY] 1769.

ADVERTISEMENT

It is therefore intended in sketching out the following little history of Comets to save the reader the expense of purchasing, and trouble of perusing, a great number of difficult and dry treatises, and to give him the sum and substance of such discoveries and conclusions as have proceeded from the most laborious and operose calculations which human intelligence can reach. . . .

Though the foregoing Letter [of Maupertuis] is written in a familiar and sportive style, and accommodated to the perception of the ladies, it is founded on true science.

DEDICATION

To the right honourable the Countess of Pembroke.

MADAM,

In looking through the kingdom for a Lady to whom I might address the following sheets, no one could be found who seemed with such propriety entitled to them as your Ladyship. The Great are so narrowly watched, that neither their virtues nor their vices, their perfections nor deficiencies, can long remain secret; and to say that your Ladyship is not only a lover, but a judge of astronomical subjects, is telling the public nothing new, since it was from the public I gained my information. It is a power inherent in your Ladyship's family,

to confer celebrity on works of genius. Even the great
Sir Philip Sidney's name is lost in that of his Patroness,
—his famous Romance being never mentioned by any
other title than that of The Countess of Pembroke's
Arcadia.

The Comet of 1759 is known throughout Europe by
the name of Dr. Halley's Comet : Deign then, Madam,
to suffer the history of that Comet and the present one,
to be honoured with your ladyship's name. There is
a shyness, or perhaps a pride, in English philosophers,
which renders them superior to the common arts of
acquiring fame, by means of retailing and explaining
their discoveries ; they are not more solicitous of arriving
at those discoveries by the shortest road, than of relating them in the fewest words : and, by this means, our
neighbours the French, are generally not only better
acquainted with the labours of their own astronomers,
but even with those of this nation, than ourselves.

I have, therefore, no pretentions, Madam, in the following Essay, to any other merit than that of laying
before your Ladyship and the public, the discoveries of
men who disdain the task of doing it themselves.

This makes me hope that the presumption of an anonymous writer (who only knows your Ladyship by the fame
of your virtues and accomplishments) will be pardoned ;
as his most powerful motive for writing is the love of
astronomy, and his highest ambition that of subscribing
himself, with the most profound respect, Madam,

Your Ladyships, most humble, and most devoted
Servant,

THE AUTHOR.

SUPERSTITION

It has been said above by M. Maupertuis, that D^r
Gregory has established the Comets again in all their
terrors. In supposing such dreadful consequences from
a Comet's tail being in contact with our earth, etc.—if
the learned Doctor were still living, one would be inclined to ask him, why the poor old ladies are still to be

frightened with Comets ? Do they either portend or
occasion anything worse than always subsists ? When
was the world without its plague, pestilence and famine ;
battle, murder and sudden death ? Though Comets are
doubtless placed in the heavens for some wise purpose,
wholly inscrutable to us, yet, for anything we have
hitherto discovered, they have no more influence or
effect upon our globe, or its inhabitants, than a will-o'-
th'-wisp or ignis fatuus ;—and yet everything that is
mischievous or disagreeable is placed to the account of
the poor Comet. If it rains, " it is the Comet " ;—if the
weather be hot, " it is the Comet " ;—if it be cold, it is
the same.—Pray let us be a little equitable, and allow
that such things as abundant rain, intemperate heat, and
intense cold, have happened in this climate before now,
without the agency of a Comet ; unless by some Comet
that has appeared in disguise, like Mr Bayes's army.

PRESENT STATE OF MUSIC IN FRANCE AND ITALY

1771

Perhaps the grave and wise may regard music as a
frivolous and enervating luxury ; but, in its defence,
Montesquieu has said that " it is the only one of all
the arts which does not corrupt the mind." Electricity
is universally allowed to be a very entertaining and surprising phenomenon, but it has frequently been lamented
that it has never yet, with much certainty, been applied
to any very useful purpose. The same reflection has
often been made, no doubt, as to music. It is a charming resource, in an idle hour, to the rich and luxurious
part of the world. But say the sour and the worldly,
what is its use to the rest of mankind ? To this it may
be answered, that, in England, perhaps more than in
any other country, it is easy to point out the humane
and important purposes to which it has been applied.
Its assistance has been called in by the most respectable
profession in this kingdom, in order to open the purses
of the affluent, for the support of the distressed offspring

of their deceased brethren.[1] Many an orphan is cherished
by its influence.[2] The pangs of child-birth are softened
and rendered less dangerous and dreadful by the effects
of its power.[3] It helps perhaps to stop the ravages of a
disease which attacks the very source of life.[4] And, lastly,
it enables its own professors to do what few others can
boast—to maintain their own poor ; by that admirable
and well-directed institution, known by the name of The
Society for the Support of decayed Musicians and their
Families. Music has indeed ever been the delight of
accomplished princes, and the most elegant amusement
of polite courts : but at present it is so combined with
things sacred and important, as well as with our pleasures,
that mankind seems wholly unable to subsist without
it : it forms a considerable part of divine service in our
churches : it is essential to military discipline : and the
theatres would languish without it. Add to this, that
there is hardly a private family in a civilized nation
without its flute, its fiddle, its harpsichord, or guitar :
that it alleviates labour and mitigates pain ; and is still
a greater blessing to humanity, when it keeps us out of
mischief, or blunts the edge of care.

TAKING THE VEIL

This morning I went to the convent of St Ursula,
to see a nun take the veil. The company was very
numerous, and composed chiefly of the first people of
Rome, who were all in full dress. I was placed close to
the altar, where I could see the whole ceremony, and
hear every word that was uttered. The service was
begun by saying mass, then Cardinal de Rossi entered in
great state ; while the organ was playing, and the mass
was singing : the music, both vocal and instrumental,
was performed by the nuns and ladies of the convent

---

[1] At the Feast of the Sons of the Clergy.

[2] The *Messiah* is annually performed for the benefit of the Foundling
Hospital.

[3] The benefit every year for the Lying-in Hospital.

[4] The musical performance for the Lock Hospital.

who were placed in the organ gallery. The composition
was pretty, but ill executed ; the organ was a bad one,
and too powerful for the band : most of the best bands,
as I was informed, were occupied in the convent with
the internal ceremony, the external was all performed
in the chapel. When the Cardinal was robed, the novi-
tiate was led into the chapel by a lady of the first rank in
Rome, and brought to the altar in exceeding high dress.
Her hair was of a beautiful light brown, and curled *en
tête de mouton* all over her head. Her gown was of the
richest, embroidered, and, I believe, embossed blue and
silver, I ever saw. She had on a large stage hoop ; and
a great quantity of diamonds ; the train of her robe
dragged full two yards on the ground ; she seemed rather
a pretty sort of young person than a beauty. When she
first appeared, she looked very pale, and more dead than
alive ; she made a most profound reverence to the Cardinal, who was seated on the step of the altar in his mitre
and all his rich vestments, ready to receive her. She
threw herself upon her knees at the foot of the altar,
and remained in that posture some time, while other
parts of the ceremony were adjusting ; then she walked
up to the Cardinal, who said, *Figlia mia, che domandate?*
My child, what is your request ? She said, that she
begged to be admitted into that convent as a sister of
the order of St Ursula ; Have you well, said the Cardinal, considered of what you ask ? She answered, chearfully, that she had ; and was well informed of all she
was about to do. Then she kneeled down again, and
kissed the Cardinal's hands, and received from him a
little crucifix, which she also kissed ; after which she
retired again to the foot of the altar, where she threw
herself on her knees, while the Cardinal said mass, which
was sung at the same time in the organ loft. After this,
there was a sermon in the Italian language, and that
being over, the Cardinal led the nun-elect into the convent, where she was divested of all her gorgeous attire
and worldly vanities, and had her hair cut off. She then
came to the gate in her religious dress, to receive the white

veil, with which she was invested by the lady abbess, the Cardinal and the other assistants standing by. After this there was more pretty music badly performed. The organ, by executing all the symphonies and accompaniments, overpowered the violins, and had a bad effect, though neatly played. When her veil was on, the new sister came to the convent door, to receive the congratulations of her friends and of the company; but first, with a lighted taper in her hand, she went round the convent to salute all the nuns, who had likewise tapers in their hands. When she was at the door, with the veil and crown on, but her face uncovered, I, among the rest, went close to her, and found she was much prettier than I had before imagined. She had a sweet mouth and the finest teeth in the world, with lively sparkling eyes, and a genteel shaped visage; she would, anywhere else, have been stiled a very pretty woman; but here, so circumstanced, a beauty. At the altar she changed countenance several times, first pale, then red, and seemed to pant, and to be in danger of either bursting into tears, or fainting: but she recovered before the ceremony was ended, and at the convent door assumed an air of great cheerfulness; talked to several of her friends and acquaintance, and seemed to give up the world very heroically.—And thus ended this human sacrifice!

A GENERAL HISTORY OF MUSIC FROM THE EARLIEST AGES TO THE PRESENT PERIOD, WITH A DISSERTATION ON THE MUSIC OF THE ANCIENTS. 4 VOLS, 1776

"Composed in moments stolen from sleep, from refection, and from an occupation which required all my attention, during more than twelve hours a day, for a great part of the year." It occupied "thirty years in meditation, twenty in writing and printing."

[The motive of composition, as Dr. Burney explains, was "to fill up a chasm in English Literature." He declares that he studied innumerable volumes, "of which

the dulness and pedantry were almost petrific "; while
—for himself : " I would rather be pronounced trivial
than tiresome."]

Vol. I.—Egyptian, Hebrew, Greek Pagan Divinities,
Demi-gods, etc.

Vol. II.—Counterpoint, Modern Provençal, Continental Contrapuntists.

Vol. III.—Mary and Elizabeth. Italy sixteenth
century. Germany, France, Spain. Church Music from
Purcell to eighteenth century.

Vol. IV.—Oratorio. Opera Bouffé, Cantatas, Dramatic, Italian, and other continental opera.

DEDICATION
To the Queen

MADAM,
    The condescension with which your Majesty has
been pleased to permit your name to stand before the
following History, may justly reconcile the author to his
favourite study, and convince him, that whatever may
be said by the possessors of severer wisdom, the hours
which he has bestowed upon Music have been neither
dishonourably, nor unprofitably spent.

The science of musical sounds, though it may have been
depreciated as appealing only to the ear, and affording
nothing more than a momentary and fugitive delight, may
be with justice considered as the art which unites corporal
with intellectual pleasure, by a species of enjoyment which
gratifies sense, without weakening reason ; and which,
therefore, the Great may cultify without debasement
and the Good enjoy without depravation.

Those who have most diligently contemplated the state
of man, have found it beset with vexations, which can
neither be repelled by splendour, nor eluded by obscurity ;
to the necessity of combating these intrusions of discontent,
the ministers of pleasure were indebted for that kind
reception, which they have perhaps too indiscriminately
obtained. Pleasure and innocence ought never to be

separated ; yet we seldom find them otherwise than at variance, except when Music brings them together.

To those who know that Music is among your Majesty's recreations, it is not necessary to display its purity, or assert its dignity. May it long amuse your leisure, not as a relief from evil, but as an augmentation of good ; not as a diversion from care, but as a variation of felicity. Such, Madam, is my sincerest wish, in which I can however boast no peculiarity of reverence or zeal ; for the virtues of your Majesty are universally confessed ; and however the inhabitants of the British empire may differ in their opinions upon other questions, they all behold your excellencies with the same eye, and celebrate them with the same voice ; and to that name which one nation is echoing to another, nothing can be added by the respectful admiration, and humble gratitude of, Madam, your Majesty's most obedient and most devoted Servant,

CHARLES BURNEY.

FROM THE PREFACE

What is Music ? An innocent luxury, unnecessary, indeed, to our existence, but a great improvement and gratification to the sense of hearing. It consists, at present, of Melody, Consonance and Dissonance.

What is Melody ? A series of sounds more fixed, and generally more lengthened, than those of common speech ; arranged with grace, and of proportional lengths, such as the mind can easily measure, and the voice express. These sounds are regulated by a scale, consisting of tones, and semitones, but admit a variety of arrangement as unbounded as imagination.

What is Consonance ? A coincidence of two or more sounds, which being heard together, by their agreement and union, afford to ears capable of judging and feeling, a delight of a most grateful kind.

What is Dissonance ? It is the want of that agreeable union between two or more sounds, which constitutes consonance : in musical composition it is occasioned by the suspension or anticipation of some sound before, or after, it becomes a concord.   It is the *Dolce piccante* of music, and operates on the ear as a poignant sauce on the palate : it is a zest, without which the auditory sense would be as much cloyed as the appetite, if it had nothing to feed on but sweets.

What kind of musical tones are most grateful to the ear ?   Such as are produced by the vocal organ.   And, next to singing, what kinds of sound are most pleasing ? Those which approach the nearest to vocal.   Which are they ?   Such as can be sustained, swelled, and diminished, at pleasure.   Of these the first in rank are the Violin, Flute, and Hautbois.   But what instrument is capable of the greatest effects ?   The Organ ;   which can not only imitate a number of other instruments, but is so comprehensive as to possess the power of a numerous orchestra.   But has it no imperfections ?   Yes.   It wants expression, and a more perfect intonation.

What kind of music is most pleasing to mankind ?   To practised ears, such as has the merit of novelty, added to refinement, and ingenious contrivance ;   to the ignorant, such as is most familiar and common.

What was the music of the Greeks, concerning which the learned talk so much ?   It is impossible to speak of it with certainty ;   however, the chief part of what I have to say concerning both the theory and practice of ancient music, is thrown into a Preliminary Dissertation, in order that the narrative might not be interrupted by discussions concerning dark and disputable points, which will be generally uninteresting even to musical readers ; and in which it is very doubtful, whether I shall be able either to amuse or satisfy the learned.

[The " Dissertation " deals with " ancient notation or tablature, modes, rhythm, etc."]

From Vol. IV

The Beggar's Opera forms a memorable epoch in our national Music : for though not a single new air was composed for this pasticcio in our vulgar tongue, it has proved the best opera to the patentees of our playhouses that ever was brought on the stage. The morality and the music are equally intelligible and acceptable to the galleries ; and a favourite singer can always fill the rest of the house.

[Of his own days, Dr. Burney complains that " Church Music was old-fashioned and playhouse music vulgar." He described a scheme originated by the Earl of Sandwich in 1776 and " supported with spirit and dignity by other noblemen "—to which he himself, in fact, gave active support—" for *Concerts of Ancient Music* in favour of such solid and valuable productions of old masters as an intemperate rage for novelty had too soon laid aside as superannuated " ; where he said " venerable old masters were performed by a select and powerful band, with correctness and energy."]

MEMOIRS OF DR. BURNEY: FROM MANUSCRIPTS AND PERSONAL RECOLLECTIONS. 3 VOLS, BY MADAME D'ARBLAY. 1832

[Madame d'Arblay fully explained her reasons for destroying all the MSS. which " could not have been spread, even in a general family review, without causing pain or mischief." From his " twelve volumes of manuscript memoirs, his countless, fathomless mass of papers," she—indeed—included no more than a few brief quotations. The following selections are all taken from passages which were actually printed in his own words.]

A FRAGMENT OF AUTOBIOGRAPHY

If the life of a humble individual, on whom neither splendid appointments, important transactions, nor atrocious crimes have called the attention of the public, can afford amusement to the friends he leaves behind, without being offered either as a model to follow, or a precipice to shun, the intention of the writer of these Memoirs will be fully accomplished. But there is no member of society who, by diligence, talents, or conduct, leaves his name and his race a little better than those from which he sprung, who is totally without some claim to attention on the means by which such advantages were achieved.

My life, though it has frequently been a tissue of toil, sickness, and sorrow, has yet been, upon the whole, so much more pleasant and prosperous than I had a title to expect, or than many others with higher claims have enjoyed, that its incidents, when related, may, perhaps, help to put mediocrity in good-humour, and to repress the pride and overrated worth and expectations of indolence. Perhaps few have been better enabled to describe, from an actual survey, the manners and customs of the age in which he lived than myself; ascending from those of the most humble cottagers, and lowest mechanics, to the first nobility, and most elevated personages, with whom circumstances, situation, and accident, at different periods of my life, have rendered me familiar. Oppressed and laborious husbandmen; insolent and illiberal yeomanry; overgrown farmers; generous and hospitable merchants; men of business and men of pleasure; men of letters; men of science; artists; sportsmen and country 'squires; dissipated and extravagant voluptuaries, gamesters; ambassadors; statesmen; and even sovereign princes, I have had opportunities of examining in almost every point of view: all these it is my intention to display in their respective situations; and to delineate their virtues, vices, and apparent degrees of happiness and misery. A book of this kind, though it may mortify and offend a few persons of the present age, may be read with avidity at the distance of some centuries, by antiquaries and lovers of anecdotes; though it will have lost the poignancy of personality.

My grandfather, James Macburney, who, by letters which I have seen of his writing, and circumstances concerning him which I have remembered to have heard from my father and mother, was a gentleman of a considerable patrimony, at Great Hanwood a village in Shropshire,

had received a very good education ; but, from what
cause does not appear, in the latter years of his life, was
appointed land steward to the Earl of Ashburnham. He
had a house in Privy Garden, Whitehall. In the year
1727, he walked as esquire to one of the knights, at the
coronation of King George the Second. My father,
James, born likewise at Hanwood, was well educated also,
both in school learning and accomplishments. He was
a day scholar at Westminster School under the celebrated
Dr Busby, while my father resided in Whitehall. I
remember his telling a story of the severe chastisement
he received from that terrific disciplinarian, Dr Busby,
for playing truant after school hours, instead of returning
home. My grandfather, who had frequently admonished
him not to loiter in the street, lest he should make improper and mischievous acquaintance, finding no attention was paid to his injunctions, gave him a letter addressed to the Rev. Dr Busby ; which he did not fail to
deliver, with ignorant cheerfulness, on his entrance into
the school. The Doctor, when he had perused it, called
my father to him, and, in a very mild, and seemingly
goodhumoured voice, said, " Burney, can you read writing ? " " Yes, Sir," answered my father, with great
courage and flippancy. " Then read this letter aloud,"
says the Doctor ; when my father, with an audible voice,
began : " Sir, My son, the bearer of this letter, having
long disregarded my admonitions against stopping to play
with idle boys in his way home from school ——" Here
my father's voice faultered. " Go on " says his master ;
" you read very well." " I am sorry to be under the
necessity of entreating you to—to—to—to cor " Here
he threw down the letter, and fell on his knees, crying
out : " Indeed, Sir, I'll never do so again !—Pray forgive
me ! " " O, you read perfectly well," the Doctor again
tells him, " pray finish the Letter : " And making him
pronounce aloud the words, " correct him " ; complied
with my grandfather's request in a very liberal manner.
Whether my father was intended for any particular profession, I know not, but, during his youth, besides his

school learning, he acquired several talents and accomplishments, which, in the course of his life, he was obliged professionally to turn to account.

He danced remarkably well; performed well on the violin, and was a portrait painter of no mean talents. Notwithstanding the Mac which was prefixed to my grandfather's name, and which my father retained for some time, I could never find at what period any of my ancestors lived in Scotland or in Ireland, from one of which it must have been derived. My father and grandfather were both born in Shropshire, and never even visited either of those countries.

Early in his life, my father lost the favour of his sire, by eloping from home, to marry a young actress of Goodman's-fields theatre, by whom he had a very large family. My grandfather's affection was completely alienated by this marriage; joined to disapproving of his son's conduct in other respects. To the usual obduracy of old age, he afterwards added a far more singular indiscretion himself, by marrying a female domestic to whom, and to a son, the consequence of that marriage, he bequeathed all his possessions, which were very considerable. Joseph, this son, was not more prudent than my father; for he contrived, early in life, to dissipate his patrimony; and he subsisted for many years in Norfolk, by teaching to dance. I visited him in 1756, in a tour I made to Yarmouth. He lived then at Ormsby, a beautiful village near that town, with an amiable wife, and a large family of beautiful children, in an elegant villa, with a considerable garden; and he appeared, at that time, in perfectly restored and easy circumstances.

Furious Industry

The celebrated Felton, and after him, the first Dr. Hayes, came from Oxford to Shrewsbury on a tour, while I was studying hard, without instruction or example; and they amazed and stimulated me so forcibly by their performance on the organ, as well as by their encourage-

DR. CHARLES BURNEY.
Probably by Miss Reynolds.

ment, that I thenceforward went to work with an ambition and fury that would hardly allow me to eat or sleep.

"The quantity of music that I copied at this time, of all kinds, was prodigious; and my activity and industry surprised everybody; for, besides writing, teaching, tuning, and playing for my brother, at my *momens perdus*, I was educating myself in every way I was able. With copy books, I improved my handwriting so much, that my father did not believe I wrote my letters to him myself. I tried hard to at least keep up the little Latin I had learned; and I diligently practiced both the spinet and violin; which, with reading, transcribing music for business, and poetry for pleasure; attempts at composition, and attention to my brother's affairs, filled up every minute of the longest day.

"I had, also, a great passion for angling; but whenever I could get leisure to pursue that sport, I ran no risk of losing my time, if the fish did not bite; for I had always a book in my pocket, which enabled me to wait with patience their pleasure."

LETTER TO HIS WIFE: ESTHER SLEEPE

LYNN REGIS, *Monday.*

Now, my amiable friend, let me unbosom myself to thee, as if I were to enjoy the incomparable felicity of thy presence. And first—let me exclaim at the unreasonableness of man's desires; at his unbounded ambition and avarice, and at the inconstancy of his temper, which compels him, the moment he is in possession of the thing that once employed all his thoughts and wishes, to relinquish it, and to fix his " mind's eye " on some bauble that next becomes his point of view, and that, if attained, he would wish as much to change for still another toy, of still less consequence to his interest and quiet. Oh thou constant tenant of my heart! to apply the above to myself,—thou art the only good I have been constant to; the only blessing I have been thankful to Provi-

dence for : the only one, I feel, I shall ever continue to
have a true sense of ! Ought I not to blush at this
character's suiting me ? Indeed I ought, and I do.
Not that I think it one peculiar to myself ; I believe it
would fit more than half mankind. But it shames me
to think how little I knew myself, when I fancied I should
be happy in this place. Oh God ! I find it impossible
I should ever be so. Would you believe it, that I have
more than a hundred times wished I had never heard
its name ! Nothing but the hope of acquiring an independent fortune in a short space of time will keep me here ;
though I am too deeply entered to retreat without great
loss. But happiness cannot be too dearly purchased.
In short, I would gladly change again for London, at
any rate.

.   .   .   .   .   .

The organ is execrably bad ; and, add to that, a total
ignorance of the most known and common musical merits
runs through the whole body of the people I have yet
conversed with. Even Sir J. T., who is the oracle of
Apollo in this country is, in these matters, extremely
shallow. Now the bad organ, with the ignorance of
my auditors, must totally extinguish the few sparks of
genius for composition that I may have, and entirely
discourage practice ; for where would any pains I may
take to execute the most difficult piece of music be
repaid, if, like poor Orpheus, I am to perform to stocks
and stones ? "

Letter to Fanny—at Bookham

I have been such an *evaporé* lately, that if I were near
enough to accost you *de vive voix*, it would be with Susey's
exclamation, when she was just arrived from France, at
only eleven years old, after staying at Mrs Lewis's till ten
o'clock one night, " *Que je suis libertine papa !* " And
thus, *Que je suis libertin, ma fille !* cry I. Three huge
assemblies at Spencer House ; two dinners at the Duke
and Duchess of Leeds ; two ditto at Mr Crewe's ; two

clubs ; a dejeuner at Mrs Crewe's villa, at Hampstead ;
a dinner at Lord Macartney's ; ditto at Mr Locke's ;
ditto at Mr. Coxe's ; two ditto at Sir George Howards',
at Chelsea ; two philosophical *conversationes* at Sir
Joseph Bankes' ; two operas ; two professional concerts ;
Haydn's benefit ; Saloman's three ancient musics, etc.
etc. etc. " What dissipating profligacy ! But what
argufies all this festivity ? 'Tis all vanity, and exhale-
ment of spirit. I was tired to death of it all before it
was over ; whilst your domestic occupations and pleasures are as fresh every morning as the roses of your
garden."

On Death of his Wife—Elizabeth Allen

On the 26th of October, she was interred in the bury-
ing ground of Chelsea College. On the 27th, I returned
to my melancholy home, disconsolate and stupefied.
Though long expected, this calamity was very severely
felt. I missed her counsel, converse, and family regulations ; and a companion of thirty years, whose mind was
cultivated, whose intellects were above the general level
of her sex, and whose curiosity after knowledge was insatiable to the last. These were losses that caused a
vacuum in my habitation and in my mind, that has never
been filled up. My four eldest daughters, all dutiful,
intelligent, and affectionate, were married, and had
families of their own to superintend, or they might have
administered comfort. My youngest daughter, Sarah
Harriet, by my second marriage, had quick intellects,
and distinguished talents ; but she had no experience in
household affairs. However, though she had native
spirits of the highest gaiety, she became a steady and
prudent character, and a kind and good girl. There is,
I think, considerable merit in her novel, Geraldine, particularly in the conversations ; and I think the scene at
the emigrant cottage really touching. At least it drew
tears from me, when I was not so prone to shed them—
as I am at present. . . . [Afterwards, recurring again to his
departed wife, he says :] In the course of nature, she

should not have gone before me. She was the admirer and sincere friend of that first wife, whose virtues and intellectual powers were perhaps her model in early life. Without neglecting domestic and maternal duties, she cultivated her mind in such a manner by extensive reading, and the assistance of a tenacious and happy memory, as to enable her to converse with persons of learning and talents on all subjects to which female studies are commonly allowed to extend ; and through a coincidence of taste and principles in all matters of which the discussion is apt to ruffle the temper, and alienate affection, our conversation and intercourse was sincere, cordial, and cheering.

She had read far more books of divinity and controversy than myself, and was as much mistress of the theological points of general dispute as reading and reflection could make her ; but, within a few days, if not hours, of her death, she lamented having perused so many polemical works ; and advised a female friend, fond of such researches, who was with her, not to waste her time on such enquiries ; saying, " they will disturb your faith— by leading to endless controversy ; they have done me no good."

Of Old Age

In 1804, in the month of April, I completed my 78th year, and decided to relinquish teaching and my musical patients ; for both my ears and eyes were beginning to fail me. I could still hear the most minute musical sounds ; but in conversation I lost the articulation, and was forced to make people at the least distance from me repeat everything that they said. Sometimes the mere tone of voice, and the countenance of the speaker, told me whether I was to smile or to frown ; but never so explicitly as to allow me to venture at any reply to what was said ! Yet I never, seemingly, have been more *in fashion* at any period of my life than this spring ; never invited to more conversaziones, assemblies, dinners, and concerts. But I feel myself less and less able to bear a part in general conversation every day, from the failure of memory, particularly in names; and I have become fearful of beginning any story that occurs to me, lest I should be stopped short by hunting for Mr How d'ye call him's style and titles.

I was very near-sighted from about my 30th year; but though it is usually thought that that sort of sight improves with age, I have not discovered that the notion was well founded. My sight became not only more short, but more feeble. Instead of a concave glass, I was forced to have recourse to one that was convex, and that magnified highly, for pale ink and small types.

MISCELLANEOUS VERSE

William Fribble, Esq.

To her who was once Miss Biddy Bellair, Greeting

No boisterous hackney coachman clown,
No frisky fair nymph of the town
E'er wore so insolent a brow
As Captain Flash, since Hymen's vow
To him in silken bonds has tied,
So sweet, so fair, so kind a bride.
Well! curse me, now, if I can bear it!—
Though to his face I'd not declare it—
To think that you should take a dance
With such a roister into France
And leave poor Will in torturing anguish
To sigh and pine, to grieve and languish.
  'Twas—let me tell you Ma'am—quite cruel!
Though Jack and I shall fight a duel
If ever he to England come
And does not skulk behind a drum.
  But—apropos to coming over,
I hope you soon will land at Dover
That I may fly, more swift than hawk,
With you to have some *serus* talk
The while, how great will be my bliss
Should you but deign to let me kiss—

O may these ardent vows prevail !—
Your little finger's vermeil nail !
      Who am,
Till direful death to dust shall crumble,
My dearest *cretur!* yours,
          most humble
             " WILL FRIBBLE."

FOR AN EPITAPH

In Memory of Mrs Susanna Elizabeth Phillips

Learn, pensive reader, who may pass this way,
That underneath this stone remains the clay
That held a soul as pure, inform'd, refin'd,
As e'er to erring mortal was assign'd.
Closed are those eyes whose radiance, mild, yet bright,
Beamed all that gives to feeling souls delight !
Quench'd are those rays of spirit, taste, and sense,
Pure emanations of benevolence,
That could alike instruct, appease, control,
And speak the genuine dictates of the soul.

                              C. B.

AS THE YEARS PASS

[It was apparently Dr. Burney's custom to introduce the Journal for each year by a short poem upon the person or event which stood out in his mind as the most striking.]

DR. JOHNSON, 1776

This year I acquaintance began with the Thrales,
Where I met with great talents 'mongst females and
    males,
But the best thing that happened from that time to this,
Was the freedom it gave me to sound the abyss,
At my ease and my leisure, of Johnson's great mind,
Where new treasures unnumber'd I constantly find.
Huge Briareus's head, if old bards have not blunder'd,
Amounted in all to the sum of one hundred ;

And Johnson—so wide his intelligence spreads,
Has the brains of—at least—the same number of heads.

PACCHIEROTTI, 1778

This year Pacchierotti was order'd by fate
Every vocal expression to teach us to hate,
Save his exquisite tones ; which delight and surprise,
And lift us at once from the earth to the skies.

GARRICK, 1779

This year joy and sorrow alike put on sable
For losses sustained by the stage and the table,
For Garrick, the master of passion, retired,
And Nature and Shakespeare together expired.
Thalia's as well as Melpomene's magic,
With him at once vanished, both comic and tragic.
Long, long will it be, now by Death he is slain,
Before we shall see his true likeness again.
Such dignified beauties he threw in each part,
Such resources of humour, of passion, and art ;—
Hilarity missed him, each Muse dropped a tear,
And Genius and Feeling attended his bier.

V

ADMIRAL JAMES BURNEY

1750—1822

CURIOUSLY enough, it was "Sailor" James, everywhere welcomed for his wit and humour, who, after his professional fame as an intimate of Captain Cook, carried the family associations with literature into a later generation, *and* provided Fanny herself with "connections in the trade" for the publication of *Camilla*.

He had been a pupil of Eugene Aram and Hood's poem "was founded on his recollections of how the gentle usher paced the playground at Lynn arm-in-arm with one of the elder boys, talking of strange murders," and "how he had shuddered on seeing Aram taken to prison"—for a murder committed fourteen years before.

He went to sea as a boy of fourteen, and was with Captain Cook in the famous second and third voyages; returning from the last fatal adventure in command of the *Discovery*. When he took part in the action of June 20, 1783, off Cuddalore, Dr. Johnson wrote to Mrs. Thrale: "I question if any ship upon the ocean goes out attended with more good wishes than that which carries the fate of Burney."

It was, in fact, the close of his career. The Histories of Discoveries in the South Sea (1803–17) and of North-Eastern Voyages (1819) occupied the remainder of his life and were recognised as standard works.

In old age he entertained the Lambs and the Lake Poets at his house in James Street, Buckingham Gate; though Hazlitt was "dropped out of the famous whist-parties" because he ventured to criticise *Evelina*. Crabb Robinson describes him, at this period, as "a fine old

man, a humorous old man—a character, a fine noble
creature, with a rough exterior, as became the associate
of Captain Cook"; and Lamb wrote of his death to
Wordsworth: "There's Captain Burney gone! What
fun has whist now? What matters it what you lead if
you can no longer fancy him looking over you?" elsewhere referring to his "flashes of wild spirit."

There were times, indeed, when his fastidious sisters
were a little uneasy about bluff James, who had fought in
a duel and whose clothes and manners—unless prepared
for the occasion—were not of the most refined. He
would crack a bottle and tell sea-tales with brother-in-law
Phillips, scarcely suited to delicate ears. But their
criticism never diminished their love; he was trusted
with their most intimate secrets, generously admired and
a favourite with all. They were always anxious at any
hint of his "going into action," eager to hear of his
promotion and fame. Johnson wondered at his "gentle
and humane manner," after he had "lived so long among
sailors and savages."

In early days the girls had been "very strongly recommended to the two pretty and motherless daughters of
Mr. Payne, the bookseller at the Meuse Gate," and James
afterwards married Sarah Payne.

Messrs. Payne and Foss (rechristened *Pain and Fuss* by
the incorrigible punster, Charles Lamb) then occupied
"an elbow-shed rather than a shop, lighted by a skylight,
at the gate of the lower mews, opening in Castle Street,
Leicester Fields"; where, however, men of letters and
other literary "loungers" "chose to resort every day,
about one o'clock,"—"very much in the way" of Mr.
Payne's strictly business occupations.

The other partner, Ross, had a brother, Edward, who
married the sister of Charles junior's wife.

James apparently wrote books in part from a keen
interest in his profession; but in the same spirit as his
father—to save the labour of his readers by the industry
of his own research. As his wife Sarah was the "original"
Mrs. Battle, his views on whist should be attentively read.

An able and distinguished man, quite obviously domestic, who met life with a smile.

He died of apoplexy, only two months after the long-delayed promotion to " rear-admiral." This kindly, and not undeserved, obituary appeared in *nearly all the London newspapers :*

Rear-Admiral Burney, F.R.S., eldest son of the learned and elegant historian, Dr. Burney, and brother to two very distinguished persons of the present age : Madame D'Arblay and Dr. Charles Burney ; a member of that triumvirate of professed scholars which has adorned our own immediate times. Admiral Burney entered into the Royal Navy at a very early period of his life, and, first as midshipman, afterwards as Lieutenant, accompanied Captain Cook in the two last enterprizing voyages (perilous and important) which have reflected so much honour on the late reign, and proved so very beneficial to the general interests of mankind.

He was one of the most scientific and best geographers that this country has produced ; of which his laborious, accurate, and voluminous history of voyages of discovery, his account of the Eastern navigation of the Russians, and other works, bear the amplest testimony.

As an officer, he was particularly remarkable for his great and enlightened humanity to those under his command, at a period too when severity in discipline was generally considered a proof of zeal, of spirit, and of ability, and when the wiser and more generous principles of the present day were considered as heterodox and pernicious. His humanity was characteristic of him, and united to the most inflexible integrity and love of truth ; attended him through all the offices of life ; and he will be long remembered, by an extensive circle of friends who loved him for his disinterestedness and honesty ; and for the simplicity and kindness of his manners, and the cheerfulness of his disposition ; for his good nature and genuine humour in conversation, and for his true, though antiquated, hospitality.

Copied into the " Worcester " Journal.

Sarah, daughter of James, married her cousin, a younger John Payne of the same firm. She is described when a girl as "full of fun and high spirits, given to madcap doings." Elsewhere we read that "after sowing her wild oats, she lived much on the Continent, but chiefly at Rome with her husband." She is the heroine of Elia's essay " The Wedding."

Lamb's *Rosamond Gray* Poems, Essays, etc., was dedicated to James's son—

MARTIN CHARLES BURNEY

Forgive me, Burney, if to thee these late
And hasty products of a critic pen,
Thyself no common judge of books and men,
In feeling of thy worth I dedicate.
My *verse* was offered to an older friend ;
The humbler *prose* has fallen to thy share:
Nor could I miss the occasion to declare,
What spoken in thy presence must offend—
That, set aside some few caprices wild,
Those humourous clouds that flit o'er brightest days.
In all my threadings of this worldly maze,
(And I have watched thee almost from a child),
Free from self-seeking, envy, low design,
I have not found a whiter soul than thine.

and he " refused to be comforted when he saw Mary laid beside her brother." Of him also it was said that " he never told a lie in his life."

A CHRONOLOGICAL HISTORY OF THE VOYAGES AND DISCOVERIES IN THE SOUTH SEA OR PACIFIC OCEAN, 5 VOLS, 1803

ADVERTISEMENT TO THE READER

Some Observations which have been made on the First Volume of this History, render it necessary for me to explain to the Reader the method which has been pursued in adducing the authorities throughout the work ; and to remark, that from the attention which I have constantly shewn to original documents, it ought not to be inferred that I have neglected to examine modern collections. These are not admissible as evidence to early facts; but in matters of opinion, and for interpretation of passages in the old narratives, it will be found that writers of late date have been consulted with much advantage.

To each voyage is prefixed, either in a note or as an introductory remark, a short account of the original journals or early publications; and those which have been followed are specified.

By this general notice is obviated the necessity of interrupting the narrative with too great a frequency of notes of reference. In all the geographical facts the particular authority is invariably pointed out, and the same rule has been observed in every case where the nature of the fact or the veracity of the original account appeared doubtful. I have been faithful to my authorities, but have no where departed from the respect due to truth, by negligently suffering to pass with silent acquiescence any representation that might impress the reader with a belief which I did not myself entertain. In relating circumstances of suspicious credit, the original authors are called on to speak for themselves, and to their accounts such remarks are added as may assist to remove doubts. On many occasions I have cited the words of an original journal for another reason, and have adopted them in the narrative in preference to any others which occurred.

The words of an eye-witness, flowing naturally from first impressions, are frequently more expressive, and convey ideas more just than studied descriptions; though the language may often be such as it would scarcely be allowable in other persons to write. Attention has been exerted on every convenience which might facilitate reference to any part of the work. Besides a copious Table of Contents, the head and margin of each page shews the subject matter, the number of the chapter, the date, and place of the transactions there narrated. This I mention, because omission in these particulars occasions much labour to be expended in researches for what such helps would have readily supplied.

An investigation of the situation of the lands discovered is given with each voyage, generally at the conclusion of the narrative. In performing this task, I have delivered my opinions freely on geographical questions, and on a few occasions have offered conjectures; for liable as conjectures are to error, instances must frequently occur where there is a necessity to resort to them. This is experienced by the navigator in seas imperfectly known, where he is inspirited with a degree of confidence if his conjectures, instead of wandering at random, are directed by the knowledge of any circumstance affording inference that will limit the uncertainty.

In the second volume, occasion has arisen in two instances to correct geographical errors committed in the first. These errors were brought to light by the examination of the journals of two of the voyages contained in this second volume. Throughout the composition of successive Volumes, the study of a subject is necessarily continued; yet in a long work requiring much search and investigation, there are very sufficient reasons to induce an author to publish by parts rather than to wait until his manuscript is compleated. The most important of these is, to secure an opportunity of revisal in the press; for large manuscripts on scientific subjects, when deprived of the fostering care of their author, are seldom fortunate. If they escape total neglect, they often fall into a worse evil, that of being published by a negligent or unskilful editor.

Concerning the extent to which this Work may be continued, I cannot speak with any confidence. As well as I am able to judge from the progress already made, another volume may be expected to carry the History of South Seas Discoveries to the commencement of the reign of His present Majesty.

THE ETHICS OF BUCCANEERING

The Accounts given by the Buccaneers who extended their enterprises to the Pacific Ocean, are the best authenticated of any which have been published by that class of

Adventurers. They are interspersed with nautical and geographical descriptions, corroborative of the events related, and more worth being preserved than the memory of what was performed. The materials of this portion of Buccaneer History, which it was necessary should be included in a History of South Sea Navigations, could not be collected without bringing other parts into view ; whence it appeared, that with a moderate increase of labour, and without much enlarging the bulk of the narrative, a regular history might be formed of their career, from their first rise, to their suppression ; and that such a work would not be without its use.

No practice is more common in literature, than for an author to endeavour to clear the ground before him, by mowing down the labours of his predecessors on the same subject. To do this, where the labour they have bestowed is of good tendency, or even to treat with harshness the commission of error where no bad intention is manifest, is in no small degree illiberal. But all the Buccaneer histories that hitherto have appeared, and the number is not small, are boastful compositions, which have delighted in exagerations : and, what is most mischievous, they have lavished commendation on acts which demanded reprobation, and have endeavoured to raise miscreants, notorious for their want of humanity, to the rank of heroes, lessening thereby the stain upon robbery, and the abhorrence naturally conceived against cruelty.

There is some excuse for the Buccaneer, who tells his own story. Vanity, and his prejudices, without any intention to deceive, lead him to magnify his own exploits ; and the reader naturally makes allowances.

The men whose enterprises are to be related, were natives of different European nations, but chiefly of Great Britain and France, and most of them seafaring people, who being disappointed, by accidents or the enmity of the Spaniards, in their more sober pursuits in the West Indies, and also instigated by thirst for plunder as much as by desire for vengeance, embodied themselves,

under different leaders of their own choosing, to make
predatory war upon the Spaniards. These men the
Spaniards naturally treated as pirates ; but some peculiar
circumstances which provoked their first enterprises,
and a general feeling of enmity against that nation on
account of their American conquests, procured them the
connivance of the rest of the maritime States of Europe,
and to be distinguished first by the softened appellations
of Freebooters and Adventurers, and afterwards by that
of Buccaneers. Spain, or, more strictly speaking Castile, on the merit of a first discovery, claimed an exclusive right to the possession of the whole of America,
with the exception of the Brasils, which were conceded
to the Portuguese. These claims, and this division, the
Pope sanctioned by an instrument, entitled a Bull of
Donation, which was granted at a time when all the
maritime powers of Europe were under the spiritual
dominion of the See of Rome. The Spaniards, however,
did not flatter themselves that they should be left in
the sole and undisputed enjoyment of so large a portion
of the newly discovered countries ; but they were principally anxious to preserve wholly to themselves the
West Indies : and, such was the monopolising spirit of
the Castilians, that during the life of the Queen Ysabel
of Castile, who was regarded as the patroness of Columbus's discovery, it was difficult even for Spaniards, not
subjects born of the crown of Castile, to gain access to
this New World, prohibitions being repeatedly published
against the admission of all other persons into the ships
bound thither. Ferdinand, King of Arragon, the husband of Ysabel, had refused to contribute towards the
outfit of Columbus's first voyage, having no opinion of
the probability that it would produce him an adequate
return ; and the undertaking being at the expense of
Castile, the countries discovered were considered as
appendages to the crown of Castile.

If such jealousy was entertained by the Spaniards of
each other, what must not have been their feelings
respecting other European nations ? " Whoever," says

Hakluyt, "is conversant with the Portugal and Spanish writers, shall find that they account all other nations for pirates, rovers, and thieves, which visit any heathen coast, that they have sailed by or looked on."

Spain considered the New World as what in our law books is called Treasure-trove, of which she became lawfully and exclusively entitled to take possession, as fully as if it had been found without any owner, or proprietor. Spain has not been singular in her maxims respecting the rights of discoverers. Our books of Voyages abound in instances of the same disregard shewn to the rights of the native inhabitants, the only rightful proprietors, by the navigators of other European nations, who, with a solemnity due only to offices of a religious nature, have continually put in practice the form of taking possession of Countries which to them were new discoveries, their being inhabited or desert making no difference.

Not infrequently has the ceremony been performed in the presence, but not within the understanding, of the wondering natives : and on this formality is grounded a claim to usurp the actual possession, in preference to other Europeans. Nothing can be more opposed to common sense, than that strangers should pretend to acquire by discovery, a title to countries they find with inhabitants ; as if in those very inhabitants the right of prior discovery was not inherent. On some occasions, however, Europeans have thought it expedient to acknowledge the rights of the natives, as when, in disputing each other's claims, a title by gift from the natives has been pretended.

In uninhabited lands, a right of occupancy results from the discovery ; but actual and bonâ fide possession is requisite to perfect appropriation. If real possession be not taken, or if taken shall not be retained, the right acquired by the mere discovery is not indefinite and a perpetual bar of exclusion to all others ; for that would amount to discovery giving a right equivalent to annihilation. Moveable effects may be hoarded and kept out

ADMIRAL JAMES BURNEY.

of use, or be destroyed, and it will not always be easy to prove whether with injury or benefit to mankind : but the necessities of human life will not admit, unless under the strong hand of a power, that a right should be pretended to keep extensive and fertile countries waste and secluded from their use, without other reason than the will of a proprietor or claimant.

Particular local circumstances have created objections to the occupancy of territory ; for instance, between the confines of the Russian and Chinese Empires, large tracts of country are left waste, it being held, that their being occupied by the subjects of either Empire would affect the security of the other. Several similar instances might be mentioned.

There is in many cases difficulty to settle what constitutes occupancy. On a small Island, any first settlement is acknowledged an occupancy of the whole ; and sometimes, the occupancy of a single Island of a group is supposed to comprehend an exclusive title to the possession of the remainder of the group. In the West Indies, the Spaniards regarded their making settlements on a few Islands, to be an actual taking possession of the whole, as far as European pretentions were concerned.

The first discovery of Columbus set in activity the curiosity and speculative dispositions of all the European maritime Powers. King Henry the VIIth, of England, as soon as he was certified of the existence of countries in the Western Hemisphere, sent ships thither, whereby Newfoundland, and parts of the continent of North America, were first discovered. South America was also visited very early, both by the English and the French ; "which nations," the Historian of Brasil remarks, "had neglected to ask a share of the undiscovered world, when Pope Alexander VIth partitioned it, who would as willingly have drawn two lines as one ; and, because they derived no advantage from that partition, refused to admit its validity." The West Indies, however, which doubtless was the part most coveted by all, seem to have been considered as more particularly the dis-

22

covery and right of the Spaniards; and, either from respect to their pretentions, or from the opinion entertained of their force in those parts, they remained many years undisturbed by intruders in the West Indian Seas. But their homeward-bound ships, and also those of the Portuguese from the East Indies, did not escape being molested by pirates; sometimes by those of their own, as well as of other nations.

AN ESSAY BY WAY OF LECTURE ON THE GAME OF WHIST. 1821

Brief Instructions for Young Whist Players

The kind of play recommended in this short treatise is on the most plain, and what the author considers the most safe, principles. Refinements cannot well be taught; they are mostly particular experiments, and must proceed from the imagination and genius of the experienced whist-player.

Maxims proposed for regular instruction in any art or science are for the most part, in the commencement at least, obvious truisms, strung together in connected and coadjutory order, so as to form a system for practice. In this mode of instruction, the ascent from the foundation is made easy, and the summit to appear not difficult of approach. In the game of whist, however, what deserves to be called good play is not attainable without long practice, and an earnestness of attention which only a strong partiality for the game can insure.

The varieties of whist are capable of furnishing dissertation without end. I have limited my endeavours to the most necessary instructions, classing them, as much as the subjects enabled me, under separate heads, to facilitate their being rightly comprehended and easily remembered. For the greater encouragement of the learner, I have studied brevity; but not in a degree to have prevented my endeavouring more to make the principles of the game, and the rationality of them, intelligible, than to furnish a young player with a set

of rules to get by rote, that he might go blindly right.
When many writers give lectures on the same science, it
must happen, however they may differ on particular
points, that there will be so much of general agreement
among them, that if the lecturer who comes last was to
be precluded from adopting or making use of that which
he approved in his predecessors, he would be nearly
fenced out of the field. In this respect I have waved
ceremony, and given the best rules I could find or think
of ; and as the authorities consulted are neither numerous
nor voluminous, I have thought it necessary only in a
few remarkable cases to give references. Of games of
skill Whist and common Draughts appear to me to
merit, in preference to all others, the character of being
simple in construction, with the least capricious rules,
and at the same time requiring greater exercise of judgment to be well played, than any other games that can
be mentioned. Whist, however, is not like draughts, a
game wholly of skill, but depending as much on chance
as on good play ; and to know how to take the better
chance in preference to the smaller, is the principal art
in conducting the game. It is well observed, in
Matthews's advice to a young whist player, that bad
play may sometimes succeed where good would not ;
but, he adds, never accustom yourself to judge by consequences. That play doubtless affords the best chance
of winning, which would succeed in the greatest number
and variety of cases. Nothing can be more simple, or
more easy of comprehension, than the principal rules of
whist. The highest cards in each suit run in the same
order, the ace being first, the king next, and so, in natural
succession, down to the deuce. The highest card of the
suit led wins the trick, unless it is trumped. Everyone
must follow the suit led, if able. If they have not a
card of that suit, they are at liberty to trump, or not.
The reckoning is according to the majority of tricks and
honours. For every trick obtained, beyond six, one is
reckoned. The honours (except at nine) are reckoned
by the difference of the number held by the parties.

These rules, on being first explained to a young friend of mine, who was desirous of learning the game, were so immediately comprehended, and appeared to him so plain and artless, that he exclaimed, "Oh! if that is all, I shall be able to play at whist as well as anybody in four and twenty hours!" When he was some twenty four hours older he discovered his mistake. As I write for persons whom I suppose to have previously advanced thus far, and to have begun to reason on the modes of playing I shall proceed to lay down a few :—

General Maxims for the Conduct of the Game

1. In the commencement of a game (or of a hand, unless in far advanced stages of the game,) it is right to play on the supposition, that the cards you have not yourself, (the trump card turned up also excepted) are divided equally, or nearly so, between the other players. As the contrary shall appear, you are to alter or modify your plan, exercising your judgment in so doing, according to the circumstances.

2. As the cards are played, some judgment is to be formed of what cards are, or are not, in the hands of the several players; as for example, the card played to an ace, or other king [1] card, is to be supposed the lowest of that suit which the player held, and if it is a high card, that he can have few or none of the suit remaining. It is reasonably to be supposed that the last player will win the trick as cheaply as he can, and, therefore, if he wins over the nine or ten with the ace, it may be considered that he has no intermediate card of that suit in his hand. Other examples it would be premature to mention thus early.

3. In general, your play should be such as may give your partner an insight into your hand; for though you may thereby give equal information to your opponents, it is in the most material cases, of greater importance to

[1] By the term king card is meant the highest remaining card in a suit.

inform your partner, than to keep them in ignorance. It is held an axiom, that the nearer your play approaches to that of a dumb partner, (i.e. whose cards are exposed), the better; and it is usual, when one of three equal players has the dumb partner, for him to give one point in the game to each of his opponents, unless when the dumb partner is taken in turn.

4. There are cases, however, where it is evidently advantageous to play a deceptive game; also some where deceptive play is a hazardous speculation; but these are particular cases, concerning which some notices will appear in the sequel. Your general play, as above observed, should be as intelligible to your partner as you can make it.

5. " Be as careful of what you play to a card you cannot win, as of what you lead. It may be of bad consequence to put down a tray with the deuce of a suit in your hand. Suppose your partner to lead the four, and the next player to play the five: if you put down the tray, it ought to be a certainty, that you will rough the next round of the suit." This is a good illustration, and shews how much an attentive player may be deceived by the negligence of his partner in playing his small cards incorrectly.

6. There are some things which should be habitually present to the mind of the player. Of these, the most difficult, from its continually varying, seems to be the keeping in mind who dealt, and the trump card turned up. By a predetermined attention to these particulars for six following deals, the observance will come to be a habit.

7. There are a few calculations on the chances of your partner or other player holding a particular card, or one of two or more certain named cards, which being permanent are more easily remembered, and should be as fixtures in the mind; if not the calculations, the results. De Mowre jocosely observes, without being at the pains of studying the demonstrations, the conclusions may be used, taking it for granted that the demonstrations are

right. It is not, however, demanded that everyone shall be so satisfied.

8. The chance against your partner, or other player, holding any named card which you have not, is two to one. This is not exactly correct, except when you are the dealer. When your partner has dealt, the chance against his holding a certain unknown card is 26 to 12 ; and against either of the other players, only 25 to 13 ; but these are small differences, which to attend to, would be a discouragement to the learner, and perplexing to the memory of a good player. Not to trouble the learner or myself with giving anything of abstruse calculation, it will be sufficiently near for practical use in play, and is so allowed by all writers on the game, to state the chances recommended to the memory of the player, to be as follows :—

1. That it is an even chance which of the two, your partner or the last player, holds the highest card in any suit.

2. That it is two to one against your partner (or other named player) holding a card which you have not.

3. That the chance is five to four in favour of his holding one of two named cards.

4. And that it is very nearly five to two in favour of his holding one of three named cards.

These chances, well remembered, will often be a direction to your play.

9. With two honours in your hand at the point of eight, it is frequently best not to call, if your game is not in danger. But if you are so deficient in winning cards that you think, if the hand is played out, the adversaries will save their lurch by tricks, it is right to call. The chance is five to four in favour of your partner holding an honour, you having two, and an honour not having been turned up.

10. Hoyle has given, what he calls, " an artificial memory," which consists of the manner of the player placing the cards in his hand ; but his invention in this is much too complicated. Matthews has also given a

method a little perplexing, as it requires being put into execution whilst the cards are playing, and according as they are played. A method I have constantly practised, is, the trumps to the left. Next to trumps, my most numerous suit; if numbers are equal, that which is headed by the highest card to be to the left. The remaining suits in the same order, the smallest suit being to the right of all. This method may assist an absent person to recollect how many, and what, cards of any suit he had originally.

OF IMPROPRIETIES

1. It is improper in a leader to play a card with emphasis which is the highest remaining card of a suit and not the ace, as it may assist his partner to recollect its being such.

2. And still more so, to draw a second card, or to make any motion of readiness to lead again, before all the players have played to his first card.

3. It is improper to pretend to hesitate when there is no cause for hesitation, as when the person who is to play has only one card in his hand of the suit led.

4. To name the trump card turned up by the dealer after the first trick is turned and quitted, should be attended with a penalty.

5. It is improper that any bet should be made which is in the least liable to occasion alteration in the play. Finding fault with a partner during the play of the hand may not merit being classed with the improprieties above complained against; but instructing players will do well to reserve their lecture till the hand is played out.

N.B. TO " LAWS "

Betting, whether of the byestanders or the players, is not in any manner to be allowed to interfere with the game; and if any such interference shall be judged to have affected the play or score of the game, the satisfaction to be made to the party or parties prejudiced, ought to be submitted to reference.

VI

CHARLES BURNEY, D.D.

1757—1817

" THE sweetest tempered boy in the Charterhouse school " achieved what we may call a more solid reputation than any other of the family. There was a party one day at his house when Dr. Parr gave as a toast—" the *third* Greek scholar in Europe." When asked to explain, the great man replied, " Our excellent host. The first Greek scholar is my friend here," (indicating Porson). " Don't blush, Dickey. The second modesty does not permit me to name." That, in fact, was the general opinion of Charles Burney in his own generation.

Educated at Cambridge and Aberdeen he became an assistant master at Highgate College and then at Chiswick, where he married the head's daughter ; soon afterwards setting up for himself at Hammersmith and ultimately moving to Greenwich. As a teacher, he seems to have attained great wealth and respect.

His classical writings are not, indeed, considered to justify his reputation ; but he amassed an enormous classical Library—of some thirteen or fourteen thousand texts, with MSS. notes by himself and other scholars— " so arranged that the state of the texts could be seen from their first known production to their latest change " ; with some three or four hundred quarto volumes of MS. and printed (i.e. on Playbills) material for a History of the Stage ; a collection of newspapers from 1603 ; and theatrical prints from the age of Elizabeth. Parliament purchased the collection for the British Museum at £13,500.

Such amazing industry in a schoolmaster and dignitary of the Church, holding a prebendary stall in Lincoln

Cathedral, fairly rivals, if it does not exceed, his father's. Yet few, one fancies, were more affectionate and simple-minded in his home life. The family one and all clearly expected, and received from him, ungrudging help in all trouble.

We must recognise that his style is more professional and easy than most of the Burney's, though the allusion below to " schools planned for Female education," the " extraordinary indulgences with which children are now gratified," and the " settled rules of our wiser Ancestors," will appear strange to-day.

In 1804 Southey wrote to Coleridge of a dinner at Sothebys where he met some " lions " ; among them Charles Burney, who " after a long silence broke out into a discourse upon the properties of the conjunction *Quam*. Except his quamical knowledge, which is as profound as you will imagine, he knows nothing but bibliography, or the science of title-pages, impresses, and dates. It was a relief to leave him, and find his brother the Captain, at Rickman's, smoking after supper, letting out puffs at one corner of his mouth and puns at the other."

REMARKS ON THE GREEK VERSES OF MILTON. [Printed at the end of Warton's " New Edition of Milton's Poems ": but " a Few Separate Copies " sent to Friends.] 1790

Introductory

When it is considered how frequently the life of Milton has been written, and how numerous the annotations have been, on different parts of his works, it seems strange that his Greek verses, which, indeed, are but few, should have passed almost wholly without notice. They have neither been mentioned, as proofs of learning, by his admirers, nor exposed to the ordeal of criticism, by his enemies. Both parties seem to have shrunk from the subject.

To investigate the motives for this silence is not necessary, and the search might possibly prove fruitless.

The present observations attempt to apply the deficiency of former Commentators, whose stores of critical knowledge have been lavished, ὅλῳ δύλακι, merely on the English poetry of Milton.

It will, perhaps, be asserted, that the following remarks are frequently too minute. Yet it seems the duty of a commentator, *on the Greek production of a modern*, to point out, in general, the sources from which each expression flowed, and to defend by collected authorities, what to some readers may appear incontrovertibly right, as well as to animadvert on passages, of which the errors will be discovered by those only, who have devoted a large portion of their time and attention to the study of the Ancients. Critical strictures on such works should be written to direct the judgment of the less learned, and not merely to confirm the opinions of profound scholars.

In these Remarks, the reader will find some objections stated, which are to be considered as relating rather to points of taste, than of authority.—In passages of which the propriety or impropriety could be decided by appeals to the Ancients, reference has generally been made to Euripides, in preference to all other writers. It is well known, that he was much studied by Milton, and he is properly termed *his favourite poet* by Mr. Warton, in his *Notes on Comus*, ver. 297.

Those, who have long and justly entertained an high idea of Milton's Greek erudition, on perusing these notes, will probably feel disappointed ; and may ascribe to spleen and temerity, what, it is hoped, merits at least a milder title.—To Milton's claim of extensive, and, indeed, wonderful learning, who shall refuse their suffrage ! It requires not our commendation, and may defy our censure.—If Dr. Johnson, however, observes of some Latin Verse of Milton, that it is not secure against a stern grammarian, what would he have said, if he had bestowed his time, in examining part of his Greek poetry, with the same exactness of taste, and with equal accuracy of criticism ?

If Milton had lived in the present age, the necessity of these remarks would, in all probability, have been superseded. His native powers of mind, and his studious researches, would have been assisted by the learned labours of Bentley, Hemsterhusius, Valckenaer, Toup, and Ruhnkenius, under whose auspices Greek criticism has flourished, in this century, with a degree of vigour wholly unknown in any period, since the revival of letters.

THE EXPOSITION OF THE CREED BY JOHN PEARSON, D.D.:
ABRIDGED FOR THE USE OF YOUNG PERSONS. BY THE REV. C.
BURNEY, LL.D., F.R.S. 1810. DEDICATED TO CHARLES MANNERS
SUTTON, ARCHBISHOP OF CANTERBURY

PREFACE

The elementary works, which have been published with a view of qualifying Students in Divinity for becoming sound Preachers of " the faith and discipline of the Church of England, against all opposers," form no inconsiderable Catalogue. . . . Those, however, which are calculated for young Persons of both sexes, at any earlier age, and which have been written expressly for the use of schools, are comparatively few in number. . . .

Whether this abridgment of the EXPOSITION OF THE CREED—the luminous production of the profound and eloquent Bishop Pearson—may be allowed, at due distance, to follow these performances, is now most respectfully left to the decision of the Publick.

With regard to the PLAN of this Abridgment, I must beg leave to assure the Reader, that every passage, which has been omitted, was omitted with reluctance. Whenever an erasure was made some beautiful thought, some learned remark, some energetick expression was expunged ; but abridgment was necessary, though it was not a task of easy performance. To the original Work scarcely more than single words have been added in any place ; and those principally where connective particles were requisite. The Notes, though replete with the purest theology and the deepest erudition, have not been inserted. From the nature of their subjects, they would have bewildered the youthful mind, much more than they would have contributed to its improvement. The Readers, therefore, who wish to peruse the history of theological controversies, and the refutation of heretical opinions, must search for them in the original Volume.

With regard to the OBJECT of this Abridgment, it has been made chiefly with a wish of promoting the religious education of youth in the Upper Forms of our Publick Schools and Classical Seminaries. It is recommended to their use, as an Exercise Book for Saturday evenings, in which the scholar should be directed to translate a portion of it, into Latin or Greek; and should be required to insert, in their proper places, the passages from the original of the New Testament, which are cited or to which the marginal notes refer. This Abridgment may also be made a book of general perusal in ALL Schools, if, while one of the upper boys reads it aloud, the rest are taught to bring forward the citations, from the Greek, Latin, or English Testament, according to their progress and advancement in these languages. From this plan the younger readers must derive an early facility of reference to the Scriptures, as well as of quotations from their sacred pages.—By confining the references also to the New Testament in modern languages, this Abridgment may, in nearly the same manner, be admitted as a Work of Sacred Instruction into Schools, planned for Female Education; and into private Houses, in which the Family Circle, on Sunday evenings, may be wisely desirous of cultivating Religious Knowledge.

Let me trespass a little further on the patience of the Reader; in order to recommend this Abridgment, with affectionate respect, to my Brethren, who are employed in the laudable, but anxious, duty of instructing the RISING GENERATION; to which service, between twenty and thirty years of my life have been constantly devoted. During the latter part of this period the difficulties, the toils, and the solicitude of a Schoolmaster's occupation have been gradually and greatly increased: not nearly so much, let me add, by the *evil days*, on which *we have fallen*; as by those extraordinary and destructive indulgences, with which children are now gratified, during the seasons, at which they are under the roof of their Parents.

As long as the domestick system of Education preserves its present form, it will inevitably produce a distaste for study at School, which the active exertions of a Master must combat ; a repugnance to regulations, which he must vigorously correct ; and a defiance of authority, which he must incessantly labour to restrain : lest his professional duties should first become insupportable, and then nugatory. If these Efforts should fail, the consequences may be readily foreseen : Learning will by degrees decay ; and Society will in vain deplore the loss ; while the " settled rules " of our wiser Ancestors, who assigned their proper Places, as well as their proper Duties, to Individuals of all Ages and all Ranks, will speedily lose their influence ; and become useless, like repealed Statutes, instead of being cherished as the guides and lights of Society.

Let not my Brethren, however, though the prospect is gloomy, and their cares are augmented, shrink from the active fulfilment of their arduous task ; but let them recollect, amidst watchfulness which must enfeeble the stoutest frame, and amidst exertions, which must enervate the most vigorous understanding, that no occupation can be more eminently useful, than that in which they are engaged. Let THEM also feel, with conscious pride, that the real dignity of every profession rests solely on its utility. Let them train their Pupils to early and steady habits of industry and obedience, and let them indicate the necessity of thinking with seriousness and reverence on sacred subjects :—let them be especially careful, that the foundation of a virtuous and religious life may be established in their docile minds, by an early introduction to the knowledge of a Christian's duties.

If they uniformly pursue this course, they may be assured, that the Publick will justly and gratefully appreciate their efforts.—Then will they reflect with unalloyed satisfaction, that by such a discharge of their obligations towards those, whose education has been entrusted to their direction, they have contributed essentially to the promotion of Learning, to the interests of Virtue and Religion, and to the prosperity of their Country.

CHARLES BURNEY.

GREENWICH,
Jan. 1, 1810.

VII

SARAH HARRIET BURNEY

1770—1844

SARAH HARRIET, daughter of the second Mrs. Burney, was a droll and clever child, with " native spirits of the highest order, and distinguished ability " ; whose novels were, in her own day, almost as popular and well thought-of as *Evelina* and *Cecilia.*

She was, also, something of a learned lady in her youth, playing interpreter for her uncle Arthur Young (the agriculturist) to some of the *émigrés.*

It is however at Rome, in later days, that we meet the most personal impressions of Sarah, who unconvention-ally—for those days—made friends with the diarist Crabb Robinson ; though when he mentioned knowing her brother James, she frankly replied that she'd never heard of him.

Yet " our acquaintance ripened into friendship which did not end but with her life. She was a very amiable person, of whom I think with respect."

He taught her how to live cheaply in Rome, at a " respectable, but cheap, restaurant in the Corso, frequented by German artists, and occasionally Italian (not English) ladies. . . . I introduced Miss Burney to our party. She became our *pet*, and generally dined with us. When I was engaged elsewhere there were several proud to take her."

One can believe that the good Robinson liked merry ladies ; but later testimony from the ferocious Landor should carry weight :—" I have made my visit to Miss Burney," he writes, " and spent above an hour with her.

She is one of the most agreeable and intelligent women I have met abroad."

Sarah's first novel *Clarentine* appeared anonymously in 1796 ; *Geraldine Fauconberg* in 1808 (2nd ed. 1813) ; and the first edition of *Traits of Nature* (1812) was sold out in three months.

The *Tales of Fancy* 1815 and *Romances of Private Life* 1839, are generally considered to contain her best work ; but I fear that none of it really calls for prolonged attention from posterity.

It is interesting, however, to find the family traits so vigorous and successful in a younger member : and the passage below " of Heroes and Heroines " reveals a timid stirring towards natural characters and truth to life, which may be dramatically set side by side with the witty excuse for writing " Romance " in the " Dedication " to *The Shipwreck* :—

" Considering my true oriental taste for coca-trees and mangoes, for fragrant gales and unclouded skies . . . I did wisely in confining myself to a track where local description and mere adventure might supply the place of sense."

MORNING CHRONICLE, 13 *July*, 1820

To Miss Burney on her character of Blanche in " Country Neighbours "

Bright spirits conspired to grace the Burney name,
    Some in letters, some in tasteful arts,
    In learning some have borne distinguished parts ;
Or sought through science of sweet sounds their fame.
And foremost *she* renowned for many a tale
    Of faithful love perplex'd ; and of that good
    Old man, who as *Camilla*'s guardian stood
In obstinate virtue clad like coat of mail.
Nor dost thou, Sarah, with unequal pace
    Her steps pursue.   The pure romantic vein
    No gentler creature ever knew to feign
Than thy fine *Blanch*, young with an elder grace,
    In all respects without rebuke or blame,
    Answering the Antique freshness of her name.

CHARLES LAMB.

REV. CHARLES BURNEY, D.D.
From bust by Nollekens.

RICHARD THOMAS BURNEY
1768—1808 OR 1811

Richard belonged to the second family and appears in the records as a handsome and high-spirited boy, more or less petted by all. But after Charterhouse and Harrow he went into the Indian Civil Service, where he was known as "Bengal Dick," and inevitably passed out of the circle.

He married Janet Ross of Bengal, and their son Henry had six children, most of whom returned to England. The following record of Major Henry throws an interesting light upon his character and position :—

"1830.—The latter end of this year, letters were received by Government, from the East Indies, announcing that Major Burney (a grandson of Dr. Burney, Senr.) who was sent as a new Resident at the court of Ava, in the Burman Empire, had met with a very flattering reception at Rangoon, to which place he was deputed, in order to enter into some preliminaries, in which he was to represent the British Authorities at Ava. The account says that the Woonghee sent two magistrates in full robes to receive him ; and 200 or 300 followers to escort him and his suite to the hall of Audience ; where the Woonghee and his principal officers of State in their Court dresses received them, with every possible mark of respect. Chairs were placed for the Resident, and the English Gentlemen (merchants of the place) who followed him. The object of his Mission was to get certain duties and fees which were charged to Traders and Boats leaving Alva regulated and fixed, so as to put some stop to the exaction of the Burmese subordinate officers, who all live upon what they can extort from foreign merchants."

The account then goes on to state the nature of the exactions and the means proposed for the future management of them ; adding that Major Burney continued on the best possible terms with the Ministers : their Excellencies often dining with him. "The king gives

23

him audience three or four times in the month : and the
Monarch in the overflowings of Royal favour and grace
it seems, has conferred upon him the lofty sounding title
of Maha Zayd Raja Nauratha ; which being interpreted
means My great, victorious, and Noble son ! with the
present of a shoulder-belt of nine gold chains. . . . It is
a matter of congratulation in our opinion that Government has discovered, and availed itself of the singular
qualifications which Major Burney appears to possess
for the Post which he so ably fills."—*Morning Herald*,
11 June, 1831. From a Calcutta paper, 1830.
"Worcester" Journal.

Of Heroes and Heroines
FROM "GERALDINE FAUCONBERG"

" The truth is," said he, " the heroines of romance
are described as being so bewitchingly amiable, that they
put me out of humour with women in real life ; and the
heroes are so perfect, that they fill me with a mortifying
sense of my own inferiority."

" I differ from you entirely," cried Mrs Neville.
" One of the strongest objections that might be urged
against novels is, the passionate, impatient, and overbearing character assigned to most of the lovers. The
authors tell you a prodigious deal of their generosity,
courage, and enthusiastic sensibility ; but many of them
are so quarrelsome, have so little self command, or are
so blindly and furiously jealous ; that one might live
as securely and as peaceably with a half intoxicated
savage ! The perfect heroes you describe were formerly,
I allow, in fashion ; but you read of no Sir Charles
Grandisons now : the present *ton* among that class of
imaginary persons, particularly in foreign publications,
is rashness, selfishness, and a sort of mad irritability, for
which any actually existing creature would deserve to
be shut up in a dark room, and fed upon bread and
water ! "

" There is so much justice in this criticism," said

Madame de St. Hermine " that good temper, one of the first requisites to happiness in social life, and fortitude to endure evil, one of the noblest virtues of the human mind, seem to be totally put out of the question, in the enumeration of a hero's merits."

" What has most provoked me," cried Geraldine, " in the very limited number of these sort of books which I have been permitted to read is, the intuitive and supernatural genius, for all kinds of accomplishments, attributed to the heroines. Brought up, many of them, in profound retirement, often poor and dependent, they acquire, nobody knows how, a skill in languages, in music, in dancing and drawing, such as we have often found, to our sorrow, the most assiduous application, under the direction of the best masters, will not enable us to attain. And these self-educated ladies are always described as out-soaring every girl of real fashion, who ventures to vie with them in talent and cultivation."

" I hold these vulgar exaggerations in such profound contempt," cried Mrs Neville, " that, were the innate endowments they record credible, I would rather forfeit the chance of ever hearing another note of music, or of ever again beholding another picture, than be condemned to listen to, or look at, the effects produced by them."

From " Country Neighbours "

Jealousy

" You have bestowed your heart upon a man who, without the taint of a single vice, is, however, with all his excellences, not wholly exempted from human imperfections. It appears to me that the fault of his nature is a tendency to jealousy, which it behoves the woman he marries to be particularly careful not to arouse. . . . Do not, because confident of the innocence of your intentions, suffer yourself to disregard the danger of irritating his feelings. Always bear in mind that it rests with you to aggravate or allay the one known fault of your husband's temper, and that it is equally your interest and your most imperious duty, to guard against the remotest possibility of destroying his and your own peace, by any inconsiderate or even playful defiance of his inborn master passion."

"Oh, how much greater justice I do him," cried Blanche, with energy, "than to believe that he is infected, in so alarming a degree, with this horrible failing which you attribute to him. . . . He has indeed taught me what his symptoms are, and I should know them at half a glance. Should they (which Heaven forbid) ever, in the slightest degree recur, I would avail myself of my right to clear away every unfounded apprehension from his mind ; the solicitude I should feel to regain his confidence ; and the honest joy he would behold in me when I had succeeded—would not these soon convince him, that he had a wife too sincerely devoted to him ; too anxious to set his heart at ease, and too determined to make him confess to her every uneasy suspicion as it arose, to become a voluntary disturber of the mutual happiness which, I trust, will be our portion."

THE PERFECT BRIDE

Blanche, always so beautiful, appeared to have acquired a new character of beauty. It was no longer her glowing youthfulness, her symmetry of face and form, nor even the perfection of grace in all her movements that struck the eye :—it was the heavenly air of serene, because entire reliance, on the worth of him she had chosen ; the subdued but touching sensibility on her countenance that attracted and fixed the delighted gazer.

VIII

CHARLOTTE ANN BURNEY, HER CHILDREN, AND GRAND-CHILDREN

Born 1759

THE " nanny-goats " of the lively Charlotte are well-known to readers of the *Early Diary* ; but we have no evidence of her later writing, and are here concerned with the continued literary activity (incidentally of her second husband), of her children and grandchildren.

She married first (in 1786) Mr. Clement Francis who, as Secretary to Warren Hastings in India, had so admired *Evelina*, that he came home determined to make the authoress his wife. His reasons for choosing Charlotte, perhaps, scarcely concern us to-day ; but he set up as a surgeon in Aylsham, Norfolk, died suddenly towards the end of 1792, leaving Charlotte with two daughters and a son. Six years later she married Captain Ralph Broome, of the Bengal Army, whose two volumes of political verse—on *Burke* 1796 and on *The Trial of Warren Hastings* in 1789—were composed in the manner of Anstey's *New Bath Guide*, and contain some sprightly couplets.

"Her only and very promising son died in London in 1829. He had long been an invalid ; althô his fond and anxious mother had sorrowfully seen his declining health, and was therefore in some measure prepared for it, yet the sad event, when it took place, was a very severe blow to her, and likewise to his sisters. He was of the Cambridge University and aged 36."

"Worcester" Journal.

But the daughters, Marianne and Charlotte Francis are of more importance for us to-day. They were, it appears, somewhat alarming blue-stockings ; and Dr. Burney, describing Marianne's great learning to Fanny, " privately " calls her " a monster."

Charlotte Francis, literally compelled by his impetuosity to marry, at sixteen, the elderly Mr. Barrett, is—of course—well known as the Editor of Fanny Burney's *Diary and Letters*. But she appears to have spent a great part of her life in nursing her own family, although she produced a *Handbook to the Marbles, Castes, and Antiquities in the Fitzwilliam Museum*, Cambridge, 1855 ; and was herself nearly as proud of the anonymous *Charades, Enigmas and Riddles by a Cantab*, 1859, of which the characteristic " Preface " is given below. Her granddaughter described her, about 1907, as " a very little old lady, with bright blue eyes, and soft brown hair, and the neatest, trimmest little figure imaginable. She never grew *old*, though she lived so long. On Sunday evenings, she always spelt out her Hebrew psalm, and Dr. Greenhill (of Hastings) remarked that she was the only woman he knew who could read Hebrew *and* make a jelly " ; as Johnson had once declared that Miss Carter could make puddings and translate Epictetus.

Finally *her* daughter, *Julia Charlotte*, when a " young girl universally admired, extremely pretty, witty and lively " ; copied out " sheets of Hebrew on blue paper " to assist her scholar-brother's failing eyesight ; and helped her second husband Dr. Maitland in his *The Church in the Catacombs* and other books. Her own *Letters from Madras, by a Lady* 1843 (quoted below) was highly praised and successfully reprinted.

CHARADES, ENIGMAS, AND RIDDLES: COLLECTED BY A CANTAB [CHARLOTTE BARRETT].

PREFACE
Cambridge, 1859.

Light and trifling as these pastimes may be, they have the sanction of high antiquity. Œdipus received a kingdom for solving the Enigma of the Sphinx, while the poor monster dashed out what brains she had, in despair at his penetration. In less fabulous times, warriors and Legislations have heeded their warnings, and among the Athenians it was customary at festivals to propound Enigmas and to bestow rewards and garlands on those who solved them.

Dr. Johnson defines a Rebus to be "a word represented by a picture": perhaps the Scythians admonished Darius by a Rebus; when he had invaded their country and was in great straits, they sent him a bird, a frog, a mouse, and five arrows:—the Persian Monarch considered this as a surrender of their Land, their streams, and their forces; but Gobriyas, a Looker-on, interpreted these objects as follows:—"Unless, O Persians, ye become birds and fly in the air, or become mice and hide yourselves beneath the Earth, or become frogs and leap into the Lakes, ye shall never return, but be stricken by these arrows!"

The word Riddle is thought to be of Saxon origin and to have implied a trial of skill; it is used as a verb by Milton:

> "Be less abstruce, my *riddling* days are o'er."

As a specimen of Mediæval Riddles we may give the following, upon the River Vulturnus in Italy:

> "Candam tolle, volat; Caput aufer, splendit in armis;
> Totum deme fluit viscera, deme dolet." [1]

There is in the British Museum a Black Letter *Boke* of such puzzles, and Lord Bacon records the enigmatical prophecy,

> "When Hempe is spun
> England's done."

telling us how it was explained in his day.

In more modern times, Dumay, a French Councillor who was blind, hearing that his friend Ménage was laid up with the gout, sent him the following query:

> "Qui mala nostra tulit præstanti dote valebat.
> Ede viri nomen, dos tibi tales erit."

[1] Vultur, Turnus, Vultus.

Thus translated by the Poet Gray :

> " He who our ills united bare
> The Art of Divination knew ;
> If you the Prophet's name declare
> I'll hail you Prophet too."

Ménage's answer was the following :

> " Œdipodem tecum facio.   Tumet œger uterque
> Pes mihi.   Caligat lumen utrumqui tibi ! "

Translated by Mrs. Thrale :

> " In Œdipus alone I read
> Our miseries united ;
> My lameness was to him decreed.
> His eyes, like yours, benighted."

The charade is of French or Italian origin ; the name perhaps derived from the Italian, *Schiarare*, to disentangle, to clear up : *Schiarato, a, cleared, unravelled* :—Its ingenuity consists in making two or more words or syllables, each having a separate meaning, combine in the whole word.—A well-known example was written during the Duke of Northumberland's administration :

" I will dedicate my First to the owner of my Second, provided he will give me the Third for my pains."

We can offer no derivation of the word Conundrum : *Johnson* and *Walker* call it " a Quibble, a low Jest, a play upon words " ; " in which," says a French writer, " all your wit is exerted to play the fool successfully."

The Double Acrostic is of very recent invention : it requires that two names or words should be spelled by the first and last letters of the several words indicated.

Various modifications exist, which cannot be classed under any of the above-mentioned heads.   Such may be the reply of the great scholar who was found under the table, his candle burnt out and his bottle empty : " How is this ? " cried the visitor—" here is neither drink nor light ! "

" No," murmued the Grecian,

> οὐδε τόδε οὐδε τάλλο
> oude toddy oude tallow.

To which we might add the following Queries and Answers, said to have been contributed to *Punch* by a Rugby schoolboy.

Q. " What is mind ? "
A. " No matter."
Q. " What is matter ? "
A. " Never mind."

Having endeavoured to collect such harmless speci-mens of these fancies as may exercise ingenuity or amuse an idle moment, we now commend them to the reader's kind indulgence.

JULIA CHARLOTTE MAITLAND
Letters from Madras during the years 1836–1839. By a Lady, 1843.

A NATIVE FEAST

The other day a very rich native, an old protégé of A——s, came to say that he and his son wished to make a feast for me, if I would come to their home. I was extremely glad, for I was longing to get into one of their native houses ; so last night we all went to him by appointment—M^r and Mrs Staunton, A——, and I. It was a most curious entertainment ; but I was surprised to find that the Stauntons, who have been so long in the country, had never seen anything of the kind before. It is wonderful how little interested most of the English ladies seem by all the strange habits and ways of the natives ; and it is not merely that they have grown used to it all, but that, by their own accounts, they never cared more about what goes on around them than they do now. I can only suppose they have forgotten their first impressions. But this makes me wish to try and see everything that I can while the bloom of my Orientalism is fresh upon me, and before this apathy and listlessness have laid hold on me, as no doubt they will.

I asked one lady what she had seen of the country and the natives since she had been in India. " Oh, nothing ! " said she : " thank goodness, I know nothing at all about them, nor I don't wish to : really I think the less one sees and knows of them the better ! "

Armagum and Sooboo, our two entertainers, met us
at their garden-gate, with numbers of lanterns, and rows
of natives, some of them friends and some servants, all
the way up to the house. The whole house was lighted
up like a show, with chandeliers, and lustres in every
possible corner, and hung from the ceiling and festooned
to the walls besides : it looked very bright and pretty.
The house consisted of one very large verandah, in which
stood the native company; that opened into a large
drawing-room, with a smaller room at each end, and
sleeping rooms beyond; and on the other side of the
drawing-room another verandah leading into another
garden. The house was furnished very much like a
French lodging-house, only with more comfortable
ottomans and sofas; but the general effect was very
French : quantities of French nicknacks set out upon
different tables, and the walls quite covered with looking-
glasses.

We were led into the great drawing-room, and placed
upon sofas, and servants stationed at our sides to fan us :
then Armagum and Sooboo brought us each a nosegay
of roses, and poured rose water over them and over our
hands ; and they gave me a queer kind of sprig made of
rice and beads, like a twelfth-cake ornament : then they
gave us each a garland of scented flowers, so powerful that
even now, at the end of the next day, I cannot get rid
of the perfume on my hands and arms. Then the entertainment began : they had procured the musicians,
dancers, and cooks belonging to the Nabob, in order that
I might see all the Mussulman amusements, as well as
those of the Hindoos. First, then, came in an old man
with a white beard, to play and sing to the Vina, an
instrument like a large mandolin, very pretty, graceful,
and antique to look at, but not much to hear. His
music was miserable, just a mixture of twang and whine,
and quite monotonous, without even a pretence to a
tune. When we were quite tired of him, he was dismissed, and the Nabob's dancing-girls came in : most
graceful creatures, walking, or rather sailing about like

queens, with long muslin robes from their throats to
their feet. They were covered with gold and jewels,
earrings, nose-rings, bracelets, armlets, anklets, bands
round their heads, sévignés, and rings on all their fingers
and all their toes. Their dancing consisted of sailing
about, waving their hands, turning slowly round and
round, and bending from side to side : It was graceful,
but very tame : there were neither steps nor figure, as
far as I could make out. The prettiest of their performances was their beautiful swan like march. Then they
sang, bawling like bad street-singers—a most fearful
noise, and no tune. Then we had a concert of orchestra
music, with different-looking instruments, but in tone
like every modification of bagpipes—every variety of
drone and squeak : you can form no idea of such sounds
under the name of music : the chimney-sweeper's clatter
on May-day would be harmonious in comparison.
Imagine a succession of unresolved discords, selected at
random, and played on twenty or thirty loud instruments,
all out of tune with themselves and with each other,
and you will have a fair idea of Hindoo music and its
effect upon the nerves.

When my teeth had been set on edge till I could really
bear it no longer, I was obliged to beg A—— to give the
musicians a hint to stop. Then there came in a man
to imitate the notes of various birds : this sounded promising, but unfortunately the Madras birds are scream-
ing, and not singing, birds ; and my ears were assailed
by screech owls, crows, parrots, peacocks, Etc., so well
imitated that I was again obliged to beg relief from such
torture. Then we had a Hindoo dancing-girl, with the
most magnificent jewellery I ever saw : her dancing was
very much like that of the Mahomedans, only a little
more difficult. There was a good deal of running backwards and forwards upon her heels, and shaking her silver
bangles or armlets, which jingled like bells : then glis-
sading up to me, waving her pretty little hands, and
making a number of graceful, unmeaning antics, with
her eyes fixed on mine in a strange unnatural stare, like

animal magnetism. I really think those magnetic actings and starings must first have been imitated from some Indian dancing-girl, and in fact the effect is much the same : for I defy any one to have watched this girl's dull, unvarying dance long, without going to sleep. The natives I believe can sit quite contented for hours without any more enlivening amusement ; but then they are always half asleep by nature, and like to be quite asleep by choice at any opportunity.

After her performance was ended we had a conjurer, some of whose tricks were quite marvellous. He had on a turban and cummerbund (or piece of muslin wrapped round him), but no jacket, so that one could not imagine a possibility of his concealing any of his apparatus about him ; but, among other tricks, he took a small twig of a tree, ran his fingers down it to strip the leaves off— small leaves, like those of a sensitive plant—and showered down among us, with the leaves, five or six great live scorpions ; not little things like Italian scorpions, but formidable animals almost as long as my hand : I did not admire their company, creeping about the room, so he crumpled them up in his hand, and they disappeared : then he waved his bare arms in the air, and threw a live cobra into the midst of us. Most of his other tricks were juggling with cups and balls Etc., like any English conjurer, but the scorpions and cobra were quite beyond my comprehension.

Our gentlemen were surprised at seeing the string which is always worn by Bramins round this man's neck, and said, that twenty years ago no Bramin could possibly have so degraded himself as to show off before us as a common juggler. After he was dismissed we had another gold and silver girl, to dance upon sharp swords, to music as sharp ; then a fire-eater ; and last of all a great supper laid out in the back verandah. The first course consisted of all the Nabob's favourite dishes of meat, and curries and pillaws set out in China plates ; the second course all Hindoo cookery, set out in cups and saucers. A—— whispered to me that I must eat as much as I could to please poor old Armagum; so I did my best, till I was almost choked with cayenne-pepper. The Moorman pillaws were very good; but among the Hindoo messes I at last came to something so queer, slimy, and oily, that I was obliged to stop.

After supper Armagum made me a speech, to inform me that he was aware that the Hindoos did not know how to treat ladies: that he had therefore been that morning to consult an English friend of his, Mr Tracey, concerning the proper mode of showing the respect that was my due; and that Mr Tracey had informed him that English ladies were accustomed to exact the same respect as if they were gentlemen, and that he had better behave to me accordingly. He begged I would consider that, if there had been any deficiency, it was owing to ignorance, and not to want of affection; for that he looked upon me as his mother! Then he perfumed us all with attar of roses, and we came away, after thanking him very cordially for his hospitality and all the amusement he had given us. I was very curious to see the ladies of the family, but they could not appear before English gentlemen. I peeped about in hopes of catching a glimpse of them, and I did descry some black eyes and white dresses through one of the half open doors, but I could not see them distinctly.

IX

FRANCES BURNEY (DAUGHTER OF ESTHER)
1826

IT is with feelings of real sorrow that circumstances of a distressing nature must now be introduced : they had been occurring at uncertain intervals for some time, and finally terminated fatally.

Frances, the second daughter of Mr. Charles Rousseau Burney, was unfortunately subject to violent attacks of pain in the stomach, attended with extreme sickness, and followed by jaundice. Much medical aid was resorted to : and when she had overcome each seizure, her spirits were so good, that her friends, as well as herself, hoped that she had overcome the disease. The latter end of the year 1827, and the beginning of the next year (1828) she was engaged in paying long visits to her friends : and having been free from her terrible complaint during that period, her appearance was extremely improved ; and her vivacity, and talent for vocal music, as well as conversation, made her a desirable companion in all companies. Her last visit was at Bath. She had been staying some time with her sisters Mrs. Bourdois and Sophia, and had left them to go to her mother, who lived likewise in Bath.

Very early in the beginning of March, she went with one of her sisters to the play, in seemingly as good health as she had latterly enjoy'd. In the middle of the night, she was heard to groan : her mother, sister Amelia, and a servant, were soon at her bedside ; and all relief that they could administer, was had recourse to. The next day she was under the care of a very eminent Practitioner ; but alas ! this was her last, and terminating attack.

She linger'd till the 28th of March, when she expired to the great grief of her Relations and friends.

In settling the affairs of their lamented niece and disposing of her effects . . . Mrs. Sandford and her Brother [Edward], were much surprised at the great number of attainments of various kinds (but chiefly literary) which their indefatigable niece had acquired. In collecting her library together, they found grammars and books, in French, Italian, Spanish, German, Greek and Latin, M.S. works of her own composition, both in Music and poetry ; for which she had a decided talent. She had indeed published a set of Tragic dramas, in very elegant language, but they were not intended for the stage. Had she lived, she would probably have brought out a Tragedy, on the subject of Foscari at Venice, which was ready for representation, but was postponed, in consequence of Lord Byron, and Miss Mitford having been beforehand with her, in selecting the same story : the former for publication only ; but the latter for representation. It was perform'd ; and met with success. Miss Frances Burney therefore judged it expedient to defer her Tragedy till some future time. The having been forestall'd was an unfortunate circumstance for her ; as her composition had been seen, and much admired by many excellent judges of theatrical performances.

From the " Worcester " Journal.

TRAGIC DRAMAS CHIEFLY INTENDED FOR REPRESENTATION IN PRIVATE FAMILIES, WITH A TRAGEDY FROM THE ITALIAN. By FRANCES BURNEY, 1818.

Preface

A long apology for a short work may be liable to just censure, as annexing to a trifle an undue importance. Various motives, nevertheless, having combined to induce the Writer of the following pages to bring them before the Public, she is desirous, by stating a few of them, to obviate as much as possible, the imputation of temerity, to which the publication of them may subject her : more especially since, wholly unknown herself in the world of literature, she can adduce the name, only, of her family, to attract attention, and stimulate curiosity, unaccompanied by any pretensions to the abilities requisite to fix the one, or gratify the other.

It has always appeared to her, that the objections which may be urged against private Theatres in general, are not, in justice, applicable to those domestic Representations, in which the younger branches of a family perform select pieces ; and to which only parents, relations, or friends particularly intimate, are admitted : and she has the sanction of judgments far superior to her own, and even clerical authority, for deeming the innocent and interesting recreation of speaking in character, to a little circle of chosen friends, an exercise not more obviously calculated to afford general entertainment, than to promote individual improvement.

Most people, at some period of their lives, are fond of what is usually termed *spouting* ; while such as have, for themselves, outlived that inclination, often derive nearly equal amusement from witnessing the scenic efforts of their juniors. Recourse, therefore, is not unfrequently had to *Stage-plays*, for the purpose of private exhibition : but even where these are not objectionable in any other respect, which is by no means invariably the case, it is a task, demanding no inconsiderable skill and pains, to modify or curtail, so as to accomodate them completely to the purpose ; while to perform them in their pristine state, would frequently be attended with difficulties yet more insurmountable.

Something therefore, distinct from these, yet of more continuity of interest, than can be maintained by the recitation of detached *Speeches*, *Dialogues*, or *Scenes*, though selected from dramatic works of even the highest excellence ;—Something, also, which consistently with propriety, and perfect freedom from any evil tendency, may admit of more impassioned action and diversified effect, than is usually thought within the province of

SARAH HARRIET BURNEY.
By Zoffany.

the *Sacred Drama*, appears desirable in our literature. The Writer is well aware that she is, herself, incapable of supplying the deficiency she indicates ; having neither the time nor the talents needful for the purpose ; but ventures to offer both her little sketches, in the hope that, not only, some hand more skilful than her own, will hereafter improve on the imperfect plan which she merely shadows out ; but that, notwithstanding their acknowledged faults of structure and execution ; their feebleness, and perhaps inaccuracy, of diction, since they have received no corrections but such as she has herself been able to give them ; they will yet be found not inadequate to the purpose for which they were designed, and unexceptional, at all events, in their moral tendency.

A plot and scenery, of a simple, or at least, not complicated description ; and characters, few in number, or if otherwise, attired in a *costume* easily adopted by either sex ; are among the lesser *desiderata* of the domestic drama. An attempt has been made to combine them, respectively, in the two first pieces : little being aimed at, beyond furnishing materials for occasional amusement, which, if not esteemed as profitable, may at least be admitted to be harmless.

It is, perhaps, a recommendation to these little Dramas, which would not advantageously be withheld, that they have both already been, more than once, represented by the junior members of a Family of distinction, and of the first respectability. That the performance of amiable and intelligent young persons should elicit applause from an auditory composed of their parents and private friends, could tend neither to excite the surprise, nor flatter the vanity of the writer. But she derives her chief encouragement to make them public, from the sympathy, apparently felt, and unequivocally expressed, on the part of the audience, with which every representation has been honoured. Such demonstrations of interest, however, as are the result, in general, of something more than mere complaisance to either actors or author, she now adduces, gratifying as they

24

must be, only as affording, perhaps, the best palliation she can offer for her apparent presumption.

The publication of this little work has also been, in some measure, accelerated, by the circumstance of several transcripts of the Dramas having been disseminated among friends who have requested copies. It seemed not impossible, that, by a casualty for which they might not be responsible, a more defective specimen might make its appearance, *in these publishing times*, to the manifest detriment of the Writer in a variety of ways.

Honoured as she must, of necessity, feel herself, by the flattering permission so kindly accorded her, to ascribe these inconsiderable labours of her pen to Three Ladies,[1] all less distinguished, even by their elevated rank, than by their eminently amiable and estimable qualities ; she is yet, from the very circumstance of the honour so conferred on her little volume, compelled to feel, more sensibly, its intrinsic unimportance : and the pride with which she would naturally contemplate names attached to *her* work, which would bestow consequence on *any*, is thence, not merely abated in her mind, but even converted into a sense of humiliation.

Sensations of a similar kind, alike the result of conscious inferiority, accrue to the Writer from her bearing the names, which once designated her Aunt *Madame* D'Arblay ; an Author, whose deservedly-admired compositions of another class, it is as needless, as, at this juncture, impolitic, to recall to the minds of the Readers.

FitzOrmond, the only piece in this collection, which has any pretension to originality, or rather, perhaps, which owes nothing to a foreign hand, (for similitude may exist, but none has been intended,) will, nevertheless, as a *juvenile* attempt, make large demands on the indulgence of the Reader. This is stated, in strict justice to the piece itself ; although to the majority, in all probability, of those who may peruse it, the internal evidence it

---

[1] The Duchess of Dorset. The Countess of Pembroke. The Dowager Duchess of Northumberland.

exhibits, will sufficiently demonstrate the fact. It was indeed, begun at the age of seventeen : and though laid aside for a time, was concluded within a short period of its commencement. As will be evident, it was written for a very limited, as well as youthful *company* ; and this circumstance, added to the great restrictions which the Writer was under in regard to scenery, occasioned her no small difficulty in the construction and conduct of her little plot ; to which her ignorance, at the time, of the established laws of the Drama, not inconsiderably contributed.

Malek Adhel was expressly put into English verse, and into a dramatic form, for a young family, *amateurs* of tragic acting, to some among whom, the brevity of the parts allotted to themselves furnished their best recommendation. In consequence, the characters are by no means fully deveolped. To exhibit them in a more interesting point of view, perhaps, the action should have been begun at an earlier period of the story, and continued through five acts, to the close. But this would have required more leisure than could, at the time, be commanded for the experiment ; and would probably, when done, have unfitted the piece, in some measure, for the purpose intended. The Prologue originally spoken at the performance, has been adjoined to this Drama, only as affording an introduction, apparently necessary, to the local and relative situations of the characters at its commencement. It has been attempted to preserve in a certain degree, the unity of place, by substituting the plains of *Cesarea* for *Ascalon*, the true scene of the decisive battle against the Saracens : but in other respects, the Romance of *Madame* Cottin has been as closely adhered to, and her sentiments as faithfully retained as possible ; from every motive of respect and justice to her, the Spectators, and the Reader, as well as to the obvious assistance and advantage of the *translating Dramatist.*

X

THE "WORCESTER" JOURNAL

THIS neatly typed folio ledger of ninety-eight pages was, apparently, put together from family papers, by Henry Edward Burney, great-grandson of Charles Rousseau.

The records are succinctly entered under consecutive years ; many of them mere dry statements of fact, others containing comment—quaintly expressed—or most interesting stories of individual adventure and misfortune. The strict chronological order, inevitably carries us to and fro from one individual, or even one generation, to another ; and I have entirely rearranged the narrative so as to present consecutive records of each Burney mentioned, using quotation marks where the actual text is copied, and adding a few " links " from statements elsewhere in the volume itself or from other sources. I have also used many dates and other items of information ; to supplement other parts of this volume—where " quotations " are given, naturally, naming the source.

It will be seen from what follows that the " Worcester " Burneys were as enterprising and industrious as their more famous cousins ; and for the most part, no less professional.

The most important new lights thrown on the family history are the particulars of " Uncle Richard " himself ; and the somewhat remarkable series of tragic misfortunes disclosed among the children of Esther and Charles Rousseau.

Curiously enough we find least about the two cousins who appear most frequently in the " Diaries " and in Susan's " Letters " :—Richard Gustavus and Edward Francisco.

Richard's extravagant gallantry and delightful non-sense is recorded on many occasions by Fanny, whose editors kindly dismiss the youth as a "conscious cox-comb" who "imitated his own airs and graces"—no doubt acquired on the dance-floor—and "entered into *games* of coquetry with the ladies." He is said, more-over, to have been so captivated by *Lord Orville*, that he adopted that charming hero as his ideal, and henceforth led a serious life!

Edward Francisco (1760-1848), on the other hand, was always distinguished for his gentle and unassuming manners. Susan declares that "he was too modest to seek even a baby"; and we meet with him, at every turn, in some quiet corner, engaged upon "obliging" his family or friends with an affectionate readiness for "back seats," on which they all had learned to depend. It has been remarked as evidence of a domestic and simple nature that as an artist he found his ideals of beauty—successively in Fanny, in one of her nieces, and in that niece's daughter.

Yet, it is clear, that there was somewhere within his mask of restrained composure some spark of the artist's wilder vision, that may be seen in some of the earlier sketches.

Sir Joshua Reynolds spoke of his first attempts as "finely drawn" and said "that his propensity to paint-ing was so strong I believe we must call it genius." He did actually study, and exhibit some illustrations to *Evelina*, at the Academy: Dr. Burney was always eager to encourage him, against his father's influence and expressed wish; but we can see, especially from Susan's letters, that he was more ready to admire the work of others than to pursue his own.

He was the original of the bashful artist in the Elia essay on *Valentines*.

There are, however, several charming illustrations by him, in Dr. Burney's many volumes, and some in the *Discoveries* by Admiral James; he did some sketches to Gay's *Fables* and to *Leonidas*, a poem by R. Glover.

Others were published in *The Cabinet of the Arts, Engravings from Designs by Stothard, Burney, Hardy, etc.,* 1799, which does, in fact, also contain reproductions from Vandyck, Turner, and Cruikshank.

But he was chiefly known, in his own day for the delicate, somewhat " finicky," popular and " pretty " drawings of the annuals, " pocket tablets," albums, " inlaid work-boxes and other feminine trifles," that can still be picked up occasionally in dingy print-shops.

THE BURNEY FAMILY
1603-1845
THE MACBURNEYS, RICHARD OF WORCESTER AND DR. CHARLES

The first recorded James MacBurney, son or grandson of a James MacBurney who came over from Scotland with James I, was " a very respectable gentleman," born about 1653 ; who " walked in the Coronation of George I, and studied painting as an amateur."

[Tradition has it that when his son ran away with an actress from Goodman's Fields, the old gentleman forthwith married his own cook, leaving his fortune to her handsome son Joseph, afterwards a dancing-master, " whose children vanish from this chronicle."]

As here recorded, however, the second James (1678–1749) " a painter thô he ought to have been a physician, in his 19th year, married Rebecca Ellis, a genteel and handsome young lady in her 16th year, who brought him fifteen children.

" His life was a succession of gaieties and troubles, and the number of places he liv'd at, proves the unsteadiness of his conduct."

In 1720, shortly after the death of Rebecca, he " married Ann Cooper of Shrewsbury daughter to a Herald Painter, who had a small fortune, and had refused an offer of marriage from the celebrated Wycherley, the Poet.

" About this time, he had taken a great liberty with

the family name, by leaving out the *Mac*. It was, therefore, after this period, called Burney alone. His particular reason for this alteration has not been preserved.

" The varieties, and eccentricities, of this gentleman's life, might, if collected together, make an entertaining history, *to any* who were not sufferers by his volatile, and improvident conduct. It might, at least afford an excellent moral lesson on the happy effects of prudence and application, where exertions are necessary for the support of a family ;   but his ready wit, and great flow of spirits, made him always an acceptable guest ; and he found it more to his taste and disposition to shine at convivial meetings, than to study his real advantage. The consequences of which were, that as his health declined in his Old Age, his circumstances kept pace, and his family were left to lament, that his talent for pleasantry, and love of sociability, overcame his prudential care, either for himself or them.   Lord Cholmondely, who was his great friend and Patron, offered his widow and daughters, apartments in Chester Castle, of which he was governor, and they enjoy'd that situation many years."

By his second marriage, James—now Burney—had five more children ; the eldest Richard ; born in Dog Lane, Shrewsbury, 1723, being the father of the " Worcester-Burneys " ; while Charles (Fanny's father), and his twin-sister Susanna, were born at Shrewsbury in 1726.

" At the age of fifteen, Richard was placed in London under Thomas Burney (his step-brother) an eminent dancing master," whose son had " so unimprovable a disposition that he became a cog on the family " ; while his daughter, " a weak and inoffensive young woman, was found dead in her bed."

Here Richard was treated with great severity, but " shut himself up from the hearing of the family, to improve himself in the violin," taught himself French, and " had small-pox to a dangerous degree."

In 1743, Thomas " grew tired of his life " and went to America, leaving his family to take care of themselves.

Richard, apparently, took over the school, and " now paid his addresses to the amiable Miss Humpherys, supposed descendant of Dudley, Earl of Leicester," whom he married in 1745.

In 1754 he " heard that a respectable gentleman of his profession was much wish'd for by the inhabitants of Worcester " ; where, after inquiries, he was able to settle as successor to " an elderly gentleman of the name of Weaver."

He had first taken a large house in the " narrow and dark Powick Lane," but, in 1759, moved a mile out of town, to Barborne Lodge, " an airy, pleasant, and respectable situation."   This was purchased for £380 and, forty-six years later, sold by the family for £1,200.

Mrs. Richard Burney, aged fifty-one, " was released from her sufferings on Oct. 8, 1771, after a painful and lingering disease.   A woman universally belov'd and esteemed, so was her loss very generally lamented."

Richard Burney had been a little time in London to settle some business, in 1792 :

" He had at different times been indisposed by complaints, to which he had been for some years subject : he however at that time appear'd as well as usual, and in remarkable good spirits.

" The family therefore were not only surprised, but extremely alarm'd, early on Saturday the 10th of March, by the person with whom he lodged, calling to enquire if they had seen or heard anything of Mr. Burney, who had quitted his house the evening before and his servant had sat up great part of the night expecting his return, but as they had not seen him, they concluded that he must be with some of his family.

" The consternation which this account occasioned may be easily supposed ; and all that day was spent in an anxious and fruitless search.   The houses of all the relations were first resorted to, and afterwards every place where it seem'd most likely to meet with him; but without success! Night came on, but their father was not to be heard of. Early the next morning, the melancholy and anxious business commenced again, and as the time advanced, their fears encreased. Edward Francisco went to the Coffee-houses, and look'd over all the papers to see if they contain'd any intelligence that would be a guide to their pursuits; this plan likewise fail'd. He from the first information, thought it probable that his Father had partaken of his favourite amusement at the Play, as he set out from home about the time of the Theatre opening; therefore it occurred to him that perhaps some scuffle might have ensued afterwards, in which he had been assaulted; he now determined on making inquiries at the different Watch-houses in the vicinity of Covent Garden, and Drury Lane. When he arriv'd at one of them, he was inform'd that an elderly gentleman had been brought there the preceding Friday evening, by a Hackney Coachman who said he did not know what to do with him; he therefore left him there for that night; and the next day, they had convey'd him to Covent Garden Workhouse, as he was then incapable of speech, and there were no papers in his pockets by which they could find out his name or place of residence. The account the Coachman gave them was, that the Gentleman had been he supposed at the Play, and having got into his Coach, had order'd him to drive to a part of the town, where he had a house for a short time, when he was first married! On arriving there, his senses were in so confused a state, that after some search for a supposed house, he was obliged to give it up. He then told the man to take him to York Street, Covent Garden, where he said he had sisters living. This not having been the case for a number of years, and no such name, or house to be found, the man began to get angry; and supposing him in an intoxicated state, said he would take him to the watch-house, and no further. On his getting out of the Coach, he stagger'd and fell down upon the pavement, and the man carried him into the house. Edward Francisco immediately repaired to the workhouse, where he beheld the melancholy and afflicting sight of his Father lying on a bed in a state of insensibility. As soon as he had sufficiently recover'd the shock, he return'd home to inform his family of the event. His eldest Brother, and 2 cousins accompanied him to the Workhouse, but he knew none of them. Their next care was to get him removed ; they therefore applied to an apothecary near at hand, to know the best method of removal. This gentleman advised a coach, as he might be supported on each side. They therefore convey'd him in this manner safe to his lodgings, where he was put to bed, and every possible care taken of him by his family. At times he appear'd to have some recollection of his situation, and his children, but in a few seconds, it was gone again, and his speech became quite incoherent. After some days, the Physician, Dr. Bradley, began to suspect that some mischief must have been done to the head, particularly as he observed a small quantity of blood come from his ear : it was therefore determin'd on, that a celebrated surgeon and anatomist (Mr. Cruikshank) should be sent for, who, on examining the head, pronounced it necessary to trapan. . . .

"On the morning of the 20th Mr. Cruikshank perform'd the terrible operation of trapanning. He had, after scalping the morning before, discover'd a large fracture on the skull, and it now appear'd, that the brain had suffered an incurable injury ; a large quantity of coagulated blood being found upon it ; which he carefully removed, and put on proper dressings, etc.

"During the remaining part of the day, the poor Patient grew more exhausted, restless, and insensible, appearing evidently worse. At night, convulsions came on, which continued till between 11 and 12 o'clock the next morning (March the 21st), when death put a final end to his sufferings, at the age of 69.

"All his children who were in Town, were constantly

with him, at this awful period : and could he have witness'd their affection, care, and solicitude, he must have felt a pleasure, even in his last moments ; but as he was insensible to that, it is likewise to be hoped that he was in a great measure insensible to the pain he seem'd to endure.

" His Remains were interred in Marybone Churchyd. and the funeral follow [*sic*] by three sons, and two nephews.

" After this melancholy event, Edward Francisco attempted to gain more intelligence concerning his poor Father's first attack.   But the people at the watchhouse, only repeated what they had said before, and either could not, or would not, give any information of the Coach-man who convey'd him to their house.   Much is there-fore left for conjecture ; but that he did not take much money with him, seems probable, as he had left his watch at home ; there was however none left in his pockets, when he was found ; thô his silver buckles were in his shoes.   That he had experienced a slight paraletic seizure when in the Coach, appears rather evident, by the confused state of his intellects, in recollecting the place of his former abode, but not that of his present ! It was likewise suspected, that the Coachman had taken care to pay himself, by his not applying afterwards to the family for any reward.

" Mr. Burney possess'd a happy flow of spirits, when well, which made his company much desired by his friends.   He had likewise a great taste for literature. He had collected together a very good library, with a choice collection of books ; but during the latter part of his life, his chief pleasure seem'd to consist in collecting Prints and arranging them in Portfolios (of which he had about 20,) besides those that decorated his house. He had likewise a considerable number of paintings, some very good.   He was extremely active himself, and en-couraged industry in his children having a rooted dis-like to idleness ; and when he had nothing else to do, he used to amuse himself with writing Poetry, for which he had a good deal of talent; but he shone most in humorous compositions."

Charles had, as a boy, remained with the family at Chester; where he early "commenced music," and was later advanced in his profession by another step-brother, James, then organist of Shrewsbury.

In 1748, having come to London to secure more pupils and more profitable engagements, he married Esther Sleepe, "a lady of great strength of mind, possessing a taste for literature, with an engaging manner and much beauty."

But, having overworked himself, as was his custom, he retired—on doctor's orders, in 1752—to Lynn Regis; where "he was much caressed, had a pleasant and excellent house, got into good business and recovered his health."

He went back to London in 1760, and a year later his wife died of "an inflammatory fever, after a severe lying in."

In October 1767 he married Elizabeth, widow of Stephen Allen, Lynn Regis; whose children became friends of the family. They had two children, Richard Thomas and Sarah Harriet. She died in 1796.

"On the 12th of April, 1813, the family had to mourn for the death of the celebrated, and much respected, Dr. Burney. He had attained the great age of 88, with his faculties very little impaired, and indeed not at all, till within a very few weeks of his death. He remembered his numerous relations in his will, and his son Charles had had a marble bust taken of him by Nollikins, which was an excellent likeness, and is now at Greenwich."

The sisters of Charles and Richard received a legacy in 1785 from one of their uncles, which did not take effect earlier; because it depended upon "the death of his favourite servant, Ann Lloyd, who was left a very handsome annuity. She had been for some time in the habit of taking strong Rum or Brandy and water, to which she at last fell a victim."

Of these sisters, Rebecca died on May 21, 1809 :— " She was an amiable woman, and was much beloved by her family, but as she had almost outlived her intellects, having arrived at the great age of 85, her death was considered as a happy release."

RICHARD'S CHILDREN

No more is told of Dr. Burney's generation in this Journal ; of which the remaining pages are concerned with Richard's eight children :—Charles Rousseau, 1747 ; Richard Gustavus, 1751 ; James Adolphus, 1753 ; Edward Francisco, 1760 ; Thomas Frederick, 1765 ; Ann or Hannah (called Nancy), Mrs. Hawkins ; Elizabeth Warren ; Rebecca (Mrs Sandford) ; and with his grand-children, the sons and daughters of Charles Rousseau and Esther, Dr. Burney's eldest daughter.

Richard Gustavus and James Adolphus were brought up to their father's profession. " In 1777 they visited Paris for the sake of improving themselves in their pro-fession, which plan answered the fullest expectations of themselves and their friends." James settled in Shrews-bury (with his half-uncle) in 1778, " business opening at Ludlow and Bridgnorth." He died in 1798, " univer-sally and deservedly respected." Richard died in 1790, " a valuable member of Society, whose loss will be felt, and regretted so long as moral worth and amiable manners shall continue to be esteem'd and ad-mired amongst men . . . an elegance of mind, associated with the most uniform good temper, augmented the pleasure his presence and social qualities never fail'd to inspire."

The " droll and good-humoured artist son Thomas Frederick displayed an uncommon genius for pen and ink drawings," but died of influenza, in 1785, at the age of 20.

Mrs. Hawkins was " released from her pain " in 1819.

" To give a character of Elizabeth Warren Burney, b. 1755, would only be to enumerate all the virtues belonging to a woman, without one drawback to counterbalance. She was not a shining character, but she had a cheerful mind, well stored, not only with useful knowledge, but with good taste ; and her judgment could always be consulted with conviction that she was right. She was pious without gloom, or fanaticism, charitable without ostentation, and made herself useful to her family, without officiousness ; she was a general favourite with them all.

" On April 22nd, Easter Sunday, 1832, she was sufficiently recovered to be able to receive the holy sacrament at Church. To take it from her nephew [Richard Allen's] hand, and to end her days at Rympton, was a wish she had long indulged. She went to church again in the evening ; and did not seem worse than usual : but on the 26th her symptoms encreasing, medical advice was call'd in, and an eminent professional gentleman visited her every other day : but dropsy in the legs came on, and from that time, she could not go to the Parsonage, althô her ingenious nephew constructed a seat with poles, to carry her backwards and forwards. He wrote an account of the alarming state she was in, to his dear uncle, Mr. Edward Burney ; and that good uncle lost no time în coming to see his dear sister, which gave her as much pleasure as she could then receive. She survived this meeting but a week ; for on the 20th early in the morning, her pure spirit departed this life ; well prepared for a better ; and left an afflicted family to deplore their loss. But not only her family, but all those Parishioners who had known her formerly, bore testimony to her worth, by the sorrow they felt. Her nephew paid the last tribute to her beloved Remains by having a vault built near the communion table to receive them. The funeral was a most respectable one."

Charles Rousseau was born in 1747, and at six years of age " began to show symptoms of an extraordinary ear for music." In 1756, " the extraordinary and promising musical talents of this young gentleman began to be so conspicuous, that he was look'd upon as a prodigy. The Harpsichord was the instrument he most excell'd on, but he play'd the violin exceedingly well, thô only nine years old."

In 1760 Esther (eldest daughter of Dr. Charles), for her part, " then about twelve years old, obtain'd great notice in the musical world, by her performance on the Harpsichord, which was in a very superior style."

In 1770 Charles had made such satisfactory progress in London that he was allowed to marry his cousin Esther. In 1776 they took a small house in Worcester for the summer.

In 1795, Charles Rousseau and Edward Francisco " paid a visit of three weeks to Mr. and Mrs. Sandford, (then living opposite the bridge at Worcester). Many musical parties were formed in consequence of the acquisition of two such excellent performers."

In 1816 " the family enjoyed much happiness in being more concentrated than usual . . . frequent pleasant intercourses took place . . . the time passed most pleasantly, but by far too rapidly. . . . The latter part of this year appeared a sad blank . . . for in proportion as the pleasure is great in the company of those who are dear to us, so is the pang severe when the time arrives that it is necessary to separate ! But this alas is a natural consequence where an affectionate family is large and therefore obliged to be widely dispersed."

Mr. and Mrs. Burney, "wishing to enjoy the tranquillity of the country, more than they could at Turnham Green," took a house near Bath, in 1817. Only two years later, September 23, 1819, Charles Rousseau died, and was buried at Bath Easton.

New Monthly Magazine, December 1, 1819

" Charles Rousseau Burney of Luckhall Place Bath. A gentleman as estimable and eminent for his private virtues, as for his high reputation, for his extensive and scientific and classical skill as a musical professor.

Though towards the close of his life his sufferings were great, he met them with unshaken fortitude and resignation ; and in the intervals of extreme pain, his habitual equanimity and sweetness of disposition were such, that nearly to the last of life, he enjoy'd and exercised the power of executing the most delightful melodies on his instrument, fully equal in point of effect and merit, to the happiest efforts of his earlier life.

By the death of this gentleman, society has lost an example of the friendly and domestic virtues, seldom equalled, and perhaps never exceeded ; for through a long life, he bore his faculties so meekly, so like the bright expanse of a cloudless sky his spotless life, that the lustre of truth will never be injured by saying that a purer spirit never winged its way to immortality.

His genius for music was vivid and extraordinary ; and that excellence which many dedicate a whole life to the endeavour to attain, beamed over his early years ; for when scarcely 20 years of age, he was allowed to be, by the best judges of harmony, one of the finest performers in the British Empire.

Such promising talents were at once honoured and patronized by the powerful assistance of his uncle the late celebrated Dr. Burney of Chelsea College, a gentleman long the ornament of the first circles, and whose memory will long live in the estimation of mankind. This eminent character gave Mr. Burney the highest and most flattering testimony of his regard, by bestowing on him his eldest daughter in marriage, a Lady whose worth and talents are too well known to need eulogium in this place ; with whom he lived in uninterrupted felicity during life and now leaves with a numerous, and esteemed family, to sorrow over his remains, and to emulate his virtues.

Mr. Burney excelled on a variety of instruments, but the Pianoforte was his favourite. On this he called forth such combinations of harmony, such richness and variety

CHARLOTTE BARRETT.
By Edward Burney.

of expressions, regulated by such correct taste as were astonishing. From his very early years, it seemed that his fingers grew and accomodated themselves to the keys with uncommon power. His execution was rapid and brilliant, his precision and feeling were exquisite, his taste matured by the finest judgment; his very soul formed for harmony, embraced every subject, from the sweet pathos of Hadyn and Mozart, to the sublimity of Handel, the Homer of Melody.

The enumeration of one point more shall conclude our account of this gentleman. His fancy and invention were manifested in the highest degree by the powers of extempore performances, a talent in him so varied and unlimited, that for hours and days he poured forth unpremeditated strains of harmony, at once original, energetic and impressive; an excellence which few men, amongst Professors, can attempt with success; but which this gentleman possessed to that degree, which must ever exalt him to the highest rank of Musical Professors."

In 1831, "so many of the family had met together that eleven of the name dined together some days. This was a source of great happiness to them all : they little forseeing how soon the number of this affectionate family was to be diminish'd, or that in about a month afterwards, they were to be deprived of one, who thô the elder, (having turn'd her 80th year), was nevertheless the most animated of the company. This amiable woman was Richard Allen's mother (Dr. Burney's eldest daughter [Esther]). She possessed all the attractions both mental and personal to make her company desirable to a large and admiring acquaintance, and her affectionate disposition to her family, was returned by reciprocal attachment on their side. Her death was occasioned by the Influenza which raged at that time very generally. She was buried at Batheaston, Feb. 24, 1832, near her dear departed husband, and daughter Frances. Her son, the Rev. Richard Allen Burney, drew up an elegant inscription for a tablet to her memory."

The Third Generation

" Anna Maria eldest daughter of Charles Rousseau, was born in 1792 and married in 1800 Anthony Bourdois, Eq., a native of France ; which match seem'd to promise much happiness to both parties ; each of them possessing every requisite for rendering the married state desirable. on searching the church register, it was discover'd that Anna Maria's name had by mistake been spelt with an H. Her Christian name was therefore, according to law—*Hannah Maria.*

" Mrs. Bourdois whose marriage with Mr. Bourdois had given the family so much pleasure, only 3 years later experienced the sad reverse of all her happiness. She had resided since the year 1802, with her husband in France, enjoying all the comforts, and even luxuries of life ; till the death of her kind and indulgent Husband, at once deprived her not only of his society, but of all the pleasures she had been so largely partaking of. He died on the 7th of August, 1806, of a liver complaint, after suffering excruciating pain for some time.

" However, her inclinations might prompt her to come to England after this sad event, prudence and propriety suggested to her the necessity of staying till her husband's affairs could be settled ; which would require some time. In her forlorn state it was a consolation, the having her uncle and aunt Mr. and Mrs. D'Arblay with her in Paris, as they had removed to that place about the time that Mr. and Mrs. Bourdois went there. She had likewise many friends amongst her acquaintance who were much attach'd to her. Having finished the settling of her affairs, the beginning of the following year, she was fortunate to meet with a very agreeable Lady who had likewise lost her husband, and was going to return to England with her family. This lady (Mrs. Newland) and she, therefore, took a coach between them, which was a pleasant circumstance for both parties ;

but as all travelling was forbidden to England on the usual roads, they were obliged to go through a part of Germany and Holland, which made their journey up- wards of 600 miles! They however arrived safe in London May the 22d. without having any loss, or meet- ing with any accident, and to the great joy of her family. After paying visits to all her Relations, which occupied sometime, she purchased a pretty small house, beauti- fully situated at Batheaston, 2 miles from Bath, to which place she repaired somewhere about May the following year and took her sister Sophia to reside with her."

In April 1821 Cecilia, another daughter of Charles Rousseau, " resigned her innocent life in so calm and tranquil a state, that her Mother, Mrs. Bourdois, and Mrs. Sandford, would have thought she had only fallen asleep, had not the affliction of Mrs. Sandford, who knew to the contrary, convinced them that it was otherwise. . . . She was deservedly beloved by her Relations and friends, as she possessed estimable and amiable qualities : to which were added great talents ; particularly for music ; this was discovered at an early age, as she began composing elegant little songs, in her 13th year. Those which she produced later in life, were masterly composi- tions, and her Pianoforte playing was executed with taste, neatness and expression. She had acquired a competent knowledge of the French and Italian lan- guages, and possessed a genus for poetry. . . . She died at the age of 32."

In 1786—
" Charles Rousseau offer'd to send their second son, Charles Crisp, a fine sensible boy, little more than 11 years old, to his grandfather hoping that youthful vivacity would in some measure beguile his solitary hours. This proposal was readily accepted, and as he attended a very good free school, and received instruction from his grandfather in music, it was an advantage to both. This plan, however, which bore so promising an appearance at first, did not prove a per-

manent comfort; for Charles Crisp, having an uncommon share of youthful volatility, had so great a dislike to anything that required application, and perseverance, that he could no longer endure the restraints of a school life; and imagined that if he could return home, he should again lead the same easy, playful life with his brothers and sisters, that he had formerly done. For this purpose, he form'd the romantic, and dangerous plan of walking alone up to London! It was in the month of August, and his grandfather and the family at Barborne Lodge were for a few days perfectly wretched, at his being missing, and they not knowing where to seek him, for he had entrusted nobody with his secret. At length they were relieved by a tradesman of the town calling and informing them that he had seen the young gentleman two days before, near Pershore, on his way to London, whither he was walking!

This relieved the great anxiety of his family, respecting his present danger, but left sufficient room for apprehensions concerning his future safety.

His grandfather immediately wrote to his Father and Mother to apprise them of their son's adventure; and the letter fortunately reach'd them, time enough to prevent the surprise and shock his appearance would otherwise have occasion'd. He was no doubt somewhat disappointed to find himself received with the coldness and disapprobation, which his conduct merited, especially as he could give no substantial plea for having deserted his friends at Worcester, except what idleness had dictated.

He was for a time kept separate from his brothers and sisters, and by remonstrance and admonition made to acknowledge his error. In the meantime, his grandfather wrote to beg that he might not return, unless by his own voluntary choice; he *did* desire it, and therefore after about a fortnight's residence in London, he was put into a coach, and sent back to Worcester again.

The fatigues and hardships he underwent in this exploit, were sufficiently great, to make him heartily repent his rash design. Not many months elapsed e'er his violent spirits occasioned his meeting with an accident, which obliged him to keep to his bed for about a month ; for early in the following year, he ran with so much violence, that on falling down he was unable to rise. The rest of the Boys carried him back into the school-room, where he fainted away. He was convey'd home in a chair, and an eminent Surgeon sent for, who pronounced the thigh bone broken, very near the hip. He bore his misfortune with great fortitude and patience, but thus paid dear for his love of boisterous play."

In 1788, Esther and Charles Rousseau offered Charles Crisp as an apprentice to Mr. Sandford ; "who thought that C.C. was in most respects well adapted for the profession, and approved the plan, and he arrived at Wellington the 17th of July, in his 14th year, where he began upon his new occupation with very promising success : the novelty of his studies and of his situation, being for a time, a sufficient stimulus to activity and mental exertion. He was possess'd of many excellent qualities, and had his perseverance and application been equal to his abilities, he must in time have acquired proportionate eminence."

Before the commencement of 1791, "poor Charles Crisp was become so completely tired of the profession of medicine, that no means were sufficiently forcible to stimulate him to the exertion it required. The charms of novelty were fled ; and application, attention, and diligence were contrary to his natural character : yet as he was possessed of genius, and capability, Mr. Sandford was willing to hope that an encrease of Steadiness would attend his increase of years ; but on the 15th of February he was missing ! enquiries were made at various places, but he was nowhere to be found. Soon after a respectable Tradesman call'd to inform Mr. Sandford, that an apprentice of his, of the name of Kinder, was likewise missing ; but that he had left a letter behind him ; by which it appear'd that he was set off on foot for London, in company with Charles and he assured his master that all search after them would be in vain.

"Mr. Sandford immediately wrote to London, to apprize the family of this event ; not doubting that it was the intention of Charles Crisp to go to his Father's house, as he had done on a former similar occasion : and his Parents accordingly prepared themselves for his reception ; instead of which, to their great surprise, they received on the 20th a short letter to the following effect ; that if they wish'd to save their son Charles from ruin, they must send someone who knew him, to London Bridge the next day, where he would endeavour to detain him till one oclock, after which, all further search, would be fruitless. Sign'd KINDER.

"This letter, sent by the penny post, unfortunately did not arrive till the evening of the day specified ; the next morning, however, several of his family loiter'd about the Bridge for several hours, without success. They repeated their search and enquired ineffectually the day following. They then concluded that either the letter had arrived too late, or that he had caught a distant glimpse of some of his family, and had hastened away ; and that, as he had always shown a taste for travelling, his intention must certainly have been to go abroad. This idea gave them great uneasiness, as he was very ill-prepared for any arduous enterprise ; and they continued in anxious, and daily expectation of either seeing or hearing from him."

Seven years now elapsed before "the family had heard anything of Mr. Charles Rousseau Burney's youngest son, Charles Crisp. They therefore concluded that he was gone abroad, and at times suffer'd great anxiety and uneasiness while uncertain of his destiny. In 1799, Mr. Sandford having occasion to write to Wellington, it occurred to him that he might possibly gain some intelligence concerning Mr. Kinder (who accompanied C. C.) from his former master there, a Mr. Ridding ; Mr. S. therefore made the enquiry, and in answer had the satisfaction of hearing that Mr. Kinder was return'd from abroad, and settled in the grocery business at Nuneaton in Warwickshire.

"Mr. Sandford immediately wrote to Mr. Kinder, requesting some account of his former companion, at the same time telling him how unfortunate the family had been in their researches in London at the time his note was received, etc.

"Two very obliging and circumstantial letters were received from Mr. Kinder upon this melancholy subject, the contents of which, being of a very interesting nature, are comprised in the following words :

NUNEATON,
20 Feb., 1799.

SIR,

It is some satisfaction to me, however gloomy the detail may be, that I have it in my power to reply to every minute circumstance connected with our unfortunate adventurer, from the time of our leaving Wellington. It seems necessary however for me to apologise,—or rather to exculpate myself for not having immediately on my arrival given the Relatives of my dear friend, information of the awful event of his death : the fact is, I address'd a letter to Mr. Burney, No 2, Titchfield Street from Calcutta, dated January 7th 1792, informing him of the death of my friend, on the 24th of the preceding month, not doubting that this letter had been received, obvious motives withheld me from reviving his friends' grief, which from my *then* supposition that he had been neglected, I thought must be poignant indeed.

"We set out from Wellington the 15th of Feby. 1791, with the quixotic scheme in our heads of proceeding immediately to Dover, and embarking for France, our pecuniary resources in a common purse, amounted to only 3 shill^s and 6 pence ! We travelled all night and arrived much fatigued at Wolverhampton, about 6 oclock the ensuing morning. After a little refreshment we proceeded on to Birmingham ; but so weary and footsore were we, that we found it impossible to walk any further. Here I sold my watch; and Charles's, with a surgical pocket-book were only reserved for a further pressing occasion. We now took places in the coach, and arrived in London on the 19th of February, procuring lodgings in Water Lane, Tooley Street, as a place where we could live at a little expense. Our project of going to France was now abandoned, as we found, after the disposal of all our little valuables, that the money arising was by no means adequate to the undertaking.

"In consequence of the latter I sent to Mr. Burney (which letter I now find arrived too late) I drew Charles to London Bridge, on the day, and at the time specified in that letter, but no friends appearing, fully justified me in the opinion that his conduct had so irritated them, that they were determined to give him up to his fate. Oftentimes I have accused myself for not making a personal application, but shame, the certain concomitant of rash, and ill-concocted projects in youth, prevented me.

"Charles was extremely solicitous to see his Brother, hoping by his mediation to be restored to the affection of his parents, and for this purpose, we saunter'd one evening about Mr. Burney's house in Titchfield Street more than 2 hours, during which time an Uncle enter'd but no Brother appearing, we return'd to our lodging.

"In the beginning of March, our finances were quite exhausted, and nothing at last seem'd to offer but (what we then thought), a disgraceful submission on one hand, or a voluntary transportation on the other. We fatally made choice of the latter. And after many unsuccessful efforts to engage on any terms, a passage to the West Indies,—we engaged in the East India's Company, Charles having changed his name to that of *Barnes*.

"At the public house where we took up our temporary residence, there was frequently one of those miscreants who engage men for the Company's service, and who described in forcible terms, the advantages the Com-

pany's soldiers enjoy'd in India, and the great probability
there was of young men of tolerable education, who
went out in subordinate situations, rising to the highest
ranks in the army.   The frequency and seeming plausi-
bility of these discourses, combined with our necessitous
condition to cajole our senses,—and we engaged with
this fellow, or rather his master, who called himself
Captain Bailey to serve in the Company's service in
India for 5 years.

   " At Bailey's house, we receiv'd every possible accomodation and were supplied with money, to enable us to
procure necessaries for the voyage.   These circumstances
served to flatter us much in our expectations ; but how
miserably were we disappointed on being shipped on
board the Woodford (Captn. Lenox).   Instead of those
conveniences we were taught to expect, we were associated with the very lowest order of human Beings !

   " Now it was that we heartily repented our whole pro-
ceedings.   The punishment attach'd to premature and
ill-judged pursuits was now pending over us.

   " Nothing served to soothe us more than finding a few
young men amongst the crowd, whose manner and
behaviour evinced that they had moved in a better
sphere.   This should have been a melancholy consideration, but harass'd and suffering minds are willing to fly
to the resources which sympathy points out to them.

   " The ship sailed from the Downs on the 27th of March
and arrived at Bencoolen in the Island of Sumatra, on
the 28th of July following.   During the passage, Charles
enjoy'd an uninterrupted state of good health ; but on
his arrival there, was attack'd with a Dysentery, of which
he was perfectly recover'd, before we left the Island.
The Malady which proved fatal to him, originated in
the bite of the musquito, which irritated by scratching,
and the blood at the same time being impregnated with
scorbutic humours, produced malignant ulcers on both
legs, which encreased in size, and gangrenous appearance,
during the passage to Calcutta.   The ship Deptford was
dispatch'd from that place to convey us there, and we

embark'd in number about 330, on the 17th of September. 1791.

" Our accomodation in this ship was miserable indeed, being much smaller than the Woodford, and to this circumstance and the great scarcity of water that prevail'd on the passage, may be attributed the unhealthy state of the ship, and the malignant progress of those ulcers with which more than 50 were afflicted.

" We arrived at Calcutta on the 7th of Novr., and those that were sick, were immediately sent to the hospital; amongst whom were Charles, and myself. Chas. was visited in his illness by Mr. Allison, a surgeon on the Bengal establishment, and it is but justice to the humanity of that gentleman, to declare that the most refined attention was paid to my friend. Attentions much beyond the comforts of a military hospital, for his purse, and heart were equally open to Charles's wants.

" My friend was possess'd of that Noble and manly spirit which always resisted the least inducement to complain, nor did I ever hear him during his painful illness, repine at the dispensations of Providence. He often exulted in the idea of having changed his name; so delicately sensible was he of avoiding the least imputation of disgrace that might alight on his friends from his imprudent conduct.

" I was at the time of his death, so much emaciated by the dysentry, that it was with great difficulty I quitted my bed, to witness the aweful exit of my dear friend. Aweful, did I say? Judge, Sir, what must have been my feelings,—worn out by a disorder which evidently threatened my own existence, far distant from other dear connexions—deprived at such a time of the cheering voice of friendship, this was a stroke almost too powerful for the utmost efforts of humanity to sustain! I should then have met death, as I would a welcome friend.

" Charles had been for 3 or 4 days, sensible of his approaching dissolution, and often in that time spoke in the most feeling manner of his Parents, and particularly of a Brother, for whom he had unbounded affection. He requested that I would inform them of his death, (which happen'd on the 24th of December 1791) with an assurance of his sincere penitence, which I did in a letter address'd to his Father, dated Hospital Calcutta, Jany. 7th 1792.

"I was not able to see the last sad duties perform'd over the mortal part of my friend ; but have oftentimes since, visited the spot, sacred to the remains of friendship and integrity.

"It may now be sufficient to say that after a lingering confinement of 6 months, I recovered, and afterwards found my little education of great service to me. I officiated as a clerk the greatest part of my 5 years.

"Determin'd on revisiting my native country, I procured my discharge, and arrived in England in December 1797, and by the assistance of an Uncle, am now settled in a comfortable business : fully determined to expiate for the gross follies of youth, by a rigid attention to the duties of maturer age.

"I am Sir, your very obedt. servant

S. KINDER.

"This account, however circumstantial, and satisfactorily given, was of a nature so truly melancholy, as to give great affliction, not only to the parents of poor Charles, but his relations in general. Had the letter been received, which Mr. Kinder mentions having written from Calcutta, it would have saved his family much uncertainty, and painful suspense. It was likewise perhaps an unfortunate circumstance for Charles, that he had changed his name ; for soon after his departure, Mrs. Burney wrote to her son Richard[1] (who was settled at Calcutta) giving him a particular account of him, and of his elopement. Mr. R. Burney, in return, said that he had made many fruitless researches

---

[1] This must really have been her *step-brother*, Richard Thomas, not her son, Richard Allen.—ED.

for him at that place. Thus at the early age of seventeen did this ill-fated young man fall a victim to rash enterprise, and immature projects."

Richard Allen (1773–1836), eldest son of Charles Rousseau, " was become a very fine player on the pianoforte " as early as 1795 ; but in the same year he was offered a living by the Bishop of Winchester, " if he would like to undergo the necessary preparation. This being too flattering an offer to reject, he recommenced his studies with such assiduity and perseverence that about the 15th of January following he was ready to be enter'd at Magdalene Hall, Oxford."

He took orders in 1798 ; and became rector of Kimpton (or Rympton), Somersetshire in 1802.

" The commencement of 1799 was memorable for the severity of the season, and there was a greater fall of snow than had been remember'd for years. Poor Mr. Richard Allen Burney was among the number of sufferers, and perhaps few escaped death more narrowly. He unfortunately set out from Bridge Street (in his way to Oxford) the very day it began ; but till his departure it seem'd very trifling. As the Coach proceeded (Thursy. Jan. 31) the darkness, the great depth of snow, and the merciless fury of the wind encreased : till at last, it was impossible for the Postillion (for they had 6 horses) to see the road ; and about half past nine, when within nearly 5 miles of Chipping Norton, the Coach was overturned in a hollow way, where the snow was 7 feet deep. In this wretched condition they were obliged to continue, while the Coachman and guard went to a hedge Alehouse, about a mile off, for additional horses ; they return'd with 3, and attempted to drag out the Coach, but in vain ! They were therefore obliged to give it up, and accompany the Passengers to the Alehouse. They went stumbling and plunging about in a manner truly miserable, sometimes sinking up to their breasts in snow : if they went before the horses, they were in danger of being trampled on by them before they could get out,—if behind, in fear of being stuck or smother'd, unnoticed by their companions, for the wind was so violent, they could not hear each other, and the snow so thick in their faces they could not see. Mr. R. Burney at length lost all sense of feeling in his cheek and ear, became breathless and giddy,—almost blinded with Ice sticking to his eyelids, and extremely faint. In lucky time, however, they reached the cottage, for had he continued a few minutes longer in that state, the consequences might have been fatal. His great precaution in warming gradually, prevented any future sufferings from the event. No beds being to be had in the cottage, they were obliged to sit up all night.

"The next day, after some fearful deliberation, they determined on walking to Chipping Norton. This walk was in every respect (except that they had light) as bad as that the preceeding night; and Mr. R. A. B., much fear'd he should never live to accomplish it! To his extreme joy, however, they arrived there safe. He had an Icicle of 2 inches length hanging from his hat, and his clothes were cover'd with a coat of thick transparent ice.

"At Chipping Norton they were confined till Monday Feby. 4th when the roads being made passable, they proceeded to Oxford without further troubles, or difficulties."

In 1811, Richard Allen married Elizabeth, daughter of the Rev. John Williams, rector of Marston. His aunt (Elizabeth Warren) who had been looking after his house,

"Took this opportunity of visiting her friends, particularly at Bath Easton and Worcester; to the latter place she was accompanied by her 2 nieces, Mrs. Bourdois, and Miss Sophia Burney, and during their stay, their curiosity was much gratified by being introduced to the Bonaparte family, Monsieur Lucien and his family being confined at this time as Prisoners of War, at Thorn Grove, 4 miles from Worcester. This circumstance proved a

source of great animation and gaiety to the select party
who were favored with their acquaintance, for notwithstanding they were considered as Prisoners of War ; they
inherited so much of the natural liveliness of character,
that they seemed to forget their situation, which caused
much surprise among the serious inhabitants of Worcester ; sometimes indeed mixed with observations of
a rather sarcastic nature ; but which were entirely
confined to those who were not acquainted with this
pleasant family.   They remain'd at Thorn Grove about 3
years : and treated their friends with many Balls, Concerts, and French Plays : but when the news arrived of
the dethroning of the French Emperor, which was the
9th of April, 1814, they were liberated, and suffered to
return to Rome.   They left Worcester Aug. the 24th,
1814.

"In 1812.—This family honoured Mr. and Mrs.
Sandford with their Company in Bridge Street Jany.
the 9th, and with some of their principal friends, spent
the eveng. there.

"On the 21st of February 1814, they gave a very brilliant masquerade, an amusement never before exhibited
either in, or near Worcester.   Mr. and Mrs. Sandford and
their niece, Miss Cecilia Burney, were highly entertain'd
by it ; as it was conducted with great humour, spirit and
decorum ; and most of the characters were well sustained."

In 1815 Richard Allen acquired, also, the curacy and
a house at Brightswell, in Berkshire :

"In November 1830, the Parish was kept in a state of
great agitation and alarm, by the expectation of having
similar outrages committed as had taken place in the
neighbouring villages, by a set of unruly Rioters, who
vowed vengeance against the Farmers, for making use
of thrashing Machines, and other impliments of hus-
bandry, which they thought was depriving them of some
of their employment.

"The damages they had been guilty of, occasioned the
collecting of the yeomanry, who drill'd themselves into

order, with pikes and bludgings, to be prepared for the attack : but it was supposed that they were apprised of the great resistance they would meet with, for they gave up their intention of visiting Brightwell : althô amongst other victims, an opulent Farmer resided very near the Parsonnage. Happily for the place, order and tranquility were by degrees restored."

In 1831, he was compelled to return to Rympton, where the " smallness of the house could not accomodate Mr. B's family : that being encreased since he had formerly resided there. It was necessary, therefore, to enlarge it by 3 additional rooms, but this could not be done till the house was vacated, and as there was an interval of near a quarter of year to pass before that could take place ; he determined on spending the time with his family at Bath.

" As a proof of the estimation with which he was regarded by his Parishioners, they one and all, on the 25th of Feby. signed a petition to the Bishop of Winchester, entreating him to give the living to Mr. Burney. This could not be granted, as a promise had been given to the Revd. Marmaduke Thomson who had married the Bishop's niece to succeed to it on the vacancy. Accordingly that gentleman call'd on the 13th of September, to see the place, and settle some preparatory measures ; and on the 27th of the same month, a general packing commenced. An inventory having been made for the sale of such articles of furniture as it was thought best not to take : the rest were sent partly by water, and partly by land, the distance from Brightswell to Rympton 100 miles.

" He immediately commenced the work of building and making alterations at Rympton. They found their furniture arrived ; thô with some damage ; particularly to a beautiful grand pianoforte, which suffered much from the damp. Putting everything to rights, and superintending work-people employed him unpleasantly for some time. Altogether the expenses ran to a considerable amount."

About 1832, " a Ladies School at Taunton, Somerset" was so much extolled for the excellent character it bore for tuition, morals, and each branch of Education, that Mr. R. A. Burney was induced to place his eldest daughter Clara there for a short time : not because she was deficient either in accomplishments, or mental acquirements : for the first she had been well-prepared, and literature was her great delight; but there being no young Lady in the immediate neighbourhood, with whom she could at her age, associate with advantage ; it was judged expedient that she should pass some time in a situation where she could have instruction and good society blended. She therefore went with great alacrity to this school, where only a limited number of scholars were admitted."

His second daughter, Arabella Sophia, was born in 1843.

Henry Burney, son of Richard Allen, married in 1842 :

His son, Henry Edward, was born—1845—in Queen Square Place, at a house belonging to P. R. Hoare [his maternal grandfather] and was baptized in Beckenham Church on June 8th, and is trying to continue this family memoranda—June 20, '99—from scraps he found in his father's papers at Wavendon Rectory.

SOPHY, CHARLES, AND FRANCES BURNEY.
(Children of Esther.)
By Edward Burney.

INDEX

Allen, Mr. Moxey, 127

Angerstein, Miss, 154, 156, 157, 244

— Mrs., continues to *intend* being handsome, 157

Ansell, Mr. (dentist), 149, 180, 181, 263

Anspach, Margravine of, 82

Arnold, Mrs., 208

Auguste, M., 65

Baker, Miss, 220

Barnewall, Mrs., 237

Bateman, Mrs., 58

Bazille, M. (D'Ar.'s uncle), his character, 70 ; 85, 86

— Madame, her character, 70, 71 ; 85 ; 101, 103

Bazille, M. Amiable, cousin of M. D'Ar., 39 ; 48

Beauharnais, son of Madame Bonaparte, 72

Beauvau, Madame Marechale de, her history and character, 82, 83

Beranger, Mrs., a vulgar governess, 163

Beverley, Lady, 207

Blaizeau, Madame, 31

Bonaparte, 44 and note

— Colonel Louis, his character and manners, 86 seq.

— Madame Louis, 72, 75, 80, 82

— Madame, 72

— Lucien, arranges festivities at Bath, 397, 398

Bood. See Anthony Bourdois

Boscawen, Mrs., 71, 217

Boucherett, M., 102

Bourdois, M. et Madame ("in-laws" of Maria B.), 58

— Anna Maria (eldest daughter of Charles Rousseau), 38 ; 49, 52 ; some account of, 386, 387 ; 397

— Anthony Bood (husband of Anna Maria, eldest daughter of Charles Rousseau), 38 ; 49, 52,

386 ; his marriage and death, 385

Bourdois, a physician (father of Anthony B.), 44, 49, 56

Brabazon, Harry, 255

— Mr., 216, 250, 251, 255, 256, 259, 267 ; nearest neighbour in Ireland, 245

— Mrs., to call on Burneys, 251, 270, 283, 293

— Mrs. Ann, 251

— Jane ("Janey-paney"), described, 250 ; history and character of, 266–271 ; her love for Norbury, 268 ; engaged to Mr. Disney, 290 seq. ; 120, 255, 274, 275, 284, 290, 294, 297, 305

Bradley, Dr., 378

Browne, Colonel, 289

— Mrs., 289

Bunbury, Mrs., 225

Burney, Arabella Sophia (daughter of Richard Allen), 400

— Cecilia (daughter of Charles Rousseau), 213, 398 ; her character and death, 387

— Dr. (father of F. B.), 19, 120, 147, 165, 212, 213, 216, 219, 226, 228, 240, 254, 257, 258, 262, 264, 279, 285, 287, 294, 302, 373, 384 ; views on *Camilla*, 206 ; 210, 211, 222 ; his praise quoted, 223, 224 ; F. B. able to go to him on his wife's death, 232 ; in " Worcester " Journal, 380 ; marries (1) Esther Sleepe, (2) Mrs. Elizabeth Allen, 380

— Mrs. Dr. Charles, " The Lady," " The Invalide " (stepmother of F. B.), 165, 169, 207, 219 ; welcomes Susan, 221 ; and enjoys *Camilla*, 222 ; in bad health, 227 ; her death, 232 seq.

— Charles. D.D. (F. B.'s brother), 49, 121, 212, 217, 222, 258, 277,

278, 285, 302, 304, 380 ; plans for *Camilla*, 205, 209, 210 ; will not take offence, 211 ; praise of *Camilla*, 220

Burney, Mrs. Charles, D.D., 288

— Charles Crisp (2nd son of Ch. Rousseau), the tragic story of his life, 387–396

— Charles Rousseau (generally called *Mr.* Burney), son of Richard B., husband of Esther, his hearty laugh, 192 ; his life and genius, 383 ; notice of his death, 383–385 ; 141, 152, 227, 387, 388, 389

— Charlotte (F. B.'s sister), 123, 167, 168, 205, 206, 207, 212, 225, 227, 237, 277, 301 ; gives a dance, 216, 218

— Clara (daughter of Richard Allen), 400

— Edward Francisco (artist cousin of F. B.), 156, 196, 197, 198, 199, 200, 202, 226, 381, 382, 383 seq. ; a visit from, 184 ; admires Norbury, 184 ; affection for Wm. Locke, 185 ; hesitates to draw Norbury, 190 ; "a sweet young man," 192 ; devoted to the children, 193 ; his life and work, 373, 374 ; search for his father, 377 seq. ; the "artist" in Elia Essay "Valentines," 373

— Elizabeth Warren (cousin of F. B.), 381 ; her character, 382 ; 397

— Esther (sister of F. B., married to her cousin Charles Rousseau), her suffering, 167, 168 ; gives a dance, 197, 198 ; her praise of *Camilla*, 220 ; notice of her death, 385, 386 ; 131, 152, 180, 203, 205, 206, 217, 227, 233, 237, 272, 275, 277, 281, 282, 288, 294, 297, 302, 387, 389

— Fanny, always copying and revising, 18 ; her journey to Paris, 20 seq. ; at the Customs, 26 ; her fellow travellers, 28 seq. ; Paris and London, 32, 33 ; up three pairs of stairs, 34 ; an embarrassing friendship, 35 ; a perfect maid, 38 ; all Parisians not profligate, 38 ; why some children are fair, 39 ; at the Italian Opera-buffa, 41 ; Alex ill, 43 ; will not meet Madame de Staël, 35, 47 seq. ; an Assembly at

Madame d'Henins, 54 seq. ; at the Parade of Gen. Hulin, 60 seq. ; a visit to Passy, 62 seq. ; fête at the Tuileries, 64 seq. ; D'Arblay's home and family, 69 seq. ; quarrel with Mrs. Thrale, 104 seq. ; D'Arblay's death, 107 seq. ; objects to *Camilla* being called a novel, 214 ; offers to go to Susan, 264 ; 386

Burney, Fanny and Sophy (daughters of Charles Rousseau), a visit to Susan B., 199 ; their characters, 199, 200 ; not taught to be grateful, 201, 202 ; kindness from Lady Beverley, etc., 207 ; 201, 220, 221

— Major Henry (son of Richard Thomas B., F. B.'s half-brother), distinguished himself in India, 353, 354

— *Mr.* See Charles Rousseau B.

— Henry (son of Richard Allen), 400

— Henry Edward (grandson of Richard Allen), 373, 400

— James (born MacBurney, father of Richard and Dr. B.), 374, 375

— James (F. B.'s brother), reading too much, 126 ; looking for a house near Susan, 156–160 ; and his wife, 176 ; his own "babe," 176 ; eager to help about *Camilla*, 205, 206, 209 seq. ; full of kindness, 207 ; his children scuffle and romp, 207 ; 122, 123, 129, 148, 149, 151, 152, 158, 159, 161, 170, 177, 178, 214, 215, 217, 218, 225, 227, 230, 231, 258, 267, 273, 274, 277, 278, 373

— Mrs. James, 127 ; "wish there were more warmth of heart," 176 ; offended at possibility of *Camilla* not being given to her brother, 209, 210 ; the original Mrs. Battle, 329

— James Adolphus (cousin of F. B.), taught dancing, 381

— Martin (son of James B.), "a sad romp," 207 ; Lamb's poem to, 331

— Richard (of Worcester, uncle of F. B.), story of his life, 375, 376 ; his tragic death, 376–380 ; 163, 387, 388

— Richard Allen (eldest son of Ch. Rousseau), anecdotes of his life, 396–400 ; his children, 400 ; 382, 385

Burney, Richard Gustavus (cousin of F. B.), taught dancing ; some account of, 156, 372, 373, 381 ; 230
— Richard Thomas (step-brother of F. B.), 353, 395 ; in India, 169 ; most lovely fair boy, 190
— Sarah Harriet (Sally, step-sister of F. B.), 165, 351
— Sophia (daughter of Ch. Rousseau), 397
— Susan, her letters, 18 ; her death, 34 note ; her life and character, 118 seq. ; farewell letter from Madame de Staël, 123 ; her husband goes to Ireland, 160, 161 ; 121 ; invited to town with Lockes, 164, 165 ; comments on F. B.'s tales of Royalty-flower-names, 172–175 ; a visit from the dentist, 180, 181 ; discusses plans for *Camilla*, 204–206, 209 seq. ; visits to her relations, 204 seq. ; political differences with Dr. B., 214 ; defends the novel, 214 ; reading aloud of *Camilla*, 219 seq. ; dreads going to Ireland, 225 ; on road to Ireland (with Fanny and William), 226 seq. ; in Dublin, 228 ; waiting to see Norbury, 229 ; cheered by sight of Norbury, 230 seq. ; first impressions of their Irish cottage, 239, 240 ; devotion of her maid Susan, 243 seq. ; further description of their home Belcotton, 244 seq. ; 259 seq. ; parting with Norbury, 252 ; no fear of the French or of the rebels, 254 ; cannot make peace with the sea, 259 ; friendship with Jane Brabazon, 266–271 ; family urge her return, 273 ; hopes and doubts of going home, 277 seq. ; anxieties about the French, 281 ; must leave Norbury behind, 283 ; no philosopher submits to inevitable, 286 ; fear that Dr. B. wants her for his *own* comfort, 287 ; decides to return, 302 seq.
— Thomas Frederick (cousin of F. B.), 381

Cadell, Mr. (bookseller), 204, 212
Cambridge, Mrs., 158, 159
— Miss, 217
— Richard Owen, his death, 84 note
Camilla (by F. B.), quoted, 110,

discussed, 204 ; Paynes' offer for, 204–206 ; further discussions, 120, 209 seq. ; public expecting another *Cecilia*, 212 ; read aloud in family, 219 seq. ; keenly enjoyed, 222 ; Dr. B. on, 223, 224 ; liked in Ireland, 236 ; Norbury recognises Mrs. and William Locke, 297, 298
Campan, Madame, prize-giving at her famous school, 71 seq.
Cartland, Mrs., 233, 237, 247, 252, 289, 303
Castelfrate, Mrs., 152
Charlemont, Lord, has *Camilla*, 247
Chevallier, M., 48, 49
Chollet, Mlle, " an ancient virgin," 69
Clarke, Mr., 218
Coët, Dr., 44, 56
Cole, Mrs., 80
Cornwallis, Lord, 274, 281, 283
Cradock, General, 284
Crewe, Mrs., 206, 211
Crillon, Mr., and his son, 42
Crokatt, Miss, 149, 152, 156, 157, 161, 162, 169, 185

Damer, Mrs., 52
D'Arblay, Madame. See Fanny Burney
— Alex (F. B.'s son), 19, 21, 23, 25, 27, 33, 34, 35, 39, 64, 66, 69, 99, 100, 107, 208, 220, 240, 251, 257, 277, 292, 293, 295, 296, 301, 302, 304 ; a bad sailor, 24 ; his illness, 44 ; ill again, 53, 57, 68 ; a letter from, 102 seq. ; to be inoculated, 263
— M., meets his wife at the Hotel, 33 ; respected by officers, 60 ; his home and family, 69 seq. ; his death, 107 ; kindness to Norbury, etc., 208 ; 38, 43, 44, 45, 47, 52, 54, 56, 57, 61, 62, 65, 75, 81, 83, 85, 89, 94, 231, 232, 240, 257, 265, 279, 301, 386
d'Ayen, Duc, 54, 97
— Duchess, 98
de Beaufremont, Madame, an old friend of M. D'Ar., 58, 59
de Beauvau, Madame, her character and life, 40 ; her charm, 45, 46 ; her children, 51, 67 ; 41, 42, 44, 53, 55, 61, 83
— M., 41, 42, 63 ; described, 45, 46
de Belloy, Madame, 83

de Biron, Madame, 63
de Boinville, M., 59
de Boisvouvray, Mlle, 218
de Bouillon, Mme, 63
de Chastel, Madame, a French American, 59
de Chavagnac, Adrienne (taken to Paris by F. B.), 21, 23, 27, 34, 38, 39, 60, 103, 242, 257; at the Customs, 22; her gaiety on board, 24; meets her father and friends, 36; and her brother, 37
— M., 36, 60; meets Adrienne, 36, 37; 218, 220, 242, 257
— Madame, 103, 218, 225
de Choiseul, M., 41, 57
de Crillon, M., 55
de Damas, M., 42, 56
de Genlis, Madame, 73
de Guignes, M., 41, 42, 56
d'Hénin d'Alsace, Princess; welcomes F. B., 34; her poverty, 49 seq.; takes F. B. to Passy, 62 seq.; 40, 41, 42, 53, 55, 56, 57, 61, 63, 64, 67, 72, 74, 75, 76, 77, 81, 82, 83, 100
d'Hennezel, Gen. and Madame, 59
Delany, Mrs., 148, 178, 280; expected on visit to Norbury, 177
de la Fayette, Madame, a visit to, 95; 96, 101
— M., 101
— M. George, 96
— Mme Virginie, 97
de la Harpe, M., his death, 92
de la Landelle, M. and daughters, 218, 231, 232, 242, 243
de la Tour Maubourg, M., 96
de Lally, M. and Princess, 218, 242, 257, 266, 297
— Tolendahl, 83
Delille, Mr., 100
de Listenois, Madame, a comedy of etiquette, 59, 90
de Luynes, Madame, 58
de Maisonneuve, Madame, an intimate friend of M. D'Ar., described, 62, 63; 64
de Mansigny, Madame, 231
de Maurville, Mlle, 218, 242
de Meulan, M., a gaily amiable man, 87
de Meun, M., 42, 56
de Montagu, M., 42, 58
de Monteclerc, Madame, austere though kind, 36, 37; 60
de Montrond, Mme, 231
de Mortemar, Made., 40, 41, 51, 53,

55, 56, 61, 67, 94; talk of English royalty, 42; her charm, 45, 47
de Muras, Madame, 58
de Narbonne, M., early visitor, 34; 36, 49, 103, 215
de Noailles, Mon., 42, 56, 98
de Poix, Prince, 50, 54
— Princess, remained in Paris through the Terror, 50; story of her sorrows, 66 seq.; talks of English royalty, 67; 42, 51, 55, 56, 57, 58, 62, 63, 83
— Charles, 41, 42, 53
de Sessa, Madame, wishes to meet F. B., 39
de Sousa, Madame, 90
de Staël, Madame; F. B.'s refusal to meet, 35; 47 seq.; leaves cards, 51; 92–94; her farewell letters to Susan, 123; 54
de Terney, Mᵉ, 218, 242
de Tessé, M. and Madame, 42, 51; 53, 55, 56, 57, 58, 97; described, 54
de Thièny, Mme, 218
de Tracy, Madame, 97
de Valence, Mme, 73, 79 note
Dickens, Mrs., 207
Disney, Mrs., 290
— Mr., engaged to Jane Brabazon, 121, 290
Dobson, Austen, his edition of the Diary, 19
Dorset, Duchess of, 99
Dubarry, Madame, 72
Duroc, M., 75
Dusaussoy, Mᵉ, 218

Eckersall, Mrs., 158, 162, 167, 195
Egerton, Mrs., 203

Farren, Miss, 300
Filewood, Mr., 149
Fitzgerald, Mr., 227, 234
Fitzwilliam, Lord, 284
Francis, Mr. (Charlotte's father-in-law), 225
— Robert (Charlotte's brother-in-law), 225
— Marianne (Charlotte's daughter), 216

Ganzelle, M., teaches French, 250
Gourdeau, "little Madle," 218

Harrington, Lady, 224
Harcourt, Lord and Lady, 40
— Mrs., 40, 41, 47

Hartsinck, M. and Madame, 149, 152, 156, 159, 161, 162, 168
— Mr., " a very great f—l," 152, 156, 157
Hawkins, Rev. Mr., 128
— Nancy, daughter of Richard B., 128, 163, 381
Hill, Mrs., 236, 237, 293
Hinde, Mr., 161, 164, 167, 169
Hoole, " Young," 127, 195, 199, 201, 202, 203
— Senior, 160, 196, 199, 202
Hooles, the, 148
— Mrs., 201
Huber, Mr. and Mrs., 38
Hulin, Gen., his Parade at the Tuileries, 60 seq.

" *Janey-paney*." See Jane Brabazon
Jerningham, General, 72, 75
— Mr., his bad manners, 75, 76, 82, 83
Johnson, Dr., 106, 127
Johnston, Henry Augustus, 125
— George Hamilton, 125

Kiernan, George, 125, 217, 226, 229, 230, 233, 238, 249, 256, 303, 304
— Augusta, 237 seq.
— Harriet, work for poor, 239
— Mrs., 235, 238
— the family, 237, 239, 275
Kinder, Charles (friend who runs away and emigrates with Charles Crisp Burney), 389–395
Kingston, Mrs. Minet (Susan's grand-daughter), 123, 124
Kirwan, Mr., 179, 236
— the Misses, 236

Laclerc, General, 75
" Lady, The." See Burney, Mrs. Dr. Charles
Lamb, Charles, and Molesworth Phillips, 122
Lajard, M., 48
La Jacqueminière, Made., 60
La Tour Maubourg, M., 62
Le Brun, Madame, 82
Leinster, Duchess of, 124
" *le Temps*." See Molesworth Phillips
Locke, Mrs. See Susan's Letters, *passim* (Freddy)
— Mr. See Susan's Letters, *passim*;

never questions his son, 158 ; detests hunting, 196
Locke, Amelia, 140, 145, 155, 158, 163, 168, 185, 189, 201, 207, 232, 256, 265, 275, 289, 295, 296, 298, 302 ; after illness, 156, 157
— Augusta, 139, 140, 141, 154, 156, 157, 162, 163, 168, 189, 200, 201 ; praise of Norbury, 166
— Charles, 148, 154, 160, 163, 189, 296 ; fond of hunting, 195
— Mrs. Ch. L., 296
— Frederic (" Feddy "), 135, 136, 145, 147, 148, 155, 178, 181, 186, 187, 188, 189 ; and Norbury, 138–139, 166 ; gallant to little Fanny, 166, 187 ; his comical whims, 167 ; jealousy and fight with Norbury, 184, 185
— George, 133, 139, 155, 161, 191, 192, 196, 201 ; promised the " mare," 195 ; obtains a living, 209
— the, 19 and note.
— William (junr.), 103, 124, 131, 134, 136, 139, 155, 156, 158, 160, 162, 163, 165, 167, 168, 169, 182, 185, 189, 191, 193, 201 ; no letters from, 137 ; greatly admires Norbury, 171, 178 ; affection for Edward Francisco, 185 ; sudden fondness for hunting, 195 ; lends Edward " eysel " and paints, 197 ; admires *Camilla*, 226 ; supposed original of Edgar Mandlebert in *Camilla*, 298
— Wm. (grandson of Mr. L.), 124
Lowock, Mrs. [? Mrs. Locke], 184

MacBurney, James (earliest Burney), 374
Malhouet, Mr., 41, 49, 72, 74, 83
Majendie, Mrs., 168
" The Major." See Phillips, Molesworth
Maturin, Ann, Phillips' second wife, 122
— Henry (Norbury's tutor), 225, 233, 234, 249, 255, 289 ; one of the best young men in the world, 237 ; praises Norbury, 246
Maturin, Gabriel, 289
— The Misses, 247
Meeke, Mrs., 246
Meignen, Madame (cousin of D'Arb.), 100
Merry, Mr., 43, 52, 81
Minchin, Mr., a tiresome M.P.;

142, 144; never speaks to his wife, 142, 143

Moore, Dr., 149, 150, 151, 154, 156, 167, 175

Mounier, M. and Mme., 42, 55, 56

Murat, Madame, 72, 80, 81

— General, 81

Newcastle, Duchess of, 224

Newland, Mrs., 386

Ogilvie, Miss, 124, 297

Osborne, Dr., respects erudition of Charles B., ii, 222, 224

Parker, Betty (Susan's nursemaid), 132, 133, 136, 138, 141

Payne, Mr. (bookseller, brother of Mrs. James B.), offers re *Camilla*, 204, 205, 206, 209 seq., 214; 224

— Sarah (daughter of James B.), 123, 206, 224; heroine of Lamb's essay "The Wedding," 331

Pelham, Lord, 43

Percy, Lady Charlotte, 207

Phillips, Fanny (afterwards Mrs. Raper—p. 123), taken to church for first time, 130; a letter to the King, 146; quaint talk about *Cecilia*, 169, 170; unselfish with James's baby daughter, 176; "a little stroke of morality," 187; giving presents, 188, 189; her character, 190, 191; takes care of her playthings, 199; will enjoy a dance, 216; ill crossing to Ireland, 229; her Irish brogue, 249; a young woman, 292; 20, 119, 123, 125, 126, 129, 131, 135, 136, 140, 144, 145, 148, 153, 154, 155, 162, 163, 164, 166, 167, 177, 179, 184, 186, 187, 199, 201, 214, 215, 216, 218, 219, 225, 243, 252, 259, 261, 267, 304

Phillips, Molesworth (married Susan Burney), The Major or The Captain, and Jane Brabazon, 120, 266; his romantic character, 122; second marriage and friendship with Charles Lamb, 122; his father and sister, 124; going to Ireland, 160; news of, 163; welcomed home, 177, 178, 179; loves Nordia beyond all things, 182; will not join the hunt, 196;

coming to England without Norbury, 225; wants all the family in Ireland, 225; passion for Belcotton, 244; his passions, etc., described by Norbury, 248; no fear of war, 255–256; his infatuation for Jane Brabazon, 266–271; will not decide to let Susan return, 278; sulks over Jane B.'s marriage, 292 seq.; argument with Norbury, 299, 300; 120, 125, 126, 127, 128, 129, 131, 133, 145, 147, 148, 149, 151, 154, 156, 158, 159, 165, 171, 182, 186, 192, 193, 194, 197, 198, 200, 201, 203, 217, 226, 229, 244, 253, 276, 302

Phillips, Norbury, his character and ways, 138, 139; strange words about his father, 121; manners with Frederic Locke, 138; praised by Lockes, 167; his prayer, 170; plays fiddle with Uncle James, 170, 171; with little Kitty, d. of James, 176; "Cork naughty," 176; wants his mother to dress "young," 180; very brave when hurt, 182, 183; "A dolly Bacchus," 183; "caressing the little lyon"—Feddy Locke—till provoked too far, 184, 185; giving presents, 188, 189; not quite so lovely as his uncle Richard, 189, 190; his games with Edward Fr., 193 seq.; loves cousin Alex, 208; left in Dublin, 225; Susan's account of him in Ireland, 232, 233; a universal favourite, 234; his good progress, 246; thinks *Camilla* "beautiful," 247; fond of Maturins, 248; understands his father, 248; love for his mother, 249; subtle description of his father, loving not the same as liking, 253, 254; to be left in Ireland, 283; finds Mrs. and William Locke in *Camilla*, 297, 298; tells his father he ought to go with his wife and leave off his tricks of biting and pinching, 299, 300; 119, 125, 126, 131, 132, 136, 137, 140, 144, 153, 154, 155, 162, 163, 164, 166, 177, 179, 185, 186, 187, 199, 202, 230, 241, 243, 252, 259, 261, 274, 286, 289, 296, 303

Phillips, William (youngest child of Susan), 120, 121, 208, 214, 218,

225, 234, 238, 240, 243, 245, 252, 261, 272, 285, 304 ; his romps, 207 ; very ill crossing, 229 ; his Irish brogue, 249 ; a little buffoon, 293 ; quotes *Camilla*, 298

Piochard, old family name of D'Arblays, 70

Piozzi, M., 106

— Mrs. See Mrs. Thrale

Planta, Miss, letters to, 18

Portland, Duchess of, 280

Price, Uredale, 182

Priestley, Dr., 179

Purcell, Dr., 234, 303

Raymond, Madame, will not feed at the Inn, 20 ; and the Gouvernante, 28

Reynolds, Sir Joshua, praises Ed. B.'s drawings, 373

Rich, Mrs., 138

Ridding, Mr., 390

Rishton, Mrs. (daughter of 2nd Mr. B. *née* Allen), 288

Robinson (bookseller), 212

Rogers, Mrs., 147, 160, 167, 259 ; a dull evening, 162

Royal Family, key to flower-names, 68

Rozely, Mr., 60

Sandford, Mrs. (Rebecca Burney, cousin), 163, 230, 381, 383, 387, 398

— Mr., 230, 383, 389, 390, 398

— Beckey (her daughter), 153–156

— Bessey (her daughter), 154, 156, 230

Schwellenburgh, Mrs., 217

Sebastiani, Colonel, 98

Shirley, Rev. Walter, 217, 301

Smith, Miss, 234 ; liked by Norbury, 248

Streatfield, Sophy and " her beau," 168, 169

Symonds, Mrs., 148

Talbot, Mr., 147, 160, 167

— Mrs., 160, 167

Templetown, Lady, 141, 147, 203 ; and her children, 163, 164

Thrale, Miss (Lady Keith), 23, 49

— Mr., 23

— Mrs., 19 ; in the Isle of Wight, 23 ; account of quarrel with, 104 seq.

Trimblestone, Lord, 237

Tucker, Mrs., 167

Upton, the Misses, 144, 145, 147, 157, 161, 162, 163, 168

Valence, General, 80, 81

Vyse, Dr., 169

Wall, Mrs., 218, 230, 251, 256

— Miss, 281, 293

Wallis, Miss, 300

Wathen, Dr., 158

Wells, Mrs., 184

Williamson, Sir A., 230

Witworth, Lord, 99

Wyse, Mr. and Mrs., who seem sensible people, 158

Young, Mr., 127

— Miss, 165

DATE DUE